AF783550

The External Relations of the European Union

Historical and Contemporary Perspectives

P.I.E. Peter Lang

Bruxelles · Bern · Berlin · Frankfurt am Main · New York · Oxford · Wien

Pascaline Winand, Andrea Benvenuti and Max Guderzo (eds.)

The External Relations of the European Union

Historical and Contemporary Perspectives

European Policy
No.52

This book is dedicated to the memory of Alan Milward and Eric Remacle. It is the outcome of a conference on the external relations of the European Union held in Melbourne in September 2009. The conference was organised by the Monash European and EU Centre at Monash University (Melbourne) in collaboration with the University of New South Wales (Sydney), the Machiavelli Inter-University Centre for Cold War Studies (CIMA, Florence and Rome), the National Centre for Research on Europe at the University of Canterbury (Christchurch) and the Institut d'études européennes of the Université libre de Bruxelles. A special thank you to Cormac McMahon for his careful editing work on the manuscript.

The book was subject to a double blind refereeing process.

No part of this book may be reproduced in any form, by print, photocopy, microfilm or any other means, without prior written permission from the publisher. All rights reserved.

© P.I.E. PETER LANG S.A.
Éditions scientifiques internationales
Brussels, 2015
1 avenue Maurice, B-1050 Brussels, Belgium
info@peterlang.com; www.peterlang.com

ISSN 1376-0890
ISBN 978-2-87574-230-8
e-ISBN 978-3-0352-6497-5
D/2014/5678/114

CIP available from the British Library and from the Library of Congress, USA.

Bibliographic information published by "Die Deutsche Nationalbibliothek".

"Die Deutsche Nationalbibliothek" lists this publication in the "Deutsche National-bibliografie"; detailed bibliographic data is available on the Internet at <http://dnb.de>.

Contents

Part V
The EU and International Organizations: Conflict and Crisis Management

Part VI
Conclusions

Abbreviations

ACP	African, Caribbean and Pacific Group of States
ASEM	Asia-Europe Meeting
APEC	Asia-Pacific Economic Cooperation
ASEAN	Association of Southeast Asian Nations
CAN	Andean Community of Nations
CAP	Common Agricultural Policy
CFDT	*Confédération Française Démocratique du Travail*
CFP	Centre for Freedom and Prosperity
CFSP	Common Foreign and Security Policy
CGT	Conféderation Générale du Travail
CIEP	Conference for International Economic Policy
CNPF	Conseil National du Patronat Français
CT	Counter-terrorism
DEA	Department of External Affairs
DG	Directorate General
DT	Department of Trade
ECSC	European Coal and Steel Community
ESDP	European Security and Defence Policy
ECHR	European Court of Human Rights
EEC	European Economic Community
EDC	European Defence Community
ESS	European Security Strategy
EPC	European Political Cooperation
EAPC	Euro-Atlantic Partnership Council
EDF	European Development Fund
EURATOM	European Atomic Energy Community
ECJ	European Court of Justice
EP	European Parliament
EC	European Community
EIDHR	European Initiative for Democracy and Human Rights

GDR	German Democratic Republic
GATT	General Agreement on Tariffs and Trade
GFC	Global Financial Crisis
ILU	Intelligence Liaison Unit
IMF	International Monetary Fund
IPAP	Industrial Policy Action Plan
MERCOSUR	Common Market of the South
MoU	Memorandum of Understanding
MoFA	Ministry of Foreign Affairs
MITI	Ministry of International Trade and Industry
NAFTA	North American Free Trade Agreement
NATO	North Atlantic Treaty Organization
NPE	Normative Power Europe
NRF	NATO Response Force
OAU	Organisation for African Unity
ODA	Overseas Development Aid
OECD	Organisation for Economic Cooperation and Development
OEEC	Organisation for European Economic Cooperation
PfP	Partnership for Peace
PMD	Prime Minister's Department
PRC	People's Republic of China
PSO	Peace Support Operation
SAARC	South Asian Association for Regional Cooperation
UNCTAD	United Nations Conference on Trade and Development
USIA	United States Information Agency
VAT	Value Added Tax
WMD	Weapons of Mass Destruction
WTO	World Trade Organization
6PT	Six-Party Talks

The EU in International Affairs

A Global Actor *Sui Generis*

Andrea BENVENUTI and Max GUDERZO

University of New South Wales and
University of Florence respectively

In 1964, British Prime Minister Harold Wilson famously quipped that a week was "a long time in politics". The Labour leader probably had in mind the dramatic change in his government's fortunes following his victory at the October 1964 general election: the elation generated by Labour's return to power after twenty-three years in the political wilderness soon gave way to serious concerns over the state of the British economy, and, more specifically, over the United Kingdom's gloomy balance of payments figures and the weakness of sterling.[1] Born of Labour's troubled early days in office, Wilson's aphorism entered British political folklore. Its validity, however, remains universal, transcending political cultures and historical circumstances; it applies to political leaders as much as governments and other political institutions. The European Union (EU), of course, is no exception. Six years ago, when turmoil engulfed the global economy and the international financial system seemed to be on the verge of a disastrous meltdown as a result of the American subprime mortgage crisis, the European Monetary Union and its flagship, the euro, appeared to provide a safe shelter for countries badly hit by the financial storm. Central and eastern European countries were reported to be keen on adopting the euro; Iceland announced its intention to apply for EU membership with a view to eventually entering the eurozone; and the idea of the UK joining the euro was even mooted in the British press although never seriously considered by the British government. Alas, six years down the track – and in an almost Dickensian turn of events – we are witnessing a serious political and economic storm, which is threatening

1 See, for instance, Newton, S., "The Two Sterling Crises of 1964 and the Decision not to Devalue," *Cardiff Historical Papers*, Vol. 7, No. 1, 2007, pp. 1-45, http://www.cardiff.ac.uk/share/resources/CHP%20Newton%20-%20sterling%20crises.pdf, accessed 31 May 2012.

the very existence of the euro and casting a dark shadow on the future of the EU itself.

How the current turbulence in Europe is going to play out and how it will impact on the eurozone's future as a viable fiscal and monetary union, on its member states, as well as on the cohesion of the wider Union, is as yet, unclear. Also uncertain are the implications of such turbulence for the rest of the world and the latter's political and economic relations with the EU. As one of the contributors to this volume suggests in an essay on Indian-EU relations, the current eurozone crisis does not seem to be conducive to the development of a close political partnership between the EU and India. Nor, it seems, would it augur well for the future of the EU's other major relationships if the economic turmoil in Europe were to spill over into the global economy and severely affect the EU's main partners.

Still, as policymakers and academic scholars are grappling with the political and economic implications of the EU's current travails, it is important not to indulge in facile euroscepticism and lose sight of the important accomplishments that have been achieved in Europe over the past sixty years as a result of the Old Continent's growing integration. During this period, not only did the EU act as a major force for the political and economic transformation of Europe, but it also emerged as a powerful trade negotiator and an important player in global issues such as the environment, development aid, social policy and human rights. Unsurprisingly, given the EU's rising profile and visibility at the international level, its role in world affairs has received increasing scholarly attention and has become the focus of intense debate among academics and practitioners. This edited volume is the outcome of a conference on the external relations of the European Union held in Melbourne in September 2009. It was organised by the European and EU Centre at Monash University (Melbourne) in collaboration with the University of New South Wales (Sydney), the Machiavelli Inter-University Centre for Cold War Studies (CIMA, Florence and Rome) and the National Centre for Research on Europe at the University of Canterbury (Christchurch) and it makes an important contribution to this ongoing debate by seeking to address a number of important questions on the nature of the EU's international role. Chief among these is no doubt the question of how the EU has been seen by non-EU countries since its inception in the 1950s. Has, for instance, the EU's view of itself as a growing political and strategic presence in the international system been shared by other international actors, and, if so, to what extent? In other words, exactly how is the EU perceived by the international community and how have these perceptions developed over time? Has the EU been perceived to be more of an economic actor or a political force? Is the EU seen as a regional model that could be emulated by others? In addressing these questions, this volume aims to throw further light on the distinctive character of European integration and its external dimension.

The first part of this book comprises two essays which examine the EU's relations with its European neighbours. Part II focuses on the EU and the Asia-Pacific region and, in so doing, examines the EU's links with a number of influential regional actors, such as China, Japan, India, Singapore, Australia and New Zealand. The third part looks at the interactions and reciprocal perceptions between the EU, on one side, and the Americas on the other, while Part IV explores EU relations with the African, Caribbean and Pacific countries (ACP), investigating the theme of a postcolonial heritage in EU external relations. Finally, the fifth part deals with the EU legal system, its possible contribution to global governance and its performance in multilateral taxation contexts.

The two essays belonging to the first section of the book are quite different in kind and perspective. Both, however, are concerned with the same (and peculiar) dimension of the European Economic Community (EEC)/European Union (EU)'s outward projection – namely, cold war and post-cold war relations between an integrated Western European bloc, the Soviet Union and the latter's former Eastern European satellites. Ambassador David Daly offers a lively personal view on the EU's eastward enlargement during the two momentous decades that followed the end of the Cold War. Karolina Pietras focuses on the diverging popular perceptions and collective memories of *Solidarność* (the Solidarity movement) (and the role played by it in the Polish crisis of the Eighties) in both Western Europe and Poland itself and how these perceptions/memories have changed over time.

More specifically, Ambassador Daly reflects on the challenges the EU has faced and the successes it has achieved in its five-decade-long expansion from the initial core of six founding partners to the current twenty-eight member states. In taking stock of what he calls a "sometimes tumultuous" process, Ambassador Daly notes how the enlargement of the EU has not only revolutionised (for the better) the political, economic and social face of post-war Europe, but has also transformed the EU itself and its member states. On this last point – which is also the focus of his chapter – he reminds us of the tremendous effort asked of candidate countries and the significant demands made upon them in their quest for EU membership. An experienced participant himself in the enlargement process, Ambassador Daly argues that, despite a certain air of near-inevitability often surrounding enlargement negotiations, the accession of candidate countries has never been a foregone conclusion, nor, as he puts it, a "pre-ordained and sealed fate". Given the complexity of the enlargement process, Daly also does well to remind us of two things: first, that it would be a mistake to consider EU membership a ready solution to every national or regional problem. Accession is a long adaptive process that continues well beyond the formal date of accession and the benefits of which are often only measurable in the longer term. Second, it would be wrong to fall into pessimism. As he points out, European integration has never been short of "nay-sayers" or "prophets of doom". Yet, it is perhaps worth remembering, as Daly does, that "almost as satisfying as all that has happened over the years of [his] involvement with enlargement is what has not happened" in terms of doom and gloom scenarios.

In her chapter, Pietras makes a valuable contribution to a better understanding of the *Solidarność* legacy in contemporary European history and culture. In so doing, she effectively shows how distant Western and Eastern Europeans still are from sharing a genuine common European identity after the long Cold War interlude – and notwithstanding all the advantages brought about by enlargement, as outlined by Ambassador Daly in his previous chapter. Noting how Polish perceptions of *Solidarność* have moved from the wide popular support that the movement enjoyed in the Eighties to quite a different, and ultimately less positive, image subsequently, Pietras tries to explain why, and in what way, things have evolved differently in the West (essentially France and Germany). Although further research based on archival documents may one day cast a different light on the period and issues examined by Pietras, the author's sound methodological approach to public opinion behaviour and the wide scope of her study, in parallel perspectives, on one of the most important inner crises of the Soviet empire, make this chapter a precious contribution in an area of key importance for the future of the EU. The building of a common European identity through a shared collective memory is, indeed, seen by many as the indispensable prerequisite for the emergence of a truly effective EU role in international affairs.

Coming to the section devoted to the EU's relations with the Asia-Pacific region, both essays by Andrea Benvenuti, Natalia Chaban and Sarah Christie examine Australasian attitudes towards the early process of European integration in the 1950s. Whereas Benvenuti focuses on the Australian government's attitude towards the establishment of the European Economic Community (EEC), which he describes as rather hesitant and uncertain, Chaban and Christie cast an interesting light on New Zealand's governmental and media perceptions of the early integration process. In their view, while generally supportive of steps towards closer continental collaboration, the New Zealand government was nonetheless awake to the risk that New Zealand might one day have to pay a heavy price for this support. As in the case of Australia, policymakers in Wellington viewed with concern the prospect of Britain's membership of the EEC since British entry would have significant economic implications for New Zealand. This attitude, Chaban and Christie show, was also broadly shared by the New Zealand media. The question of New Zealand's attitudes towards European integration is further explored in Serena Kelly's chapter on New Zealand and Singaporean contemporary perceptions of the EU. The focus here, of course, is on the present, rather than the past. Kelly finds that, while in both New Zealand and Singapore local political elites and public opinion tend to view the EU as a relatively strong economic power, uncertainty remains over the nature of the EU's role beyond the economic realm. Kelly observes that if the EU is trying to "brand" itself as a normative power, then it is clearly finding it hard to be recognised as such.

The next chapters further explore the EU's role and place in contemporary international affairs by focusing on India-EU relations. In examining the significance of the EU for Indian foreign policy and security strategy, Daniel Novotný argues that in spite of Indo-European attempts to deepen their ties through the signing of the Strategic Partnership Agreement in 2004, the bilateral relationship still lacks critical depth and sufficient closeness. The Indian foreign policy elite no doubt recognises the EU's clout in international economic affairs, yet it remains understandably sceptical of the EU's ability to give itself a coherent foreign and security policy. In Indian eyes, the problem of the EU's inability to speak with a single voice in foreign affairs is further compounded by a "perceived lack of common strategic interests" between India and the EU. Given these limitations, it is no surprise if the EU remains a marginal factor in New Delhi's foreign and defence policy calculations. Similar concerns are raised by Rajendra Jain in his chapter on contemporary Indian perspectives on the EU and its international role. Here Jain notes also the inability of both India and the EU – their strategic partnership notwithstanding – to establish a structured dialogue on security issues owing to different priorities and security concerns (with India essentially confronting traditional security threats in a largely hostile neighbourhood and the EU mostly preoccupied with non-traditional security threats). That said, Jain also reminds us of the progress that has been achieved in Indian-EU relations since the establishment of formal diplomatic ties in 1962. While such progress as has been achieved might not be exceptional, it is nonetheless real enough. Not only has Indo-European political dialogue "considerably widened and deepened" over the past fifty years, but, more importantly, there is still a growing willingness on the part of both India and the EU to engage further. More pessimistic, however, about the current (and future) state of India-EU relations is Emilian Kavalski. Despite the oft-heard claim that India and the EU are natural partners, Kavalski remarks how little there is beyond mere commercial interests that brings India and the EU together.

He also notes how often the "frenemy" pattern characterises the interactions between New Delhi and Brussels.

The peculiarities of the EU's international role and the limitations of its Common Foreign and Security Policy (CFSP) are well illustrated in a revealing chapter by Gudrun Wacker on EU's relations with East Asia. Like Novotný, Jain and Kavalski, this author also finds that the EU has been punching well below its weight in Asia. She concurs with the existing literature on EU relations towards Asia that not only has the EU traditionally focused on trade and investment in its dealings with the region, but that it has also been slow in recognising the current systemic power shift from Europe to Asia. She argues that while the EU is not a unified actor and is unlikely to become one in the foreseeable future, it has nonetheless the potential to "raise its game" and aspire to play a more prominent political role in East Asia. Much, of course, will depend on the EU itself. Unless it injects more substance, coherence and clarity into its policy towards the region, the EU is destined to become increasingly marginalised in the region.

Relations with the other emerging Asian great power, the People's Republic of China (PRC), are the focus of Marie Julie Chenard's chapter. She examines the evolution of the European Community (EC)'s policy towards the PRC between 1973 and 1975. She argues that the establishment of diplomatic relations between Brussels and Beijing "marked a decisive point in the Community's opening to China". More importantly, it indicated a readiness, on the European Commission's part, to play a foreign policy role as well as its desire to show that the EC was "more than just the sum of its member states". As Chenard points out, the EC's opening to China required answers "regarding which external relations issues the EC should tackle, how the Community as a whole should tackle them and who should speak for the Community in international politics".

No scholarly account of the EU's role in, and policy towards, the Asia-Pacific region would be complete without a proper examination of Euro-Japanese relations. Hitoshi Suzuki provides just that by examining how the EC dealt with Japan in the 1970s. In this historical chapter, Suzuki focuses on how the European Commission resisted pressure from the EC member states to impose restrictions on the importation of Japanese cars, electronic goods and textiles in order to reduce Europe's growing trade imbalances with Japan. Although it found it difficult to rein in the protectionist instincts of several member states (who still went ahead and introduced domestic safeguards against Japanese exports even at the cost of making the European Community's common foreign trade appear as lacking consistency and clarity), the European Commission nonetheless managed to impose its approach. This policy was centred on the idea that

Euro-Japanese trade imbalances should be reduced through the expansion of EC exports to Japan and not the imposition of restrictions on Japanese exports. The Commission was able to persuade the Japanese government to begin to open up its highly protected internal market and, in so doing, to make a greater contribution to sustaining the world economy.

American attitudes towards the European Community and the EU make up the third part of the volume. Flora Anderson has written a convincing essay on US perceptions of the European integration process in the 1940s and 1950s through the lens of two prominent social scientists. Max Guderzo takes the story forward by studying those perceptions from a different angle and during a different period (1962-73). For his part, Rémy Davison proposes an innovative interpretation of the NATO context and its links with the EU. Latin America also figures prominently in this section through the contribution offered by Edward Moxon-Browne, whose chapter more specifically examines Central and South American perceptions and interpretations of the European integration process.

Anderson's essay belongs to a growing body of scholarship that seeks not only to chart the gradual emergence of a transatlantic intellectual network, but also to understand its influence. The network's effect on the political, diplomatic and economic dimensions of the European integration process and its close links with the US government, have been crucial also in the formulation of the latter's policies towards Europe during and after the Second World War. Based on primary sources available at the Harvard University archives, this chapter focuses on Talcott Parsons and Karl Deutsch, their scholarly work on European issues and their interactions with the Department of State and other branches of the US government on the subject of European post-war reconstruction. Where Parsons sought to understand the roots of National Socialism in Germany with a view to avoiding the re-emergence of totalitarianism across post-war Europe, Deutsch devoted his attention to the twin questions of European modernisation and integration through innovative patterns of international organisation. Both agreed on the need to develop a new "vision" of European integration, a vision that would help secure one of the most pressing objectives at the time – the reconstruction of the Old Continent – in a manner acceptable to American interests and global aspirations. In examining Parsons and Deutsch's intellectual contributions to the making of post-war Europe, the author throws an interesting new light on the conceptual framework that underpinned the well-known contribution of the US to the birth of an integrated and stable Western Europe.

Like Anderson's contribution, Guderzo's essay also deals with the political, economic and strategic rationale behind American moves in support of European integration in the decades immediately following the end of the Second World War. Here, however, the focus is on the period beginning with John Kennedy's declaration of transatlantic interdependence in July 1962 and ending with the first EC enlargement in 1973. Starting from American responses to early Western European steps towards politico-economic co-operation in the 1950s, Guderzo identifies an important common theme between Kennedy's EC policy and that of his predecessors, Harry Truman and Dwight Eisenhower. Guderzo calls this theme "enlightened interest" and correctly views it as the main explanatory key behind the great degree of continuity that characterized American reactions to European integration between the early 1950s and mid-1960s. That said, the last years of the Johnson Administration and the new course set by Richard Nixon and Henry Kissinger saw an important change in American attitudes towards the EC and, accordingly, Guderzo examines this change through the lens of *realpolitik*. He argues that Nixon's tilt away from genuine multilateralism in favour of *realpolitik* cannot simply be ascribed to US domestic considerations and wider foreign policy calculations. It was, rather, a response to a noticeable sense of disillusionment with America's European partners that gripped the Administration in the aftermath of the latter's ill-fated attempt at transatlantic co-management of most world affairs.

Rémy Davison completes this framework of analysis centred on the United States and its relations with Western Europe by proposing a well-structured approach in eight steps to the gradual transformation of the EU-NATO partnership since the end of the Cold War. The chapter looks at the way in which NATO belied most predictions and academic analyses in the 1990s by successfully setting in motion its own transformation from its previous role as a deterrent force to an "out-of-area" offensive military force. The author rightly identifies the first Gulf War as the starting point of this metamorphosis and the intervention in the Bosnian war as its full demonstration, through air strikes on Serbian forces and the subsequent peace-keeping role played by the alliance. Emphasizing the logical connection between those developments and the development of the Military Concept introduced at the 2002 Prague Summit, the chapter also explores the 9/11 terrorist attack on the United States and its implications for EU-NATO relations. Substantial sections of the essay are devoted to the Euro-Atlantic Partnership Council, the Partnership Action Plans on Terrorism and the major challenges identified (and faced) by NATO in the period under review. The author also analyses the main elements of collaboration and competition in the EU-NATO relationship, and interprets the roots of transatlantic divergence on specific issues. In this context, Davison not only mentions the American tolerance towards EU attempts to define its own security and defence policies, but also refers to Washington's fundamental scepticism about the EU's real readiness to offer front-line contributions in an independent or joint capacity. These remarks, which may go a long way to explaining why the US has been building *ad hoc* constellations of power within and without NATO for the last two decades, once again remind us of the complex dynamics of trans-atlantic relations, as well as of the EU's tardiness in taking responsible roles in international affairs.

This "American picture" is completed by Moxon-Browne with an essay on the multi-nuanced nature of Central and South American perceptions of the European integration process. In the first part of his chapter, Moxon-Browne examines, in depth, public opinion trends for the period 1995-2000 and assesses Latin American awareness of the EU with specific attention to significant sub-regional variations, respondents' education levels, competition with other international organizations and the US in terms of "image" and presence. He shows that while no single Latin American viewpoint exists on the EU, it is nonetheless apparent that the latter does not enjoy the same well-defined profile as the United States. That said, regional elites and the more educated sections of Latin American societies are cognizant "of the nuances of EU policies in Latin America and in the world more broadly, especially in the context of upholding peace and providing international stability". In the chapter's second section, he not only investigates the suitability of Europe's path to regional integration as a model for Latin American regionalism, but also explores the extent to which the European example has directly or indirectly influenced the development of multilateralism in a context often dominated by strong nationalism. In addition, the author proposes a parallel view of MERCOSUR (Common Market of the South) and the EU. This is conveyed through an innovative perspective – that of the former as a "two-way mirror" of the EU against the backdrop of rival economic interactions due to the presence on stage of the US as a traditional strong actor.

Moving to Part IV of the book, Ferdinand Leikam and Laura Kottos offer two stimulating interpretations of Western Europe's relations with the ACP countries. More specifically, Leikam examines the EEC-Commonwealth Africa partnership from Rome to Lomé, whereas Kottos centres her attention on French, Belgian and British imperial attitudes on the eve of the establishment of the EEC in 1957-58. Leikam's work mainly relies on British and EC archival sources, but it also makes good use of available African material, including press reports and diplomatic accounts. The final product is an interesting essay articulated in four sections. The chapter's first part discusses the origins of the EEC and its association system, and focuses on the impact of these developments on British colonies and newly independent Commonwealth states in Africa. Here Leikam casts an interesting light on how these countries/colonies perceived the new European institutions from outside. Having done so, the author then moves to examine Britain's first bid to join the EEC in 1961-63 and analyses the reactions of the British (African) Commonwealth to London's plans for the extension of the EEC's association regime to its current and former colonies. The chapter's third section deals with the decision taken by some members of the African Commonwealth to pursue association agreements with the Six, also in reaction to the first Yaoundé agreement signed in July 1963. The author shows that relations between Commonwealth Africa and the EEC remained uneasy for, while the EEC insisted on reverse preferences, the African Commonwealth remained opposed to the principle of reciprocity. In his last section, Leikam covers Britain's final (and successful) bid for EEC membership in 1970-72 and explores the consequences of British EEC accession on London's former African colonies. Here Leikam also looks at the impact of the Lomé Convention and the association system as a means to build a durable structure for relations between Africa and an integrated Europe.

In her chapter, Kottos, too, aims to show the profound connections between the process of European integration and decolonization in an historical perspective. The author complements Leikam's analysis by offering a different view – in her case, from inside Europe – of the crucial transition which saw the old imperial centres reassess and "restructure" the relationship with their own colonial peripheries in the second half of the 1950s. More specifically, the essay investigates the attitudes of France, Belgium and the United Kingdom to decolonization in a comparative context. It argues that the three colonial powers viewed the future of their political and economic links with their former colonies (as well as that of these newly independent states with the emerging European Communities) pretty much in the same way – that is, as a continuation of empire by other means. In this context, modernization was the key tool (and quite an expensive tool, at that) to reach such a goal. While France and Belgium chose to achieve this through the association system, Britain initially preferred to wait and remain outside the EEC, fearing that integration in Europe could slow down *inter alia* the needed transformation of its empire. Also relying on an analysis of public opinion trends as well as on an examination of the role played by domestic pressure groups in steering governmental choices towards new and stronger links between Europe and its former colonies, this chapter offers not only a stimulating comparative analysis of Europe's role in the decolonisation process, but also an original interpretation of Europe's end of empire.

The last section of the volume includes two essays by Rostam J. Neuwirth and George Gilligan. Neuwirth singles out the main flaws that undermine the current structure of the international legal order and proposes persuasive interpretations of the debate on the relationship between international law and European law. Key issues such as the legal status of the EU, or its competences and capacities as an international actor are examined and the discussion also touches the core of external perceptions of Europe and the EU debated elsewhere in the book. The author gives specific attention to a central question, namely, why international law, based as it is on traditional relations between sovereign nation states, has not yet discovered the secret of inner dynamism characterizing European law, which has proven able to progress in sixty years from the foundation of the European Coal and Steel Community (ECSC) to the Treaty of Lisbon. The chapter also studies the reform of the United Nations system, the main trends in the related academic debate and the financial elements involved, including the taboo of supranational taxes. It examines the main features of the EU legal order, highlighting such key concepts as the single institutional framework, the subsidiarity principle and the financial aspects of the EU architecture. The concluding remarks summarise the preconditions for a reform of the international legal order as a whole, also building on the EU experience with its history of successes and failures.

Gilligan's essay adopts a different perspective to investigate the EU's interaction with other international organizations, examining its role as an efficient and proactive player in multilateral taxation contexts. The chapter devotes specific attention to the EU Savings Tax Directive (EUSTD), analysing in detail its genesis and impact, and to Organisation for Economic Cooperation and Development (OECD) activities in the area of harmful tax practices (OECDHTP), both deemed by Gilligan to be very significant anti-tax avoidance multilateral regulatory initiatives. Discussion of these issues involves parallel sets of intertwined reflections on sovereignty – in particular, national fiscal sovereignty and legitimacy – which, in turn, underpin the theoretical architecture of the essay. The author uses a wide range of sources to show the extent to which both the EUSTD and OECDHTP have either received significant support or generated strong opposition in a manner that demonstrates the force of globalization and the growing interdependence between nation states. Gilligan's conclusions not only underscore the perceptions of different jurisdictions in relation to their legitimate position on transparency in taxation and other financial domains. They also underline the crucial significance of normative issues in understanding compliance at all levels, whether at local, national or international level. The durable importance of market forces, the need for more research, empirical data collection and informed interpretations in order to assess the efficacy of international regulatory initiatives such as the EUSTD and the OECDHTP are also apparent. Each of these elements is needed to produce policy-relevant prescriptions on the benefits deriving from increased tax competition and from global, rather than regional, approaches to international tax coordination. In order to show that political economy contexts and their variations do matter in explaining the different approaches examined in this essay, Gilligan also draws attention to the contrasting attitudes of the Bush and Obama Administrations to the proactive anti-avoidance initiatives taken by the EU in multilateral taxation contexts. He concludes that the EU is likely to become an increasingly important actor in these contexts.

The concluding remarks to this volume are by Pascaline Winand, the resourceful Director of the Monash European and EU Centre from 2007 to 2014 and expert organizer of the 2009 conference, upon which this book is based. Her conclusions offer an interpretative golden thread through the five different sections of this volume, skilfully drawing attention to the EU's role in international affairs that is at once complex and in flux. As she points out, the multifaceted nature of EU's external relations requires a continuing effort on the part of academic researchers and policy analysts to grasp and explain such complexity. It is in this spirit that this book has been written. Our hope is that it will not only make a significant contribution to a better understanding of a complex institution such as the European Union, but it will also provide a stimulating stepping stone to further research into a very challenging but equally rewarding field.

Part I

EU External Relations with its Neighbours

EU Enlargement

A Success but Never a Simple Question of Time

H.E. David Daly

Ambassador and Head of Delegation of the European Union to Australia and New Zealand from 2009 to 2013

European foreign policy is an area that has seen more than its share of transformations over the years and certainly more than I personally expected to see when I started out in my career with the European Union. Thus, a book which brings together so many of the threads of the evolution of institutions and individuals in response to a changing world and context in Europe is a very useful addition to the literature in this sector. It is a great privilege for me to be asked to contribute to this volume and in so doing, share something of my own perception and experiences of what have been, by any reckoning, an extraordinary twenty years. In this chapter, I hope to offer some insights into the process of enlargement, an area with which I have had a long and, I hope, fruitful involvement.

In any discussion of enlargement of the European Union a single question seems to be asked more often than any other. That question is "when?"; "When will country X join the EU?" The EU has grown in numbers of member states many times in its history, with Ireland, the UK and Denmark being the first new member states to join in 1973 to the latest accessions – those of Romania and Bulgaria in 2007, and Croatia in 2013 now bringing us to a Union of twenty-eight. So "when?" may seem the most obvious way to ask for an accession progress report. And yet, posing the question in this manner assumes a certain inevitability, almost a pre-ordained and sealed fate. The only element left in doubt is the final date of accession. Having had a direct involvement in trade liberalisation discussions with the countries of central and eastern Europe, accession negotiations with Hungary and on-going work to stabilise the West Balkans and the accession of Croatia, I have come to the view that the question of "when?" is unhelpful. Accession and stabilisation are dynamic processes that cannot be accomplished by the serene contemplation of a ticking clock. Before setting out a new and more pertinent question with which to tackle the subject of enlargement I would like to examine the recent enlargements of the EU and their effects on the EU and the new member states.

The Most Successful Policy of the EU

At the time of the fall of the Berlin Wall the EU had 12 member states. German unification aside, enlargement to a Europe of 25 came to occupy the efforts of many in the EU for much of the 1990s, leading finally to the accession of ten very diverse new member states, most from central and eastern Europe on 1 May 2004. Chris Patten, a former European Commissioner for Competition and currently Chancellor of Oxford University, writing about the collapse of Russia's Communist empire in Europe, has noted: "We now had to cope with the results of the ending of Europe's division. We found a policy to support the emergence of open markets and democracy in central and eastern Europe – the enlargement of the EU. This has been the most successful foreign policy pursued by Europe".[1]

The success of the policy of enlargement is particularly evident in the political sphere. The prospect of accession to the EU helped candidate countries to make changes that cemented key elements of a democratic free-market system in place and guaranteed the adoption of reforms in the areas of human rights, freedom of media, equality, institution building, regulatory convergence, as well as tackling organised crime and corruption. This great raft of transformations in the candidate countries was not accomplished without difficulties, discussion and occasional stops and starts. Many times along the way we were told it would be much easier to garner support for reforms if there were a "target date", an accession deadline of sorts. Tempting though this line of thinking may be, I found myself wondering on many occasions why it was that people were so keen to ask the wrong question. There was a question that was rarely asked but that could usefully have figured a lot more prominently in people's minds. That question was not "when?", but rather "what?"; as in "What do we still have to do in order to be ready to join the EU?"

Accession – Not an Inevitable Outcome

To understand the importance of this latter question, we must remember what it means to accede to the EU. With accession comes an obligation on the new member state to implement EU law. European law has grown in breadth and in depth over the years and now is a substantial corpus of texts and accumulated jurisprudence. Any country joining the EU

1 Patten, C., *Not Quite the Diplomat: Home Truths about World Affairs*, London, Allen Lane, 2005, p. 152.

is committing itself to adopting the entire corpus and to incorporating it, where appropriate, into domestic law. It also implies an acceptance of the twin obligations to muster the political will, firstly, to implement its provisions and secondly, to enforce EU law. This is a heavy burden and demands a sophisticated public administration in the new member state. The price for a member state neglecting its obligations in this regard can be high: the European Commission has powers to bring a case against a member state to the European Court of Justice, where it forms the opinion that the member state has failed to meet its obligations under European law.

It is pertinent here to remind ourselves that at the heart of the EU is the Single Market, which can only operate on a basis of mutual confidence in the legal structure and administrative capacities between the member states. If consumers in one member state did not have confidence in the authorities of another the Single Market would unravel because barriers to the free movement of goods, workers and capital would be created. These barriers would, no doubt, further undermine confidence among ordinary consumers and the business community and would in the end be the undoing of the entire project.

Given the central importance of confidence in the operation of the Single Market, candidate countries must convince the European Commission and the other member states that they do, in fact, possess the necessary legal framework, administrative capacity and political will to implement and enforce EU law. This must be proven to the satisfaction of all parties concerned. But how is a candidate country to know what is expected of it? How is it to convince the European Commission and the member states that it has made the necessary changes to prepare for membership?

The Copenhagen Criteria

The EU adopted a set of criteria in 1993, known as the Copenhagen Criteria, which outline the general principles to be respected. The Communiqué of the Copenhagen Presidency Council (quoted in part below) sets out the essential elements to be achieved:

> Membership requires that the candidate country has achieved stability of institutions guaranteeing democracy, the rule of law, human rights, respect for and protection of minorities, the existence of a functioning market economy as well as the capacity to cope with competitive pressure and market forces within the Union. Membership presupposes the candidate's ability to take on the obligations of membership including adherence to the aims of political, economic and monetary union.[2]

2 Presidency Conclusions, Copenhagen European Council, 21-22 June 1993, Section (iii), para. 2, http://www.europarl.europa.eu/enlargement/ec/pdf/cop_en.pdf, accessed 27 September 2012.

To summarise, the criteria can be divided into four distinct groups: political (functioning democracy, respect for human rights and for minorities); economic (functioning market economy and the ability to withstand the competitive pressures of the EU single market); legal (presence of a legal system, adoption of the corpus of EU law) and administrative (an ability to implement and enforce the law). The accession of a new member state changes life, not just for that state but also for the rest of the EU states and in some ways for the character of the EU as a whole. Thus, there is also a need for the EU, for its part, to be able to absorb the new member state and for the Union to continue to function successfully.

Viewed from the perspective of a candidate country, however, principles are suitable as a starting point but they do not provide the sort of detailed guidance that is needed for that country to take practical steps towards membership. What is really needed is detailed guidance, sector by sector, that allows a candidate country to proceed in an organised fashion with the legal, economic and administrative transformation that membership demands of them. Candidate countries are assisted in their preparations by the Commission in two ways: firstly, the Commission undertakes an annual review of progress made by all candidate – and potential candidate countries. This review contains detailed recommendations under each of the Copenhagen Criteria. Secondly, the Commission sets a series of very detailed benchmarks at the start of the accession negotiation process. These benchmarks relate to "chapters" or portions of the *acquis communautaire* or corpus of EU law that the candidate countries must adopt before their candidacy can be accepted for accession. When the EU and the candidate country agree that the necessary changes have been made under a particular chapter, that chapter is said to be closed. In the case of the membership application of Estonia, for example, there were 30 chapters in all. Six were opened in 1998, seventeen in 1999, six in 2000 and one in 2002. All chapters were closed in December 2002 and an Accession Treaty was signed by the Estonian government six months later and approved by referendum in September 2003. Formal accession came on 1 May 2004.

The benchmarks are the agreed standards against which the progress of the candidate country can be measured. Some examples of these include: the correct application of State Aid law in industrial sectors undergoing restructuring, e.g. ship-building or steel; the respect of basic freedoms under law and in practice, e.g., access to courts, free media, and respect for human rights; the incorporation of a reasonable strategy for budgeting for the infrastructure investments needed to comply with EU environmental law.

How, then, does a candidate country show that it is really ready for membership? How does a country prove that it has met the conditions? The process of evaluation begins even before the candidate country has applied for membership. Each candidate country signs a "Europe Agreement" before their formal application for membership. The provisions of this agreement set the scene for many of the changes that will be required before the candidate country can accede to membership. In the case of the West Balkans, association agreements were drawn up before formal accession negotiations were entered into. Whether by Europe Agreement or by Association Agreement, the intention was the same: to provide something akin to a membership training ground for states that had many changes and transformations to adopt before they could say that they were ready to become fully fledged EU member states.

Getting to Know You

It was also an opportunity for the EU (both Commission and member states) to get to know the candidate countries, and to become aware of the strategies and policies that were intended to enact change and compliance with the *acquis*. At particular stages along the way, there were also opportunities for EU member states and the Commission to conduct "peer reviews", where public servants from member states worked alongside their candidate country counterparts and reviewed progress that had been made. Non-government organisations were also invited to take part in the process and to contribute their comments and observations at this point. Rather than concentrating on any one of these many steps along the way as a single snap-shot of progress, I like to think of the whole process as a period of engagement, shading into involvement. All of these contacts and interchanges build into a more and more complete picture of the candidate country and allow everyone involved to assess progress towards the eventual goal of incorporation of the *acquis*.

Of course, bumps along the road are part of the journey. Candidate countries will always have their difficulties along the way. Past experience tells us that some industries have more work to do than others in preparing themselves for a new competitive environment. Agriculture has often been a cause of extensive discussion and the question of state aid to particular industries or sectors is commonly another important area of negotiation. Transition towards agreed procedures and standards under the headings of Justice, Freedom and Security also commonly require a steady hand on the tiller, if I might borrow a boating metaphor. The free movement of workers and capital have both undergone a phasing-in regime across Europe as both the candidate countries and the member states assess the eventual impact of membership. None of these areas of discussion, negotiation and occasionally, of controversy, should obscure the larger picture, however. The simple fact of the matter is that the candidate countries have many excellent political, strategic, economic and social reasons for wishing to join the EU and existing member states have a direct interest in the transition to membership being a success for both the candidate country and established members. Fortified by the positive impetus that comes with membership candidacy, we have seen great development and transformation in the Western Balkans and in many other jurisdictions since those heady days that followed the fall of the Eastern bloc.

Not a Miracle Cure

It would be a mistake, however, to imagine that EU membership was a panacea or a “miracle cure” for every ill. It is not. Any country that has taken on itself the strictures of applying for candidacy and which has undergone the ensuing transformation that necessarily accompanies an application for full membership of the EU will have experienced something closer to a “dawning” EU membership than to a single “light-bulb” moment. That is to say, membership, with its ensuing advantages and obligations, is not turned on in the casual flick of a switch, nor is it entered into lightly. Although it is solemnised by a binding treaty and ratified by each of the Parliaments of the EU, it is the culmination of a whole process of transformation and development that will have lasted many years. Concentrating on the supposed end point (EU membership) is, in my opinion, a failure to apprehend the true nature of what is involved. In reality, in undergoing the process of candidacy, the candidate countries make changes that have many powerful effects, independent of any final outcome to the process.

So it is that we saw a rise in foreign direct investment (FDI) in candidate countries all through the 1990s, long before accession in 2004. A country that is actively adopting stricter and more transparent systems across all areas of public and commercial administration is a country that can attract investors who need to be reassured that their investment will bear fruit and that the jurisdiction has a stable and predictable legal and administrative platform from which to build a long-term business partnership. Not only did FDI grow in this period, so also did trade and that trade became more sophisticated in nature. Foreign direct investment in the candidate countries brought not just capital but also business and technological know-how. When companies decide to invest in an emerging market, capital is only one of many things they bring to the table. They transfer their knowledge of their home market and production methods, their experience of working in the new regulatory framework and their business and production contacts. All of these transfers are important if a country is to emerge truly prepared for the competitive environment that is Europe. To have a right to compete without access to the ramping-up process would be a right in name only. Another sign of the success of the process is that competitiveness improved and productivity increased over the candidateship period. This reflects the successful strategic nature of the partnerships that were forged at this time.

These benefits of the candidature period were not lost as time went on. Rather they continue to bear fruit, not just to the candidate countries themselves but also to the wider European Union. The formal accession of the ten candidate countries on 1 May 2004 came as the culmination of a long process of engagement that has added significant momentum to the adoption of European policies not just in the region but as a flag bearer for policies that will be emulated across the region and in the wider world.

Looking at the case of Croatia, there is no doubt that the candidacy period has proved important not just for Croatia itself but also for the wider western Balkan region. Croatia has been engaged in the candidacy and accession process since 2003 and acceded on 1 July 2013. We all know the upheaval, not to mention the terrible destruction and loss of life that accompanied the break-up of Yugoslavia. In taking upon itself the challenges of candidacy, Croatia has taken a decisive step towards a better future. Without a clear change in direction, the conflicts of the 1990s could end up casting a very dark shadow over the future peace and prosperity of a new generation coming to the fore in the western Balkans. Croatia's strategic change of direction and its accession process have succeeded in mobilising a population behind something new, a project that promises a brighter future for its people.

Wider than the immediate successes in Croatia alone, however, is the impact of the demonstration effect of the Croatian experience. In the same region, the EU has recognised Serbia, Macedonia and Montenegro as official candidate countries. Albania, Bosnia and Herzegovina, and Kosovo have also been recognised as potential candidate countries. I feel confident that the path taken by Croatia will be emulated by many of its neighbours, copper-fastening stability and prosperity in the region. It is particularly encouraging to see that Croatia has offered to cooperate with Serbia in making translations of *acquis* documents available to Belgrade. This is a very hopeful sign that Croatia is not seeking to play anything but a positive role as a future member state.

Each Path of Engagement Unique

It is opportune to mention at this point that the path that was taken by each country is a unique mix of local circumstances and engagement with the EU at a given period of time. It will not be repeated in identical fashion by new candidate countries. The newest candidate states come to the process of acclimatisation, adoption of the *acquis* and adaptation at a moment in time when international and European Union dynamics have evolved anew in light of developments. The priorities of the moment are necessarily different, the challenges of the moment have changed and as such, the process of becoming a member state of the EU will also have evolved to some degree. The saying of Heraclitus comes to mind: one can never step in the same river twice. It must be said that although some things do change and even may change drastically, the aim of the process of membership remains constant. Each new member state still needs to prepare for the rigors of the internal market and to adapt to and adopt the ground rules that form the basis of our agreed common market and common economic, social, political and legal space. Just as much as any prospective member state, the EU has an interest in every new member being a successful member. This is quite simply because standing together we are always stronger than standing apart.

Tumultuous Change, Strong Benefits

To take stock of the results of the sometimes tumultuous period of expansion, the EU is now the largest importer and exporter, particularly of agricultural products from the developing world. The expansion of the EU has brought with it a rise in GDP in the new member states in the order of 1.75-1.85%, a significant boost. EU-15 has benefited to the tune of a more modest 0.5%, but clearly from a much larger base. More countries are covered by EU climate change policies than ever before. This means that more countries are committed to the EU's ambitious greenhouse gas emission targets and other mitigating measures: a base figure of 20% carbon emissions reduction, our emissions trading scheme, a 20% energy efficiency target and a 20% renewable energy target for 2020. There are now more countries contributing to overseas development aid (ODA) than before and Europe's contributions account for 60% of all ODA given globally. More countries contribute to the EU's security operations around the world. More countries are contributing to the on-going process of developing our relationship to our new "next-door neighbours", those countries that, as a result of the enlargement process, find themselves sharing a border with the EU.

The cause of a successful and strong Europe has never lacked for nay-sayers. The prophets of doom have always had their distinctive, shrill cry. Almost as satisfying as all that has happened over the years of my involvement with enlargement is what has *not* happened. Some critics said that Western Europe would be overrun with an exodus of millions from the East. There were movements of people, of course, but nothing of that order. There were others who doubted the capacity of the new member states to assume their responsibilities in the EU institutions, but that has proven to be a false alarm. The Cypriot Presidency of 2012, the Hungarian and the Polish Presidencies of the previous year are proof positive that newer member states have taken up their duties within the administration of the EU and served with great distinction in the range of roles that they have been asked to play.

This volume, quite properly, seeks to evaluate enlargement from many different angles and points of view. Some scholars may well have their doubts about the finer points of the path that has been traversed over the years. Speaking personally however, to cast my mind back to the early 1990s is to remember a time of excitement and possibilities but also of real fears and dangers. Not every country made the sorts of choices that have brought the thirteen new member states into the EU. Not every country sought the open market, embraced open administration, adopted the supremacy of the rule of law or applied free movement principles that are so characteristic of Europe. Those that did prospered; many that did not have paid a heavy price.

For all these reasons, as Europe confronts the opportunities and the challenges of this century there is no doubt in my mind that, to use Lord Patten's words again, the "enlargement […] has been the most successful foreign policy pursued by Europe".[3]

3 Patten, C., *Not Quite the Diplomat: Home Truths about World Affairs*, *op. cit.*, p. 152.

Differences in Collective Memory

Perception of *Solidarność* in Western Europe and in Poland

Dr Karolina Pietras

Paris IV Sorbonne

Memory and history are closely connected to communal and individual identity. Memory and history are therefore also constructed according to present demands, especially recent history. Yet, the past sometimes also presses into the present.[1]

The fate of the Polish workers' movement *Solidarność* fits perfectly into this framework. *Solidarność*, the first independent labour union in a Soviet bloc country, was born during strikes in the summer of 1980 at the Lenin Shipyard (now called Gdańsk Shipyards). Initially, this great workers' movement – almost ten million workers – and its leader Lech Wałęsa enjoyed in Poland an enormous popularity and massive support. But after the imposition of martial law in December 1981 and almost eight years of conspiracy, the movement lost its popular support. After the Round Table[2] negotiations between the government and the opposition, which resulted in semi-free elections in 1989, the involvement of *Solidarność* in politics (for which the movement was unprepared), and the problematic presidency of Lech Wałęsa (1990-1995), the image of *Solidarność* within Polish society deteriorated strongly.

This is partially due to the nature of the agreement between the Polish democratic opposition and the authorities in 1989. The former dissidents broke the first rule of *Solidarność*: the transparency and accessibility of negotiations. Whereas during the Gdańsk strikes everybody heard and

---

1 Bergson, Henri, *Matter and Memory*, Trans. N. M. Paul and W. S. Palmer, New York, Zone Books, 1991.

2 The Round Table Talks took place in Warsaw from 6 February to 4 April 1989. They included *Solidarność* members such as Lech Wałęsa, Bronisław Geremek, Bogdan Lis, Lech and Jarosław Kaczyński, Tadeusz Mazowiecki, Jacek Kuron, Adam Michnik (and others) and members of the communist government such as Czesław Kiszczak, Aleksander Kwaśniewski, Leszek Miller, and others.

could participate in the discussion, in Magdalenka,[3] the first, and most important part of negotiations happened behind close doors. This secretive mode of negotiation, which broke the much-admired principle of self-management, self-administration, democracy and transparency, left a bitter taste in society. The newborn "civil society and participative democracy" never really had the chance to mature.

Of course, the first big success of *Solidarność* was the non-violent transition from a communist system to a democratic one, but according to a study by *Rzeczpospolita* conducted in 2005, the Poles who disapprove of the changes started by *Solidarność* outnumber those who approve of them.[4] Even the perception of a positive event, such as the non-violent revolution started by *Solidarność*, can change according to present demands.

In light of the celebration of the 25th anniversary of *Solidarność*, it is interesting to examine the diverging popular perceptions of this movement, and how they have changed since its conception, in Western Europe and in Poland.

The *Solidarność* movement in communist Poland and developments leading up to the imposition of martial law, attracted wide interest in several countries, especially in France, Germany, Italy and the USA. In this chapter, I would like to present my research on perceptions of the *Solidarność* movement especially in France and West Germany, from the beginning of the strikes in August 1980, through the declaration of martial law by General Jaruzelski on 13 December 1981, up until recently.

The topic will be analysed through two different lenses: geographical and temporal. The two time periods in question are the 1980s and the present time (before and after communism), and the regions of interest are two western countries: France and Germany. This will be analysed with a special focus on press coverage of the events. Comparable national newspapers such as France's *Le Monde*, and Germany's *Frankfurter Allgemeine Zeitung* make up the test field, although some reactions from *Le Figaro* and *L'Humanité* and from the German weekly magazine *Die Zeit* will be also presented.

The choice of these countries and these periods for this study is not arbitrary. On one hand, the perception of *Solidarność* deteriorated in Poland, while on the other, the union and its leader Lech Wałęsa are still positively perceived in Western societies. Sometimes a historical event is

---

3 Talks between the democratic opposition and the Communist regime in Magdalenka, near Warsaw, started on 16 September 1988. These meetings paved the way for the Round Table discussions.

4 *Rzeczpospolita* (Polish national daily newspaper), 16 August 2005.

clearer and easier to understand when looked at from the outside, from the perspective of a foreign country. Current politics in Poland have tended to cloud the perception of the historical facts in its country of origin.

As for 1980s France and Germany, they constitute interesting case-studies to observe the repercussions, in "non-communist" countries of crisis at the heart of the communist bloc.

Historical Background

Let us point out briefly the historical background. Communist Poland of 1980 was struggling with the economic crisis and gigantic debts in western banks. The raising of food prices in the summer of 1980 started a wave of labour unrest through the whole country. The strikers in Gdansk, led by an electrician Lech Wałęsa, issued far-reaching demands for labour reform and more civil rights. The workers' priority was the establishment of an independent trade union with the legal right to strike. After two weeks of strikes, an agreement between the workers and the government was signed on 31 August. It was as a social contract, authorizing citizens to introduce democratic change, nonetheless trammelled by the limits of the communist system.

Sixteen months later, on 13 December 1981, the government took a hard line against the union, and martial law was introduced by General Wojciech Jaruzelski, drastically restricting normal life. *Solidarność* was declared illegal and thousands of opposition members were arrested.

In the 1980s, *Solidarność* was perceived differently in France and in West Germany. While many remember the French as the biggest allies and supporters of *Solidarność*, Germans are remembered as having been reserved and cold to the nascent political movement. The West German reaction to the Polish crisis of the 1980s is often represented as contrasting strongly with the reaction of the French. Does this received wisdom correspond to the facts? Was the sympathy shown for altruistic or idealistic reasons or was it based on various domestic strategies?

In Germany, the prudent reaction of the government was the result of the prevailing policy of *détente*; *Ostpolitik* had priority. In France, the official rhetoric of the government seemed to be more pro-*Solidarność* than the German one. However, was it also backed by political action? The support of French society gave the impression of being almost unanimous, but was it really so?

The Hot Polish Summer of 1980

The strikes in the Baltic Sea towns in the summer of 1980 monopolized the headlines of the Western European media. All of the major newspapers sent correspondents to Poland and even local newspapers devoted many articles to the Polish crisis. At first sight, the classical dichotomy between France and Germany seemed visible from a comparison of the two countries' newspapers. While *Le Monde* was optimistic and described the events in Gdańsk as "neither revolution nor act of desperate protest: the movement to strike during this so-called 'Polish Summer' is above all clear-headed and controlled",[5] fear of the destabilization of the Communist bloc prevailed in Germany. The first page of *Der Spiegel* of 15 August 1980 presented a picture of the Gdańsk strikers with the title "Upheaval in Poland – Danger to Eastern Europe" (*Der Aufruf in Polen – Gefahr für Osteuropa*).

The West German position was indeed more complex than the French one. West Germany shared a 1,700-kilometre border with two Warsaw Pact countries (Czechoslovakia and the German Democratic Republic (GDR)) and the divided status of Berlin required a more measured reaction. Bonn's long-standing social democratic government perceived the "Polish revolt" as a danger to the good relationship it had developed with Eastern Germany. Helmut Schmidt remained committed to *détente*. He wanted to maintain a dialogue between East and West, to keep the status quo and to avoid, at any price, a general crisis that might destabilize all of Europe. The German policy was based on the concepts of "changes by rapprochement" and the "policy of small steps". The underlying idea was that the Communist regime was modifiable, but not removable.

For these reasons, the leaders of the SPD (Sozialdemocratische Partei Deutschlands/Social Democratic Party of Germany) (with some rare exceptions) looked upon *Solidarność* with scepticism. The West German Defence Minister Hans Appel warned against any involvement in the Polish crisis in order to avoid a Soviet intervention. German politicians generally preferred to see gradual reforms in Poland, conducted by "enlightened Communists", such as Edward Gierek and Mieczysław Rakowski. So it was that the agreements between the Polish strikers and the authorities on 31 August 1980 were received with relief and enthusiasm in West Germany. Willy Brandt, the SPD president and former chancellor, declared himself "satisfied and relieved" after having been "profoundly touched by the courageous and admirably sophisticated uprising of the Polish workers".[6]

The cautious position of the German federal government provoked considerable criticism from other Western nations but the picture was actually more mixed than is usually supposed. As a matter of fact, some German politicians were openly positive in their statements, while some of

5 *Le Monde*, 27 August 1980.

6 *Frankfurter Allgemeine Zeitung*, 31 August 1980.

their French counterparts were not. For example, Helmut Kohl, the CDU (Christlich Demokratische Union Deutschlands/Christian Democratic Union of Germany) president and opposition leader (who would become chancellor in October 1982), referred to the Polish events as a "crisis of Communism" and "a hopeful sign for all of Europe".[7] On the other hand, Valéry Giscard d'Estaing, then President of France, was not the biggest enthusiast of *Solidarność*, saying on *Antenne 2*, on 27 January 1981, that "Poland is inside the Soviet bloc and any communication with the Soviet bloc goes through Poland. Anybody who ignores these geographic and strategic facts of life has no chance of being acceptable to the Soviet Union".[8]

François Mitterrand (who was elected President in May 1981), for his part, also feared the political tension and its potential international implications and therefore spoke prudently on 19 August 1980 about "one of the most important events of these last years."[9]

Neither French nor German politicians reacted clearly or in a homogeneous way and some Germans seemed indeed more enthusiastic than some of their French colleagues.

Western Media Coverage of the Polish Summer

This same ambivalence applies to the German and French media. The initial phase of the Polish crisis and the birth of *Solidarność* (between August 14 and September 30) aroused more interest in the German press than in the French print media. The daily newspaper *Frankfurter Allgemeine Zeitung* devoted 114 pages to the Polish issue, including 36 out of 39 headlines (a total of 92%). In the weekly *Die Zeit*, the Polish crisis occupied 27 pages, of which 6 were headline stories, over seven editions. Conversely, the Parisian *Le Monde* published 70 pages on the Polish situation during the same period. Only 23 out of its 39 headlines (59%) concerned Poland. Apparently, the French population was less interested in the Polish events during the first weeks of the Polish crisis than the Germans.

As we have seen, German politicians demonstrated more unease about Poland (and the problems that the Polish situation could cause). However, the German media did not share their politicians' hesitations and did not

---

7 *Le Monde*, 27 August 1980.

8 Védrine, H., *Les Mondes de Francois Mitterrand: A l'Elyssée 1981-1985*, Paris, Fayard, 1996, p. 200. "*La Pologne se trouve à l'intérieur du bloc soviétique et les communications du bloc soviétique passent au travers de la Pologne. Celui qui ignorerait ces données géographiques et stratégiques n'a aucune chance d'être acceptable pour l'Union soviétique*".

9 *Le Monde*, 20 August 1980.

show particular caution. The *Frankfurter Allgemeine Zeitung* called the signing of the Gdańsk Agreements a proof of the "economic, political, and moral failure" of the Communist system.[10]

French Press Reaction

Meanwhile, the reaction of the French press to the Polish strikes was mixed. Perhaps the most remarkable attitude was that of *L'Humanité*, the French Communist Party's (*PCF Parti communiste français*) national newspaper. The French Communist Party's attitude to the Polish crisis was indeed perplexing. In the 1980s, the *PCF* was the most pro-Soviet Communist party in Europe. It is true that after the publication of *The Gulag Archipelago* (1974), the *PCF* had begun to follow a line closer to that of the Italian Communist Party's Euro-communism. However, this was only a relative change of direction and the French Communist Party globally remained loyal to Moscow, supporting, for instance, the Soviet invasion in Afghanistan in 1979.

Regarding *Solidarność*, *L'Humanité* displayed obvious bias, emphasizing the strikers' economic claims, where all other Western newspapers focused on the social and political dimensions. The tone of *L'Humanité*'s articles was rather up-beat, especially concerning the Polish Communist Party, portraying it as "tolerant, ready for dialogue and self-criticism" and claiming that "the strikes were not directed against socialism".[11] Its headlines continued to suggest the superiority of popular "democracy" over a capitalist state: "Warsaw: Tolerance, Reform and Dialogue", "Discussion throughout the country", "Listening to the workers", and even "Discussion in Gdansk, fights in Le Havre".

The French press and population as a whole, even including members of the *PCF* and the Confédération Générale du Travail (CGT) (the largest communist trade union), were quick to criticize *L'Humanité*'s apparently contradictory position. A *PCF* member suggested in *Le Monde* that "the management of the French Communist Party [had] decided to support the Polish state, even against the workers".[12]

Le Monde's reaction was not atypical: other French newspapers were less than enthusiastic about *Solidarność*. They had particular difficulties in explaining the role of the Catholic Church. Both *Le Figaro* and *Le Monde*, for instance, devoted many articles to this issue. Germans had similar difficulties in understanding this "Polish particularity". According

10 *FAZ*, 1 September 1981.

11 *L'Humanité*, 19 August 1981.

12 *Le Monde*, 17-18 August 1980.

to Jürgen Wahl (expert on German-Polish relations and a CDU politician)[13] the media misjudged the role of the Catholic Church and even sent open atheists to Poland, for whom the religious component of the *Solidarność* struggle was too much to handle. However, it was even more difficult for the French, who often perceived Poland through the French tradition of *laïcité* (the secular State) and the stereotype of *Polak-katolik* (Polish Catholic), which is very strong in French culture.

The Cold Polish winter of 1981-82 and its Impact on France

The imposition of martial law provoked a wide range of reactions in Western Europe, chief of which was fear. The concern for détente and world peace dominated reactions: "Doing everything possible to promote a peaceful solution" ("*Tout faire pour favoriser une solution pacifique*", *L'Humanité*, 17 December, 1981), "Back to the Cold War?" ("*Rückfall in den Kalten Krieg?*", *Die Zeit*, 18 December, 1981) or "Peace – Just a Fairytale?" ("*Frieden – nur ein Weinachtsmärchen?*", *Die Zeit*, 25 December, 1981).

France did not deviate from this line. *Le Figaro* understood that it could no longer pretend that a conflict between *Solidarność* and the Warsaw government was avoidable and therefore argued that, given the gravity of his country's situation, Jaruzelski "could not have acted differently. [...] He represents Poland's last hope".[14] The French Foreign Minister Claude Cheysson reacted in a very moderate way immediately after the news about martial law had reached Western Europe: "*Bien entendu, nous n'allons rien faire*". ("Of course, we are not going to do anything.")[15] This muted reaction was promptly overridden by President Mitterrand, who declared that "*Tout ce qui permettra de sortir de Yalta sera bon*" ("We are in favour of anything that heralds the end of the Yalta agreements").[16]

The sociologist and political scientist Georges Mink explains in *La force ou la raison*, the unsurprised and ambiguous reaction of the French government by the conviction that "the events in Poland" would have no influence on the French domestic situation. He also suggests that it was "as if France had been informed by the United States through Colonel

13 Publication after the conference: *From Solidarność to Freedom. 25 Year International Conference Warsaw-Gdansk, 29-31 August 2005*, The Solidarity Center Foundation, Warsaw-Gdansk, Lech Walesa Institute, 2005, p. 135.

14 *Le Figaro*, 14 December 1981.

15 Wyrwa, T., *La Résistance polonaise et la politique en Europe*, Paris, France-Empire, 1983, p. 549.

16 Brzezinski, Z., "*L'avenir de Yalta*," *Politique étrangère*, Vol. 49, No. 4, 1984, pp. 789-811; p. 802.

Ryszard Kukliński (a Polish officer working for the US intelligence) on November 1981". Moreover, he points to the fact that French leaders feared the downgrading of good Franco-Soviet relations.[17]

In any case, the French government's weak reaction had fierce repercussions in the French media. *Le Figaro*, for instance, wrote on 17 December 1981: "After three days of scandalous hiding in the undergrowth, France finally knows what to think about Poland […] it's about time. Mr Mitterrand expresses – in the name of his own country – the exact sentiments that 55 million men and women […] felt before he had".

The most forthright reaction came from *Libération*. Jean-Louis Peninou expressed his indignation in an editorial entitled "Shame": "Fear, hypocrisy, prudence, mediocre cynicism – we made use of all of the disgusting platitudes of diplomacy […] Our government carefully abstained from condemning the proclamation of martial law against the workers and Polish society".[18]

The wider French community was not slow about making its voice heard. In the days following the proclamation of martial law, ordinary French men and women clearly demonstrated their sympathy for the Polish people by turning out in their tens of thousands at protests and organized events throughout France on 14 December. The largest demonstration took place in Paris, but protests were held all over the country. A Polish historian even stated that "After 13 December, France was transformed – for several weeks – into a boundless haven of support […] News of General Jaruzelski's coup d'état evoked the greatest French popular protest since the Second World War".[19]

However, this solidarity was not as unanimous, as one is prone to remember. On the contrary, close examination reveals a more complex situation and shows that French solidarity was tainted with ambiguities. For example, neither the biggest French trade union, the Confédération Générale du Travail (CGT), nor the Communist Party participated in the 14 December demonstration that was called spontaneously by the trade unions. Also, the Communist paper *L'Humanité* was very hostile to *Solidarność*. It accused the independent Polish trade union of being the principal author of its country's problems and of having provoked martial law: "Finally and above all, responsibility certainly belongs to the heads of the *Solidarność* movement, who are doing their utmost to aggravate

17 Mink, G., *La force ou la raison*, Paris, La Découverte, 1989, p. 102.

18 *Libération*, 14 December 1981.

19 Szarek, J., "Zachód wobec Solidarności," in A. Borowski (ed.), *Droga do niepodległości. Solidarność 1980-2000*, Warszawa, Volumen, 2005, pp. 337-352; p. 338.

the situation into a state of civil war".[20] "[*Solidarność* leaders] seek neither dialogue nor national harmony, but rather have escalated blindly [...] into an arena where Poland risks dissolution, where peace and détente in Europe could be damaged".[21] According to *L'Humanité*, martial law had been introduced to "save Poland from anarchy, so that *Solidarność's* extremist elements would be openly declared as power-hungry".[22] The daily put a special emphasis on the "excesses" of the *Solidarność* movement, which had effectively "sown disorganisation in the economy and created a state of shortage, disorder, and permanent strike".[23]

Of course, others of a different political stripe in France did not share this opinion and openly showed their support for *Solidarność*. The demonstration on 14 December united both the Right and the ruling PS party, not to mention hundreds of CGT militant rebels. As a result, the Polish crisis stirred up a variety of sentiments and reactions.

However, in spite of this multi-coloured support for the Polish opposition, the French government continued its *Realpolitik*. This, too, puts the so-called unanimous French support into perspective. Indeed, Paris refused to participate in the American sanctions against Poland and Moscow, nor did it abandon its plans to construct a Siberian gas pipeline. After the contract was signed on 23 January 1982, the French Prime Minister Pierre Mauroy declared that it was inadvisable to meddle: "It was pointless to add to the Polish crisis a crisis of our own: that of French people losing their supply of gas".[24]

Some French journalists criticized their government's attitude. For instance, Jacques Ellul wrote in an article entitled *Cowardice*: "Anything that might have salved our conscience has been done. Yet none of this can be of real help to the Poles. We are steeped in self-justification. When it is time to move from words to action, the volunteers are suddenly missing".[25] However, the majority of the French media preferred to remain silent about the ambivalent attitude of their own country. Instead, they commented on the German, Italian and American reactions to the Polish crisis. The German government's position – as well as their unenthusiastic participation in pro-*Solidarność* demonstrations – was criticized by nearly all of the newspapers. Jean Wetz, a *Le Monde*

20 *L'Humanité*, 15 December 1981.

21 *L'Humanité*, 18 December 1981.

22 *L'Humanité*, 14 December 1981.

23 *Ibid.*

24 "*[...] il ne servait à rien d'ajouter au drame polonais le drame supplémentaire pour les Français de ne pas être approvisionnés en gaz*". Chambraud, A., "*Le cartel des 'non',*" *Le Point*, No. 489, 1 February 1982, p. 32.

25 *Le Monde*, 14 January 1982.

journalist, described Willy Brandt as "the champion of caution in an effort to preserve détente at any price".[26] Even François Mitterrand declared, with heavy overtones of irony, that the French, unlike the Germans, "are now a nation of 55 million heroes. They are extremely supportive of the Poles – particularly given the fact that they themselves have nothing to lose".[27]

As a matter of fact, a kind of self-satisfied, almost smug attitude can be found among the French press. Instead of criticizing their government's position, several journalists emphasized the way in which "France [was] the only Western nation to lend its voice" to the Polish situation, unlike the "cowardly relief" of the rest of the West who instead "passively" accepted the Polish normalization (*L'Express*, special issue on *Solidarność* from December 1981). *Le Nouvel Observateur* declared that "France, first, as a nation and secondly as a state, is far and away the most engaged in this solidarity".[28] In this way, the French media contributed to the creation of the myth of unanimous French support for the Polish opposition in clear contrast to other European countries.

The Repercussions of the Polish Events on West Germany

But, to what extent did the French media's negative perception of West Germany correspond to reality? At first sight, the French media seems to have been right. Bonn clearly displayed the greatest caution *vis-à-vis* the Polish crisis. When martial law was introduced in Poland, Chancellor Helmut Schmidt was paying a visit to East Germany. He declared that he supported Honecker's isolationist approach to the Polish crisis. This was interpreted as a *carte blanche* for Jaruzelski, which was later confirmed by another statement: "We do not want to act as judges of the Polish people".[29] This opinion was shared by Willy Brandt, who said that the situation in Poland "will not last a long time" and that West Germans should refrain from taking sides. During the following weeks, unlike the other Western countries, West Germany did not cut off contact with the Polish regime. As early as 30 December 1981, the Bonn government accepted an official visit from the Polish Prime Minister Mieczysław Rakowski. It was not until 6 January 1982 that the federal government admitted that the Polish soldiers acted "in the context" of the existing situation within the Eastern bloc and that the Kremlin was behind Jaruzelski's decision. But the very same month, SPD President Herbert Wehner went to Poland. Still

---

26 *Le Monde*, 30 December 1981.

27 Szarek, J., "Zachód wobec Solidarności," *op. cit.*, pp. 337-352.

28 *Le Nouvel Observateur*, 19 December 1981.

29 Helmut Schmitt during a speech in German Bundestag (9. Periode, 74 Sitzung, 18.12.1981), p. 4293.

in 1985, his predecessor Willy Brandt and his successor Hans-Joachim Vogel refused to meet Lech Wałęsa during their official visit to Poland.

German opposition was also marked by apathy. The Polish crisis did not attract any attention from the peace or ecological movements, which were very active at that time. Among the politicians only Franz Josef Strauss noted that the Chancellor had fallen into a political trap and should at least have shortened his stay in East Germany. Helmut Kohl called for solidarity with the Polish people, but at the same time stated that "the Poles are responsible for this situation, because they have pushed the envelope too far".[30] His attitude was primarily motivated by criticism of the government, whose position, according to Kohl, had damaged West German credibility abroad. Only after the CDU leader won the Bundestag elections in the autumn of 1982 was the political direction changed. The new Chancellor officially demanded that Jaruzelski rescind the prevailing state of war, liberate all political prisoners, and revoke the banning of *Solidarność*.

Martial Law's Resonance in the Media

This German indifference at the national political level was nowhere to be seen in the media. Between 13 December 1981 and 15 January 1982, *Die Zeit* published 28 pages on the Polish crisis, including seven out of seven cover stories. The *Frankfurter Allgemeine Zeitung* devoted 93 pages to the Polish issue, including 27 out of 27 headlines. These numbers do not differ fundamentally from the French figures: *Le Monde* published 139 pages about the Polish crisis, including 26 out of 29 headlines (90%), *Le Figaro* 82 pages and *L'Humanité* 67 pages.

However, a part of the German press sympathized with General Jaruzelski and was pleased that he had come to grips with the Polish problem. *Der Spiegel* supported his decision and *Die Zeit* wrote that "the state of war [with *Solidarność*] is a relief for the Poles, the Russians and the West and provides one last chance to turn back from the edge of the abyss".[31]

Generally speaking, West German commentators were nervous about the movement's impact on East-West relations and their coexistence with the GDR. They sometimes – even *Die Zeit* – suggested that Polish intellectuals were being irresponsible and unrealistic.

Nevertheless, not all the media sided with the German and the Polish authorities. Several newspapers professed admiration for the courage of

30 Deklaration 20 December 1981 "*den Polen selbst die Schuld an ihrer derzeitigen Lage mit der Begründung zuschrieben wolle, sie hätten den Bogen überspannt*".

31 *Die Zeit*, 18 December 1981.

the Poles *vis-à-vis* the danger of a Soviet intervention. Numerous dailies, such as *Tageszeitung*, *Die Welt*, and *Saarbrücker Zeitung*, criticized the weak West German popular reaction to the Polish crisis, which they compared not only with the more overt French solidarity, but also with an earlier demonstration in Bonn against the euro-missiles crisis that had mobilized 300,000 people.

Yet this does not mean that all of German society sat on their hands. On 20 December 1981, 3,000 people demonstrated in West Berlin against the declaration of martial law. Many other demonstrations took place in West German cities, such as Bremen, Hamburg, Frankfurt, Munich, Karlsruhe and Saarbrucken. The numbers were significantly lower than in France, however. While 10-15,000 people marched in Paris, the city of Munich could muster no more than 500 people. Frankfurt did little better, with demonstrator turn-out falling short of even this low number.

The media in other Western countries, not just the FRG, found some aspects of the events of August 1981 hard to interpret. The British media, for instance, was generally enthusiastic but some doubts lurked in the background. The right-wing papers were uncomfortable with the idea of a political revolution brought about by a trade union – trade unions were treated almost instinctively with the deepest suspicion by British Conservatives who were at that time engaged in a long struggle with the National Union of Miners and the print unions of Fleet Street. The religious affiliations of *Solidarność* were at least a source of some reassurance. As the former British Prime Minister Harold Macmillan was heard to quip, "How refreshing to see the working-class on its knees!"[32]

Solidarność's Ideology and Western Europe

While considering newspaper coverage of the events of the 1980s, one must not forget that the Polish crisis also entailed – for some more than for others – an ideological struggle.

In this war of ideologies, each faction aligned itself with the elements of *Solidarność* that corresponded to its own pre-existing ideology. Thus, the German and French Right adopted *Solidarność*'s anti-totalitarian ideology, as well as certain elements of liberalism and religion.[33]

Georges Mink wrote that the intelligentsia of the Right saw in *Solidarność* "a concentration of virtues, with useful consequences".[34] He added that *Solidarność* began as an anti-totalitarian movement which

---

[32] Publication after the conference: *From Solidarność to Freedom*, *op. cit.*

[33] Krasnodebski, Z., "Solidarność i jej wplyw na Europe, dawna i nowa," in "*Solidarność. Wydarzenie, Konsekwencje, Pamiec*," 2005, p. 247.

[34] Mink, G., in *Europa*, "*Sierpień widziany z perspektywy Maja*," 31 August 2005.

simultaneously stripped its adversaries of their gravest threat: anti-clericalism. Catholicism was presented unanimously and unambiguously as a positive social force.[35] Moreover, by the 1980s, the Right had already discovered, however paradoxically, a strong potential in *Solidarność* for an eventual global triumph of liberalism, largely thanks to the movement's questioning of the state order. Nevertheless, generally speaking, the Right was not uncritical of the Polish workers' movement and tended to support *Solidarność* less than did the Left.[36]

The Left, which at that time was very influential in academic and intellectual circles in Western Europe, was a more enthusiastic supporter of *Solidarność* than the Right. There was admiration for its anti-bureaucracy component, the autonomy of trade unionism, and the inherently global reach of the movement. Other elements were considered incompatible with a left-wing position: *Solidarność* was too nationalistic, too Catholic, and too anti-Communist.[37] As a consequence, some left-wing intellectuals, such as Jürgen Habermas, treated *Solidarność* with scepticism.[38] The Left marginalized the religious and nationalist elements of the movement, deeming them a "Polish particularity" in order to fit it to their ideology.

Different Faces of Assistance to Poland

In West Germany, the reaction of the population was in clear opposition to that of the government: an enormous relief action for Poland was initiated. For Christmas alone, the West German population sent two million packages, in addition to a monthly average of 750,000 packages. All in all, in two "free-postage" periods (February/June and November/December 1982) the Poles received more than 8.6 million packets and medicines worth 500,000 DM.[39] The German Caritas, a non-government organisation, in only the first six months of the martial law period, sent 41 million DM worth of gifts. Nearly every city and every organization – not to mention the German Catholic Church – sent gifts non-stop to Poland. According to representatives of *Solidarność*, West Germany was "the country with the highest amount of donations to Poland".[40]

---

35 *Ibid.*

36 Krasnodebski, Z., "Solidarność i jej wplyw na Europe, dawna i nowa," *op. cit.*, p. 248.

37 *Ibid.*

38 See, for example, Habermas, J., Michnik, A. and Fernbach, D., "Overcoming the Past," *New Left Review*, Vol. A, 1994.

39 Riechers, A., *Hilfe für Solidarność. Zivilgesellschaftliche und staatliche Beispiele aus der Bundesrepublik Deutschland in den Jahren 1980-1982*, Bonn, Friedrich Ebert Stiftung, 2006, p. 23 and p. 33.

40 Bégin, N., "*Kontakte zwischen Gewerkschaften in Ost und West. Die Auswirkungen von Solidarność* in Deutschland und Frankreich. Ein Vergleich," *Archiv für Sozialgeschichte*,

Albrecht Riechers explains this enormous material support of the German population (estimated at a value of at least one billion DM)[41] as compensation for the lack of political reaction to the Polish situation.

French charitable assistance was also enormous,[42] but unfortunately, among numerous statistics of different organizations, foundations and others it is difficult to find global statistics concerning the whole of France.

In France, the support of the trade unions for *Solidarność* had an important impact. They supported the Polish workers' movement from the very beginning; Claude Sardais visited the Gdansk shipyard on 26 August 1980 and thus had an involvement with the campaign from the earliest days. During the following years, the French trade unions helped and financed *Solidarność* and its members in numerous ways. The behaviour of French unions (except for CGT) became the symbol of West European trade union help. After the proclamation of martial law the French trade unions collected the largest amount in a single campaign – one million US dollars – for *Solidarność*.[43]

The *Confédération Française Démocratique du Travail* (CFDT) played a central role in the committee of support for *Solidarność*, in particular at a material level. For months, the trade union acted jointly with well-known figures such as philosopher Michel Foucault and humanitarians like Bernard Kouchner. CFDT hosted activists from Poland, provided the Polish trade union with educational materials and organized study internships for *Solidarność* militants.

Meanwhile, in Germany the negotiations with the *Deutsche Gewerkschafts Bund* (DGB) ran into difficulties,[44] as a *Nordsee Zeitung* article from 21 April 1982 attests: "the Polish unionists must wait a long time for official approval of German colleagues". A *Solidarność* office was finally opened in Bremen on 19 April 1982 and was financed by the DGB, although this financial support was stopped after Jaruzelski's amnesty on July 1984.[45]

It should be mentioned that material help in both countries was organized in particular through local parishes, Caritas and the Red Cross. In

---

Vol. 45, 2005, pp. 93-324; p. 300, p. 303; See also Goddeeris, I., "Western Trade Unions and Solidarnosc. A Comparison from a Polish Perspective," *The Polish Review*, Vol. 52, No. 3, 2007.

41 Riechers, A., *Hilfe für Solidarność. Zivilgesellschaftliche und staatliche Beispiele aus der Bundesrepublik Deutschland in den Jahren 1980-1982*, Bonn, Friedrich Ebert Stiftung, 2006, p. 67.

42 Testimonies of several *Solidarność* activists such as, for example, Seweryn Blumsztajn.

43 Goddeeris, I., "Western Trade Unions and Solidarnosc," *op. cit.*, pp. 305-329.

44 Riechers, A., *Hilfe für Solidarność*, *op. cit.*

45 Goddeeris, I., "Western Trade Unions and Solidarnosc," *op. cit.*, pp. 305-329.

France, some newspapers also organized convoys with gifts for Poland. For example, the readers of *Ouest-France*, being very aware of the Polish situation, sponsored 100 convoys with humanitarian help.[46] The French also organized actions like *parrainage* – a campaign in which French and Polish families were put in direct contact with each other in order to provide better support. A similar objective was shared by so-called *jumelages*, a program through which the French trade unions concluded cooperation agreements with individual branches of *Solidarność*.[47]

Another important distinction between France and Germany relates to the behaviour of the intellectual elites of both countries.[48] From the beginning, the French media were interested in the Polish crisis, but it was demonstrations and other actions, such as visits to Poland by celebrities like Simone Signoret and Yves Montand that spurred the massive success of the Polish campaign. For the French intelligentsia, the interest in Poland and *Solidarność* was also stimulated by the analyses and commentaries of personalities such as André Glucksman, Alain Touraine, Jacques Derrida, Jacques le Goff and Michel Foucault. The weak reaction of the French political leaders to the *coup d'état* in Poland mobilized the French intelligentsia against the government. Pierre Bourdieu, the French philosopher, was prompted to launch a petition, under the heading "*Les rendez-vous manqués: après 1936 et 1956, 1981?*" (After the missed calls-to-arms of 1936 and 1956, [what now of] 1981?), principally by the apathetic statement of the Minister of Foreign Affairs, Claude Cheysson. Bourdieu contacted Foucault and their petition appeared in *Libération* the day after the Minister's statement.

In Germany, with some rare exceptions, public support from the intellectuals and VIPs was conspicuous by its absence.

How do we explain this sympathy and support for *Solidarność*? The reasons might be multiple. First of all, in the French case, *Solidarność* was a sort of second part of the revolution for the generation of May 1968. For many participants of the student revolts of 1968, the Polish crisis was a sort of "epilogue" to their struggle and so, many were natural supporters of *Solidarność*. The Polish workers' movement found a receptive audience in French culture and in the tradition of "social revolution". French society was "prepared" for *Solidarność*: after the Prague Spring and Aleksandr Soljenitsyn's book of 1974, many French intellectuals

46 Frybes, M., *Merci pour votre Solidarité*, Warsaw, Adam Mickiewicza Institute, 2005, p. 72.

47 Kula, M., *Niespodzewani przyjaciele, czyli rzecz o zwykłej ludzkiej solidarności*, Warszawa, 1995; also Goddeeris, I., "Western Trade Unions and Solidarnosc," *op. cit.*

48 Bégin, N., "*Kontakte zwischen Gewerkschaften in Ost und West. Die Auswirkungen von Solidarność* in Deutschland und Frankreich. Ein Vergleich," *op. cit.*, p. 323.

had renounced Communism. *Solidarność* served as a sort of catharsis.[49] This cultural history could explain why the events in Poland were more warmly felt by the French people than by the Germans. What for the French was a sort of construction of a new world through a "self-limited revolution"[50] was, to German eyes, an unpredictable Polish revolt, which could end catastrophically.

In the case of Germany, the enormous material support of the population is partially to be explained by their recent history and geopolitics. Whether we attribute the great outpouring of generosity to a lingering sense of responsibility for the fate of Poland after the Second World War or whether we, like Albrecht Riechers, ascribe it to a desire to counterbalance their government's passivity, the fact of the scale of the operation cannot be denied.

Is there a French-German Polarity?

During this last phase of the Cold War, the Polish situation was considered very important for the political situation, *détente*, and the future of the Eastern bloc.

Both France and Germany showed some similarities in the beginning of the 1980s. They both based their policy on a triptych of *détente*, agreement, and co-operation and both faced elections in 1981. As a result, the reaction of Paris and Bonn did not differ fundamentally: both governments were cautious in their public statements. The Polish crisis was also used as a pretext to regulate domestic policy. In Germany, the Polish problem was a political battlefield for Kohl, Schmidt and Franz Josef Strauss, while in France it caused tension between the French Communist Party and factions that were trying to end the domination of the pro-Soviet Left.

However, wider society reacted differently in both countries; while millions of French citizens openly showed their support for *Solidarność* in street demonstrations, the support of the German population was above all material, rather than ideological, and was certainly less ostentatious. However, one should not exaggerate the differences between Germany and France. The image of a French-German contrast in the stand towards Poland has partly been created by the French media in order to draw attention away from their government's passive stance.

---

49 Bégin, N., "*Kontakte zwischen Gewerkschaften in Ost und West. Die Auswirkungen von Solidarność* in Deutschland und Frankreich. Ein Vergleich," *op. cit.*; Frybes, M., *Merci pour votre Solidarité*, *op. cit.*; Goddeeris, I., "Western Trade Unions and Solidarnosc," *op. cit.*

50 Term used by Jadwiga Staniszkis.

France and Germany Now

Nowadays, there are perhaps more warm feelings toward *Solidarność* and its ex-leader, Lech Wałęsa, abroad than in Poland itself. In France and Germany, there is still a lot of sympathy for *Solidarność*, and for Wałęsa, who during the 2000 Polish presidential elections received only 1% of the vote. According to a study carried out in the year 2000, some of the most widespread (positive) images of Poland among the French were still such socio-historical references as *Solidarność* and Lech Wałęsa (15%).

In Germany, *Solidarność* has not been completely forgotten, either. In 2006, the German director Volker Schlöndorff ("The Tin Drum", *Palme d'Or* at the Cannes Film Festival, 1979) made a movie about the events of the 1980s in Poland entitled "Strike", portraying the Polish peaceful revolution in a positive light.[51]

But, surprisingly, during the celebrations of the 25th anniversary of *Solidarność* in Warsaw and in Gdansk, France, the country from which the Polish trade union had received the most support, was represented by two second-line figures: Jean-Bernard Raimond, former Foreign Minister, and Cardinal Jean-Marie Lustiger, recently retired Archbishop of Paris.

Meanwhile, the conference and the anniversary celebrations reunited many important people from Poland and other countries. Statesmen such as Václav Havel, European Commission President José Manuel Barroso, German President Horst Köhler, Ukrainian President Wiktor Juszczenko and many other representatives from countries like the UK, Bulgaria, Canada, Lithuania, Estonia, Croatia, Hungary, and Belgium were present in Poland. The final speech, "Solidarity as a Foundation of European Integration" was delivered by President Barroso.

Nevertheless, the celebration had an artistic French touch. On the evening of 26 August, the French musician Jean-Michel Jarre gave a huge concert on the site of the Gdansk shipyards.

---

51 It must be noted that, in comparison to the Polish film about *Solidarność* by Andrzej Wajda "Men of Iron," winner of the Golden Palm at Cannes in 1981, which was very well received, the German one was not a big success. In Poland, it was the cause of much controversy. The portrayal of shipyard workers drinking vodka and the devout Catholicism of the main character, Agnieszka, for example, led Anna Walentynowicz to refuse to present this film as her biography.

Part II

The EU and the Asia Pacific Region

Australia, the "Messina Initiative" and the Establishment of the EEC, 1955-1958

Dr Andrea BENVENUTI

University of New South Wales

Introduction

In early June 1955 the foreign ministers of France, West Germany, Italy, Belgium, Luxembourg and the Netherlands (the so-called Six) met in the Sicilian town of Messina to discuss proposals for closer Western European integration. At the end of the three-day conference, they agreed to explore the possibility of creating an economic common market in the shape of a customs union and an atomic energy authority.[1] In order to do so, the Six set up an intergovernmental committee under the chairmanship of Belgian foreign minister Paul-Henri Spaak. In April 1956 the committee produced a report calling for the creation of Euratom and a common market with common supranational institutions. The Six endorsed its recommendations at a conference in Venice in May 1956.[2] Negotiations began in earnest in May 1956 and, on 25 March 1957, they culminated in the signing of the Rome treaties, which established both the European Economic Community (EEC) and the European Atomic Energy Community (Euratom).[3] Three years after the collapse of the European Defence Community (EDC), the process of European integration was back on track. Although this was not immediately apparent at the time, the emergence of an increasingly integrated core of continental nations was destined to reshape the political and economic landscape of Western Europe. Over time, it would also affect Western Europe's relations with the outside world.

---

1 Kaiser, W., *Using Europe, Abusing the Europeans: Britain and European Integration, 1945-63*, London, Macmillan, 1996, p. 23.

2 Benvenuti, A., "Opportunity or Challenge? Australia and European Integration, 1950-1957," *Australian Economic History Review*, Vol. 51, No. 3, 2011, p. 308.

3 *Ibid.* Euratom was designed to coordinate the Six's plans for the peaceful use of nuclear energy.

Australia was no exception and its relations with Western Europe were soon bound to enter a new phase. From a rather detached attitude towards European integration, the Australian authorities quickly began to take a less relaxed, and ultimately a less benevolent, view of it.[4] As a growing body of literature has shown, the emergence and consolidation of a political and economic bloc in Europe had a profound impact on Australia's foreign relations. Its effects were threefold: firstly, it contributed to transforming Canberra's traditional ties with Britain and the British Commonwealth; secondly, it complicated Australia's relations with Western Europe itself. Lastly, it was instrumental in pushing Canberra to seek closer political and economic ties with the Asia-Pacific region. That said, academic studies on Australian-European relations have predominantly focused on the period following the British decision in 1961 to apply for EEC membership.[5] Not much exists on the period preceding Britain's first application and, more specifically, on Australian attitudes towards the creation of the EEC in 1955-58.[6] Hence, by focusing on the period ranging from the Messina Conference in 1955 to the ratification of the Treaty of Rome in 1958, this chapter seeks to throw additional light on Australia's policy with regard to a seminal phase in the history of the European integration process.

In so doing, the chapter argues that the Australian government pursued a rather ambivalent, and ultimately ambiguous, policy towards the Six. On the one hand, it claimed that the EEC would help secure peace and prosperity in Western Europe as well as strengthen the Western alliance, of which Australia was one of the staunchest supporters. On the other hand, it appeared reluctant to extend the EEC the full diplomatic

---

4 On Australia's early attitudes towards European integration, see *Ibid.*, pp. 297-317.

5 See, for instance, Ward, S., *Australia and the British Embrace: The Demise of the Imperial Ideal*, Melbourne, Melbourne University Press, 2001; Benvenuti, A., *Australian-European Negotiations on Agriculture: A Study in Economic Diplomacy 1983-93*, MA Thesis, Monash University, 1997; Goldsworthy, D., "Menzies, Macmillan and Europe," *Australian Journal of International Affairs*, Vol. 51, No. 2, 1997, pp. 157-169; O'Brien, J., "The British Commonwealth and the European Economic Community, 1960-63: The Australian and Canadian Experiences," *Round Table*, Vol. 85, No. 340, 1996, pp. 479-491; Murray, P., Elijah, A. and O'Brien, C., "Divergence and Convergence: The Development of European Union-Australia Relations," *CERC Working Papers Series*, No. 3, 2000, pp. 1-49.

6 See O'Brien, J., "Australian Department of Trade and the EEC, 1956-61," in A. May (ed.), *Britain, the Commonwealth and Europe: The Commonwealth and Britain's Application to Join the European Communities*, Basingstoke, Palgrave, 2001, pp. 39-52; Elijah, A., *Better the Devil You Know: Australia and the British Bids for European Community Membership*, PhD Thesis, University of Melbourne, 2004, pp. 82-88. Australia's response to the EEC question is briefly discussed in A. Benvenuti "Opportunity or Challenge?," *op. cit.*, pp. 308-313.

backing that such a bold project deserved. The reason for such hesitant attitude is straightforward: it is to be ascribed to the dominant influence of the Department of Trade (DT) on policy concerning the EEC issue. As it wasted no time in claiming a central role in this area of policymaking, the DT ensured that the Australian approach would be driven by economic rather than political considerations. As a result, Australian diplomacy, while recognising the political benefits of a more integrated Europe, never went as far as the United States in embracing the Messina initiative. Instead, it adopted a narrower focus, tending to concentrate on the potential trade losses that Australia would suffer should the EEC adopt a high external tariff or a protectionist farm regime. In so doing, however, Australia sent out a mixed message about where it stood in relation to one of the most important developments in post-1945 world history.

Australia's Early Response

Australia's diplomatic response to the Messina initiative took time to emerge.[7] Following the breakdown of the EDC in 1954, Australian ministers and officials in the ruling Liberal-Country Party Coalition government led by Sir Robert Menzies were sceptical of ambitious schemes for closer continental integration.[8] Like their British counterparts, Australian policymakers doubted that anything concrete would emerge from the Messina process.[9] In any event, more pressing issues appeared to command their attention. The commitment of Australian ground forces to Malaya in 1955, the negotiation of a controversial trade treaty with Japan in 1956, the renegotiation of Australia's imperial trade preferences with Britain, the emergence and worsening of the Suez crisis in 1956 – these were only a few of the major foreign policy questions with which Australian diplomacy wrestled throughout 1955 and 1956. If to this we add the fact that Anthony Eden's Conservative government (1955-57) remained opposed to a British participation in supranational European bodies, the Australian government could clearly afford to be relatively relaxed about the Messina process.[10]

---

7 Benvenuti, A., "Opportunity or Challenge?," *op. cit.*, p. 308.

8 *Ibid.*, p. 309. For the EDC's collapse see, for instance, Ruane, K., "Agonising Reappraisals: Anthony Eden, John Foster Dulles and the Crisis of European Defence, 1953-1954," *Diplomacy and Statecraft*, Vol. 3, No. 4, 2002, p. 164.

9 On widespread scepticism in Britain towards the chances of success of the Six's initiative, see Schaad, M., "Plan G: A 'Counterblast'? British Policy towards the Messina Countries, 1956," *Contemporary European History*, Vol. 7, No. 1, 1998, p. 49.

10 On Eden's approach to Europe, see Burgess, S. and Edwards, G., "The Six Plus One: British Policy-Making and the Question of European Economic Integration, 1955," *International Affairs*, Vol. 64, No. 3, 1988, pp. 393-413; see also Milward,

In late June 1955, following an invitation by the Six to join the work of the Spaak Committee, the British Cabinet examined the opportunity of sending a ministerial representation but, in the end, only agreed to send an observer, the Under-Secretary of the Board of Trade, Russell Bretherton.[11] The choice of a Whitehall official and his restrictive brief were quite revealing of the scant significance that the Eden government attached to the Committee.[12] As it turned out, Bretherton's appointment was short-lived as the British government decided to withdraw from the Spaak Committee in November 1955. In December Eden told Menzies that Britain was not going to join an initiative that would so "substantially weaken the Commonwealth relationship, both economically and politically".[13] All the British government was prepared to consider was the creation of a European Free Trade Area (FTA) in industrial products. Better known as the "Plan G", this project sought to avert a split within the Western European camp by making participation in the FTA open to all the European members of the Organisation for European Economic Cooperation (OEEC). At the same time, by suggesting that agricultural commodities be excluded from the FTA, the British sought to protect Commonwealth farm exports to the United Kingdom (UK).[14] London, in other words, sought to achieve the best of two worlds – the perpetuation of its political influence in Europe alongside the preservation of the Commonwealth as a prop to British power and prestige in world affairs. Accordingly, in September 1956, the Eden government examined the "Plan G" and agreed to discuss it with Britain's Commonwealth partners. At this stage, ministers in London were still unsure whether the FTA should be seen as an alternative or addition to the Six's common market proposal.[15]

The prospect of British association with the Six in the economic field naturally caught the eye of Australian ministers and, in the autumn of 1956, this led to the first thorough appraisal of the whole European

---

A., *The Rise and Fall of a National Strategy 1945-63*, London, Frank Cass, 2002, chapters 7 and 8.

11 The National Archives, London (TNA), CAB 128/29, CM(55)19th mtg, 30.6.1955; CAB 129/76, CP(55)55, 29.6.1955.

12 Schaad, M., "Plan G," *op. cit.*, p. 44. Benvenuti, A., "Opportunity or Challenge?," *op. cit.*, pp. 308-309. The Six's representatives were all of junior ministerial or ministerial rank.

13 Benvenuti, A., "Opportunity or Challenge?," *op. cit.*, p. 309.

14 For the origins of the Plan G, see Schaad, M., "Plan G," *op. cit.*, pp. 39-60.

15 TNA, CAB 128/30, CM(56)65th mtg, 14.9.1956; CAB 195/15 CM(56)65, 14.9.1956; Schaad, M., "Plan G," *op. cit.*, pp. 40-60; Singleton, J. and Robertson, P., *Economic Relations between Britain and Australasia, 1945-1970*, Basingstoke, Palgrave Macmillan, 2002, pp. 150-151.

integration issue, including the question of what attitude Australia should adopt towards it. On 30 October the Cabinet gathered to discuss two documents – a submission prepared by the DT and a brief memorandum by the Department of External Affairs (DEA). In its submission, the DT adopted a positive attitude towards the FTA scheme, welcoming London's plans for preliminary consultations with the Six. Trade officials regarded this British initiative as a sensible solution, provided that the FTA did not extend to foodstuffs for this would undermine Britain's preferential trade arrangements with the Commonwealth. More importantly, the DT also approved of the Six's efforts to achieve closer political and economic cooperation. "If the [Common Market] proposal resulted in a strengthening of the European economy", DT officials argued, "Europe would be in a better position to meet the challenge of the Soviet economic offensive in the Middle and Far East". In addition, the Six's initiative would help boost their political stature in world affairs and find a permanent solution to the German question since it "would undoubtedly tie that country more closely to the western powers". These would no doubt be important achievements from which Australia could only benefit. Yet, with the political and economic advantages of a more cohesive Western Europe also came problems. The DT identified two potential dangers arising from the common market proposal. One was the establishment of a common external tariff, which could "conform to the highest rather than the lowest level of existing tariffs". The other was the introduction of restrictive trade regulations in the agricultural field.[16]

That said, concerns also existed over a French proposal for the association of Western Europe's colonial territories with the future common market for Paris was seen likely to demand that they also be included in the FTA.[17] Trade felt that such an inclusion "could have serious repercussions", for it could place Australia "at disadvantage in selling manufactures to the territories and in competing with the territories in the European market for foodstuffs and raw materials". London should therefore resist moves for the incorporation of Europe's colonies into the FTA. On the whole, however, Trade felt reassured that, "with the position on wool and foodstuffs protected, the prospect for Australia of United Kingdom association with a European Free Trade Area is a possible but not a serious loss of trade [...] This loss, if it occurs, might well be offset by increased opportunities to sell our agricultural products in

16 National Archives of Australia, Canberra (NAA), A4906, Vol. 18, Cabinet submission 444, 30.10.1956.

17 On France's successful attempts to have the colonial territories of the Six included in the common market proposal see Schenk, C., "Decolonization and European Economic Integration: The Free Trade Area Negotiations, 1956-58," *Journal of Imperial and Commonwealth History*, Vol. 24, No. 3, 1996, pp. 451-452.

Europe". More importantly, Trade officials also recognized that it would be in Australia's interest "to have the United Kingdom present at the discussions of the European powers [on the FTA question] as this may be as effective a way as any of having our viewpoint heard". In their view, in fact, the proposed FTA scheme was likely to be Australia's best opportunity to "have a more effective influence on the shape of the Customs Union".[18] All in all – and as long as the common market scheme did not develop into an inward-looking and protectionist bloc – Trade was broadly in favour of continental steps towards closer integration. In any case, it conceded that unless Britain joined the customs union, the impact of greater integration on Australia's trade interests would be limited. Quite plainly, Trade's support for the Messina initiative was rather narrow in scope and certainly did not contemplate London's participation in an eventual customs union.

As for the DEA memorandum, this struck a more positive note with regard to the political and economic implications for Australia of greater Western European cooperation. Australia, External Affairs argued, could "be optimistic about the prospects of this new development in European integration". Not only did the country stand "to gain from a stronger and more closely united Europe", but the creation of a FTA across Europe should also "provide greater trade opportunities for us particularly as there is likely to be increased concentration of activity in the manufacturing field". Like Trade, the DEA was also of the view that Britain ought to seek some form of association with the Six in order to prevent West Germany from becoming too influential economically by dominating the customs union. Association with the Six, however, should not come in the guise of a direct British participation in a customs union, but rather in the context of the FTA framework. Here the views of External Affairs and Trade were broadly coincident. Where they differed was on the question of Australia's participation in the FTA and on the latter's extension to the colonies of western European countries. Unlike Trade, the DEA favoured both options. With regard to the "dependent territories" idea, External Affairs argued that this might be "the sort of link on which we could develop a case for association [with the FTA]". For this reason, the government should avoid giving the impression that it was opposed to it. The British authorities, instead, would have to be told that the treatment of the "dependent territories" question was of special interest to Australia and that Canberra would like to know more of British intentions on this issue. Australia should also "establish direct contact with the other European countries concerned".[19]

---

[18] NAA, A4906, Vol. 18, Cabinet submission 444, 30.10.1956.

[19] NAA, A4906, Vol. 18, Notes on Cabinet Submission No. 444, October 1955.

While wary of the economic implications of an FTA for Australia, ministers were broadly in support of British plans to discuss the concept with the Six, provided, of course, that farm commodities would be on the agenda.[20] They also took a benevolent view of the Six's common market initiative, saying that they were "conscious of the important political and economic advantages which could flow from a strong and united Europe".[21] It was, however, obvious that Cabinet support for both the initiatives was strictly dependent upon London's pledge not to become too closely associated with the Six. Insofar as Britain persisted in its resolute opposition to supranational schemes, the Menzies government had nothing to fear from greater continental integration.[22] Besides, as progress among the Six remained uncertain, no further action on Australia's part was needed, at this stage. The Australian Cabinet had met at a particularly awkward time for the Six. Negotiations on the common market had bogged down on French demands for the harmonization of social costs. The French government, believing that the cost of its social system put France at a cost disadvantage *vis-à-vis* the other five, had demanded (with no apparent success) that their partners revise their social systems. A conference, convened in Paris at the end of October 1956 to break the deadlock, had produced no appreciable result.[23] In general, France still appeared somewhat lukewarm towards the common market project.

The botched Anglo-French intervention at Suez in November 1956, however, was to have important reverberations on France's European policy as Paris began to adopt a more constructive attitude towards the common market project. Fears of international isolation and loss of prestige internationally led the government of socialist Prime Minister Guy Mollet (1956-57) to the conclusion that French power and influence in international affairs could not be sustained without greater political and economic cooperation among the Six.[24] As West German Chancellor Konrad Adenauer told a French interlocutor in the aftermath of France's Suez fiasco, "there remains to them [France and other individual European states] only one way of playing a decisive role in the world; that is to unite

---

20 NAA, A4906, Vol. 18, Cabinet decision 546, 30.10.1956. Since foodstuffs represented the lion's share of Australia's exports, the Australian government had no desire to see access to the British market curtailed as a result of any Anglo-European free trade area. Benvenuti, A., "Opportunity or Challenge?," *op. cit.*, p. 309.

21 *Ibid.*; NAA, A4906, Vol. 18, Cabinet decision 546, 30.10.1956.

22 Benvenuti, A., "Opportunity or Challenge?," *op. cit.*, p. 309; NAA, A4906, Vol. 18, Cabinet decision 546, 30.10.1956.

23 Schaad, M., "Plan G," *op. cit.*, p. 59.

24 Olivi, B. and Santaniello, R., *Storia dell'Integrazione Europea*, Bologna, Il Mulino, 2005, p. 30; Bozo, F., *La Politique Etrangère de la France depuis 1945*, Paris, La Découverte, 1997, p. 29.

to make Europe; [...] Europe will be your revenge".[25] France's change of heart injected new momentum into the negotiations. In November 1956 Mollet and Adenauer found a compromise over the question of harmonization, thus breaking the deadlock.[26]

Towards the Establishment of the EEC

With negotiations in Europe finally making progress, it became increasingly evident how qualified Australian support for greater European integration really was. At the beginning of 1957, with the Six edging towards a final agreement, the Menzies government reacted with alarm to the news that, under French pressure, the Six were contemplating treaty provisions aimed at establishing a protected internal market for foodstuffs.[27] As a result, the Australian government immediately toughened its attitude and began to give serious consideration to developments in Europe. On 2 February 1957 Minister for Trade John McEwen handed a stern note to the Six, registering Australian concern at their proposed arrangements on agriculture.[28] In it, McEwen made it clear that while appreciating the politico-economic case for closer European cooperation, Australia was uneasy about the introduction of protectionist agricultural provisions in the final customs union treaty. McEwen, in particular, was concerned at "the suggestion that imports of agricultural commodities from non-member countries should not be permitted until exportable surpluses from member countries have been marketed under special price arrangements". He informed the Six that Australia would seek to convene a special session of the GATT to examine their proposed agricultural arrangements before these would be enshrined in a final treaty.[29] More generally, he warned that:

> Australia would be bound to oppose within G.A.T.T. any proposal for the extension to the Customs Union as a whole of any system of agricultural marketing or price support involving non-tariff regulation of competing imports now maintained on a national basis in any one country of the Messina group.[30]

McEwen's démarche was not without controversy. On 5 February 1957 the Secretary of the Prime Minister's Department (PMD), Allen

---

[25] Feldstein, M., "The Failure of the Euro: The Little Currency That Couldn't," *Foreign Affairs*, Vol. 91, No. 1, 2012, pp. 105-116.

[26] Schaad, M., "Plan G," *op. cit.*, pp. 56-57.

[27] Benvenuti, A., "Opportunity or Challenge?", *op. cit.*, p. 310.

[28] *Ibid.*

[29] *Ibid.*

[30] *Ibid.*; see also NAA, A1209, 1957/4595 part 1, Aide Memoire, 2.2.1957.

Brown, complained to the influential Secretary of the Department of Trade, John Crawford, that

> [Ministers'] general attitude was one of sympathy and encouragement with some reservations about possible effects on our established markets [...] It is not very helpful on the one hand to be expressing encouragement and sympathy in general terms and yet to be posing obstacles to every particular proposal which emerges. Although our message does not, of course, go to that limit, I think it must have conveyed the impression that we were inclined to take a selfish viewpoint wherever our interests were concerned.[31]

In making it clear that he would have wished a milder message had been sent to the Six, rather than a "catalogue of criticism", Brown further noted:

> We cannot exclude the possibility that at some later stage in these developments we might be prepared to overlook some possible short term losses in markets in the interests of contributing to the development of a strong and stable European community. The emphasis on the part that G.A.T.T. might play also seemed to be over-emphasised. Inevitably G.A.T.T. will be called to pass judgement on the plan but it would be unfortunate if before we had resolved our overall attitude there should be any possibility of the plan bogging down in a special session of the Contracting Parties where there could be some danger of losing sign of the fundamental purpose of the plan.[32]

So irritated were PMD officials at McEwen's diplomatic move that they brought the problem to the prime minister's attention, stressing the danger of treating the common market initiative simply "as another trade proposal". In a memorandum to Menzies, R. Durie argued that if the government had really the strengthening of Western Europe at heart, it should "be prepared to face some short term adjustments in markets in the hope of some longer term and more stable advantages". "I still think", Durie added, "there was a good reason not to be too heavy handed in these initial stages".[33]

As sound as this advice was, the PMD was the only government department to question Trade's zeal (and haste) in delivering such a note.[34] The Department of Primary Industry openly sided with Trade and strongly supported its tactics. The Treasury and DEA acquiesced with it. The DEA justified its support for the DT's diplomatic démarche on the ground that

31 NAA, A3320, 3/2/2/8/1 part 1, A. Brown to J. Crawford, 5.2.1957.

32 *Ibid.*

33 NAA, A1209, 1957/4595 part 1, R. Durie to Menzies, 7.2.1957.

34 NAA, A1209, 1957/4595 part 1, Durie to E.J.B. Foxcroft, 7.2.1957; A1838, 791/4/11 part 2, Memcon Paul Phillips, P.J. Lawler and K.G. Brennan, 1.2.1957.

> in the formative stages of the Treaty Australia should not hesitate to press hard for protection of her trade interests. At later stage when the Treaty was concluded and it was necessary to consider it in G.A.T.T. it might become necessary to weigh broad strategic and political merits against commercial de-merits.[35]

Trade's reaction was not long in coming and in a note sent to Brown on 21 February, Deputy Secretary Alan Westerman defended his department's tactics by pointing out that in order to have any effect at all, the Australian démarche had to be made before the Six's ministerial meeting in Brussels on 4 February. In any case, Westerman argued that "the points raised in the message appear to be consistent with the Government's earlier attitude to the Common Market proposals and not inconsistent with a later more sympathetic view of the proposals". He disputed that McEwen's note amounted to a "catalogue of criticism" as Brown had dubbed it; in fact, it was only "an attempt to direct the attention of the Messina powers to specific problems which were of concern to us".[36] Westerman may have been right here, yet the general tone of McEwen's note no doubt pointed to a toughening of the DT's attitude towards the Six. As 1957 progressed, this hardened further.

At the end of March 1957 the prime ministers and foreign ministers of the Six gathered in Rome to sign the treaties establishing the EEC and Euratom. Although doubts remained in Canberra and other capitals as to whether the Six would be able to complete the ratification process successfully, it was nonetheless apparent that, after several months of complex and tough negotiations, the Six had achieved a major diplomatic success. This, inevitably, prompted a further reappraisal in Canberra. On 11 April 1957, ministers met to discuss another submission tabled by McEwen.[37] In it, the Australian Trade Minister recommended that Australia recognise "the long term political and economic advantages" of the common market project. In his view, once fully implemented, the common market ought to

> bring results of considerable political, strategic and long run economic importance to Europe. The Treaty should have a uniting influence and should lead to increased European production and consumption. If an expansion of the economies of the Six Messina countries were realised we might eventually be able to look forward to an increasing export trade with Europe.[38]

---

35 NAA, A1838, 791/4/11 part 2, Memcon, Phillips, Lawler and Brennan, 1.2.1957.

36 NAA, A1209, 1957/4595 part 1, W. Westerman to Brown, 21.2.1957.

37 NAA, A571, 1959/2383 part 2, Cabinet decision 713, 11.4.1957.

38 NAA, A571, 1959/2383 part 2, Cabinet submission 577, 21.3.1957.

However, while welcoming the Six's initiative, McEwen could not help expressing his disquiet at the agricultural provisions of the Treaty of Rome since these appeared to envisage "short and long term protection for European agriculture". There was, he complained, "little in the Treaty to take account of the interests of third countries".[39] Although the Treaty provisions on agriculture were rather vague and further legislation would be needed before a common farm system could take shape, McEwen's concerns were well-founded.[40] Between 1958 and 1962, the EEC would actively work to create such system, replacing "the plethora of national agricultural protective policies which had characterized Europe in the 1950s".[41] The outcome was the adoption, in January 1962, by the Council of Ministers of a set of regulations instituting a common market for agricultural products – the so-called Common Agricultural Policy (CAP), whose central features were price support and managed markets.[42] The CAP, which became fully operational only at the end of the 1960s, created a protected, inward-looking, insulated and highly managed farm system. Yet, while McEwen and his department were right to voice their concerns about the risks for Australia of the increasing European emphasis on managed agricultural markets and internal price support, their criticism was based on shaky ground since, with the exception of agriculture, Australia of the 1950s was one of the most protectionist countries in the Western world.[43]

McEwen, however, had no time to dwell on this matter of principle. His brief was to defend Australian trade interests and, fearing the emergence of a potentially protectionist Western European economic bloc, he felt he had little option but to consider a more energetic approach. Thus, he told Cabinet that "if we learn that our fears on agricultural

39 NAA, A571, 1959/2383 part 2, Attachment to Cabinet submission 592, 4.4.1957.

40 For "agricultural" clauses of the Treaty of Rome, see Fennell, R., *The Common Agricultural Policy of the European Community: Its Institutional and Administrative Organisation*, Oxford, BSP Professional Books, 1987, pp. 7-10; Ludlow, P., "The Making of the CAP: Towards a Historical Analysis of the EU's First Major Policy," *Contemporary European History*, Vol. 14, No. 3, 2005, pp. 349-350.

41 Ludlow, P., "Too Far Away, Too Rich and Too Stable: The EEC and Trade with Australia during the 1960s," *Australian Economic History Review*, Vol. 41, No. 3, 2001, p. 272. For a succinct historical account of this period, see Tracy, M., *Government and Agriculture in Western Europe 1880-1988*, London, Harvester Wheatsheaf, 1989, pp. 252-266.

42 Benvenuti, A., *Australian-European Negotiations on Agriculture*, *op. cit.*, chapter 1.

43 Murray, P., Elijah, A. and O'Brien, C., "Common Grounds, Worlds Apart: The Development of Australia's Relationship with the European Union," *Australian Journal of International Affairs*, Vol. 56, No. 3, 2002, p. 397; Woodland, A., "Trade Policies in Australia," in S. Dominick (ed.), *National Trade Policies: Handbook of Comparative Economic Policies*, Westport, Greenwood Press, 1992, p. 239.

protection have been placed too high, we could then give greater support to the [customs union] proposals". In the meantime, however, the government should "press energetically" to see Australia's agricultural interests protected.[44] McEwen's strategy rested on three pillars: firstly, the government should seek "maximum action in G.A.T.T. prior to ratification (as distinct from signature) of the Treaty and subsequently"; secondly, it should exert significant pressure on the Six to ensure that they took account of the interests of non-EEC agricultural producers; thirdly, it should try to "to enlist as much support as possible for our position from U.S.A., Canada and the U.K. in G.A.T.T. and by other means for modification or adjustment of them".[45] Australia's objective was two-fold: first, to protect current levels of farm trade with the Six and second, to create new trade opportunities.[46] In endorsing McEwen's submission, Cabinet clearly favoured strong diplomatic action towards to the Six. Ministers brushed aside the Treasury's qualms that the Trade line went too far. In a note on the DT's submission, the Treasury had advised ministers to avoid taking steps "likely to prejudice the establishment of the Common Market". After all, Treasury contented, "it is not possible to know how far the fears expressed in the [Trade's] submission are justified". In any case, Treasury officials observed, Australia's "trade with the Messina Countries in the products likely to be affected was only £18.5 million out of total exports of A£770 million".[47]

Australian Policy in the Aftermath of the Rome Treaty

McEwen's suggested course of action, however, soon ran into difficulties. Despite his attempts to seek an early examination of the Treaty of Rome within GATT, the GATT Intercessional Committee decided at the end of April 1957 that further preparatory work was needed before an effective examination of the Treaty could be made. The US and Canada argued that any special session of the GATT on the Treaty of Rome should be deferred until its ratification was completed. The American and Canadian view was that "intensive discussion of the Treaty in G.A.T.T. could embarrass the Messina Governments, and hinder the ratification procedures". Both countries wanted the Six's ratification process completed

---

[44] NAA, A571, 1959/2383 part 2, Cabinet submission 577, 21.3.1957.

[45] *Ibid.*

[46] Benvenuti, A., "Opportunity or Challenge?," *op. cit.*, p. 310; NAA, A571, 1959/2383 part 2, Cabinet submission 577, 213, 1957, and Treasury's note on Cabinet submission 577, 26.3.1957.

[47] NAA, A571, 1959/2383 part 2, Cabinet submission 577, 21.3.1957.

first.[48] The Eisenhower administration, in particular, was strongly supportive of the Messina initiative.[49] Despite sharing some Australian economic concerns, the administration was inclined to brush them aside for the sake of greater Western European cohesion. Political motives clearly overrode American concerns about the Six's protectionist tendencies in agriculture. And, in any case, the reality was that while the prospect of an integrated agricultural policy was indeed an area of concern for the Americans, the actual legal stipulations contained in the Treaty of Rome were rather weak and sketchy when compared to other policy areas. Hence, as the Americans recognised, there would be plenty of opportunities in the years to come for the US and other interested parties to urge the Six to steer their agricultural policies in the right direction.[50]

Despite these early difficulties, the Department of Trade persevered in its efforts to thrash out a workable strategy to deal with the EEC problem. On 27 June 1957 DT officials discussed further options at an inter-departmental meeting with officials from Canberra's major departments: the DEA, PMD, Treasury and Primary Industry. Once again, Trade officials reiterated "the potential value of the European Economic Community on broad political and strategic grounds", but, in what appeared to be a further hardening of Trade's attitude, they argued that the Australian government ought not to "accept all of the provisions of the Treaty as being essential to achieve its objectives". The Treaty's provisions on agriculture were especially problematic since they were "capable of being developed and applied [...] as to make the Community a highly protectionist bloc". This posed a threat to Australia. Hence, the government should retain "full freedom to take all action open to us to safeguard Australia's trade interests" and should also aim to "ensure total marketing opportunities not less than at present in the Customs Union market as a whole for products of Australian export interest". To this end, Australia "must continue in relation to the European Economic Community [its] pressure for the harmonisation of European agricultural policies with policy obligations under G.A.T.T." More specifically, the government should "seek agreement on a programme of progressive dismantling of non-tariff protective measures for agriculture". "These lines of approach", Trade officials suggested, "should be pressed in G.A.T.T., in bilateral discussions and any

48 Benvenuti, A., "Opportunity or Challenge?," *op. cit.*, pp. 310-311; NAA, A1838, 791/4/11 part 4, Maris King to Arthur Tange, 13.5.1957; A1838, 791/4/11 part 2, AHC Ottawa to DEA, cablegram 72, 15.3.1957.

49 Winand, P., *Eisenhower, Kennedy, and the United States of Europe*, New York, St. Martin's Press, 1993, chapter 5; see also Warner, G., "Eisenhower, Dulles and the Unity of Western Europe, 1955-1957," *International Affairs*, Vol. 69, No. 2, 1993, pp. 320-324.

50 Benvenuti, A., "Opportunity or Challenge?," *op. cit.*, p. 311.

relevant negotiations with Community countries, and through the United Kingdom, the United States and Canada". Trade was clearly in favour of applying maximum pressure on the Six, but, while pushing for a rather aggressive line, it was careful not to overdo it. Part of the reason, no doubt, was that it was reluctant to alienate other departments. Thus, Trade officials argued that "we cannot assume that our objections will be fully met, or met to a significant extent, and we must contemplate that some damage to our trade interests in Europe, at least in the short term, may be an unavoidable price to be paid for whatever political and strategic advantage we may foresee arising for us from closer relations between the countries of Europe".[51]

Once again, however, the DT's line of action did not go uncontested. The hawkish Department of Primary Industry complained that it did not go far enough and that it was "deficient" in several respects.[52] At the other end of the spectrum, the PMD argued that Trade's approach to European integration remained too focused on trade issues.[53] "They [the DT] are, i[t']s true, less rabid than Primary Industry", P.J. Lawler observed in late June 1957, but "they are still approaching the whole subject too narrowly".[54] According to Lawler, European economic integration, while undoubtedly presenting some costs for Australia, need not have been, on the whole, harmful to Australian economic interests. And in any case, "the political and strategic importance of the proposals had to be recognized and we might have to be prepared to make some sacrifices in order to obtain that objective".[55] That objective was by no means completely secured. In a departmental note drafted in early June, PMD officials had warned that the successful creation of a Western European common market was not yet a foregone conclusion. In their opinion, in fact, it remained to be seen whether the EEC would succeed or whether it "will, like the European Defence Community, crash at the hurdle of ratification, whether it will clear this hurdle only to founder amidst the difficulties of practical application, whether political instability in member countries will impede and frustrate the Treaty".[56] The PMD concern was that if Australia "continued to be wholly preoccupied with the particular considerations for our export trade, events would be

51 NAA, A1209, 1957/5119 part 2, Draft Principles: EEC.

52 NAA, A1838, 791/4/11 part 3, Interdepartmental meeting on the European Common Market and Free Trade Area held in the Department of Trade, 20.6.1957.

53 NAA, A1209, 1957/5119 part 1, P.J. Lawler to John Bunting, 2.7.1957.

54 NAA, A1209, 1957/5119 part 2, Lawler to Bunting, undated (circa late June 1957).

55 *Ibid.*, see also Benvenuti, A., "Opportunity or Challenge?," *op. cit.*, p. 313.

56 NAA, A1209, 1957/5119 part 2, Lawler to Bunting, 13.6.1957; see also The European Economic and the Proposed Free Trade Area – Considerations for Australia, PMD note, June 1957.

likely to pass us by". PMD regarded "many of the difficulties which Trade foresaw" as being, "at this stage quite hypothetical". The government should therefore refrain from adopting a "firm attitude" until it "had seen illustrations of how the difficulties might, in fact, work out and their relative importance". PMD also wondered whether the government should place so much emphasis on agriculture.[57] Treasury and DEA officials spoke in much the same vein, agreeing broadly with the PMD's position.[58]

PMD's strong criticism of Trade did not have an appreciable impact on Australia's European policy. Not only did it fail to garner significant support from other government departments, but, more problematically, it cut little ice with the prime minister. Menzies was clearly reluctant to antagonise his influential coalition partner, McEwen's Country Party,[59] but, in all truth, he also remained sceptical of certain aspects of the EEC project. As he told the Liberal Party Federal Council gathered in Canberra on 21 October 1957, "the trade aspects of the Treaty including, particularly, the arrangement for agriculture, require special consideration in GATT". In his view, the adoption on the part of the Six of a protectionist domestic farm regime would no doubt be a problem and should not be ruled out. This, however, was not the only issue for Menzies. The risk also existed of the common market ending up being dominated economically by West German industry. This would threaten British exports to a growing continental market with negative consequences for the position of sterling. And "any threat to sterling, of course, affect[s] us", Menzies argued. More problematically, "the Messina Plan, unless accompanied by an associated and wider FTA, will divide Western Europe rather than unite it". It is true that Menzies, more than McEwen, tended to emphasise the positive aspects of political integration. The common market, he said, had "an obvious value to the Free World". "Politically the Treaty should have a uniting influence and increase, again politically, defensive co-operation" on the Continent.[60] The fact, however, remained that he appeared more cautious than his officials on the supposed benefits of European integration. In this context, therefore, it is not particularly surprising that the PMD failed to challenge Trade's grip on Australian policy on the EEC.

57 NAA, A1209, 1957/5119 part 1, Lawler to Bunting, 2.7.1957.

58 NAA, A1209, 1957/5119 part 1, Lawler to Bunting, 2.7.1957; A1838, 791/4/11 part 3, Interdepartmental meeting on the European Common Market and Free Trade Area held in the Department of Trade, 20.6.1957.

59 O'Brien, J., "Department of Trade," *op. cit.*, p. 48.

60 NAA, A1838, 791/4/11 part 6, Statement by the Prime Minister to the Liberal Party Federal Council, Canberra, 21.10.1957.

In mid-September 1957 Cabinet agreed to keep the EEC question under "constant" review.[61] In doing so, ministers endorsed another Trade submission outlining Australia's preferred course of action in the months to come. In it, McEwen and his officials now appeared willing to take on board some criticism and to dispel the impression that they were irremediably opposed to the establishment of the EEC. McEwen made clear that the Australian government had no intention "to wreck [European] integration as such". All Australia wanted, he said, was "to protect our markets as they now exist and our expectations in regard to future markets and gain maximum recompense in tangible trade terms for any departure from international obligations on the part of the Community countries". Nor, he added, did Canberra "want to destroy G.A.T.T. as a useful instrument" of international trade diplomacy by forcing the GATT members to take a premature stance on the EEC issue. Hence, the government's best course of action, for the time being, was to conduct a holding operation. Australia should not only "avoid any final decision by the G.A.T.T." on the EEC issue since the government did not yet have "full particulars as to how the [Rome] Treaty arrangements will be applied in practice". But it should also "oppose an unqualified support by G.A.T.T. of the Treaty".[62]

McEwen's temporizing attitude owed to the fact that, by now, it had become clear how little international consensus existed on how to deal with the EEC. As mentioned earlier, the United States was strongly behind the creation of the EEC and was unwilling to confront the EEC member states within the GATT. Without strong American backing, Australian advocacy had little chance of succeeding. This said, however, in the course of 1958, McEwen would again resort to bolder tactics and repeatedly attempt to bring the Treaty of Rome to the attention of the GATT. Once again, his tactics would be unsuccessful. GATT was unwilling to challenge the EEC and "took refuge behind procedural and technical barriers".[63] In autumn 1958 he had to settle for the rather harmless outcome of the thirteenth session of GATT, which simply agreed to establish three committees with a view to investigating agricultural protectionism and measures to expand international trade.[64] Representations to EEC governments also brought the Australian Trade Minister little joy. They invariably found his criticism of the agricultural aspects of the Treaty of Rome somewhat disingenuous given Australia's membership of the Commonwealth, a trade bloc, which also discriminated against third

61 NAA, A4926, Vol. 34, Cabinet Decision 1007, 17.9.1957.

62 NAA, A4926, Vol. 34, Cabinet submission 862, 12.9.1957.

63 O'Brien, J., "Department of Trade," *op. cit.*, p. 41.

64 *Ibid.*, p. 42.

parties.[65] As for the UK, Harold Macmillan's Conservative government (1957-63) was loath to upset the Six and simply advised Canberra to seek protection through the GATT.[66]

Conclusion

From 1957 onwards, ministers and officials in Canberra would repeatedly stress the political and economic importance of a more integrated Western Europe. The FTA proposal collapsed in November 1958, however, and, with it, the prospect of seeing Australian agricultural interests reconciled with moves towards greater continental integration. This was directly attributable to the opposition of the new de Gaulle administration to British attempts to merge the EEC into a looser free trade area.[67] One of the consequences of these developments was that Australia would struggle to articulate how exactly it would benefit from such Western European integration. As this chapter has sought to illustrate, this was in large measure due to the dominant role played by the Department of Trade in the formulation of government policy towards Western Europe. Under the leadership of its powerful minister, the DT was able to stamp its authority on Canberra's policy-making process and thus exert a disproportionate influence on Australia's European policy. This ensured that McEwen and his department would not only be able to shape Australia's European policy in keeping with their own views and objectives, but that the Australian approach to the EEC would also be informed, principally, by economic rather political considerations. It is therefore no surprise that, while aware of the positive political implications of a more cohesive Western Europe, Trade became increasingly concerned about the economic losses that Australia would incur if the EEC adopted a high common external tariff or a protectionist internal agricultural regime. Throughout 1957, therefore, the DT's attitude towards the EEC inevitably hardened. That said, however, it never reached the point at which it sought deliberately to sabotage the EEC, as O'Brien has argued.[68] Despite its growing concerns about the future of some agricultural exports to Western Europe, Trade knew that as long as Britain remained outside the EEC, potential trade losses would be, all in all, rather small. In May 1960 McEwen revealed to his Cabinet colleagues that only A£15 million of Australia's exports had been

---

65 Benvenuti, A., "Opportunity or Challenge?," *op. cit.*, p. 312; Murray, P., Elijah, A. and O'Brien, C., "Common Grounds," *op. cit.*, p. 397.

66 Benvenuti, A., "Opportunity or Challenge?," *op. cit.*, p. 312; Goldsworthy, D., "Menzies, Macmillan," *op. cit.*, p. 158.

67 Ward, S., *British Embrace*, *op. cit.*, pp. 54-55.

68 O'Brien, J., "Department of Trade," *op. cit.*, p. 40.

negatively affected by the EEC's common external tariff in 1958-59.[69] Thus, as McEwen himself made clear in late 1957, Canberra had no interest in undermining Western European integration. Nor, however, was he willing to grant his full and unconditional support to the Messina initiative.

Understandably, the Prime Minister's Department found this attitude objectionable. After all, if Western European integration was a prize worth striving for, why – the PMD correctly reasoned – should Australia risk undermining the whole common market project, then still in its formative and most delicate stage, by launching a diplomatic offensive against the EEC? Viewing Western European integration as a largely positive outcome, the PMD was loath to do anything that could jeopardise the painstakingly negotiated Messina initiative. Unfortunately for PMD officials, their department's position found little support in Canberra. As this chapter has shown, the Department of Primary Industry broadly shared Trade's hard line. As for the DEA and Treasury, these two departments, while at times critical of DT's views and tactics, were not ready to challenge its ascendancy over Australia's EEC policy. The DEA, in particular, failed to establish its credentials as a major player in this area and made little impact on policy. This ensured that the Australian approach would remain largely focused on the economic implications of European integration for Australia at the expense of a more sober political appreciation of the whole process. More importantly, not even the PMD's political head, the prime minister himself, was prepared to back fully the views of his departmental officials. Menzies remained ambivalent on the EEC question and, in any case, preferred to let McEwen do the running in this area of policy. Here, it is perhaps useful to note that, while in the United States policy towards the EEC remained firmly in the hands of the President and the State Department, in Australia the political departments remained divided and uncertain as to what strategy the government should adopt towards the EEC. In this context, the political consideration underlying the EEC project would always come second and Australia's policy would be guided by economic rather than political considerations.

This is not to say that Trade's concerns about certain economic aspects of the EEC project were misplaced or that its tactics were misguided. Indeed, as the gradual implementation of the CAP during the 1960s was to reveal, Australian concerns were more than justified. Moreover, it was entirely legitimate for the DT to ensure that growing political and economic collaboration amongst Western European nations would not be to the detriment of Australian agricultural producers. This notwithstanding, it should not be ignored that, as a member of the Commonwealth, Australia was itself part of a discriminatory trading bloc and that, as such,

[69] *Ibid.*, p. 46.

Trade's pro-free trade advocacy within GATT and its condemnation of the Community's protectionist instincts rang somewhat hollow. So, to some extent, did its stated backing for European integration for, ultimately, this support often appeared to be no more than an after-thought – always conditional, as it was, upon the EEC's approach to agricultural trade. In the end, one could be excused for thinking that the Menzies government's overall attitude towards the process of Western European integration was hesitant and uncertain. Unsure of the extent to which greater European political and economic cooperation was a political prize worth fighting for and uncertain whether the long-term pacification of Western Europe was more important than some trade losses, the Menzies government sent out a mixed message as to where it stood in relation to one of the most important developments in post-war international relations. In this respect, much more logical and straightforward appeared to be the attitude of successive American administrations in the early years of the integration process. Having identified continental integration as an overriding American foreign policy aim, Washington ensured that nothing would derail the Six's march towards greater political and economic cohesion.

Images and Perceptions of the EU in New Zealand in the 1950s

Natalia CHABAN and Sarah CHRISTIE

University of Canterbury, New Zealand

Introduction

The process of European integration that preceded the establishment of the European Economic Community (EEC) in 1957 is an important aspect of world history. Yet, there is little research into how New Zealand reacted and responded to the advent of the European integration process during the 1950s. This decade saw New Zealand move from a reliance on Britain as its main economic and political ally to a stronger connection with the USA and Australia (with the formation of the Australia, New Zealand, United States Security Treaty (ANZUS)), as well as searching for a place within the broader Asia-Pacific region. This realignment came at the same time as Britain was readjusting its political and economic priorities in the face of European integration.[1]

While a significant body of scholarship exists on this foreign policy shift in New Zealand,[2] little attention has been paid to New Zealand's understanding of the European integration processes during the 1950s. Most research focuses on New Zealand's reactions from the 1960s onwards.[3] This chapter fills this gap by investigating how New Zealand

---

1. Kennaway, R., *New Zealand Foreign Policy 1951-1971*, Wellington, Hicks Smith & Sons, 1972.
2. Singleton, J. and Robertson, P., *Economic Relations between Britain and Australasia, 1945-1970*, Basingstoke, Palgrave, 2002; see also Singleton, J., "New Zealand in the Nineteenth and Twentieth Centuries," *EH.Net Encyclopedia*, R. Whaples (ed.), 10 February 2008, http://eh.net/encyclopedia/article/Singleton.nz, accessed 10 November 2013.
3. McLuskie, R., *The Great Debate – New Zealand, Britain and the EEC: The Shaping of Attitudes*, Wellington, Decision Research Centre, Victoria University of Wellington in association with the NZIIA, 1986; King, M., *The Penguin History of New Zealand*, Auckland, Penguin Books, 2003; Mein Smith, P., *A Concise History of New Zealand*, New York, Port Melbourne, Cambridge University Press, 2005; Rice, G. (ed.), *The*

perceived and responded to the three major events in early European integration history – namely, the Schuman Declaration adopted on 9 May 1950, the Treaty of Paris establishing the European Coal and Steel Community (ECSC) on 18 April 1951, and the Treaty of Rome establishing the EEC on 25 March 1957. New Zealand's responses to these landmark events are traced firstly in the relevant official documents, and secondly in the New Zealand news media discourses. While attention to elite responses is a common element of the existing scholarship, media imagery is typically overlooked, and comparative analyses of the two discourses are non-existent. By comparing the visions of early European integration and its impacts on New Zealand across official and news media discourses, this interdisciplinary analysis adds to the existing knowledge on New Zealand's approach to European integration.

Answering a call for "multilayered perspectives"[4] in the studies of historical perceptions of European integration, this chapter considers specific *actors* involved in the communication of the process of European integration (New Zealand political elites dealing with Europe and newsmakers reporting Europe to the general public); *means* (New Zealand official correspondence and news media) and the *contents* (historical changes in the visions in the representation of the process of early European integration and its impacts in one country, New Zealand). This study is part of an empirical research project, investigating the perceptions of the European integration process in New Zealand and the profiles of the EU in the eyes of New Zealand society.[5]

The use of the term "European integration" in this chapter is a deliberate choice, based on the belief that the 1950s contemporaries did not view the adoption of the Schuman Plan and the treaties of Paris and Rome as inevitable precursors to the European Union (EU) in its present-day form. It is hoped that this study will help promote not only a better understanding of the EU's historical relevance and its modern visions in New Zealand, but also provide a greater historical insight into the perceptions of Europe outside its borders.

This analysis first focuses on New Zealand political stakeholders' responses to the initial stages of European integration. Then, it briefly

---

Oxford History of New Zealand, Second Edition, Auckland, Oxford University Press, 1992; Jackson, K. (ed.), *Fight for Life – New Zealand, Britain and the EEC*, Wellington, Price Milburn and Company for NZIIA, 1970.

4 Call for papers "Communicating European Integration," Eighth History of European Integration Research Society Conference, March 2012.

5 It is a part of a trans-national comparative project "The EU through the Eyes of the Asia-Pacific" involving twenty locations led by the National Centre for Research on Europe, University of Canterbury, NZ (www.euperceptions.canterbury.ac.nz).

discusses the methodology used in the media analysis and presents the main findings of how the New Zealand press reported the process. Finally, it discusses the main findings, which reveal a major difference between official and media discourses. In the early 1950s, New Zealand's government elites and foreign affairs bureaucracy were vigilant, nuanced and cautious in their attitudes towards the UK's imminent accession to the Community and the future consequences of this move for New Zealand. In contrast, the media discourses in the two major national papers in 1950 and 1951 reveal a lack of clarity about the possible negative outcomes of European integration to New Zealand. Only in the coverage of the Treaties of Rome in 1957 did the leading national press start preparing the New Zealand public for the shock of being "abandoned" by the UK and begin to discuss how New Zealand would be disadvantaged economically by integrating Europe – an image that continues to dominate modern public perceptions of the EU in New Zealand.[6]

New Zealand Official Discourses on Early European Integration

Historians such as Robert McLuskie pointed out that while there was limited debate within New Zealand in the 1950s on the possibility of Britain's closer alignment with continental Europe, the official reaction was essentially one of support for eventual British accession to the EEC. While New Zealand elites understood that this would hold serious implications for New Zealand, they also acknowledged the benefits of a politically and economically stable Europe and the role the European integration project could play in achieving this.[7] Singleton also noted that New Zealand decision-makers were well aware of the vulnerability of the post-war New Zealand economic model that focused so overwhelmingly on the UK.[8] In support of the latter claim, this research found a summary report on post-war European economic recovery prepared for Alister McIntosh, Secretary for External Affairs in 1948. The report

---

6 Holland, M., Chaban, N., and Benson-Rea, M., *External Perceptions of the European Union: A Survey of New Zealanders' Perceptions and Attitudes towards the European Union*, University of Canterbury, NCRE Research Series, No. 1, 2003; Chaban, N. and Holland, M., (eds.), *The EU Through the Eyes of the Asia-Pacific: Public Perceptions and Media Representations*, University of Canterbury, 2005 NCRE Research Series, No. 4; Chaban, N. and Holland, M., (eds.), *The European Union and the Asia-Pacific: Media, Public and Elite Perceptions of the EU*, London and New York, Routledge, 2008.

7 McLuskie, R., *The Great Debate – New Zealand, Britain and the EEC: The Shaping of Attitudes*, Wellington, Decision Research Centre, Victoria University of Wellington in association with the NZIIA, 1986, pp. 8-9.

8 Singleton, J., "New Zealand in the Nineteenth and Twentieth Centuries," *op. cit.*

highlighted that the UK's participation in Europe did "not so much create new problems for New Zealand as accentuate a dilemma which is already inherent in our overseas economic positions; namely, that our dollar-earning capacity is limited (so long as we supply the bulk of our exports to U.K.)".[9]

Prior to the Schuman Declaration, New Zealand officials were already engaging with the idea of greater economic and/or political integration in Europe. A telegram from the Minister of External Affairs in Wellington to the Secretary of State for Commonwealth Affairs in London in August 1947 stated that New Zealand "would be willing to give the fullest consideration to any definite proposals for an economic union in Europe involving possible participation by the Dominions, though [...] we attach great importance to maintaining the special relations between members of the Commonwealth".[10] A report canvassing the different positions of the various Commonwealth governments prepared by External Affairs in 1949 highlighted the concerns many other Commonwealth countries held – that European integration would be at the expense of the Commonwealth.[11] From as early as 1947, there was an understanding that some form of European integration was a possibility and that New Zealand could stand to lose economically in this process.

Between 1950 and 1951, the New Zealand government closely followed the Schuman Plan. In August 1950, a confidential report was prepared by External Affairs in Wellington outlining the details of the French proposal and the UK's responses to it.[12] New Zealand also received regular updates from Britain. Memoranda sent to the Commonwealth Heads of State communicated Britain's caution at the French proposal, and demonstrated a willingness to inform Commonwealth governments of the intricacies of discussions surrounding the British position on integration.[13] Based on British reassurances that Britain could reconcile

9 New Zealand National Archives, Wellington (henceforth NZNA), ABHS W5422 950157, part 1 – Report – United Kingdom and the Economic Recovery of Europe – Economic Implications for New Zealand, Summary 9/6/1948, Draft of paper prepared for Mr McIntosh by GDL White and Mr Webb from Director of Stabilization, 9 June 1948.

10 NZNA, ABHS W5422 950 157111/14/3/3, part 1, Minister of External Affairs, Wellington to Secretary of State for Commonwealth Relations, telegram 195, 28 August 1947.

11 NZNA, ABHS W5422 950 1577, Record No. 111/14/3/3, part 1, The Commonwealth and European Union.

12 NZNA, ABHS W5503 7148 75, LONB42/7/1, part 1, The Schuman Plan: Recent Developments, 7 August 1951.

13 NZNA, ABHS W5503 7148 75, LONB42/7/1, part 1, Commonwealth Relations Office to various Commonwealth Posts, French Proposals for a Franco-German Coal and Steel Authority. See also NZNA, ABHS W5503 7148 75, LONB42/7/1,

interest in greater European cooperation with its continuing support for the Commonwealth, New Zealand felt it could treat European integration as a positive step towards a stronger Europe.

Still mistrustful of German power, New Zealand wanted to ensure an active role for Britain in any European united entity. In this light, Britain was seen as a counterbalance to the growing dominance of West Germany. It was also seen as a moderating influence to the French European federalist tendencies. On 7 September 1951, New Zealand sent a telegram to the Commonwealth Relations Office in which they advised that "we are in agreement with the United Kingdom Government's decision to associate itself with the future operations of the Schuman Plan community". It also stated that the "political benefits of this decision appear to us especially important" given that it would ensure the "successful absorption of Germany into the Western European community as an equal, but not dominant partner". The proposed British responses to the Treaty were seen to offer a "possible alternative to United Kingdom participation (at the expense of the Commonwealth relationship) in hard and fast federalist solutions".[14]

Leading up to the 1957 signing of the Treaties of Rome, the documents analysed in this research revealed a growing scepticism of how Britain could juggle its responsibilities to New Zealand and the Commonwealth with the pressures of an integrating Europe. In 1953, a report was sent from the New Zealand Government Office in London to the Secretary of External Affairs in Wellington. It mentioned that the British were "genuinely determined" to support the movement towards integration in continental Europe. This extended beyond the proposals for the ECSC and included support for the European Defence Community (EDC) and NATO. Yet, the British Foreign Office kept reiterating to the Commonwealth countries that Britain's relationship with the Commonwealth prevented the UK from taking a stronger role in closer European integration.[15] The New Zealand representatives in London reassured Wellington that Britain's central motivating factor in holding itself aloof from European integration was the wish to "maintain their position as the centre and directing force of the Commonwealth". They emphasised that Britain was

part 1, Commonwealth Relations Office to various Commonwealth Posts, telegram T. 2120/361, Schuman Plan, 8 July 1950.

[14] NZNA, ABHS W5503 7148 75, LONB42/7/1, part 1, External Affairs to Commonwealth Relations Office, telegram 116, 7 September 1951.

[15] NZNA, ABHS W5422 950 157, Record No. 111/14/7, part 1, European Federation – Note of Informal Talk by Mr F.G.K. Gallagher, Foreign Office, with representatives of the four "old" Commonwealth Governments.

"intensely concerned with preserving the support of the Commonwealth, because without it Britain would lose prestige and power".[16]

However, in a follow-up memo to Mr Corner (New Zealand's Deputy High Commissioner in London), Mr McIntosh mentioned that Wellington had "wondered on occasion whether the United Kingdom were being wholly frank with us about their attitude to European integration". He queried also whether "while standing aloof from such schemes as ECSC, EDC, EPC [European Political Community] etc., they will do all they can to help make them successful".[17]

This uneasiness over the dual pressures on the UK is further evident in a 1954 letter from Mr McIntosh to the High Commissioner for the UK in Wellington. The letter expressed New Zealand's support for the UK's "closer association" with the ECSC, yet it also mentioned "certain economic aspects of the proposals" that "call for comment". Among these, the letter listed the impact of the UK's accession on New Zealand as a steel consumer (with 75% of its imports coming from Britain)[18] and an agricultural producer. The latter aspect was seen of "substantial though less immediate concern". Importantly, this letter also demonstrates that New Zealand remained convinced that political advantages would outweigh the economic impacts. In his concluding remarks, Mr McIntosh stated that the New Zealand Government was "aware of the general political advantages which are expected to flow from the United Kingdom's closer association with the E.C.S.C."[19]

By the end of the decade, the anxiety was channelled into actions, with New Zealand foreign affairs officials widening their lobbying and intensifying information gathering. They also identified new diplomatic priorities. A 1958 internal memo within the Prime Minister's Department reviewed the European Communities. It recognised the "growing importance of Brussels as the centre of European integration" and for "setting the economic pace" of Europe and suggested that New Zealand should consider "the relative merits of Brussels as a future [embassy] post". Of interest was a hand-written note on this memo: "It is apparently difficult enough to persuade Govt [*sic*] to consider Bonn. Brussels would be

[16] NZNA, ABHS W5422 950 157, Record No. 111/14/7, part 1, New Zealand High Commission London to the Secretary of External Affairs, 12 March 1952.

[17] NZNA, ABHS W5422 950 157, Record No. 111/14/7, part 1, A.D. McIntosh to F.H. Corner.

[18] NZNA, ABHS W5422 950 157, Record No. 111/14/3/7, part 1, A.D. McIntosh to United Kingdom High Commission Wellington, 6 April 1954.

[19] *Ibid.*

impossible".[20] This illustrates the difference in understanding of European integration between those New Zealand officials dealing directly with the issue and those further removed from it.

During the 1950s New Zealand political stakeholders supported the development of a strong and peaceful Europe, yet they were wary of the potential impact of European integration on New Zealand. The following section will explore the media imagery of European integration that was presented to New Zealand citizens over this time and investigate the ways in which the public view was different from the views held by the national "elites".

Methodology

It is argued that in the formation of public opinion about foreign issues, ordinary people remain largely passive targets of political text or talk.[21] Galtung and Ruge famously noted that "the regularity, ubiquity and perseverance of news media will in any case make them first-rate competitors for the number-one position as international image-former".[22] The importance of foreign news was further stressed by Wanta *et al.*[23] who empirically proved that greater negative media portrayals of a foreign nation correlated with stronger negative perceptions of and attitudes towards that nation. This research assumes that subtle but nevertheless powerful effects of mass media may lie in their selection and presentation of certain issues (and non-presentation of the other issues).[24] Respectively, the questions which lead our analysis of the media discourses are the following: what imagery was used in describing European integration key events in the 1950s news media in New Zealand?; which European-New Zealand relationships were addressed and how were these seen to be affected by European integration?

In the 1950s print media was the main means by which most New Zealanders received their foreign news. This study looks at the coverage

---

20 NZNA, ABHS W5422 950 157, Record No. 111/14/3/3, part 1, Review of European Communities 1958, 13 March 1959.

21 Van Dijk, T. A., *Ideology: A Multidisciplinary Approach*, London, Sage, 1998.

22 Galtung, J. and M. Holmboe Ruge, "The Structure of Foreign News," *Journal of Peace Research*, Vol. 2, No. 1, 1965, pp. 64-91, p. 64.

23 Wanta, W., Colan, G., and Lee, C., "Agenda Setting and International News: Media Influence on Public Perception of Foreign Nations," *Journalism and Mass Communication Quarterly*, Vol. 87, No. 2, 2004, pp. 64-77.

24 Rossler, P., "The Individual Agenda-Designing Process: How Interpersonal Communication, Egocentric Networks, and Mass Media Shape the Perception of Political Issues by Individuals," *Communication Research*, Vol. 26, No. 6, 1999, pp. 666-700.

of the Schuman Plan and the Treaties of Paris and Rome in the two main newspapers, principal sources of information for the North and South Islands of New Zealand – the *New Zealand Herald* (Auckland) and *The Press* (Christchurch). In the 1950s, New Zealand did not have one daily circulating nation-wide. Including two regionally-significant newspapers means both that our research considers more than one perspective and ensures as far as possible that a New Zealand-wide response is identified. These two papers were chosen because of their respectable status, combined circulation and the fact that they have continued to operate to the present day. In the 1950s all New Zealand newspapers were locally owned, meaning that they were likely to reflect a pronounced local agenda.

This study investigated textual images of the three major events of European integration in the 1950s. It zoomed in on the so-called "peak periods" in the coverage, in this instance, publications on the topic appearing daily for two weeks before and after the event. Only news items that referenced or addressed the three European integration events – the 1950 adoption of the Schuman Plan, the 1951 Treaty of Paris creating the ECSC and the 1957 Treaties of Rome, creating the European Economic Community (EEC) and the European Atomic Energy Community (Euratom) – were included in the study. All sections of the chosen newspapers were searched. The sample included the texts of news stories written by correspondents, submitted by the news wires, as well as editorials and letters to the editors (Table 1).

Table 1: Number of news items monitored

	The Press	The New Zealand Herald	Total
1950	46	63	109
1951	17	40	57
1957	65	72	137
Total	128	175	303

This analysis employs qualitative content analysis as a technique for gathering and analysing the content of the news texts. This method is instrumental in answering the key questions: what is trying to be evoked by the two leading New Zealand newspapers about early European integration?; what is the context?; and is the message positive or negative? This analysis is also informed by limitations on the inferences our research team can make using the method of content analysis: it does not make any inferences about newsmakers' motivation or the intent behind a particular news text, nor does it infer the effect such content would have on the reader. This analysis also treats any bias detected (and any subsequent consequences) in the news texts as unintentional.

European Integration in New Zealand Print Media Discourses

In the 1950s, *The Press* and *The Herald* featured a diverse range of topics dedicated to Europe in general and its early political integration in particular. This research registered a vivid journalistic interest towards both Western and Eastern Europe and the ideas of European integration expressed by their visionaries and leaders. The leaders of Europe's "three big powers" – France, Germany and the UK – were reported extensively. In contrast, the leaders of other nations who signed the Schuman Plan (Italy and the Benelux countries) were mentioned only occasionally. Coverage of European integration by the two leading newspapers in the 1950s revealed three trends: attention to the integration occurring on the continent, reporting on the UK's attitude towards the process, and the reaction of the Commonwealth and New Zealand in particular.

Europe in NZ Press in the Early 1950s: Schuman Declaration (1950) and Treaty of Paris (1951)

In 1950 and 1951, the process of European integration was predominantly introduced in the "International" sections of the newspapers – a placement that implies that this process is an event happening on the remote European continent and not directly relevant to the local readership. Most of the news items dealing with the subject of European integration framed this process as a major focus of the reports, presenting a detailed factual account of events inside Europe, introducing multiple actors and extensively quoting them. Both papers extensively sourced their "European" news from the New Zealand's news wire New Zealand Press Association (NZPA), which used either the services of its correspondents assigned to Europe or *Reuters*.[25] Occasionally, American sources were used (e.g. *The New York Times*) and often the news texts included numerous lengthy quotes from other media sources (e.g. various European newspapers, *The Economist*, or other New Zealand media). Both papers often published identical news stories (purchased from NZPA). Importantly, instead of expressing their own opinions and attitudes, the two papers preferred to quote the European leaders frequently and at length.

---

[25] The international UK-based wire with which the NZ media had a special preferential arrangement for news purchase as in 1947 the Australian Associated Press and the NZPA joined the Reuters Trust Reuters Group PLC, http://www.fundinguniverse.com/company-histories/Reuters-Group-PLC-Company-History.html.

Framing European Integration on the Continent

Perhaps unsurprisingly, our initial expectation was that the two papers' reportage of the early-European integration would present a positive perspective of the process. To confirm this, the adoption of the Schuman Plan was described by *The Herald* as a "historic day for Europe".[26] *The Press* hailed the plan as a "highly encouraging sign that free Europe does not mean to tarry on the road to unity, strength and security".[27] In the 1951 report of the Treaty of Paris, both papers quoted Jean Monnet, the head of French delegation at the Paris conference, who stated: "the Schuman Plan Treaty is designed to open a breach in the walls of national sovereignties by substituting for the barriers which have divided and impoverished us so far".[28]

Yet, this constructive and positive image of Europe appeared only intermittently. In 1950, *The Press* and *The Herald* frequently portrayed post-war Europe as a group of bickering nations: "No enterprise has been more heavily encumbered with fears, sensitivities and divergences of outlook".[29] On the continent, the main axis of relationship in 1950 lay between Europe's "arch-enemies" – France and Germany. France was portrayed as mistrusting Germany. *The Press* mentioned France's "age-long feud with Germany",[30] and *The Herald* cited "four generations of military strife"[31] and "the centuries-old opposition".[32] According to Western German Federal Chancellor Adenauer's vision presented in both papers, "We must do away with constant mistrust. We must make a new start".[33] *The Herald* depicted the eventual adoption of the Schuman Plan as "France's desire to bury the past and help her former arch-enemy toward the status of a prosperous and contended member of the European household".[34] Newspapers also highlighted for their readers the existence of internal competition for power and prestige in the nascent European community. *The Press*, citing the *Stuttgarter Nachrichten*, stated that "Paris may succeed in obtaining the long-sought leadership within the European community of nations".[35]

---

26 *The Herald*, 5 June 1950.

27 *The Press*, 15 May 1950, p. 7, quoting "The Marshall Plan Administrator, Mr Hoffmann".

28 *The Press*, 21 March 1951, p. 7; *The Herald*, 21 March 1951.

29 *The Herald*, 12 May 1950, quoting Mr Acheson.

30 *The Press*, 13 May 1950, p. 7.

31 *The Herald*, 1 June 1950.

32 *The Herald*, 11 May 1950.

33 *The Press*, 4 April 1950, p. 5; *The Herald*, 4 April 1950.

34 *The Herald*, 5 June 1950.

35 *The Press*, 12 May 1950, p. 7.

In 1950 Europe was also reported as a weakened international player, especially when compared to the US and the USSR. European cooperation was presented as a defence against the threat posed by the communist bloc. *The Herald* described the new Europe as a counterbalance to the Soviet Union.[36] In relation to the US (a rich and assertive benefactor who dictated the rules and even exerted influence from behind the scenes), Europe was cast as a defenceless and dependent actor. *The Herald* reported that the Americans made European co-operation "so obviously their own project".[37] According to *The Herald*, it was the US that was "urging Europe integration, economic and political".[38] Commenting on the French proposal of an international coal and steel pool, both papers suggested that "the United States had a hand in the matter" with the scheme probably being "underwritten"[39] by the US. The US-Europe relations were also compared to the relations between a doctor and a patient. A US official cited by both papers proudly noted the US's work in "rehabilitating Europe's broken economies" by introducing the Marshall Plan.

While many "stumbling blocks"[40] were noted in the 1951 reporting of the establishment of the ECSC, both papers quoted the leader of the West German delegation at the Paris Conference, who noted that "the treaty is an appeal for further progress towards a united Europe".[41]

Framing the UK's Reaction

In 1950, both papers reported extensively on "British isolationism"[42] and "hesitation"[43] in the context of the Schuman Plan. The UK's reaction was described by *The Press* as "cautious",[44] "still doubtful"[45] and (in the words of Churchill) "non-committal".[46] *The Press* also underlined a "distinct difference between the views of London and Paris".[47] *The Herald* quoted "misunderstanding"[48] between the two over British participation

36 *The Herald*, 1 June 1950.
37 *The Herald*, 4 April 1950.
38 *The Herald*, 5 June 1950.
39 *The Press*, 12 May 1950, p. 7; *The Herald*, 12 May 1950.
40 *The Press*, 17 April 1951, p. 7.
41 *The Press*, 21 March 1951, p. 7; *The Herald*, 21 March 1951.
42 *The Herald*, 20 June 1950.
43 *The Herald*, 21 June 1950, quoting Mr Schuman.
44 *The Press*, 16 May 1950, p. 5.
45 *The Press*, 12 May 1950, p. 7.
46 *The Press*, 22 May 1950, p. 5.
47 *The Press*, 29 May 1950, p. 7.
48 *The Herald*, 1 June 1950.

in the Schuman proposal. The "mutual suspicions"[49] of Britain and France were a common thread. In this light, the French Government's decision to go ahead with the plan without Britain was reported by *The Press* to have caused "a first-class crisis".[50]

In 1951, media images of the UK's reservation and suspicion towards the Schuman scheme morphed into images of open opposition. The British attitude to the plan was described as changing from "cold" to "exceedingly chilly".[51] *The Press* reported that Britain was making an "attempt to prevent the initialling of the plan"[52] and seeking to "oppose"[53] the fixed limit on the volume of coal requirements of Germany. Some British Government officials were colourfully depicted as "resolutely uncompromising" when making a "last-ditch stand against any compromise, with European federalism".[54] These positions were seen as raising "further doubts about Britain's will for genuine co-operation in Europe".[55]

Framing Commonwealth and New Zealand Responses

The Commonwealth's reaction to the Schuman Plan did not receive extensive consideration in either 1950 or 1951. The 1950 reports were sanguine about the possible consequences of European integration. Both papers quoted *The Economist*, which remarked that "Australia and New Zealand are likely to be relieved rather than disturbed by evidence of initiative in the Mother Country, whatever direction that initiative may take".[56] Patrick Gordon-Walker, the Secretary for Commonwealth Relations, was quoted in *The Herald* as promising that if "certain forms of western union" appear very difficult, "it is our business to see that those forms do not develop".[57] An earlier statement by the UK Labour Party (reported in *The Herald*) also reassured New Zealand readers that "in every respect except distance we in Britain are closer to our kinsmen in Australia and New Zealand on the far side of the world than we are to Europe".[58]

49 *The Press*, 1 June 1950, p. 5; *The Herald*, 1 June 1950.

50 *The Press*, 3 June 1950, p. 7.

51 *The Press*, 14 March 1951, p. 7.

52 *Ibid.*

53 *The Press* 6 March 1951; *The Herald*, 6 March 1951.

54 *The Herald*, 2 March 1951.

55 *The Press*, 8 March 1951, p. 6.

56 *The Press*, 4 April 1950, p. 5; *The Herald*, 4 April 1950.

57 *The Herald*, 13 May 1950.

58 *The Herald*, 4 April 1950.

Mention of the "Commonwealth and Europe" becomes slightly more visible in 1951. Both papers reported on an "unofficial"[59] London-based conference, held under the auspices of the European League for Economic Cooperation, which involved representatives from Britain and its Dominions. The agenda made mention of "difficulties of reconciling the economic interests of Europe and the British Commonwealth".[60] Winston Churchill was quoted as saying, "the economic interests of the British Commonwealth and Europe were not contradictory, but complementary".[61] He underlined that "it is important that Great Britain and the Dominions should discuss their problems with their European friends".[62] The delegates were reported to have continued the conference in Brussels where they were meeting Western European experts. It is significant that the papers reported that only the first session of the conference was held in public, while "the rest of the discussion will be held in private and the conclusions will be made public later".[63] The names of the delegates from the Commonwealth – "economists, trade union leaders, industrialists and politicians"[64] (allegedly "private citizens who do not officially represent their governments")[65] – were not disclosed by the papers.

Treaties of Rome (1957)

The coverage of the treaties of Rome which established a common market and atomic energy pool between the six ECSC European nations in 1958 was very different from the coverage of the two earlier key events in Europe's integration. In stark contrast to earlier reports, the 1957 coverage of European integration was increasingly featured in the domestic news sections of both newspapers. That year, New Zealand was pre-occupied with a new development – a previously reluctant Britain (New Zealand's key European market) that was now contemplating closer economic association with its Western European partners. It was feared that this would disadvantage the Commonwealth and harm the New Zealand economy. This was mentioned in a substantial number of news items, which, given the nature of the content, were presumably written by local authors.[66] In contrast to the 1950 and 1951 reports, the lion's share of 1957 coverage

59 *The Press*, 28 May 1951, p. 7.
60 *The Press*, 31 May 1951, p. 3; *The Herald*, 31 May 1951.
61 *The Press*, 30 May 1951, p. 7.
62 *Ibid.*
63 *The Press*, 31 May 1951, p. 3; *The Herald*, 31 May 1951.
64 *The Press*, 30 May 1951, p. 7.
65 *The Press*, 31 May 1951, p. 3; *The Herald*, 31 May 1951.
66 Most of the news items in both papers were published without by-lines.

portrayed European integration as a minor factor in both domestic New Zealand discourses and those of the wider Commonwealth, often referring to it in a brief, fleeting manner. The main focus was on the reactions from the Commonwealth and New Zealand.

Framing Actions of the Six European Nations Signing the Treaties

The internal process of setting the Common Market and Customs Union was presented as problematic – it featured "a few hotly debated clauses", the "agony" of the treaties' ratification by national Parliaments, as well as the "battle" over tariffs and the agricultural questions which "plagued much of the discussion on the Common Market".[67] The benefits were reported to be unevenly distributed – "the low-tariff countries stood to score at the expense of the high-tariff countries".[68] Integration was described as amorphous: "The whole conception of European economic union has yet to be given shape and substance".[69] Europe was also presented as ambivalent, simultaneously uniting and dividing. German Foreign Minister, Dr Von Bretano, declared "the scheme is open to other countries".[70] Yet, Western Europe was increasingly separating itself from its Eastern European neighbours: the creation of the Western European common market and the Euratom scheme were reported as "certain to intensify existing divisions in Europe".[71]

Nevertheless, the signing of the treaties in Rome proved the "remarkable vitality"[72] and "surprising progress"[73] of the Schuman scheme. Both papers noted that "the treaties launch the greatest effort in modern times to unite the people of Europe".[74]

Framing the UK's Reaction

The 1957 coverage consistently depicted British ambivalence. British leaders were reported to "have openly and enthusiastically espoused the idea of European economic union – with certain reservations".[75] On the one hand, the Common Market scheme would "impinge […] on

67 All quotes from *The Press*, 20 February 1957, p. 10.

68 *The Press*, April 16, 1957, p. 13.

69 *The Herald*, February 28, 1957.

70 *The Press*, March 20, 1957, p. 16.

71 *The Herald*, March 18, 1957.

72 *The Herald*, February 8, 1957.

73 *Ibid.*

74 *The Herald*, March 27, 1957; *The Press*, March 27, 1957, p. 13.

75 *The Herald*, February 28, 1957.

the interests of the Dominions".[76] Yet, Britain "could not afford to hold aloof from the movement for closer European integration".[77] This would explain *The Herald* noting that a free trade area and common market "had aroused much favourable comment in Britain"[78] and that in the future Britain may "sacrifice Commonwealth interests".[79]

Framing the Commonwealth and New Zealand Responses

The crucial question considered by the two papers was the probable effect of the proposed European Common Market on Commonwealth agricultural produce. *The Press* described agriculture as the "real lion in the path of negotiations".[80] *The Herald* questioned whether Britain would end up "making concessions to the demands of the European food exporting countries".[81] Yet, earlier reports in 1957 optimistically argued that "there should be no real cause for alarm".[82] *The Press* presented reassuring statements by the British government that it is undertaking "closest consultation with Commonwealth".[83]

Specifically for New Zealand, the common trade proposals in Europe were recognised to "consolidate and benefit the whole Western alliance, of which New Zealand is a part".[84] Yet, increasingly, integrating Europe was presented by both papers as having negative implications for New Zealand. The "disquieting"[85] news spoke of New Zealand as "very vulnerable"[86] and getting ready to "suffer".[87] New Zealand "feared"[88] discrimination by the European countries and the exporters of farm goods and importers of machinery were seen as the "main victims".[89]

The growing worries for New Zealand were arguably aggravated by the first signs of its "identity crisis". Both papers noted "the unconcern, even indifference, of British Government spokesmen and some influential

---

76 *The Herald*, February 8, 1957.

77 *Ibid.*

78 *The Herald*, 14 February 1957.

79 *The Herald*, 3 March 1957.

80 *The Press*, 16 February 1957, p. 11.

81 *The Herald*, 8 February 1957.

82 *The Herald*, 28 February 1957.

83 *The Press*, 16 March 1957, p. 12.

84 *The Press*, 7 February 1957, p. 10; *The Herald*, 7 February 1957, quoting Mr Holland, NZ PM; *The Herald*, 3 March 1957.

85 *The Press*, 20 March 1957, p. 14, quoting Mr Holyoake.

86 *The Herald*, 3 March 1957.

87 *The Herald*, 4 April 1957.

88 *The Press*, 4 April 1957, p. 10, quoting Mr Halstead, Minister of Industry and Commerce.

89 *The Press*, 6 February 1957, p. 11.

papers in Britain"[90] towards New Zealand's precarious situation and possible fall in national income. Both dailies inquired if it was time to treat the Commonwealth as "outdated and to be replaced by plans for closer trading relations with countries outside the British family?"[91] Both newspapers warned of an option New Zealand might have to face – i.e. be "forced to look increasingly elsewhere than Britain".[92]

New Zealand's proactive response was to send a mission consisting of leading politicians and businesspeople to London. Notably, while all members were introduced in detail by both the papers, the content of the mission's negotiations was not reported in a transparent manner. *The Press* noted that "it was agreed that no detailed information of any of the proceedings will be released to the press"[93] and "only an outline of the New Zealand mission's brief may be given to the public pending the discussion".[94] *The Herald* quoted Mr Holyoake's non-response to the question on "New Zealand's views on the proposed European free trade area"[95] during the press conference discussing the New Zealand trade mission to the UK.

Conclusions

This chapter has sought to outline the various perspectives emerging in the 1950s among New Zealand political and media commentators with regard to European integration and the impact that such views had on New Zealand and relations with Europe. Our future research into the New Zealand historical perceptions of European integration will feature a wider media sample and will include other periods of monitoring (from the 1960s to the 1990s). We also hope to widen our scope to include other Commonwealth countries. Undoubtedly, this broader view will highlight the finer peculiarities of the portrait painted of European integration in the 1950s in New Zealand.

In the early 1950s, New Zealand elites were supportive of European integration efforts in general, and the Schuman Plan in particular, as a solution to a divided Europe and as a way of maintaining Britain's influence and power in world affairs. They believed that the UK could play a part in this integration process in a way that would not be detrimental to

90 *The Press*, 7 March 1957, p. 3; *The Herald*, 3 March 1957.

91 *The Press*, 7 March 1957, p. 3; *The Herald*, 3 March 1957.

92 *The Herald*, 20 March 1957; *The Press*, 20 March 1957, p. 14, quoting Mr Ormond, chairman of NZ Meat Producers Board.

93 *The Press*, 10 April 1957, p. 13.

94 *The Press*, 2 February 1957, p. 13.

95 *The Herald*, 6 April 1957.

Commonwealth interests. However, within a decade, New Zealand had become increasingly sceptical of British assurances that London could balance its Commonwealth commitments with new European priorities. While the New Zealand elites were still supportive of integration, and the need for Britain to play a role in forging the type of Europe they wished to see, they were aware that there might be an economic price for this political stability.

This changing attitude between support for a solution to overseas political instability and a potential domestic economic problem was also reflected in the New Zealand media. It is suggested that the New Zealand media imagery in 1950 and 1951 sent New Zealand readers several peculiar messages at the dawn of European integration. First, in the monitored reports Europe seemed to appear as a weak player and thus potentially harmless to New Zealand. Secondly, 1950-51 events in Europe (or how they were framed by the two papers' newsmakers) did not affect New Zealand's interests in an obvious way. These events took place on a far away continent and they were led by a small group of European "elites" who were pre-occupied with their internal issues rather than building a dialogue with the rest of the world. Post-war Europe's external affairs did not seem to stretch beyond its relations with the US and the USSR. Thirdly, Britain had a different stance towards European integration when compared with everybody else in post-war Western Europe. Arguably, this very particular – "non-committal" and "suspicious" – attitude of Britain towards the on-going integration left its imprint on subsequent New Zealand public images and perceptions of the process of European integration.

Britain's first application to join the EEC was lodged in 1961. It was to be eleven years before the UK acceded to EEC membership. Britain's decision crucially affected New Zealand's economic well-being and faced it with a dramatic question: "To be or not to be?" as a developed and prosperous nation. Yet, only in the coverage of the 1957 treaties did the New Zealand leading press feature a more critical consideration of the process of European integration and the consequences of the British decision to join the European Community. We also argue that the 1957 coverage solidified an image critical for understanding New Zealand's historical and modern perceptions of integrating Europe; namely, it is impossible to stay away from Britain.

According to the New Zealand leading press (and later in the eyes of the general public),[96] this is a fundamentally triangular relationship – and the 1957 coverage amply illustrated the mutual entwinement of the three

[96] Chaban, N. and Holland, M. (eds.), *The European Union and the Asia-Pacific: Media, Public and Elite Perceptions of the EU*, London and New York, Routledge, 2008.

actors, New Zealand, the UK and integrating Europe. British ambivalence – the desire to preserve relations with the Commonwealth as against their economic interest in entering into closer association with their European partners – was reported by the two leading dailies, and arguably set the background to the later discourse of "abandonment" ever-popular in New Zealand since the UK joined the EEC. In particular, the "abandonment" discourse focused on the more extreme implications for New Zealand expressed in the market losses, severed cultural ties with Britain and a sense of unfair treatment.[97] Nevertheless, this explicitly negative position was later contrasted with a more pragmatic view which highlighted continuity in relationships between New Zealand and Europe and New Zealand's active role in gaining recognition for its special status and seeking new markets.[98]

Finally, the 1950, 1951 and 1957 coverage of the three key events of early European integration featured little transparent reflection on the content of New Zealand's political and business elites' negotiations with the UK and its European partners. In conclusion, this chapter argues that these "information deficits" contributed to a more acute feeling of abandonment among the New Zealand public following British accession. It is also suggested that this feeling lingered, shaping responses to later European integration events and even modern perceptions of New Zealand-Europe relations.

97 See, for example, Jackson, K., "Introduction," in K. Jackson (ed.), *Fight for Life New Zealand, Britain and the EEC*, Wellington, Price Milburn and Company for NZIIA, 1970; Jackson, K. and Harré, J., *New Zealand*, London, Thames and Hudson, 1969.

98 See, for example, Lodge, J., "The EEC and New Zealand," *New Zealand International Review*, January/February, 1976; Kennaway, R., *op. cit.*; McMillan, S., "How Much Butter?," *New Zealand International Review*, Vol. 4, No. 4, 1979.

The EU in New Zealand and Singapore

A Normative Power?

Dr Serena KELLY

University of Canterbury, New Zealand

Introduction

Since its modest beginnings as the European Coal and Steel Community (ECSC) in 1951, the EU has progressed economically in a variety of ways, with its political evolution happening at a much slower pace. This has resulted in the more traditional understanding of the Union as an "exporter" of its economic values to other parts of the globe, for example, as a model for regional economic integration. The concept of Normative Power Europe (NPE) goes beyond this notion and notes the importance of the EU's external relations in exporting values *other than* economic systems.[1] NPE is based on the idea that shared values and identity, rather than personal interests, drive the EU and it is these values which the EU wishes to export to other countries and regions of the world, as it believes that these values promote effective and legitimate governance. Using primary data gained from elite interviews and public opinion surveys, this chapter analyses the strength of NPE in New Zealand and Singapore. In doing so, it seeks to understand how effectively the EU is communicating what it is and what it stands for to the rest of the world.

Methodology

Although there has been much literature on the emergence of the EU as an international actor and many studies have examined how the EU is perceived by its own citizens,[2] there has traditionally been a deficit in

1 There may, however, be some overlaps with the former model, for example, with trade.

2 Betham, D. and Lord, C., "Legitimacy and the European Union," in A. Weale, and M. Netwich, *Political Theory and the European Union*, London, Routledge, 2011; See also Egeberg, M., "Transcending Intergovernmentalism? Identity and Role Perceptions

external perceptions of the EU, something which has been addressed by a number of academics, including Martin Holland and Natalia Chaban at the National Centre for Research on Europe, University of Canterbury. In order to understand how the EU is understood, conveyed and portrayed in the Asia-Pacific, they have undertaken a number of studies in the region. They found a dearth of studies exploring how the EU is perceived *externally*, and thus embarked on a number of multi-tiered projects with the aim of addressing this academic gap.[3]

Others who have addressed this deficit include Philomena Murray, who investigated Australian elite perceptions of the EU,[4] and Ole Elgström,[5] who analysed perceptions of the EU in multilateral and trade negotiations. In addition, Sonia Lucarelli has also highlighted the importance of examining EU external perceptions, noting that "we fail to understand a fundamental component of the EU's international role as well as of the Europeans' self-identification process if we do not investigate what the external images of the EU are".[6]

This study draws on data collected from Singapore and New Zealand public and elite opinions utilising Holland and Chaban's methodology. In order to understand how normative the EU is viewed in Singapore (2007) and New Zealand (2004), a two-fold methodology has been adopted – elite interviews and public opinion surveys.

---

of National Officials in EU Decision-making," *Journal of European Public Policy*, Vol. 6, No. 3, 1999; Bruter, M., "On What Citizens Mean by Feeling 'European': Perceptions of News, Symbols and Borderless-ness," *Journal of Ethnic and Migration Studies*, Vol. 30, No. 1, 2004.

3 "EU External Perceptions," National Centre for Research on Europe, University of Canterbury, www.euperceptions.canterbury.ac.nz, accessed 11 March 2011.

4 Murray, P., "Australian Voices: Some Elite Reflections on the European Union," *CESAA Review*, Vol. 29, 2002, pp. 5-18, http://www.cesaa.org.au/forms/Cesaapercent20Review percent20October percent202002.pdf, accessed 10 March 2009.

5 Elgström, O., "Leader or Foot-Dragger? Perceptions of the European Union in Multilateral International Negotiations," *Swedish Institute for European Policy Studies Report* 1, 2006, www.sieps.se/publ/rapporter/bilagor/20061.pdf, accessed 11 March 2011; Elgström, O., "Outsiders' Perceptions of the European Union in International Trade Negotiations," *Journal of Common Market Studies*, Vol. 45, No. 4, 2007, pp. 949-967.

6 Lucarelli, S., "EU Political Identity, Foreign Policy and External Image," The External Image of the European Union: A Global Survey, *GARNET Working Paper Series* 17, 2007, http://www.garneteu.org/fileadmin/documents/working_papers/1707/1 percent20Surveypercent20Frontpercent20Page-Content-Authors-acknowledgments.pdf, accessed 11 March 2011.

Jerry Yeric and John Todd have defined public opinion as "the shared opinions of a collection of individuals on a common concern".[7] For the surveys, 400 telephone interviews were conducted in New Zealand and 400 people completed an online survey in Singapore. Professional companies were contracted in both countries to carry out the survey. A total of twenty-three questions were asked of respondents.

Secondly, semi-structured elite interviews were used to determine opinions about the EU held by Singaporean and New Zealand elites. The expression "elite" refers to people who are "in positions to make decisions having major consequences".[8] Elites are important as they have the ability to influence their country's choice of international partners, and their views were included in this study for that reason. The elites were drawn equally from four sectors – political, business, media and civil society. These interviews were conducted in English by trained local researchers.

Thirty-two interviews were conducted in Singapore and twenty-eight in New Zealand. The elites were chosen at random, and asked the same question from the public surveys: "When thinking about the term 'the European Union', what *three* thoughts come to your mind?" The reason for introducing these questions is that it gives an honest, unprejudiced answer about initial impressions about how the EU is perceived in the public, thus providing a unique insight. The answers were categorised and analysed according to the outline presented in the theoretical framework, making for an interesting comparison between the opinions of "movers and shakers" of Singapore and New Zealand, and those of ordinary citizens.

The Case Studies: Singapore and New Zealand

While it is acknowledged that the Asia-Pacific region is larger than Singapore and New Zealand, for comparability purposes, these countries have been chosen for a number of reasons. The study of their relationships with the EU provides a unique perspective, given that EU involvement in the area is usually focused on the bigger countries such as Japan or China in Asia, and Australia in the Pacific. This traditional focus on the EU in the literature means that these "third tier" states have been overlooked in the past.

7 Yeric, J. and Todd, J., *Public Opinion: The Visible Politics*, Illinois, F.E. Peacock Publishers, 1983, p. 4.

8 Mills, C. *The Power Elite*, New York, Oxford University Press, 1956, http://www.thirdworldtraveler.com/Book_Excerpts/HigherCircles_PE.html, accessed 11 March 2011.

Although the countries are geo-politically distinct, they have a number of commonalities. For instance, both are stable, (largely) democratic, traditional allies of the EU (but not the major players), English-speaking, former British colonies and maritime states. In addition, both countries rely heavily on international trade, making a prosperous, stable relationship with the EU crucial. Indeed, both are interested in signing Free Trade Agreements (FTAs) with the EU. Both states have a similar population size – the New Zealand population is officially 4,328,994[9] while the Singaporean population is slightly higher at 5,353,494,[10] meaning they are larger than seven of the current EU member states, and within 4% of the population of Ireland.[11]

The two share a cooperative relationship with the European Union. Whereas in many parts of the world the EU, and the former Commission delegations (now known as EU delegations) in particular, place a strong emphasis on developmental assistance, the relatively affluent economies of Singapore and New Zealand mean that the relationships have instead focused on areas such as the arts and culture, research and development, education, and health.

Their geopolitical locations mean that the EU cooperates with New Zealand and Singapore for their highly developed strategies in dealing with their neighbouring, developing countries. For New Zealand, it is the country's proximity and paternal interest in the politically turbulent Pacific region (part of the African, Caribbean and Pacific Group of States (ACP)) which solidifies the EU relationship. By contrast, Singapore is situated in the middle of a somewhat volatile Asian region, where the EU is engaged in several regional forums aimed at promoting development and stability in the region (such as cooperation with the Association of Southeast Asian Nations (ASEAN) and in the Asia-Europe Meeting (ASEM) process).

The following section outlines the characteristics and capabilities of the EU as a normative power. There are a number of conditions and values which need to be taken into account when considering NPE. They are based on the reasoning that the EU is a *sui generis* entity; it acts multilaterally, has a sound legal base for its actions, is a "soft" power, and promotes a set of values. In short, it is, overall, a force for good in the world. Section three then looks at how prominent these ideas are in the minds of Singaporean and New Zealand citizens.

9 https://www.cia.gov/library/publications/the-world-factbook/geos/nz.html.

10 https://www.cia.gov/library/publications/the-world-factbook/geos/sn.html.

11 https://www.cia.gov/library/publications/the-world-factbook/geos/ei.html.

Internal and External Constructions of NPE

The EU as a Sui Generis, Multilateral and Legal Entity

Although the idea that the EU needs to be understood as a *sui generis* entity has been debated in academic circles,[12] according to Ian Manners the EU is *sui generis*, because "it changes the norms, standards and prescriptions of world politics away from the bounded expectations of state-centricity".[13] One part of the unique way the EU is structured is its preference for operating multilaterally – through international organisations like the United Nations (UN), World Trade Organization (WTO) and North Atlantic Treaty Organization (NATO). According to Michael Smith multilateralism is an important tool for the EU because its economic weight means it is able to use and shape international institutions.[14] The sheer number of member states at the UN also gives it an advantage in voting sessions.

Operating multilaterally also serves to enhance the legitimacy and legality of the EU. The legal platform on which the EU operates is another element of NPE – to perform as a normative power is to operate within the law.[15] The legal basis of the EU, reflected in the myriad of treaties that govern it, has important implications for NPE. These treaties have evolved over time, from the Treaty on European Union which included "liberty, democracy, respect for human rights and fundamental freedoms" and the "rule of law" (Article 6), to the more recent Treaty of Lisbon (2007) which provided for the establishment and practice of the EU's foreign policy, stating that:

> The Union's action on the international scene shall be guided by the principles which have inspired its own creation, development and enlargement, and which it seeks to advance in the wider world: democracy, the rule of law, the universality and indivisibility of human rights and fundamental freedoms, respect for human dignity, the principles of equality and solidarity, and respect for the principles of the United Nations Charter and international law (Article 21 [10a]).

---

12 See, for example, Moravscik, A., "Preferences and Power in the European Community: A Liberal Intergovernmentalist Approach," *Journal of Common Market Studies*, Vol. 31, No. 4, 1993, p. 474.

13 Manners, I., "The Normative Ethics of the European Union," *International Affairs*, Vol. 84, No. 1, 2008, p. 45.

14 Smith, M., "The European Union and International Order: European and Global Dimensions," *European Foreign Affairs Review*, Vol. 12, 2007, pp. 437-456.

15 Sjursen, J., "The EU as a 'Normative' Power: How Can This Be?," *Journal of European Public Policy*, Vol. 13, No. 2, March, 2006, p. 245.

(Semi-)Soft Power Politics?

NPE is aligned with the EU's "soft power". Whereas in the 1970s a military capability for the European Communities was hardly on the cards,[16] the EU's capability in this area is now less clear-cut. Until the end of the 1990s, the EU had no military capability and therefore relied on non-military tactics to promote its set of values to the world. Because of this, the EU was often deemed to be a "soft-power" actor in its international relations, juxtaposed with the United States' "hard-power" status.

The EU's soft power is based on its desire to create peace without the use of overt force.[17] Joseph Nye[18] defined power as "the ability to alter the behaviour of others to get what you want", in particular, an entity's soft power "rests on its resources of culture, values, and policies".[19] Soft power is also linked to attraction as "[w]hen policies and positions of states or non-state actors have moral authority, or are seen as legitimate in the eyes of others, their soft power is increased".[20] In this way, the EU relies on its ability to shape the views of its partners.

The EU's Common Foreign and Security Policy (CFSP) was first introduced in order to safeguard European values. Since then, its structure and role have been amended in reaction to a perceived "expectations-capabilities gap", the failure of the EU to react to civilian crises in the Balkans.[21] Whether the EU is being "militarised", is subject to debate. Although the EU does not have an army, (member states remain responsible for their own security and defence) its military capabilities have been increasingly improved in order to fulfil the 1992 "Petersberg tasks". In addition, the European Security and Defence Policy (ESDP) aimed at strengthening the EU's ability to act through the development of civilian and military capabilities and was designed to complement the EU's soft power capabilities. Further, although the development of the Rapid Reaction Force gave the EU the capacity to coordinate and deploy a force

---

16 Duchêne, F., "Europe's Role in World Peace," in R. Mayne, *Europe Tomorrow*, London, Fontana, 1972.

17 Sjursen, H., "The EU as a 'Normative' Power," *op. cit.* See also, Smith, K., *European Union Foreign Policy in a Changing World*, Cambridge, Polity Press, 2003.

18 Nye, J., "Think again: Soft power," *Foreign Policy*, 2006, http://www.foreignpolicy.com/story/cms.php?story_ id=3393.

19 Nye, J., "Public Diplomacy and Soft Power," *The ANNALs of the American Academy of Political and Social Science*, Vol. 616, 2008.

20 Gilboa, E., "Searching for a Theory of Public Diplomacy," *The ANNALS of the American Academy of Political and Social Science*, Vol. 616, 2008, p. 61.

21 Hill, C., "The Capability-Expectations Gap, or Conceptualising Europe's International Role," *Journal of Common Market Studies*, Vol. 31, No. 3, 1993.

of 60,000, such deployments remain within the control of individual countries. Anne Deighton has noted that ESDP was a way for the EU "to project power beyond its borders".[22] This analysis does not seek to assess whether or not the EU is being militarised, but rather to evaluate whether the EU is *perceived* as being a military power or not. An increasingly militarised profile could endanger the EU's normative identity,[23] because its international "presence" has been built on its normative actions, which gained and kept the trust of its world partners and beneficiaries. Others do not believe that it is contradictory for the Union to develop a military capability to work alongside its soft-power politics. It may even be complementary, strengthening the exportation of normative values.[24] This is how the EU's military capability currently operates, i.e., supporting EU normative goals.

There have been many critiques of the EU's softpower capability. Javier Noya concluded that "soft power is not a type of power at all".[25] Furthermore, Thomas Diez noted that the question is not whether a state is a power, but the extent to which it is one.[26] In other words, the two concepts, military power and the promotion of norms, are not mutually exclusive. For example, when the European Security Strategy (ESS) was introduced as a reaction to the war in Iraq, it was threat-driven and emphasised the importance of multilateralism, and included a focus on the potential of the NPE policies of trade and development:

> Active policies are needed to counter the new dynamic threats. We need to develop a strategic culture that fosters early, rapid, and when necessary, robust intervention […] Trade and development policies can be powerful tools for promoting reform. A world seen as offering justice and opportunity for everyone will be more secure for the European Union and its citizens.[27]

The New Zealand Minister for Finance, Bill English, controversially noted the ineffectiveness of the EU's soft power. In a secretly taped discussion he noted; "Europe has turned out to be particularly ineffective

---

22 Deighton, A., "The European Security and Defence Policy," *Journal of Common Market Studies*, Vol. 40, No. 4, 2002, p. 720.

23 Manners, I., "The Normative Ethics of the European Union," *op. cit.*

24 Petiteville, F., "Exporting 'Values'? EU External Co-operation as a 'Soft Diplomacy'," in M. Knodt and S. Princen (eds.), *Understanding the European Union's External Relations*, New York, Routledge, 2003, p. 137.

25 Noya, J., "The Symbolic Power of Nations," *Working Paper 35, Real Instituto Elcano*, Madrid, 2005, http://www.isn.ethz.ch/isn/Digital-Library/Publications/Detail/?ots591=0C54E3B3-1E9C-BE1E-2C24-A6A8C7060233&lng=en&id=13678, accessed 9 March 2011.

26 Diez, T., "Constructing the Self and Changing Others: Reconsidering 'Normative Power Europe'," *Millennium – Journal of International Studies*, Vol. 33, 2005, p. 620.

27 "European Security Strategy," *A Secure Europe in a Better World*, 12 December 2003.

even in its own backyard [...] There still needs [to be] someone willing to pull the trigger".[28] Because of the number of military and security capabilities that the EU currently possesses, being a "soft power" no longer adequately describes the EU, therefore, perhaps the term "semi-soft power" may be more fitting. The data presented in Section Five will examine whether the EU is viewed in Singapore and New Zealand as a soft power or whether its increasing militarisation is changing the perception of the EU.

The EU's Values

The EU's success at integration has influenced its global vision; it now wishes to export its values. According to Manners,[29] there are nine normative principles that the EU wishes to promote in other regions and nations globally. These are (but not limited to): peace, freedom, democracy, human rights, the rule of law, equality, social solidarity, sustainable development and good governance. The promotion of environmental issues, regionalism, and the peaceful resolution of conflicts have also been listed as values the EU seeks to promote.

Like multilateralism, the promotion of regionalism heavily influences how the EU deals with the rest of the world, as it promotes this policy amongst its partners. According to the EU, its promotion of regionalism enables it to be more effective and efficient. This means that New Zealand, as a participant of the Pacific Island's Forum, is often involved with the EU through the Forum's relationship with the EU and perhaps more significantly, Singapore's communication with the EU is often conducted at one step removed through ASEAN.

Human rights have tended to be the most researched of the values, maybe because this is the most visible, tangible and distinct feature of NPE. However, even in human rights the EU faces criticism. The separation between how the Commission and the intergovernmental CFSP actors approach human rights means that it has been criticised as lacking coherence and consistency, particularly pre-Lisbon. In first-pillar competences "democracy, rule of law and human rights" were treated together. Within CFSP, the focus on human rights was treated as separate from the promotion and defence of democracy and the rule of law, with the former receiving much less emphasis.[30] EU human rights initiatives are often declaratory only and the emphasis in CFSP on human rights is often

[28] Young, A., "Tape Shows Nationals' War Ethic, says Clark," *New Zealand Herald*, 5 November 2008.

[29] Manners, I., "The Normative Ethics of the European Union," *op. cit.*

[30] Smith, K., *European Union Foreign Policy in a Changing World*, Cambridge, Polity Press, 2003, p. 140.

viewed as a diversion from the fact that member states find other areas more difficult to agree on. Nevertheless, the promotion of human rights has been seen as an important mechanism for the EU's capability and visibility.

The EU's emphasis on democracy and human rights has been prominent in its dealings in the Pacific, and has been strongly supported by New Zealand. For the Singaporean relationship, and the whole of Asia, the emphasis on human rights has been "the most significant field of intellectual debate and contention within EU-Asia relations".[31] For example, the first meeting between the EU and ASEAN highlighted a marked difference in their approaches as "[h]uman rights were a European concern whereas the Asian participants preferred an exclusive focus on trade".[32] The EU Delegation in Singapore also emphasises human rights in Singapore on its website.[33]

The EU's development policies are a key part of the strategy of the EU delegations as they are ideally placed to be a strong network for the EU to promote and export its norms.[34] Singapore and New Zealand's cooperation with the EU in neighbouring countries has been viewed as being important for bilateral relations. More recently, concern has been raised that the Lisbon Treaty has merged EU development policy with its so-called "hard power" capabilities.[35]

Normative rules are important to how the EU deals with post-colonial states, with trade, conditionality and sanctions often being used as tools to persuade third parties to take on European norms. Conditionality covers the promotion of democracy, human rights, the rule of law, good governance, and market liberalism. From Europe's point of view, these are all key areas for promoting growth in developing countries, although from

31 Wiessala, G., "Promoting Human Rights in EU-Asia Relations, Burma, China and Indonesia," *EurAsia Bulletin*, Vol. 8, Nos. 1 and 2 (Jan.-Feb.), 2004, http://www.eias.org/publications/bulletin/2004/janfeb04/ebjanfeb04p3.pdf, accessed 9 March 2009.

32 Holland, M., *The European Union and the Third World*, Hampshire, Palgrave, 2002, p. 68.

33 See http://www.eeas.europa.eu/delegations/singapore/key_eu_policies/human_rights/index_en.htm, accessed 28 November 2011.

34 Eeckhart, P., *External Relations of the European Union – Legal and Constitutional Foundations*, Oxford, Oxford University Press, 2004.

35 Anderson, S. and Williams, J., "The Securitization of Development Policy or the Developmentalization of Security Policy?: Legitimacy, Public Opinion, and the EU External Action Service (EAS)," presented at the 2011 European Union Studies Association Conference, Boston, MA, http://euce.org/eusa/2011/papers/8l_anderson.pdf, accessed 10 June 2011.

the viewpoint of developing countries this focus is sometimes criticised as being driven by EU self-interest.

Finally, the EU's environmental strategies are also part of NPE. Although the EU does not have a common environmental initiative on the same level as the Common Agricultural Policy (CAP), it has arguably overtaken America as the world environmental leader, and its success in environmental matters supports multilateralism.

It is clear that the EU employs a myriad of tools and values in its role as a normative global actor. Internally, the norms espoused by the EU have been mostly successful in promoting stability in Europe. What is less clear is its success further afield. The remainder of this analysis focuses on evaluating the success of NPE from the perspective of the public and elites in Singapore and New Zealand.

Beyond the EU's Borders

Evaluating NPE in Singapore and New Zealand

Helene Sjursen has noted that it is one thing to call the EU a normative power for good, but it is also important to systematically analyse it.[36] The strength of NPE lies in the EU's ability to convince others to follow it, consequently placing a reliance on world opinion.[37] Although the way the EU is represented beyond its borders (for example, through its Delegations) is connected to its aspirations to export its core values, the representation of the EU abroad does not necessarily correlate with reality.[38] While the EU might define itself as a force for good, this is subjective and as such "the EU's 'normative' power might simply be an expression of Eurocentric cultural imperialism".[39] Because of this, NPE has been described as "a practice of discursive representation".[40]

External perceptions of the EU are important for a number of reasons. In order for an entity to be considered legitimate, it requires acceptance and recognition not only from those it wishes to represent, but also from beyond the borders of the entity itself. With approval comes legitimacy

36 Sjursen, H., "The EU as a 'Normative' Power," *op. cit.*

37 Laïdi, Z., "European Preferences and Their Reception," in Z. Laïdi, *EU Foreign Policy in a Globalised World, Normative Power and Social Preferences*, New York, Routledge, 2008, p. 5.

38 Although some people argue that perception is reality, that is to say, we act in accordance with our perception of reality and not in accordance with reality itself, therefore perception is perhaps even more important.

39 Sjursen, H., "The EU as a 'Normative' Power," *op. cit.*, p. 248.

40 Diez, T., "Constructing the Self and Changing Others: Reconsidering 'Normative Power Europe'," *op. cit.*, p. 626.

and this legitimacy forms the basis of claims by governments that they should be listened to.[41] Moreover, external perceptions of the EU are "argued to be instrumental in understanding the images which potentially impact the Union's external actions and consequently affect its internal rhetoric and self-visions of foreign policy".[42]

Images of the EU in the Eyes of the Singaporean Public

The answers from this study's public opinion surveys were categorised according to the values outlined above and are demonstrated in Figure 1. Because of the traditional, economic vision of the EU, any answers containing inferences of an economic character were categorised together. The EU's economic identity was overwhelmingly the dominant image in Singapore, with 20% of the sample pointing to the economic and business spheres as dominant areas of activity. Such answers included references to the euro, as well as trade and the single market. Only a very small number of respondents mentioned the EU as a security and/or defence actor (1%), indicating that the image of the EU as a hard power is close to non-existent, a finding which is positive for NPE and understandable given the EU's deficiency in this area. The majority of responses were categorised under the "other" category. In other words, they did not refer to the EU as a normative, economic and on the whole powerful actor. These included the EU as a travel destination, or the EU as part of the Western world.

Importantly for this research, the survey was designed to ascertain whether the EU's self-belief as a normative/soft power had been communicated to publics outside of the Union. The total number of any answers that mentioned normative ideals was also recorded. In Singapore this accounted for a relatively low 5% of the overall answers. Although a vision of the EU as a normative actor was relatively low in the minds of the Singaporean public, nevertheless it was seen as being powerful.[43]

---

41 Koppell, J. G. S., "Global Governance Organisations: Legitimacy and Authority in Conflict," *Journal of Public Administration Research and Theory*, Vol. 18, 2008.

42 Chaban, N., Kelly, S. and Bain, J., "European Commission Delegations and EU Public Policy: Stakeholders' Perceptions from the Asia-Pacific," *European Foreign Affairs Review*, Vol. 14, 2009, p. 279.

43 The numbers displayed reflect the total number of responses. Respondents were often unable to think of "3 images".

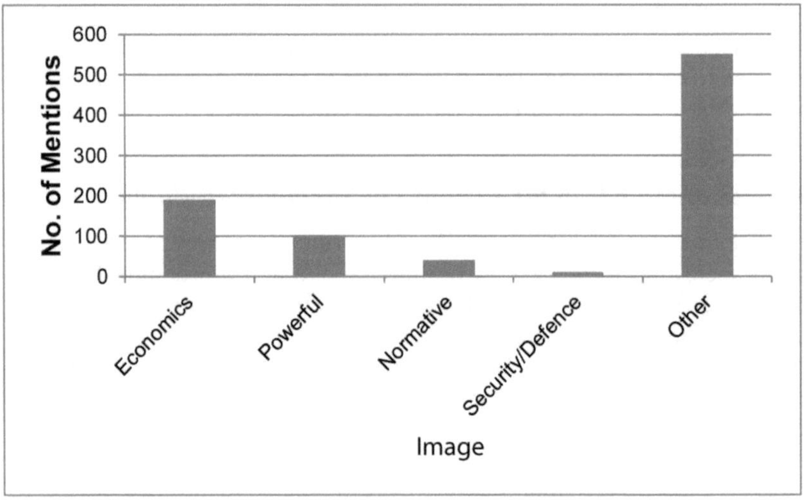

Figure 1: *Images of the EU in the Singaporean Public.*

Figure 2 further extrapolates concepts and visions related to NPE. When normative EU ideals were mentioned by the Singaporean public respondents, they referred to EU ideals in general, which could be interpreted as both internal and external ideals. For example, "peace" was mentioned, as was "law" and also general "stability".

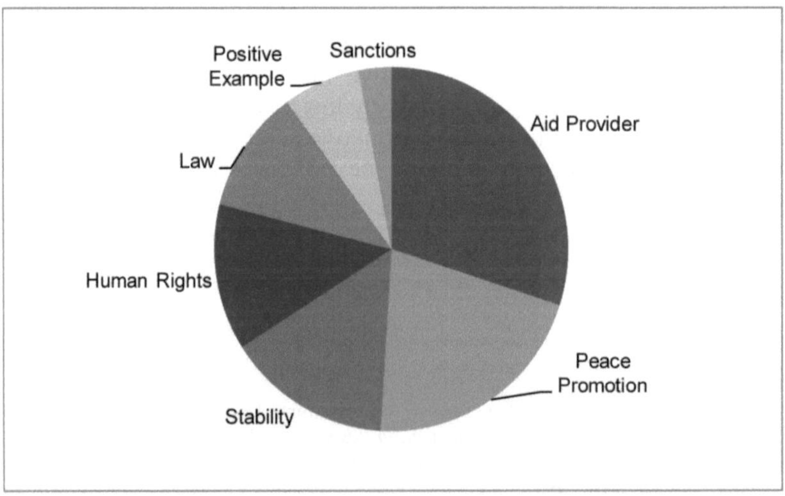

Figure 2: *Singapore Public Opinion: A Normative EU?*

Judging from these findings, although the overall image of the EU as a normative actor was quite low when compared to the EU's economic activities, it was still present and thus, significant. Out of the normative categories presented above, the EU as an aid provider was the dominant image for the Singaporean public (30%). This was followed by the EU's action as a promoter of peace (21%) and stability (15%). A reference to EU law and regulations (excluding economics) was also acknowledged (11%). Surprisingly, human rights were relatively very low on the agenda (13%), despite it being a clear goal of the EU in its dealings with that country. Clearly then, the communication of the EU as a promoter of human rights is not as successful as it could be in Singapore. Although there is a strong internal public support for the EU to promote human rights, Balfour[44] has noted that human rights is "a cross pillar activity". There are inherent difficulties in trying to explain a finding such as this in Singapore, but it may be that the cross-pillar nature of the activity "robs" the area of the promotion of human rights of its stand-alone visibility.

The final finding among the Singaporean public highlights the link between the EU and the regional grouping of ASEAN. Although the EU engages with ASEAN and it has been noted that the EU is a positive role model in regional integration which some ASEAN officials wish to emulate, in total only eight responses (2% of the sample) mentioned ASEAN in some form. The political relationship between Singapore and the EU also stresses the promotion of human rights, something which was also noticeably absent from the respondents' comments. Perhaps, therefore, this supports Rüland's viewpoint that Asia, and ASEAN in particular, view the EU's value of human rights protection as a form of neo-colonialism.[45]

44 Balfour, R., "Human rights promotion," in F. Cerutti and S. Lucarelli (eds.), *The Search for European Identity*, London and New York, Routledge, 2008, p. 163.

45 Rüland, J., "ASEAN and the European Union: A Bumpy Interregional Relationship," Zentrum für Europäische Integrationsforschung, Rheinische Friedrich Wilhelms-Universität Bonn, Discussion Paper, C95, 2001, http://www.zei.de/download/zei_dp/dp_c95_rueland.pdf, accessed 9 March 2009.

Images of the EU in the Eyes of the New Zealand Public

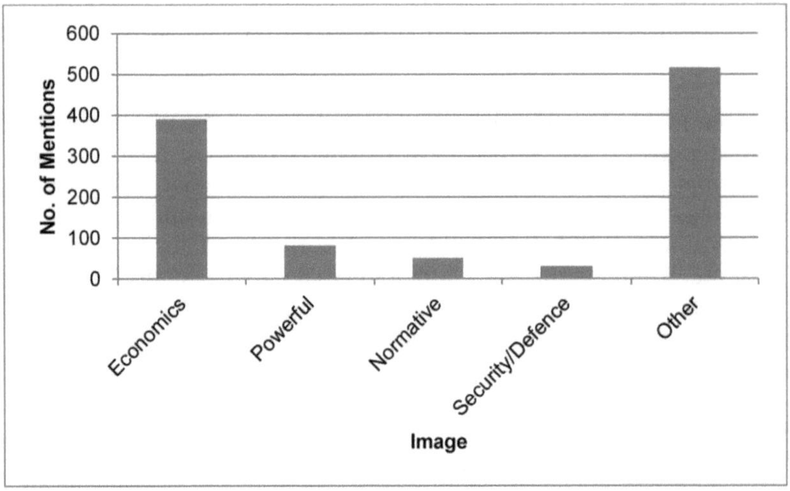

Figure 3: *Images of the EU in the Eyes of the New Zealand Public.*

Comparing the Singaporean public opinion responses with those from New Zealand, many points of similarity between the two samples can be seen. There were also a few telling differences, however. For example, references to the EU's economic role was markedly higher than in Singapore: 35% versus 20%. This is a surprising finding, given that Singapore is seen as the economic hub of Asia. The explanation might lie in the fact that the New Zealand-EU relationship has always been predominately focused on trade, and particularly trade in agricultural goods.

An awareness of the EU as a normative actor by the New Zealand public was approximately the same as in Singapore – 5% of the total "spontaneous image" answers. This gives the indication that efforts to promote the EU as such have been consistently, albeit weakly, received around the world (see Figure 4).

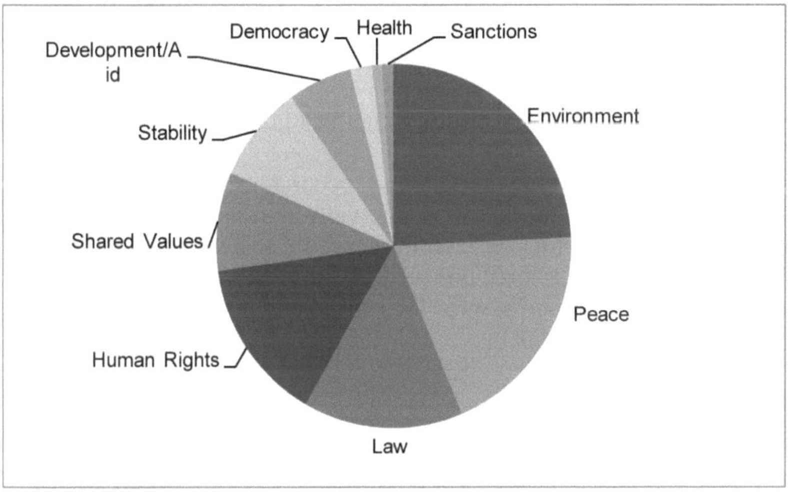

Figure 4: *New Zealand Public Opinion: A Normative EU?*

When compared to Singapore, there was a difference in the type of norms the EU was associated with in New Zealand. Whereas the focus in Singapore was primarily on development aid, in New Zealand the EU as a champion of environmental matters received the highest mention at 25% of respondents, followed by a perception that the EU is both a human rights actor, and involved in establishing legal regulations.

Something which was noticeably absent in the Singaporean answers was the general perception that the citizens and countries of the EU share common values. In New Zealand, this accounted for 9% of the total answers pertaining to EU norms. The same percentage of respondents mentioned the EU promoting "stability", in contrast to the Singaporean answers where stability was the second most mentioned norm. Perhaps the biggest difference in how the Singaporean and New Zealand public view the EU was in its role as a development aid provider. Although both countries consider themselves as developed, there was a much bigger awareness in Singapore of the EU's development assistance role than in New Zealand: 30% versus 6% respectively. This is in contrast to the emphasis placed by both countries on the importance of the cooperative relationship between the host country and the EU in promoting development and stability in the nearby Pacific and Asian regions. Likewise, democracy also featured low in New Zealand respondents' minds, with only two responses mentioning democracy at all, the same number as in Singapore.

Perceptions of Singaporean Elites on the European Union

Expanding on how the EU is perceived by the public in Singapore and New Zealand, the following section incorporates the findings of face-to-face semi-structured interviews with elites in each country from four different cohorts. Once again, and as per the stereotyped image, the EU as an economic actor, or issues pertaining to economics, were at the forefront of the minds of the elites that were interviewed in Singapore (see Figure 5). Interestingly, the elites representing the civil society sector were more likely to view the EU as both powerful and normative, whereas the elites in the business community were the only cohort to think of the EU in security and defence terms.

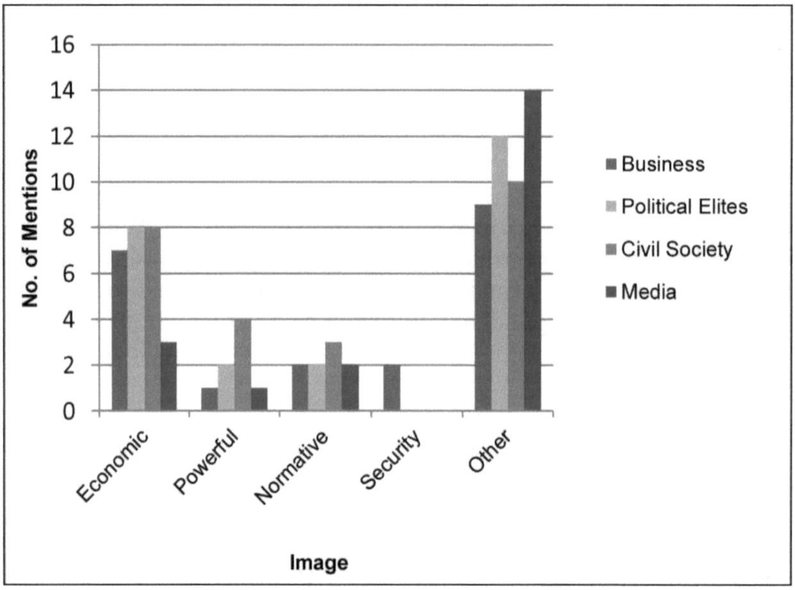

Figure 5: *Images of the EU among Singaporean Elites.*

Significantly, the mentions displayed in the "other" category were again dominant. These answers covered general ideas associated with the EU such as culture or people. This supports Krzeminski's comment that when one thinks of Europe, one thinks of it in terms of culture and herein lies Europe's power.[46] The high number of cultural identity images

46 Krzeminski, A., "Culture (em)power(s) Europe," Conférences en ligne du Centre canadien d'études allemandes et européennes, Vol. 1, No. 1, 2004, http://www.cceae.umontreal.ca/IMG/pdf/CEL_0101.pdf, accessed 1 May 2009.

may be related to what van Ham describes as "place branding".[47] This means that the EU is associated with a wider cultural identity which does not necessarily relate to the EU or its specific borders but rather a more inclusive notion of a "cultural Europe". There were also many negative images raised by the interviewed elites including conflict, excessive costs and protectionism.

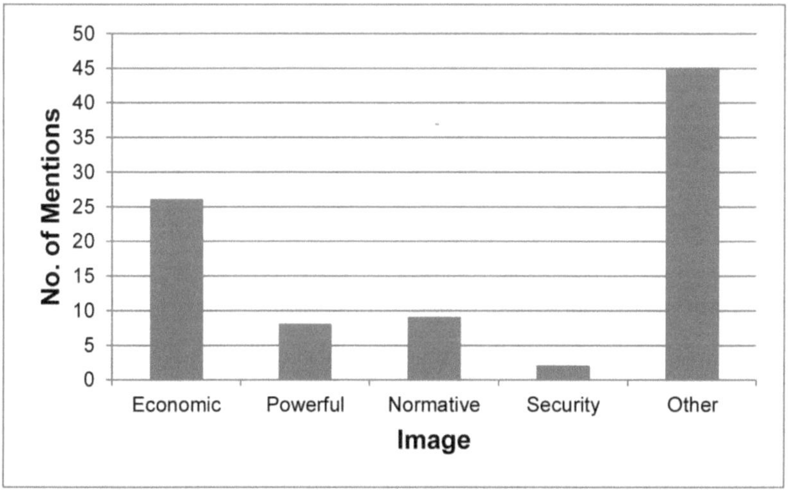

Figure 6: *Images of the EU amongst the Singaporean Elites: Combined Cohorts.*

As Figure 6 shows, generally the EU was viewed more as a normative actor than as a military power and even slightly more of a normative actor than as a generically powerful entity. This shows that the normative values of the EU are generally better known and understood amongst the elites across all cohorts than amongst the general public (10% versus 5% of respondents).[48]

47 Van Ham, P., "Place Branding: The State of the Art," in G. Cowan and N. Cull, *The ANNALS of the American Academy of Political and Social Science*, University of Pennsylvania, SAGE, Vol. 616, 2008.

48 As noted above, sometimes respondents were unable to think of "3 images".

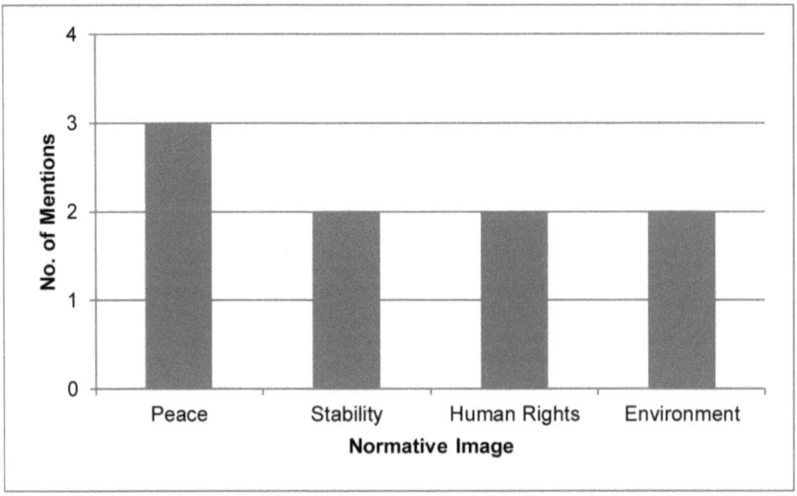

Figure 7: *Normative images of the EU amongst Singaporean elites.*

The normative paradigms in which the EU was influential and which were mentioned by the elites in Singapore were divided almost equally between the four issues raised – peace, stability, human rights, and the environment. Interestingly, the latter category was absent from the answers of the general public, although the EU stated on its Europa website that its "priorities are combating climate change, protecting biodiversity, reducing the impact of pollution on health and better use of natural resources".[49] D'Andrea has noted the potential impact of the EU's environmental promotion on the formation of an internal EU identity.[50] A failure by the EU to communicate this goal (of environmental protection) to the wider public, including abroad, may be to its detriment.

[49] Europa website, "Activities of the European Union: Environment," http://europa.eu/pol/env/index_en.htm, accessed 23 March 2009.

[50] D'Andrea, D., "Global Warming and European Political Identity," in F. Cerutti, and S. Lucarelli (eds.), *The Search for European Identity*, Routledge, London and New York, 2008, pp. 83-84.

Perceptions of New Zealand Elites on the European Union

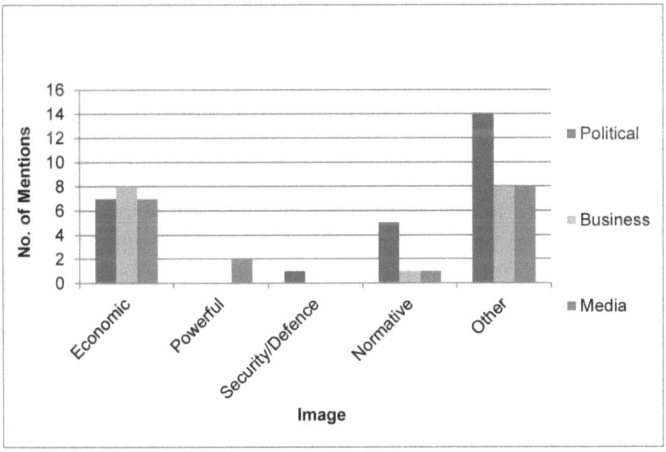

Figure 8: *Images of the EU amongst New Zealand Elites.*

As with the other results presented in this chapter, aside from the references to "other" areas of influence, the EU as an economic actor was the most prominent amongst all three cohorts in New Zealand (see Figure 8). Interestingly, only the media elites spoke of an image of the EU as a powerful actor. Likewise, only one New Zealand political official had a perception of the EU as any kind of military actor. Furthermore, the EU as a normative actor was most prominent amongst the political actors.

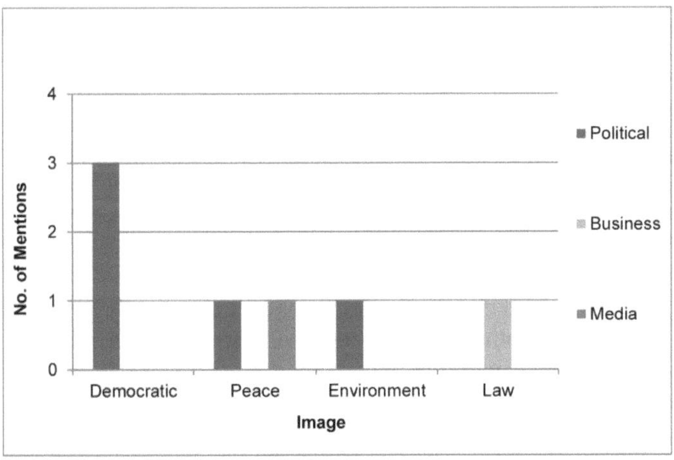

Figure 9: *Normative Images of the EU amongst the NZ Elite.*

The EU as a promoter of democratic principles was by far the most prominent image of EU normative principles in New Zealand elite interviews, but this was identified only amongst the political cohort. This was followed, although on a relatively small scale, by the EU as a promoter of peace and stability and as a protector of the environment. Only one business actor mentioned the EU as a legal entity, but it must be noted that in this instance it was probably more in relation to rules and regulations pertaining to accessing the EU markets.

Lorenzo Fioramonti and Sonia Lucarelli have noted that political elites "frequently view the EU as a key player in a future 'multipolar' world, and, at times, as a champion of 'multilateralism'".[51] Because multilateralism is a key factor of NPE, terms referring to this were anticipated, but were glaringly absent from the images of the EU. Similarly, Fioramonti has mentioned that the EU is seen an environmental actor.[52] However, this was not the case in the two case studies presented here.

Conclusion

Unsurprisingly, the EU was overwhelmingly viewed as an economic power, whether this was through trade or the euro. Although the EU is a political and economic entity, the findings above demonstrate that there is a myriad of images and perceptions related to what "outsiders" think of when thinking about the EU and which are often unrelated to the political identity of the European Union, for example, culture, history, tourism and tradition.

Whilst the case studies are from two distinct geopolitical regions, the findings are remarkably similar. Indeed, in comparing these images a clear pattern emerges indicating that although NPE has been used as an effective theory for understanding the EU's role as an international actor, this does not in reality reflect how the EU is viewed from outside its borders, thus highlighting some of the current shortcomings in the EU's external relations. If the EU is trying to "brand" itself as a normative power, as the literature suggests, then in these case studies at least, it is failing to be a success at doing so. Conversely, and positively for the EU, it is viewed as a relatively strong power, although what sort of power this is beyond the economic sphere is unclear at this stage.

It is acknowledged that the findings may be influenced by the relatively stable relationship both countries have with the EU. Therefore, a similar study in developing countries that benefit from the EU's development

51 Fioramonti, L. and Lucarelli, S., in F. Cerutti, and S. Lucarelli (eds.), *The Search for European Identity*, London and New York, Routledge, 2008, p. 200.

52 *Ibid.*, p. 203.

policies would paint a clearer picture of the EU's global, normative role. Nevertheless, the results of this study are significant given that the EU relies on the two countries to support its external (and thus normative) role and to give internal and external legitimacy to its actions in third countries.

Although there were variations in the emphasis and understanding of the EU's values amongst the respondents, in Singapore the EU as a peaceful entity was overwhelmingly prominent. In New Zealand, the EU as an environmental actor was most prominent in the eyes of the public, in contrast with the opinion of the elites, who saw the EU as first and foremost a democratic entity.

Surprisingly, human rights were relatively low on the agenda, despite it being at the forefront of the minds of the EU policy implementers. Clearly then, the communication of the EU as a promoter of human rights could be improved in both countries. Cross-pillared competencies could have been a reason for the EU's inefficiency in communicating the EU's human rights focus to the rest of the world.

Given that an actor's identity needs to be both constructed and communicated, a lack of a common understanding about the Union could potentially have negative consequences. Although it is beyond the scope of the chapter to evaluate the reasons behind the lack of awareness of third publics in Singapore and New Zealand, one reason may be in a lack of communication. If the EU wishes to become a more effective normative actor, then this needs to be communicated.

The EU's Place in India's Foreign and Security Policy

Daniel Novotný

Adjunct Fellow, Monash European and EU Centre

Introduction

In 2004 the European Union and India signed a Strategic Partnership Agreement. In spite of all the efforts made by both sides, EU-India relations have generally lagged behind the expectations of many policymakers involved in this process. While still evolving, the partnership with the EU has been greatly overshadowed by India's pre-occupation with its Strategic Partnership with the United States and its complex and uneasy relations with immediate neighbours, particularly China and Pakistan. Several European diplomats interviewed by the author expressed their frustration at New Delhi's apparent lacklustre efforts to further advance India's Strategic Partnership with the EU.

This chapter focuses on EU-India relations and examines the significance of the EU for Indian foreign and security strategy. This is first explored in the context of the Indian foreign policy elite's perceptions about external threats facing the country and their views of India's external security environment and, secondly, in the context of the enduring tension in New Delhi between idealist and realist approaches to international politics. The discussion essentially places the evolving relations between the EU and India in the broader context of India's security predicament or conundrum: how to take advantage of the country's unique geopolitical location against the backdrop of a rather hostile neighbourhood, being permanent hostage to the multiplicity of internal and external security challenges, while simultaneously aspiring to become a "great power" of the 21st century. The chapter is divided into seven parts. Part one and two highlight India's unique geopolitical location and the influence of the idealist and realist political thinking on the country's foreign and security policies. Part three examines India's generally ambivalent perceptions of and attitudes towards Europe and part four analyses why the EU is currently not seen as an important security partner but "only" an important and truly powerful "trading bloc". Part five discusses the significance of the fact that the EU does not constitute a vital element within the so-called "strategic triangular" relationships in South Asia. Part six looks at where the EU fits in New Delhi's "grand strategy" for the 21st century which would allow India to realize its potential to acquire the greatly desired "great power status". The concluding part evaluates the shared interest of Brussels and New Delhi in promoting a "symmetrical" multi-polar international system.

India and Geopolitical Imperatives of South Asia

In international relations the geographical factor is widely accepted as a paramount determinant in foreign policy making. India occupies a strategic geopolitical position in Asia, on a subcontinent jutting deep into the Indian Ocean, sitting astride major sea lines of communication linking the Persian Gulf with the Asia-Pacific, thus providing a kind of connecting link between East and West. It is obvious that the country's geographical location has significantly shaped the Indian elite's worldview and strategic outlook. There is a clear notion that because of its strategic location in South Asia, its sheer geographical size and large population, India is a geopolitically important player that is entitled to play a central role in solving major world problems. As Jawaharlal Nehru earlier asserted, "India is too big a country herself to be bound down to any country, however big it may be. India is going to be and is bound to be a big country that counts in world affairs".[1] Accordingly, India's central and dominant position in South Asia and the Indian Ocean has and will increasingly affect the foreign, economic and military policies of the European Union, the United States, China and other major powers – and vice versa.

However, the Indian elite view their country's geographical location as both a blessing and a curse for national security. Since gaining independence, the external security environment has never been very favourable to India as the country has faced complex and multiple threats and challenges to its security that are often both external and internal in origin. India has been a hostage to its geography, flanked on both sides by not-so-friendly neighbours, China and Pakistan. India has fought three full-blown wars with Pakistan since their partition in 1947 and one border war with China that ended with India's defeat. New Delhi's inescapable dilemma over the last sixty years has been how to provide India with enough security and maintain a favourable power equation in the region in the face of the persistence of this two-front problem.

1 Bandyopadhyaya, J., *The Making of India's Foreign Policy: Determinants, Institutions, Processes and Personalities*, Bombay, Allied Publishers, 1970, pp. 30-31.

Over the last decade, India has tripled its defence spending, a development that is widely interpreted as principally a race against China's military buildup.[2] While the question of the "Chinese threat" tends to be underplayed on the official level, as one Indian IR expert asserted, "in reality there is a great concern about 'China threat' among the Indian elites".[3] There is a prevalent perception that India currently has to deal with some kind of "encirclement" or "containment" by China, whereby Beijing employs neighbouring Pakistan, Bangladesh, Myanmar and lately also Sri Lanka as proxies to achieve its offensive strategic objectives. Indian leaders tend to compare China's "aggressive" and "assertive" policies with India's "peaceful" policies – in the words of one respondent, "the 'peaceful rise' of China is questionable".[4] A former senior Indian diplomat even asked explicitly: "Will China dominate the 21st century world?"[5]

India's Foreign Policy Tradition: Idealist versus Realist

Elite ideational influences and threat perceptions have a real effect on the decision-making process and selection of policies and, as Alagappa contends, both are "crucial to the security thinking and behaviour of Asian governments and must therefore feature in their explanation".[6] Indian strategic culture and the elite's thinking about international relations have been shaped by many influences, the most prominent being the idealist political thinking represented by Asoka and Mahatma Gandhi and the realist trend advocated by a renowned Hindu thinker and statesman Kautilya in his *Arthasastra*, characterized as "one of the greatest political books of the ancient world".[7] Kautilya highlighted the importance of enhancing a country's relative power in its struggle for victory against the rival neighbouring states while accentuating the weakness of human nature – thus inviting a comparison with Machiavelli. On the

---

2 "China's Military Build-up Figures in India-US Talks," *Thaindian News*, 20 January 2010, http://www.thaindian.com/newsportal/uncategorized/chinas-military-build-up-figures-in-india-us-talks_100306767.html, accessed 1 April 2010.

3 Interview, Singapore, 27 November 2008.

4 Interview, Prague, 20 August 2008.

5 Sikri, R., *Challenge and Strategy: Rethinking India's Foreign Strategy*, New Delhi, Sage Publications, 2009, p. 8; Interview, Singapore, 10 November, 2008.

6 Alagappa, M., *Asian Security Practice: Material and Ideational Influences*, Stanford, Stanford University Press, 1998, p. 649.

7 Kautilya was a key adviser to the Indian king Chandragupta Maurya (c. 317-293 B.C.E.); Zaman, R. U., "Kautilya: The Indian Strategic Thinker and Indian Strategic Culture," *Comparative Strategy*, Vol. 25, Issue 3, 2006, pp. 231-247; quoted in: Boesche, R., "Kautilya's Arthasastra on War and Diplomacy in Ancient India," *The Journal of Military History*, Vol. 67, 2003, p. 9.

other hand, many Indian policy-makers during the first three decades after independence, including the first prime minister of India, Jawaharlal Nehru, were greatly influenced by the idealist political tradition and, as Bandyopadhyaya points out, "[…] also strongly criticized the purely realist view of international politics based on military and economic power".[8] This influence of the idealist and realist political thinking, as Kapur argues, has fed "the constant tension between the importance of morality and power politics in India's external policies".[9]

India's nuclear arms test in 1998 could be seen as a harbinger of the growing prominence of realist thinking in the Indian national security discourse that had long been dominated by idealist approaches to international relations. During the Cold War, India was affected by triangular power relationships in the region as Indo-Pakistani and Indo-Chinese rivalry developed within the broader context of the global bipolar conflict between the US and the USSR. India's 1998 nuclear action effectively meant that New Delhi abandoned Nehru's non-realist foreign and security policy based on "playing off the great powers against each other diplomatically from a position of military and economic weakness".[10] Kapur observed that "the Nehru paradigm effectively made India a weak status quo country. After 1998, India sought a position as a strong status quo power. […] The 1998 test decision secured long-term gain and an increase in India's negotiating space with the powers".[11]

The shift in the ideational influences on the Indian elite's security thinking and in turn the country's strategic behaviour from the late 1990s had perhaps two main conceptual and policy implications: first, India unambiguously set out to pull itself out of China's shadow – as George Fernandes, the then Indian defence minister, famously proclaimed in 1998, "China was India's potential enemy No. 1".[12] The increased realist emphasis on an interest-based approach to international affairs has also prompted India to seek a closer relationship, both on the political and defence levels, with China's immediate neighbours including Japan, South Korea, Mongolia and Vietnam. Sikri argues that "such measures will help to exert counter psychological pressure on China. India

8 Bandyopadhyaya, J., *The Making of India's Foreign Policy: Determinant*, *op. cit.*, p. 67.

9 Kapur, A., *India – From Regional to World Power*, Oxford, Routledge, 2006, p. 24.

10 *Ibid.*, p. 12.

11 *Ibid.*, pp. 12 and 14.

12 Singh, B. K., "George Fernandes and Sino-Indian Relations," Institute of Peace & Conflict Studies, 27 May 2003, http://www.ipcs.org/article/china/george-fernandes-and-sino-indian-relations-1044.html, accessed 30 March 2010.

must shed its diffidence in dealing with China".[13] Second, following the breakup of its main Cold War-era ally, the Soviet Union, New Delhi has sought to expand its hitherto underdeveloped relations simultaneously with all the major powers. India thus began a new pattern of strategic dialogue on political, economic and military issues with a number a partners, including France and the United Kingdom, and signed landmark Strategic Partnership Agreements with the European Union and the United States.

It is in the context of the now predominant realist thinking underlying the Indian elite's national security considerations that the EU-India Strategic Partnership has evolved in the last decade. The EU is said to have started taking India seriously only after the 1998 nuclear arms test – by signing the Strategic Partnership Agreement six years later, Brussels "acknowledged the political and the economic importance of India for the European Union [...] Just as Europe should take India seriously, I want India to take Europe seriously".[14] During the Cold War, it was principally the USSR that saved India from a complete and crushing isolation within the Pakistan-US-China versus India-USSR triangular relationship. Mindful of this historical precedent and in the face of China's current rapid economic growth and global diplomatic offensive, New Delhi is acutely aware that it needs to engage simultaneously all the major powers to be capable of responding to China's rising clout from a position of strength. From India's perspective, the EU has potentially the capacity to play an important role – economically and politically, if not militarily – in New Delhi's realist approach to achieving security characterized by efforts aimed at "managing asymmetries, not eliminating them, [and managing] the multi-cornered strategic context to India's advantage".[15]

Indian Ambivalence Towards Europe

Indian perceptions of and attitudes towards Europe have generally tended to be dichotomous and deeply ambivalent. They have been shaped – on both sides – by what Verma characterizes as "the 'repertoire of images' which both India and Europe fabricated for each other when they came in contact with one another for the first time. [...] Their images of each other oscillated so wildly, from one extreme of exaggerated praise and

13 Sikri, R., *Challenge and Strategy: Rethinking India's Foreign Strategy*, *op. cit.*, p. 108.

14 From the speech by EU Trade Commissioner Peter Mandelson "The Global Economic Agenda: Europe and India's Challenge Confederation of Indian Industry Partnership Summit," Kolkata, 13 January 2005, official website of the Delegation of the European Union to India, http://www.delind.ec.europa.eu/eu-india-hlm-cv-jan05-1.asp?links=dia-link3, accessed 25 March 2010.

15 Kapur, A., *India – From Regional to World Power*, *op. cit.*, p. 43.

admiration, to the other extreme of contempt and rejection [...]".[16] Throughout the 18th and 19th Centuries, the "idealized image" of Europe as the pinnacle of human achievement gradually gave way to a more balanced and nuanced view. Many Indian elites educated in European universities were bewildered by and hence questioned the seemingly inherent contradiction between the classic texts highlighting humanist values of justice and freedom, on the one hand, and the cruelty and arrogance the European colonial powers demonstrated in India and other parts of Asia, on the other. As Verma observed, "It was a strange situation in which two cultures had to live in a state of togetherness, a situation demeaning to both; two cultures loving and hating each other mostly for wrong reasons".[17]

Today, after the two bloody world wars and having watched the European realist, hard-power approach to international politics during the Cold War that led to Western implication in various violent armed conflicts around the globe, its blatant support for brutal dictatorial regimes as well as the perpetuation of the perceived contemporary patterns of global economic exploitation, Indians have long since repudiated any romanticized image of the "Old Continent". But current Indian perceptions of Europe continue to be dichotomous and full of ambivalence, albeit of a somewhat different nature. This is in part because of the pervasive notion that the EU is difficult to comprehend – a typical description characterizes the EU as "a strange creature [that] defies easy and simple classification. It is unique, with attributes of a state but it is not a state [...] [it is] a multifaceted actor".[18]

Indians admittedly have a high regard for Europe as an economic superpower, for its technological prowess, and the unique success of its integration process. Yet, Indian policy-makers also point to Europe's military and strategic impotence due to the lack of the Union's cohesion and the overall relative decline of Europe's influence in world affairs which is why "the EU is not a hegemon and is no counterweight to the US".[19] A series of interviews with Indian policy-makers, diplomats and IR scholars conducted in New Delhi, Singapore and Prague in 2008 demonstrated that, at the end of the Cold War, Indian elites initially anticipated that 21st century global international relations architecture would be

16 Bhalla, A. (ed.), *India and Europe – Selected Essays by Nirmal Verma*, Rashtrapati Nivas, Shimla, Indian Institute of Advanced Study, 2000, p. 31.

17 *Ibid.*, p. 35.

18 Bava, U. S., "India and EU," in N. S. Sisodia and C. U. Bhaskar (eds.), *Emerging India: Security and Foreign Policy Perspectives*, New Delhi, Institute for Defence Studies and Analyses, 2005, p. 180.

19 *Ibid.*, p. 190.

structured and shaped around three main pillars: the US, the EU and East Asia (particularly China). However, contrary to these expectations, the reality is that at present "the EU can not be considered an important actor, a significant factor in Asian security".[20] More specifically, based on the quantitative and qualitative analysis of relevant studies and all interviews conducted by the author, we can identify the following priorities – as seen by the country's elite – that in turn shape the dynamics of India's contemporary foreign and security policy: India's relations with the US; India's relations with East Asian powers China and Japan and the Association of Southeast Asian Nations (ASEAN); India's relations with the EU and Russia; and relations with other countries and regions.[21]

The EU as a "Trading Superpower"

In New Delhi, the EU is generally perceived as an "emerging new actor in international politics" which, from the military-security perspective, does not have much to offer to India, particularly when compared with the US.[22] Though most EU states are also members of the NATO, it is the US that is currently seen as India's main security partner, while the EU is primarily treated as an important and powerful "trading bloc".[23] Baru vividly describes the experience of the Indian delegation during the Doha trade negotiations that "is writ large on the psyche of Indian negotiations". According to him, thanks to the Indian commerce minister's "brave stand against the US and European Union bullying on the Doha Development Agenda […] India was left standing alone towards the end as one developing country after another succumbed to trans-Atlantic pressure".[24] Indian analyses on trade and economic issues stop short of portraying the EU as a powerful but ruthless and exploitative economic power that largely pays lip service to the liberalization of international trade.[25]

---

[20] Interview, Singapore, 27 November 2008.

[21] Interviews: Prague, 25 June 2008; New Delhi, July 2008; Singapore, 10 and 27 November 2008.

[22] Bava, U. S., "India and EU," in N. S. Sisodia and C. U. Bhaskar (eds.), *Emerging India: Security and Foreign Policy Perspectives*, *op. cit.*, p. 180.

[23] Interview, New Delhi, July 2008.

[24] Baru, S., *Strategic Consequences of India's Economic Performance: Essays & Columns*, New Delhi, Academic Foundation, 2006, p. 203.

[25] In particular, Indian exporters are negatively affected by the implementation of a variety of non-tariff barriers (NTBs) in the form of so-called "standards" that are alleged to be protecting the European countries from the ever-increasing competition from developing countries. Among the major NTBs in the EU market have been quoted subsidy in agriculture and quota on textiles and clothing. For more on this issue, see Bhattacharya, S. K., "Non-Tariff Barriers, Indo-EU Trade and the World Trade

Indian foreign-policy elites clearly recognize a substantial difference between the relatively unified and cohesive economic policy of the EU and its divided and inconsistent Common Foreign and Security Policy (CFSP). On the one hand, the EU is frequently mentioned in India as the world's most successful example of how regional economic integration can be utilized as an instrument of regional security: achieving peace and regional political stability by means of promoting economic engagement.[26] But, on the other, the EU as an entity that has been struggling to define its own identity and to design and implement its CFSP, cannot aspire to play a more important political and security role on the Indian subcontinent that goes beyond the influence derived from its economic and financial muscle.

These ideas were commonly expressed during the interviews conducted as part of this research project. For example, a senior Indian diplomat paraphrased the remark supposedly made by Henry Kissinger: "So, whom should I call if I want to talk with the European Union?" He argued that "the EU does not really exist. The Europeans are not really ready to completely submerge their national identities. The EU must sort out its internal political differences first and [...] then it will also be more respected".[27] To that end, the interviewed members of the Indian foreign policy elites cited some examples of perceived European disunity: firstly, the divergent attitudes of different EU member states affiliated with the Nuclear Suppliers Group (NSG) to the Nuclear Agreement in 2008 that was to give a waiver to India to accommodate civilian nuclear trade with that country. The eventual formal approval of the NSG came only after several days of intense US diplomacy. Secondly, when Morocco in 2002 occupied the Perejil Island just off its northern coast, whose sovereignty has long been disputed by Morocco and Spain, the EU member states were again divided on how to respond to the crisis. "How then can the EU get its weight around the world?" asked one respondent, citing the relative lack of European cohesion and concluding: "Over the last 10 years, the EU has done well [...] it has gained some weight [...] but it is not enough".[28]

Hence, while New Delhi deals directly with the EU Commission on Trade and Commerce on the economic and trade issues, it has long maintained robust bilateral relations and dialogue on political-security issues with individual EU member countries, particularly the UK, France and

Organization," in R. K. Jain, and H. Elsenhans, *India, the European Union and the WTO*, New Delhi, Radiant Publishers, 2006, pp. 266-269.

26 Baru, S., *Strategic Consequences of India's Economic Performance: Essays & Columns*, *op. cit.*, p. 124.

27 Interview, Prague, 20 August 2008.

28 Interview, Singapore, 10 November 2008 and Prague 20 August 2008.

Germany. As a senior Indian policy-maker, who has attended all of the EU-India Summits to date, explained, "when we deal with a company based in California, they say we are an American company and not a Californian company. But as an editor of an Indian newspaper, for example, I do not deal with the EU but with individual countries".[29] Brussels has been granted a full mandate on trade and, consequently, is seen in India as a powerful player both at the regional and international levels. Conversely, in the political and security field, where Brussels lacks the instruments to ensure this kind of unanimity between its member states, the EU is by and large perceived as an inconclusive and incoherent political-security actor.[30] More specifically, the broader discourse on the EU foreign and security policy is characterized by two major political and national cleavages about "what the EU should and should not do in international politics". The cleavages stem from the disagreement over the value the EU should place on its relationship with the United States and also how to approach military power and the use of military force.[31]

The EU and "Strategic Triangles" in South Asia

If we are to understand geopolitical developments on the Indian subcontinent over the last six decades and the place of the EU in New Delhi's strategic calculations, rather than analysing bilateral relations, we need to focus on "triangular" and "multi-cornered" power relations in the region – namely, those between India, regional countries and extraterritorial powers. Before 1947, British colonial rule over India lasting almost two centuries was largely conditioned upon Britain's famous imperial policy of "divide and rule" and based on a carefully calculated policy of "strategic triangle". This strategy involved a systematic reinforcement of respective religious identities of the Hindus and the Muslims and deliberate cultivation of mutual intolerance between the two communities whereby their "security" was guaranteed by Great Britain. Later during the Cold War, from the 1960s onwards, there was a different kind of "strategic triangle" relationship in operation on the Indian subcontinent: India was then supported by the Soviet Union while Pakistan was backed by the US and China. Much like the British policy of promoting tensions between the Hindu and Muslim communities, the US-Chinese approach was characterized as "[maintaining] a system of manageable instability between India and Pakistan. Conflict management, not conflict resolution, was the

29 Interview, Singapore, 10 November 2008.

30 Vennesson, P., "Competing Visions for the European Union Grand Strategy," *European Foreign Affairs Review*, Vol. 15, Issue 1, 2010, pp. 57-75.

31 *Ibid.*, pp. 58 and 62.

aim".[32] We can thus see a striking similarity between the earlier British strategy and the strategies employed by the major powers during the Cold War.

The contemporary "strategic triangle" power relations are as complex as ever and they are principally characterized by a close strategic partnership between India and the US on the one hand and Pakistan with China on the other. In this new South Asian power equation, Beijing is keen to use "Pakistan as a key partner in keeping India off balance in the Sino-Indian rivalry" within a system of manageable instability, while New Delhi seeks to cultivate its relations particularly with the US along with other major actors to increase its space for manoeuvring and advance its geopolitical standing.[33] It could be argued that we can understand India's attitude to the EU in a broader context of "triangular" and "multicornered" power relations in South Asia. While Europe dominated the world for centuries, the EU is currently not seen – despite its undisputed economic strength – as "a major military power or a serious global geopolitical player, with most of its diplomatic energies focused on trying to handle the problems of EU integration and expansion, and in preventing the re-emergence of old fault lines".[34] In other words, neither the EU as a whole nor any of the European states individually currently constitute a vital element in the "triangular" power relationships and consequently do not significantly figure in India's strategic calculations.

The EU with its emphasis on "soft power" as revealed in its slogan "Power for Good" stands in stark contrast with India's contemporary effort to enhance its "hard power" capabilities. From the Indian perspective,

> the EU is well-endowed with soft power and some hard power. It now seeks to increase its hard power with the new political identity as defined by the Common Foreign and Security Policy and also by creating a force structure that can respond to conflict both on the continent and abroad. In contrast (or rather *similarly* – author's remark), India has tremendous soft power (culture, value and institutions) and needs to build up its hard power (the economic and military).[35]

Indian policy-makers point to the divergent geopolitical developments in Europe and South Asia since the late 1940s. While the contemporary

---

32 Kapur, A., *India – From Regional to World Power*, *op. cit.*, p. 47.

33 Ahrari, E. M., "Pakistan as a 'Key Non-NATO Ally'," *Asia Times Online*, 20 March 2004, http://www.atimes.com/atimes/South_Asia/FC20Df01.html, accessed 2 April 2010.

34 Sikri, R., *Challenge and Strategy: Rethinking India's Foreign Strategy*, *op. cit.*, p. 14.

35 Bava, U. S., "India and EU," in N. S. Sisodia and C. U. Bhaskar (eds.), *Emerging India: Security and Foreign Policy Perspectives*, *op. cit.*, p. 189.

thinking of European elites is influenced by the continent's successful integration process and desire to actively promote European norms and values around the world, inter-state relations in Asia and particularly in South Asia are heavily affected by threat perceptions, mutual enmities and historically determined distrust between states. In sum, the European elites' thinking accentuating foreign policy instruments of "soft power" to defend national security is largely incompatible with the strategic thinking of Indian elites that places a high value on the utility of *realpolitik*, military capabilities and the balance of power.

The EU and the US in India's Grand Strategy

Indian elites generally anticipate the existence of a multi-polar or perhaps rather semi-multi-polar make-up of the international relations around the mid-21st century. The United States, China, Japan and India have been identified as the main pillars of the security architecture in Asia in the short and medium-term. However, as Sikri aptly points out, "uncertainties remain about the relative global weight of the major powers in the coming decades [...] [particularly] whether the US can retain its 'full spectrum' domination of the world for too long".[36] The prevailing sense among the Indian elite is that while international relations by the mid-21st century will essentially be multi-polar in nature, the system will also be characterized by the predominance of two main powers: the US and China. Though American influence in the world will decrease *vis-à-vis* the other major powers, the US will most likely be able to defend and preserve its position as *primus inter pares* in this, to use Huntington's depiction, "strange hybrid, [...] *uni-multi-polar* system with one superpower and several major powers".[37]

The elite predicts that India will maintain very friendly and close relations particularly with the US, the EU, along with Japan, Russia, Canada, Australia, and the ASEAN countries – to name the most frequently mentioned actors. They also anticipate a further strengthening in the coordination of military and security strategies with other regional powers, namely Australia, Vietnam and Indonesia. On the other hand, the interviewed policy-makers on the whole agree that China will constitute the principal state-based security threat for India.

The policy-makers I interviewed were by and large inclined to hold the view that the current global economic and financial crisis, among other factors, will contribute during the next two decades to the weakening of

---

36 Sikri, R., *Challenge and Strategy: Rethinking India's Foreign Strategy*, *op. cit.*, p. 6.

37 Huntington, S. P., "The Lonely Superpower," *Foreign Affairs*, Vol. 78, No. 2, March/April, 1999.

US and EU clout in the economic and political spheres and, conversely, the relative increase in the Chinese and Russian influence in the international system. Sikri argues that the US "influence has probably reached a plateau […] the US is an empire, albeit a declining one".[38] In this, what Fareed Zakaria characterizes as the "post-American world", first and foremost China and Russia, will be competing with the US over the spheres of influence in the regions of Central Asia, Southeast Asia, and East Asia.[39] Furthermore, it is important to note that despite the continuing high intensity of the EU-India trade relations, the relative, albeit very slow and gradual, decline of the EU economic influence in Asia in general and India in particular is quite obvious. Chauvin's study shows that both export and import intensity in the EU-India trade relations has tended to decline, and has concluded that India's trade has increasingly displayed a reorientation away from the European continent towards the new industrialized Asian economies.[40]

New Delhi's overarching goal in its "grand strategy" for the 21st century is to implement foreign and security policies that would allow India to realize its potential to acquire the greatly desired "great power status". Owing to its geographic location, India stands largely outside of the economic and political integration processes that are currently taking place in both Europe and East Asia. Consequently, India needs to enhance its economic, political and military capabilities through engaging and gradually expanding its relations with the EU and other major powers and establishing diverse partnerships at the global level. It has been observed that Prime Minister Manmohan Singh "ha[d] begun to play with the big ideas underlying India's foreign policy […] that […] reflects a new national confidence that […] India will begin to matter much more in world affairs in the years to come".[41]

While the US is set to retain its position as a central factor in Indian foreign and security policy for the foreseeable future, the EU is not regarded in India as an important regional security actor because of the perceived lack of common strategic interest between the two entities.[42]

---

38 Sikri, R., *Challenge and Strategy: Rethinking India's Foreign Strategy*, *op. cit.*, pp. 5 and 8.

39 Zakaria, F., *The Post-American World*, New York, W. W. Norton & Co., 2008.

40 Chauvin, S. *et al.*, "EU-India Trade and Investment Relations," in R. K. Jain and H. Elsenhans, *India, the European Union and the WTO*, New Delhi, Radiant Publishers, 2006, pp. 266-269.

41 Mohan, C. R., "Rethinking India's Grand Strategy," in N. S. Sisodia and C. U. Bhaskar (eds.), *Emerging India: Security and Foreign Policy Perspectives*, New Delhi, Institute for Defence Studies and Analyses, 2005, p. 37.

42 Bava, U. S., "India and EU," in N. S. Sisodia, and C. U. Bhaskar (eds.), *Emerging India: Security and Foreign Policy Perspectives*, *op. cit.*, p. 188.

Although both Brussels and Washington have similarly maintained bilateral relations with India at the level described as "Strategic Partnership", the Indian elite recognize a substantial difference between the EU and the US in terms of how the two entities have in the last decade approached their relations with India. In contrast with the rather indecisive and faltering approach of the EU during the diplomatic and political negotiations with India, the US has demonstrated its determination to support India in its aspirations to become a global power and help create a special "privileged" position for India within the system of global politics. For India, as an aspiring "great power", the diplomatic, political and also military support from Washington will in the immediate future be absolutely essential. The EU is at the moment largely perceived as a political-economic grouping that has hardly any strategic vision and perspective with regards to the character and scope of its "strategic partnership" with India.[43]

Indian policy-makers accentuate the fact that, unlike Washington, Brussels seems to have so far failed to comprehend the multi-layered nature and complexities of South Asian geopolitics, its implications for the Indian elite's threat perceptions and in turn the dynamics of the country's foreign and security policy. More specifically, referring to the apparent perception gap between Brussels and New Delhi, it is argued that "compared with its long history full of warfare, now the EU has gone too soft. [The EU policy-makers] do not know what it means having neighbours like China and Pakistan".[44] By contrast, it is the "China policy" that is often identified as "an overarching factor in the India-US relationship".[45] Insofar as both New Delhi and Washington are concerned about maintaining a favourable balance of power in the context of the "strategic triangles" framework, "the US has clearly chosen India to be the balancer of Asia".[46] For the EU, which does not have any direct geopolitical interest in South and East Asia, the rising power of China does not signify a major security issue. Unlike the US with its forward military deployment in East Asia and vital geopolitical interests spanning the globe, "the EU and China dominate their respective 'near abroads', their two spheres of influence do not overlap, which further reduces the potential for conflict".[47] In contrast to the EU attitude, the process of strategic realignment and

---

43 Jain, R. K., "India and the European Union: The Parameters and Potential of Strategic Partnership," paper presented at the seminar "India and the European Union," New Delhi, 23-24 March 2006, p. 8.

44 Interview, Singapore, 27 November 2008.

45 *Ibid.*

46 Kaur K. and Mann, B. S., *South Asia: Dynamics of Politics, Economy and Security*. New Delhi, Knowledge World, 2006, p. 173.

47 Gros, D., "The EU and the Rise of China," in *The Rise of China: Policies of the EU, Russia and the US*, ESF Working Paper No. 30, European Security Forum, 2008, p. 1.

the ensuing "strategic partnership" between the US and India have been founded upon overlapping vital national interests between the two actors whereby, according to the US Chief Policy Advisor for South Asia, the three most important ones are "China, Pakistan and Counter Terrorism".[48]

The difference in European and American attitudes to India was also reflected in two important bilateral agreements – the *Political Declaration on the India-EU Strategic Partnership* of 7 September 2005 and the *US-India Joint Declaration* of 18 July 2005. While the first, rather complex document dubbed "Action Plan" talks about "exchanging ideas", "strengthening dialogue" and "discussing problems", the latter is a much shorter Joint Statement that appeals to both sides to take joint action to tackle global threats to international security. Whereas the *EU-India Action Plan* appears as a preliminary, tentative document that still awaits completion, the *US-India Joint Statement* was later followed by another important document entitled *New Framework for US-India Defense Relationship* that demonstrates the US resolution to encourage and assist India to become a major power in the international system. In short, the above two documents mirror two very different worldviews and geopolitical perspectives of Brussels and Washington and, by extension, highlight their diverging approaches to their respective relations with India.[49]

India, the EU and a Multi-polar World

Notwithstanding the Indian elite's contemporary attitudes to the EU discussed above, medium to long-term prospects for the EU-India relations seem to be relatively bright because, on balance, the two entities share more common ground on strategic issues than differences. For one, India's relations with the West are shaped by a sense of linguistic and cultural affinity because "the Indian elite's strategic thinking and lifestyle is [...] oriented towards the West. Culture, language and a democratic polity bring India and the West together".[50] Secondly, there are still expectations in New Delhi underlying its relations with Brussels that the EU will help India on the way to increasing its prestige and becoming a major power. Brussels has sent some positive messages in that direction in the important document on the European security strategy titled *A Secure Europe in a Better World*. In reference to this policy document, a senior EU Commission representative publicly recognized that "India is gaining

48 Kaur, K. and Mann, B. S., *South Asia: Dynamics of Politics, Economy and Security*, *op. cit.*, p. 172.

49 Racine, J.-L., "The India-Europe Relationship in the U.S. Shadow," in R. K. Jain (ed.), *India and the European Union: Building a Strategic Partnership*, New Delhi, Radiant Publishers, 2007.

50 Sikri, R., *Challenge and Strategy: Rethinking India's Foreign Strategy*, *op. cit.*, p. 161.

in real importance for the EU. Before, we looked more to China, and saw India rather as a leader in the developing world. Now it's an equal partner. […] The relationship has to be of the same parity, density, quality as the relationship we [the EU] have with the United States, Canada, China, Russia and Japan".[51]

Thirdly, as both India and the EU lay great emphasis on the imperatives of opposing unilateralist tendencies in the world political order, the EU-India Strategic Partnership effectively adds yet another "pole" to the emerging multi-polar global balance of power. As a senior EU source pointedly affirmed following President George W. Bush's re-election in 2004, "both the European Union and India have always been strong defenders of multilateralism".[52] Yet, we should note here that New Delhi is and will be increasingly faced with the apparent contradiction between embracing and promoting "multi-polarity" in the international system and being involved in a "strategic partnership" with Washington. While India, along with the EU, China and Russia, share the interest in constructing a multi-polar international system, it has been argued that "China's quest for multi-polarity is self-serving and somewhat one-sided or asymmetrical".[53] Beijing has traditionally shown a certain degree of contempt for India's power capabilities and its great power ambitions which have been demonstrated, for example, in China's fierce opposition to the admission of India and also Japan as new permanent members of the reformed and enlarged UN Security Council.

Notwithstanding growing trade ties and increasingly frequent exchange of high-level visits between the two countries, geopolitical competition between India and China has in fact increased since the end of the Cold War. Beijing's approach in the last decade favoured the creation of an "asymmetrical multi-polarity" through the selective and carefully measured expansion of bilateral relations with other regional powers, particularly Russia and the EU (especially the UK, France and Germany). By further advancing its relations with the EU and expanding them to include political-security cooperation, New Delhi may be able to respond more effectively to China's asymmetrical approach to multi-polarity. Importantly, in contrast to China's foreign policy strategy, in the EU (as well as Russian) scheme of a "multi-polar world" India is accorded a due position as one of the principal "poles" – Russia and some European

---

51 "EU, India Eye Counterterrorism," *The Washington Times*, 5 November 2004; see also "A Secure Europe in a Better World: European Security Strategy," Brussels, 12 December 2003.

52 *Ibid.*

53 Boquerat, G. and Grare, F. (eds.), *India, China, Russia: Intricacies of an Asian Triangle*, Singapore, India Research Press and Marshall Cavendish Academic, 2004, p. 90.

countries, though formally not the EU as a whole, support India's aspiration to become a permanent member of the UN Security Council. In short, there is a fundamental difference in China's and India's approaches to multi-polarity and consequently their respective motivations for expanding their relations with the EU. Cabestan has found that "the former wants multi-polarity to be anti-US (adding another "pole" to counter the US influence – author's remark) while the latter hopes that multi-polarity can remain much more fluid and adaptable to the circumstances".[54]

Conclusion

In sum, due to its unique geopolitical position, India has to deal with a very complex and dynamic external security environment that gives rise to multiple threats and challenges. There is particularly a great concern among the Indian elite about China's "aggressive" and "assertive" policies in South Asia and beyond. India's nuclear arms test in 1998 heralded the growing influence of realist thinking on the Indian national security strategy that had long been dominated by idealist approaches to international relations. It is in this context that we can see the differences in the way New Delhi has approached its relations with the European Union in contrast with the United States.

New Delhi now concentrates on the building of its economic, political and military capabilities that would allow it to respond to China's rising clout from a position of strength and not weakness as in the Cold War era. For that reason, India has sought – following the demise of the USSR, its Cold War-era main ally – to expand its relations simultaneously with all the major powers to be able to increase the country's space for manoeuvre and advance its geopolitical standing. While maintaining a new pattern of strategic dialogue on political, economic and military level within a Strategic Partnership framework with both the EU and US, it is only the latter that is widely considered to be a central factor in India's foreign and security policy. The EU, on the other hand, is not regarded in India as an important regional security actor largely owing to the perceived lack of common strategic interest between the two entities.

Indian foreign-policy elite clearly recognize a substantial difference between the relatively unified and cohesive economic policy of the EU – earning it a reputation of "economic superpower" – and its divided and inconsistent foreign and security policy. Although some attempts have been made to shift the focus of the EU-India Strategic Partnership from trade and investment to the political-security scene, including discussions

54 Cabestan, J. P., "The Chinese Factor: China between Multi-polarity and Bipolarity," in G. Boquerat and F. Grare (eds.), *India, China, Russia: Intricacies of an Asian Triangle*, *op. cit.*, 2004, p. 100.

on problems such as global terrorism, Indian policy-makers would clearly like to see much closer cooperation in defence and security areas, along with more frequent and intensive consultations on issues of common strategic interest.

Indian elites generally believe that if the EU were able to achieve and implement a coherent political-security strategy, it could potentially figure more prominently in India's strategic thinking and its aspirations to become a "great power" of the 21st century. India's global standing and whether the country achieves the much desired "great power status" in the 21st century will largely depend on the country's assessment of the likely evolution, which is a process fraught with uncertainty, of the power distribution within the emerging global multi-polar system.

Contemporary Indian Perspectives on the EU and its Role in South Asia and the World

Rajendra K. JAIN

Jawaharlal Nehru University, New Delhi

Introduction

India was one of the first developing countries and the first Asian country to establish diplomatic relations with the European Economic Community (EEC) and accredit its Diplomatic Mission to the Community in January 1962. Over time, the European Union (EU) has emerged as India's largest trading partner, biggest source of foreign direct investment, major contributor of developmental aid, and an important source of technology. The EU is also home to a large and influential Indian diaspora, mostly in the United Kingdom.

This chapter is divided into five parts. Parts one and two highlight how India and the European Union perceive each other. Part three examines how India perceives the EU as a global actor and discusses the convergence and divergence on several key issues like global governance and climate change. Part four looks at the growing engagement of the EU in South Asia, especially Pakistan and Afghanistan since the turn of the millennium. It discusses South Asia's role in the promotion of democracy in the region and goes on to evaluate EU-SAARC relations and whether the EU can be a model for SAARC (South Asian Association for Regional Cooperation). The concluding part makes some reflections on the current state of India-EU relations after a decade of annual summitry.

Indian Perceptions of the EU

The Indian encounter with Europe has been unprecedented in human history, as no comparable rich and complex civilization had such a long period of direct European domination. European ideas and values profoundly influenced the English-educated elite and gave rise to various movements by Indian leaders from the 19th century onwards. Many Indian national leaders were educated in Europe and many Indian activists found refuge in Europe. Two broad strands were visible in the century after the second half of the 19th century: one sought to emulate the West, trying to adopt and adapt Western value systems and Western institutions to the Indian milieu; the second strand asserted the importance of basic Indian values, criticized the arrogance of the Western rulers, and passionately questioned Western analysis and assessments regarding India's history, its intellectual heritage as well as its cultural and religious identity.

The Indian elites' perception of the EU has been and continues to be essentially conditioned by the Anglo-Saxon media, which impedes a more nuanced understanding of the processes and dynamics of European integration as well as the intricacies and roles of EU institutions. Despite the growing knowledge and awareness about the EU in India in recent years, there continues to be a lack of comprehensive understanding of India-EU relations in the media. There is a considerable divide between reality and an individual's perception of it. This is particularly true of the image that Europeans have of India and vice versa. The average Indians encounter the "3 Ds" and have considerable difficulty in understanding the strange political and economic animal that the EU is, especially given the complexity of EU institutions, proliferating regulations and rotating presidency. For them, the EU is *difficult* to comprehend; it is *different* from their friendly, neighbourhood, regional organization (SAARC); and since it is *distant*, Indians are generally reluctant to make the necessary effort to understand it. For the average Indian, the EC (European Commission) stands for the "Election Commission". And if the EU Delegation is said to be an embassy, the usual query is for which country does it issue visas? To many Indians, Europe is like "the dowdy old lady", known for over four centuries. There is "no excitement, no passion" between India and Europe.[1] India, the Europeans often complain, "like" Europe, but "love" the United States even though it is "tough love".

When it comes to South Asia (or India), there are three categories of people in Europe: there are those who are otherwise very well informed and knowledgeable but who do not try to understand South Asia because they are convinced that others have tried it before and have failed in the effort; the second category consists of those who neither understand anything nor have a great desire to understand anything. India is simply too big, too distant, and too complex for them to make the effort. There is a small minority which falls in between these categories – those who have the courage and perseverance to understand the more complex problems of India and wish to do something about it. The Nordic countries have

1 Raja Mohan, C., "India, Europe and the United States," in R. K. Jain (ed.), *India and the European Union in the 21st Century*, New Delhi, Radiant Publishers, 2002, p. 62.

long been perceived as the "moral superpowers": "white knights" championing issues like non-proliferation and human rights.

Many of the historical and cultural bonds and terms of reference which traditionally linked India with Britain – the "Oxbridge" legacy – and, in turn, Europe have largely withered away with time, and the rise of globalisation. A wired-in middle class is no longer greatly interested in European history, art or society. India's youth dream not of going to Oxford or Cambridge, but to American universities. Europe is not seen as a land of opportunity for further growth like the US in business and academic circles despite their close historical relationship.

Relations with India are driven by "very small circles" in Brussels. In the first circle are those which have substantial economic stakes – primarily the Big Three (France, Germany and the United Kingdom). They are the ones which bring the requisite energy, especially when push comes to shove, to move forward in an increasingly heterogeneous Union of 28 member states. In the second circle are those member states which have interests in certain sectors, but which do not quite have the big picture. In the third circle are the remaining member states, which broadly feel that if some things are good for others, it is fine with them.

Most Europeans, including academics, were traditionally interested primarily in Indian languages, scriptures and culture. Indologists in many European countries have had a very uneasy cohabitation with those who sought to study contemporary India. For most German India specialists, the golden period of Indian history was the Gupta Period; nothing before and nothing thereafter.

Most stakeholders in India maintain that policy-makers and think-tanks in the EU have a fixation with China and that India's democratic polity and shared values do not necessarily earn it any brownie points in Europe.

Many in India feel that Europe very often tends to have a patronizing attitude. "Engage and we shall teach you". Amongst those involved in the development aid business, this is usually called the "Mother Teresa" mentality.

EU Perceptions of India

Most people in Brussels have generally tended to feel that Indian policy-makers appeared to need convincing that the EU is "a player that matters".[2] Europeans have often urged India to shed its so-called narrow

2 Comment by Chris Patten, cited in Ahmed, R. Z., "EU asks India to ditch narrow view of Pakistan," *The Times of India*, 10 October 2002.

"prism of Pakistan" once and for all and develop a wider "world-view like that of China" in order to create a more meaningful partnership.

Europeans rightly complain about the structural constraints of the Ministry of External Affairs in terms of the handful of personnel dealing with Europe or the EU.[3] The Ministry is addressing this, though things may not necessarily change in the near future. EU officials also argue that when it comes to a meeting with India they usually confront a random democracy rather than a structured dialogue.

Europeans tend to consider India as a regional South Asian power, as still "an emerging country" whose status is being slowly enhanced, but the process of its global empowerment is just beginning whereas China is clearly ahead in terms of GDP, defence capabilities and diplomatic clout.[4] EU officials often argue that unlike China, which functions as a *demandeur* continuously seeking to widen interaction and dialogue, India has been neither proactive nor entrepreneurial enough to avail of existing opportunities. Indian policymakers usually respond by stressing that on most things which are of vital concern to India, the EU as a single entity is either unable or unwilling to make a difference with the result that most deliverables continue to lie in bilateral agreements.

To most European policy-makers, Europe does not yet seem to be central to Indian priorities and they note a US-centric tendency. India accords greater importance to the US than the EU because, as the principal foreign policy interlocutor, the US is perceived as having the biggest impact on its national security environment. There is a societal bias towards the US in terms of the importance given to Washington, cultural and intellectual ties with the US, and the nearly two million-strong Indian diaspora that has chosen the US as their home. The US has the capacity to act in ways which are of greater benefit to India than long European declaratory statements. The hallmark of the Union is incrementalism through dialogue and discussion whereas the Americans have a more practical, direct, American approach, which focuses on vital issues to India like geopolitical considerations, energy and technology.[5] India also finds it comparatively easier to deal with the US on a one-to-one basis, characterized as it is by an effective leadership. Decision-making in the EU, by contrast, is inherently time-consuming in an increasingly heterogeneous EU-28 driven forward by committees and compromises.

3 Markey, D., "Developing India's Foreign Policy Software," *Asia Policy*, July 2009, http://www.nbr.org/Publications/Asia_Policy/AP8/AP8_Marley_India.pdf, pp. 73-96.

4 Racine, J.-L., "The India-Europe Relationship in the US Shadow," in R. K. Jain (ed.), *India and the European Union: Building a Strategic Partnership*, New Delhi, Radiant Publishers, 2007, pp. 41-62.

5 Racine, J.-L., "The India-Europe Relationship in the US Shadow," *op. cit.*

The EU as a Global Actor

Most stakeholders in India regard the EU not merely as an economic and trading partner but as a global actor with a growing profile and presence in international politics. To them, the EU displays a lack of geopolitical coherence and has not yet shown signs of acting as a credible power.[6] On many foreign policy issues, Europe is not a single voice, but multiple voices competing for attention. Indians feel that it is going to be a long, long way before Europe acts as a coherent foreign policy actor given the inherent constraints of the Common Foreign and Security Policy. It is still "a group of nations and not an integral union of nations. It does not appear to have formulated for itself an independent role in the emerging world order".[7] Indian analysts do not think the EU can function as a counterweight or play the role of a "balancer" to the US.[8] There is scepticism in India as to whether Europe can acquire a mature military identity. The Union continues to be dependent on the US and its political will to exercise its military capability remains to be seen. Some stakeholders in India feel that the Union could possibly play a more coherent role now that the Lisbon Treaty has come into force.

Europe is perceived to be in relative decline in terms of the rise of Asia and in terms of where it stands in the world distribution of power at this stage.[9] To most Indians, postmodern Europe seems to be a lonely power in what is basically a Westphalian world with pre-modern and modern mindsets. Europeans seem to endorse Chinese views of a unipolar Asia, and not a multipolar Asia which also takes into account the growing profile of India and Japan in the region. The notion that Asia is a "naturally" Sino-centric continent, Indian observers argue, should be discarded.[10]

India and the EU have many common interests, but the success in transforming these into coordinated policies has proved rather elusive. India believes in strengthening multilateral institutions and mechanisms

---

6 Lisbonne-de Vergeron, K., *Contemporary Indian Views of Europe*, London, Chatham House, 2006, p. 5.

7 Subrahmanyam, K., "Lessons from Dialogues with European Security Experts," in K. Voll, and D. Beierlein (eds.), *Rising India – Europe's Partner*, New Delhi, Mosaic Books, 2006, p. 321.

8 Subrahmanyam, K., "Lessons from Dialogues with European Security Experts," *op. cit.*, p. 315.

9 Raja Mohan, C., "Prerequisitees for Foreign Policy and Security Interactions between Europe and India," in K. Voll, and D., Beierlein (eds.), *Rising India – Europe's Partner*, *op. cit.*, p. 259.

10 Sahni, V., "China-India Partnership: Defining an Agenda," *China Report*, Vol. 44, No. 1, 2008, p. 37; Raja Mohan, C., "India and the Emerging Non-Proliferation Order: the Second Nuclear Age," in H. V. Pant (ed.), *Indian Foreign Policy in a Unipolar World*, London and New Delhi, Routledge, 2009, p. 51.

for addressing global challenges such as terrorism, proliferation, drug trafficking, and spread of diseases like HIV/AIDS. But Indian and EU perceptions differ on the restructuring of international institutions, multilateral trade negotiations, climate change, the International Criminal Court, to name just four. Indian elites are convinced that on most issues which are most important to India – like enlargement of the UN Security Council – the EU either has no common policy or will be unable to formulate one now or in the near future. The real reason why India and Europe have not really been able to work together is because there are fundamental differences in terms of "where we are coming from to this debate and they relate to our relative positions in the international system and what we think are the most important issues and how we must approach them".[11]

India argues that inclusiveness, legitimacy and democracy must be enhanced in existing international institutions to reflect more appropriately the changing balance of power, both economic and political. While Europe has often talked about making India a full partner in the management of the global order, it is yet to take definitive steps or play a leadership role for the inclusion of India at the High Table. At the same time, India does not seem too keen to join EU-run institutions or clubs, which would entail taking on additional responsibilities, all for minimal gain or misplaced prestige.

A guiding principle of EU foreign policy is effective multilateralism and a means to shape an international system based on norms and rules. But this is not a view that is shared by many of the new global powers that have "a more traditional" perspective of multilateralism based on balance of power.[12] For India, multilateralism essentially means meaningful and achievable multilateralism. It cannot simply be reduced to common values; it is a process of constant political negotiation.

Most of the existing financial and trade rules reflect the power realities at the end of the Second World War. India has discovered that it is extremely difficult to change or incrementally reform existing norms because existing international institutions have in-built rules and norms that prevent erosion or dilution of their power and mission.[13] India, from long experience of its negative impact, has become acutely sensitive to

[11] Raja Mohan, C., *Rising India – Europe's Partner*, *op. cit.*, 2006, p. 258.

[12] de Vasconcelos, A., *The European Security Strategy 2003-2008, Building on Common Interests*, ISS Report, No. 5, Paris, EU Institute of Security Studies, 2009, p. 20.

[13] Johnston, A. I., "Is China a Status Quo Power?," *International Security*, Vol. 27, No. 4, Spring 2003, p. 23.

this "regulatory imperialism" of the West, as it has been termed.[14] It is therefore determined to play an active role in the framing of new rules, which must reflect the needs and aspirations of one sixth of humanity. As an aspiring power, India is more sympathetic to the American effort to "rework" the rules of the global game whereas Europe is perceived to be a staunch defender of the present order. Although India's position was well understood on the Indo-US nuclear deal, there was very strong opposition to the Nuclear Suppliers Group waiver by several European countries, which needed persuasion. Thus, while the hyperpower may change the rules, the support of others, especially the EU as a whole or at least its key members, is still needed.

Climate change has been a major irritant in EU-India relations, with the Europeans insisting that so long as the so-called "major emitters" like China and India remain outside the emissions reduction regime, their own efforts will make little difference to the global goal of stabilizing and reducing CO_2 emissions. India argues that climate change is taking place, not due to the current level of greenhouse gas (GHG) emissions, but because of the accumulated stock of GHGs in the atmosphere which is the result of carbon-based industrial activity in developed countries over the past two centuries and more. India has sought an outcome to the negotiations which is fair and equitable and in accordance with the principle of common but differentiated responsibilities and respective capabilities. India has announced a National Action Plan on Climate Change, with eight National Missions, which incorporates its vision of sustainable development and the steps it must take to realize it. India is unwilling to accept any mandatory carbon emission limits because only continuous growth offers a real possibility of lifting millions out of poverty and because 400 million people in India out of 1.8 billion worldwide still do not have access to electricity. India has argued that it is imperative to maintain a distinction between the "lifestyle emissions" of the West and "survival emissions" of developing countries.[15] It is necessary for low-emission technologies to be made available to poorer countries at a price they can afford and technology needs to be shared generously and easily without stringent constraints of intellectual property rights. Climate change is increasingly becoming the next WTO-type of North-South divide.

---

[14] Horn, H., Mavroidis, P. C. and Sapir, A., "Beyond the WTO? A Study of EU and US Preferential Trade Agreements," *The World Economy*, Vol. 33, No. 11, 2010, pp. 1565-1588.

[15] Saran, S., Speech by Special Envoy of the Prime Minister, on Climate Change at Mumbai, 21 April 2008, http://www.meaindia.nic.in/speeches/13883, accessed 12 February 2009.

Growing Engagement with South Asia

Despite a long and deep experience of social, cultural, commercial and political interaction, South Asia has never been a region of front-line policy for the EU because of low levels of trade and investment. Politically, it was perceived as a complex region with intractable problems. The Union's first "EU Asia Strategy" (July 1994) hardly mentioned South Asia. It merely expressed a desire to "generally" strengthen relations with regional groupings like SAARC.[16] The revised Asia Strategy (September 2001) had a separate section on South Asia, which expressed concern about tensions between India and Pakistan over Kashmir. It highlighted the importance of political and security challenges in the region and threats to regional stability posed by terrorism, religious fundamentalism and ethnic conflict (notably in Afghanistan and Sri Lanka). It urged the Union to "reflect more deeply" on the major political challenges facing the region, and be ready to adopt "a more assertive and forward-looking approach" to its policy dialogue with the key countries of the region.[17]

At the turn of the century, the Union began to take greater interest in India – a consistently growing economy of a billion-plus people, which had doubled its share of world GDP and which had been logging nine per cent and more growth for many years; the acquisition of nuclear weapons; the steadily improving relations with the US; and recognition of India's growing stature and influence regionally and globally – all these factors prompted Brussels to enhance its engagement with India and hold annual summits since 2000.

In the years since the attacks of 9/11, the EU's engagement in South Asia has grown significantly. This includes a strategic partnership with India; the mutation of the "non-relationship" with Pakistan into a growing political and economic engagement and annual summits since 2009; an active role in dealing with the Maoist insurgency and the restoration of democracy in Nepal; and greater involvement as one of the four Co-Chairs to support Norway's facilitation effort and monitor progress of the peace process in Sri Lanka. In 2007, the EU became an Observer in SAARC. The Union and several member states have been actively engaged in trying to stabilize the situation in Afghanistan as part of the International Security Assistance Force.

The draft of the EU's first regional strategy for South Asia was presented at the South Asian Envoys meeting in Mumbai (March 2007) and

---

16 European Commission, Communication from the Commission to the Council, "Towards a new Asia Strategy," COM(94)314 final, 13 July 1994.

17 European Commission, Communication from the Commission, "Europe and Asia: A Strategic Framework for Enhanced Partnerships," COM(2001)469 final, 4 September 2001, pp. 8 and 20.

was chaired by the visiting External Affairs Commissioner Benita Ferrero-Waldner. It was a limited document, amounting to no more than a compilation of bilateral issues. The head of the relevant Commission unit was advised to prepare another draft. Subsequently, the idea of outlining a South Asia strategy died a quiet political death because a regional strategy would necessarily involve grappling with sensitive issues between India, Pakistan and Afghanistan and because not much inherent added value was evident in a South Asia strategy. Moreover, since the Union already had annual summits with India (and more recently Pakistan), Brussels had come to the conclusion that a South Asia regional strategy was rather premature in the present circumstances: let things move first in terms of concrete cooperation and then one could revisit it at a later point of time. As long as SAARC remains the least economically integrated region in the world, prospects of closer EU-SAARC relations do not seem to be bright.

The EU and Afghanistan-Pakistan

The EU's relationship with Pakistan was historically an isolated one, or what could be termed as "normal relations", characterized by low economic trade, low levels of development aid and a general lack of interest. However, after September 11, the stakes were particularly high in Pakistan – a country of 145 million people, a nuclear power that has been "a hotbed of radical militancy, the godfather of the Taliban in Afghanistan and the sponsor of *jihadi* organizations operating in Kashmir".[18] With Pakistan's transformation into a frontline state in the war against terrorism, the EU came out in strong support of a fragile regime with economic aid[19] and trade preferences[20] and the conclusion of a "third generation" agreement with Pakistan. There are continuing concerns about Pakistani

[18] Racine, J.-L., "The Case of Pakistan: A Strategy for Europe," in I. H. Daalder, N. Gnessotto and P. H. Gordon (eds.), *Crescent of Crisis: US-European Strategy for the Greater Middle East*, Washington, D.C., Brookings Institution Press, 2006, p. 200.

[19] During the period 2002-2006, a total of Euro 145 million was allocated (original aid allocation of Euro 75 million with a "one-off" additional allocation of Euro 70 million for financial service sector reforms in 2002 and education in 2006.) After the October 2005 earthquake, the EU provided a further € 93.6 million in humanitarian aid. For the period 2007-2013, the EU made a four-fold increase in development aid from the annual Euro 15 million to Euro 60 million for the period 2007-2013, providing an indicative amount of Euro 398 million focusing primarily on a poverty-alleviation agenda.

[20] On 16 October 2001, the Commission presented a package of trade measures worth approximately €1 billion to Pakistan over the four year period to December 2004 giving Pakistan the best possible access to the EU short of a Free Trade Agreement by making it eligible for the new Special Generalised System of Preferences (GSP) Scheme for countries combating drug production and trafficking by increasing quotas for Pakistani textiles and clothing, which accounted for about 60 per cent of Pakistani exports to the EU.

madrassas being a preferred destination for European home-grown terrorists. Security, counter-terrorism considerations, and a push by large member states, especially Britain, led to the holding of the first-ever EU-Pakistan summit on 17 June 2009. However, this is unlikely to lead to an overnight change in what is still "a relatively desultory and uninspiring relationship".[21]

In the aftermath of 9/11, the EU became involved in the post-war reconstruction of Afghanistan and appointed a Special Representative for Afghanistan.[22] Unlike Iraq, the war in Afghanistan was viewed by Europeans to be "necessary and just". They committed themselves to it through NATO, perhaps with "a premature view of an Afghanistan that would mainly need peacekeeping and reconstruction following the US military intervention to oust the former regime in Kabul, rather than combat forces ready to engage in a resurgent Taliban".[23] The European Security Strategy of December 2003 projected Afghanistan as an example of state failure which was the source of 90 per cent of heroin that arrives in Europe. The Union and its member states are engaged in diverse activities such as police training, building of democratic institutions, counter-narcotics and judicial training. But there is a clear implementation deficit with only 265 of the planned 400 trainers being stationed in Afghanistan.

As a result of intense pressure from the Obama administration to do more in Afghanistan, the American troop surge of 2009, led by Gen. David Petraeus was accompanied by a European surge. The total number of European troops in Afghanistan grew from approximately 17,400 in November 2006 to over 27,000 in March 2009.[24] However, there has been growing domestic disenchantment with European engagement in Afghanistan. Given the inability of the combined might of NATO to actually win the war in Afghanistan, President Obama's Af-Pak policy has sought to enable the US and others to pull out of Afghanistan, leaving behind a semblance of governance in the country.

---

[21] Islam, S., "EU-Pakistan: A Crucial Summit," *Dawn* internet edition, 13 June 2009.

[22] Apart from the EU, five member states now have special envoys to Afghanistan-Pakistan, viz. France, Germany, Italy, Sweden and the UK.

[23] Asmus, R. D. and Lindberg, T., "Rue de la Loi: The Global Ambition of the European Project," Stanley Foundation Working Paper, September 2008, p. 7, http://www.gmfus.org/publications/article.cfm?id=491.

[24] "EU Engagement in Afghanistan," EU Council Secretariat Factsheet, AFG/04, March 2009, http://www.consilium.europa.eu/uedocs/cmsUpload/090330-EU_engagement_Afghanistan.pdf.

Democracy Promotion in South Asia

In South Asia, the EU has incorporated an "essential element" clause in third generation agreements concluded with India (1994), Pakistan (2001), Bangladesh (2000), and Sri Lanka (1994). From 1994-2002, no project under the European Initiative for Democracy and Human Rights (EIDHR) (1994-2006) – renamed the European Instrument for Democracy and Human Rights in 2007 – was undertaken in South Asia, primarily because the lion's share of fiscal allocations went to the politically more important regions of Central and Eastern Europe and the Newly Independent States. During the period 2002-2006, South Asia received a meagre financial allocation of only 6.85 per cent (€7.23 million) of the total funds allocated.[25] In order to promote democracy in South Asia, the European Union and EU member states fund more work on human rights than on the political elements of democracy promotion. South Asia has also received only a tiny share of good governance projects.

The policy of the EU towards Pakistan on democracy has sometimes been led by pragmatists who favoured a *realpolitik* view of Pakistan and its usefulness in the fight against terrorism and sometimes by pro-democracy hardliners, especially in the European Parliament, who want democracy and the rule of law to get top priority. The war against terrorism weakened the commitment to democracy and human rights in countries which were valuable allies like Pakistan with most European governments stressing the TINA ("There is No Alternative") factor. The key problem areas in Pakistan are the persistence of Islamic extremism, the lopsided economy, and "the two steps-forward, two-steps-backward approach to human rights, democratization, and political openness".[26]

The EU took an active interest and played a proactive role in the restoration of parliamentary democracy in Nepal where the assassination of the ruling monarch and the Maoist insurgency led to a virtual civil war from 2004. India facilitated a peace process in Nepal in coordination with the US, the UK, the EU and the UN. Out of the total allocation of €70 million for the period 2002-2006, the EU allocated €10 million for the consolidation of democracy, improving the judicial system through Conflict Mitigation Packages to defuse the situation. However, in the wake of the royal takeover in 2005, the European Commission suspended all programming activities and the launch of new projects was put on hold until the King restored Parliament in April 2006. An *ad hoc* commitment of

---

25 European Commission, "Furthering Human Rights and Democracy across the Globe," Brussels, 2007, p. 17.

26 Cohen, S. P., "Pakistan and the Crescent of Crisis," in I. H. Daalder, N. Gnessotto and P. H. Gordon (eds.), *Crescent of Crisis: US-European Strategy for the Greater Middle East*, *op. cit.*, p. 188.

€7 million was made to support the People's Movement and Nepal's return to democracy. This essentially sought to embrace the capacity and effectiveness of the National Human Rights Commission to monitor human rights violations.

Since the turn of the millennium, the European Commission has undertaken Election Observation Missions (EOMs) in South Asia – Bangladesh (2008), Bhutan (2008), Nepal (2008), Pakistan (2002 and 2008), Sri Lanka (2000, 2001, 2004 and 2005). Since the focus of EIDHR is largely on human rights, EOMs have become the major means of promoting good governance, though some doubt the extent to which election observation can contribute to institutionalizing democracy.

In South Asia, the EU has preferred a "bottom-up" approach by essentially concentrating on civil society and non-governmental organizations (NGOs), which have been the main channels and recipients of aid by the European Commission. The enthusiasm for the role of civil society derives chiefly from it being perceived as the key to the implosion of communism in Eastern Europe and the former Soviet Union and to the subsequent transition to democracy. This approach has been criticized because it tends to narrowly identify civil society with NGOs, especially the Western-advocacy type and de-emphasizes the role of institutions. Moreover, it enables the EU to "avoid tackling controversial issues" with partner countries while maintaining the profile of an international actor keen on supporting human rights and democracy.[27] Some South Asian scholars even question whether civil society "can be politically manufactured in the ways that appear to be implicit in some of the writing on democratization and explicit in the work of multinational agencies engaged in development".[28] Thus, external players can only play a supportive role and their capabilities to bring about fundamental changes are necessarily limited.

EU as an Observer in SAARC

SAARC is perhaps the only regional organization in Asia with which the EU does not have a treaty relationship but a Memorandum of Understanding, signed in 1996. Internal divisions within SAARC have however prevented any effective implementation of the MoU; its financial section has never been activated, making it extremely difficult to

---

27 Balfour, R., "Principles of Democracy and Human Rights: A Review of the European Union's Strategies towards its Neighbours," in S. Lucarelli and I. Manners (eds.), *Values and Principles in European Union Foreign Policy*, London, Routledge, 2006, pp. 118-119.

28 Singh, G., "South Asia," in P. Burnell, *Democratization through the Looking-Glass*, Manchester, Manchester University Press, 2003, p. 224.

implement any meaningful EU-SAARC projects. The lack of political cohesion among the SAARC members themselves, especially the uneasy relationship between India and Pakistan, makes the organization unsuitable as a political dialogue partner. An *ad hoc*, informal Ministerial-level dialogue with the Union had been held with SAARC on the sidelines of the UN General Assembly from 1998 to 2002, but it has not been resumed. The EU has time and again reiterated its willingness to share expertise and experiences in all areas of interest to SAARC and implement the South Asian Free Trade Area so that it does not have to reinvent the wheel, but it has not been possible to move things forward.

The EU took the initiative and became an Observer in SAARC at the 14th SAARC summit (New Delhi, April 2007). However, unlike the foreign ministers of China, Japan and South Korea who attended the summit, Brussels was only represented by the German Ambassador to India because it felt that it was problematic to send a Commissioner merely to make an Opening Statement. Several cooperation projects have been under discussion (customs, civil society and civil aviation), and although Brussels has become rather frustrated with SAARC's highly bureaucratic and procedural approach, it nonetheless perseveres in the hope that things may improve in the near future.

The EU as a Model for South Asia

Since the turn of the century, Indian leaders have on many occasions appreciatively referred to the EU as an example which can be emulated in South Asia. In January 2003, Foreign Minister Yashwant Sinha urged that "we move forward from SAARC and think of a South Asian Union [...] [which] will not merely be an economic entity. It will acquire a political dimension in the same manner which the European Union has come to acquire a political and strategic dimension".[29] At the Islamabad SAARC summit (January 2004), Prime Minister Atal Behari Vajpayee had even proposed a common currency for South Asia. President Abdul Kalam said that the greatest contribution of the EU is that it has demonstrated to the world that it is possible to build "a strong union of nations without compromising national identities". The Union has become "an inspirational model and an example to emulate for every region of the world".[30] The EU, according to Pakistani Foreign Minister Kasuri, offered a model and other

[29] Sinha, Y., Inaugural address at the seminar on "South Asian Cooperation" organized by the South Asian Centre for Policy Studies, Dhaka, 10 January 2003, http://www.meaindia.nic.in/speeches/eam-10jan.htm.

[30] Abdul Kalam, A. P. J., Address to the European Parliament at Strasbourg, 25 April 2007, http://pib.nic.in/release/rel_print_age.asp?relid=27125.

regional organizations can "learn immensely" from their experience.[31] Prime Minister Shaukat Aziz also remarked that the EU was the "best example of multilateral cooperation".[32]

The differences in the evolution and the respective geo-political milieux of the EU and SAARC are significant in the identification of problems, of how policies are formulated, and what instruments are used for implementing those policies. Each region has developed its own approach towards regional cooperation and it is based on its unique characteristics. While the EU may serve as a reference point, the "European integration process is "absolutely exceptional and impossible to export" elsewhere in the world.[33]

Conclusion: India-EU Relations Now

For the most part, the driving force behind EU-India relations has been, is, and will continue to be trade and commerce. With the conclusion of an India-EU trade and investment agreement, trade is likely to grow significantly. If trade goes forward, then many more things may well move forward as well. Political dialogue has also considerably widened and deepened. In recent years, there have been growing discussions between India and the EU on regional issues as India cannot solve the problems by itself and needs good collaborators. There is a growing willingness to discuss and engage, but this is not necessarily accompanied by a mindset change. As one senior EU official put it: "First there has to be a basic similarity of analysis. Only when you understand the country, you understand the issue. This gradually builds confidence in one another. Only when you have confidence, can you collaborate".[34]

Despite a strategic partnership, India and the EU have not been able to have a structured dialogue on security issues partly because of disparate priorities and different security contexts.

India is confronting traditional security threats in an increasingly difficult and dangerous neighbourhood whereas the EU mostly confronts non-traditional security threats. Unlike any of the previous security dialogues, the one held in November 2008 shortly after the Mumbai attacks was

31 Kasuri, K., Remarks by Foreign Minister Khurshid Kasuri at a reception to mark EU enlargement, 1 May 2004, http://www.hipakistan.com/en/pdetail.php?newsId=en63700&F_catID=13&f_type=source.

32 Aziz, S., Remarks by Aziz to a delegation of EU ambassadors, Islamabad, 7 July 2005, "Shaukat asks EU for market access and technological help," *Daily Times*, 8 July 2005.

33 Telo, M., "Multilateralism and Regionalism in European Union and South Asia Relations," in B. Vivekanandan and D. K. Giri (eds.), *Contemporary Europe and South Asia*, New Delhi, Concept Publishing, 2001, p. 206.

34 Interview in Brussels, November 2006.

more substantive partly because of Indian keenness to discuss security issues, partly because France (with which India already has a broad and dense bilateral strategic dialogue) had the Presidency, and partly because a lot of the undercurrents of the attack had linkages with Europe. There is not much enthusiasm amongst EU member states to get involved in the inordinately time-consuming exercise of declaring terrorist groups since they resurface under new names. Getting the EU to cooperate even in "soft" areas of cooperation such as money laundering, technical cooperation, and exchange of information has not fructified though cooperation with Europol is likely to happen in the near future. The prospects of practical, ground-level, hard-core security cooperation are rather limited because assets and competences are really with the member states and not the Union.

After many summits, India and the EU are gradually getting used to working together. There is a widening and deepening of political dialogue and a variety of consultation mechanisms on around 45 issues, which have enabled the two sides to better understand and appreciate each other's positions, perspectives and perceptions. However, shared values do not necessarily translate into greater cooperation; one needs to have shared interests and priorities. Mutual long-term interest is going to be in areas like scientific and technological cooperation, movement of skilled persons, and so on. The time to build and enhance existing frameworks is now.

There are many things that India needs to do in order to deal with the growing profile and role of the EU in world politics. It needs to intensify its engagement with EU institutions – especially the European Parliament – and enhance its contact and interaction with the Council. It needs to promote civil society exchanges and linkages between India and Europe and foster greater intellectual and elite interactions, as well as build greater expertise in Indian universities and the think tank community on the EU.

Europeans have to revise their mental maps about the growing profile of emerging powers. This is not easy and old habits die hard. Europeans are used to wielding influence, and in the past, whether one was listened to, or not, depended on Europe. But today Europe tends to be seen by many Asians as increasingly a region in relative power decline.

Europe should think and cooperate with emerging powers and other key countries in the construction of a new international system, rather than demanding that they "prove" themselves to be responsible stakeholders. Emerging powers need to be made full partners in the writing of new rules for institutions in a rapidly changing world.

The European Union and India

Birds of a Feather or Frenemies for Ever?

Emilian KAVALSKI

Australian Catholic University

> The European community is, in fact [...] an object of literary curiosity; the means are defective, the guides incompetent, the same difficulties obstruct the eager progress of the student, and they are only to be overcome by a like display of energy and perseverance.[1]

Introduction

While having a different "European community" in mind, the 1820s depiction by the Bombay correspondent of *The Asiatic Journal* in the above epigraph will resonate with most Indian commentators today as a relevant account of the European Union (EU). In short, the EU provokes a certain "curiosity", yet its external affairs management is perceived as "incompetent" at best and "defective" at worst. This has obliged even the most eager of Indian observers to "display [a lot] of energy and perseverance" in coming to terms with the complexity of the Brussels-based bloc. But even the most persistent among them have had to conclude that for India, "the EU is a marginal player".[2]

This result appears to reflect a paradoxical pattern of interactions. On the one hand, both the EU and India assert that as the largest democracies in the world they share common values and a normative outlook. Hence, the suggestion is that these birds of a democratic feather should have no problem flocking together around a common strategic vision. On the other hand, the EU and India remain rather aloof from one another while showering their affections on other international partners: China, for the EU, and the United States, for India. In this respect, both Brussels and

1 "Literary and Philosophical Intelligence," *The Asiatic Journal*, Vol. 14, 1822, p. 38.

2 Jain, R. K., "India's Relations with the European Union," in D. Scott (ed.), *Handbook of India's International Relations*, London, Routledge, 2011, p. 227.

New Delhi have often not only neglected and disregarded each other's interest, but have actively competed with one another. In this respect, they appear increasingly to act like "frenemies" on the world stage.

While concurring that such labels are simplistic, the generalisations that they provide can offer worthwhile insights into the complex strategic contexts within which the foreign policy engagements of the EU and India function. This chapter, therefore, engages in a close reading of the declarations, documents and testimonies that mark the cornerstones of EU-India interactions. Such narrative process-tracing is premised on the appraisal of the bilateral relationship between India and the EU. Such an overview provides the context for the analysis of the composite genealogy, distinct grammars (of the *untimely*, *socialisation* and *parity*) and pervasive contradictions of India-EU relations. While this assessment draws attention to the complexity of world affairs, at the same time, it also offers a background for detailing the dominant themes underwriting Indian perceptions of the "strategic partnership" between Brussels and New Delhi. The chapter concludes with a brief discussion of the implications and possible trajectories of the EU-India relationship.

Genealogy, Grammars and Contradictions of the EU-India Relationship

By engaging in close reading of key documents and statements, this section outlines the narrative underpinnings of the institutional and ideational framework of the EU-India relationship.[3] The import of discourses to the study of foreign policy has been largely sidelined in the study of world affairs owing to their alleged abstruseness, which purportedly obscures the understanding of interests and agency in the international arena. The claim here is that the focus on discourses has important explanatory potential in regard to the various scenarios of foreign policy developments. In this respect, the consideration of the narrative constructions that underwrite the formulation of foreign policy takes into account "the developments of a few key concepts, their historical origins, their transformations, [and] their constitutive relationship to other concepts".[4]

The conjecture, therefore, is that public articulations of foreign policy choices are not independent of the context in which they emerge. Such assessment makes use of Michel Foucault's notion of "genealogy". Thus, the textual analysis of international interactions can be said to

---

3 This is an update on the argument developed in E. Kavalski, "Venus and the Porcupine: Assessing the European Union-India Strategic Partnership," *South Asian Survey*, Vol. 15, No. 1, 2008, pp. 63-81.

4 Ole Wæver cited in E. Kavalski, *India and Central Asia: The Mythmaking and International Relations of a Rising Power*, London, Routledge, 2010, p. 8.

"begin with the present and goes backwards in time until a difference is located. Then [it] proceeds forward again tracing the transformations and taking care to preserve the discontinuities as well as the continuities".[5] Following the Foucauldian perspective this chapter approaches foreign policy articulations as (concurrently) *discursively enabled* and *discursively limited*. The effects of these narratives are exposed not as *causal*, but rather as creating the *horizon of the possible*. Foreign policy narratives are, thereby, intertwined with the narrative process-tracing of their explanation. Such suggestion recalls Ludwig Wittgenstein's concept of "grammar". It refers to the practice of rules that do not have defining characteristics which would be "common to them all, but [rather] similarities, resemblances". The Wittgensteinian perspective implies that "every instance of [a] rule's use modifies the rule as such, it cannot be said that a rule is being applied, but that it is being constantly constructed and reconstructed".[6] In this respect, the grammars of EU-India interactions simultaneously *facilitate* and *restrict* the practice of foreign-policy-articulations.

The relationship between the EU and India reflects the complex historical genealogy of the connections between Europe and South Asia, as well as the significance of the distinct grammars animating the social, political, and economic exchanges between these regions.[7] The engagement in textual process-tracing is intended as a sketch for a prolegomenon to the conceptual contexts of the EU-India relationship. In other words, the motivation here is not only to *discover* new and previously untouched perspectives on the complex relationship between Brussels and New Delhi, but also the *uncovery* (i.e., the *excavation*) of viewpoints from underneath layers of ossified or never-problematized knowledge.[8] By elaborating the contradictions of their foreign policy approaches, this investigation suggests that the discursive interpretation of international affairs can be read not only as the reproduction of policy-goals, but it also pays attention to what remains figurative, implicit and inter-textual.

---

5 Foucault cited in E. Kavalski, "Venus and the Porcupine," *op. cit.*, p. 69.

6 Zolkos, M., *Conceptual Analysis of the Human Rights and Democracy Nexus*, Copenhagen, Copenhagen University Press, 2005, p. 192.

7 Khosla, I. P. (ed.), *India and the New Europe*, New Delhi, Konark, 2004; Lisbonne de Vergeron, K., *Contemporary Indian Views of Europe*, London, Chatham House, 2006.

8 Janice Bially-Mattern cited in E. Kavalski, *India and Central Asia*, *op. cit.*, p. 22. For a detailed analysis of such uncovery see Kavalski, E., "The Fifth Debate and the Emergence of Complex International Relations Theory: Notes on the Application of Complexity Theory to the Study of International Life," *Cambridge Review of International Affairs*, Vol. 20, No. 3, 2007, pp. 435-454.

Genealogy of EU-India Relations

Brussels routinely acknowledges that during the 1960s India was one of the first countries to set up relations with the emerging European Union.[9] The relationship between India and the then European Community was formalised with the 1981 Agreement for Commercial and Economic Cooperation. As the title of this document suggests, the interaction between Brussels and New Delhi was limited to the areas of trade and commerce. This pattern of essentially economic relations was reiterated by the 1994 Cooperation Agreement on Partnership and Development. Despite its alleged broader scope, the preamble asserts that its main aim is

> to enhance commercial and economic contacts between India and the EU [by] creating favourable conditions for a substantial development and diversification of trade and industry within the framework of a more dynamic relationship which will further their development needs, investment flows, commercial and economic cooperation.[10]

In fact, the centrality of economic interests is stated in Article 4, which spells out the three main areas of the EU-India interactions: (i) "improving the economic environment in India by facilitating access to Community know-how and technology"; (ii) "facilitating contracts between economic operators and other measures designed to promote commercial exchanges and investments"; and (iii) "reinforcing mutual understanding of their respective economic, social and cultural environment as a basis for effective cooperation".[11] Within these three areas, the 1994 Cooperation Agreement outlines a set of seventeen targets stretching from "improvement in the economic environment and the business climate" to "cooperation in the fields of information and culture".[12] In this respect, the EU and India agreed upon ten "means" for achieving these objectives, ranging from the "exchange of information and ideas", "provision of technical assistance and training programmes" to the "establishment of links between research and training centres, specialised agencies and business organisations".[13]

At the same time, the 1994 Cooperation Agreement made explicit the non-committal nature of this relationship by acknowledging that Brussels and New Delhi "will, within the limits of their available financial means

---

9 Cameron, F., Berkofsky, A., Bhandari M. *et al.*, *The EU-India Relations*, Brussels, European Policy Centre, 2005, p. 6.

10 European Commission, "Cooperation Agreement between the European Community and the Republic of India," *Official Journal of the European Communities* L223 (27/8/1994), p. 24.

11 *Ibid.*, p. 26.

12 *Ibid.*

13 *Ibid.*, p. 27.

and within the framework of their respective procedures and instruments, make available funds to facilitate the aims set out in this document especially as concerns economic cooperation". Therefore, it recommended that the EU and India "hold friendly *ad hoc* consultations".[14] Yet, as the decade of the 1990s was coming to an end, there seemed to be a shared understanding both in Brussels and in New Delhi that the two polities were operating in a qualitatively new international environment. Thus, intent on increasing its visibility, the EU unfolded a "Strategic Partnership" with India. Such strategic partnership between Brussels and New Delhi has been translated as a "new-found reciprocity and recognition of each other's potential and relevance", which occurred against the backdrop of transforming external contexts.[15]

As suggested, this discursive enhancement in the external relations of Brussels reflects the increasing awareness of the EU's global reach. The *European Security Strategy* maintains that "our [the EU's] history, geography and cultural ties give us links with every part of the world [...] These relationships are an important asset to build on. In particular, we should look to develop strategic partnerships with Japan, China, Canada and India as well as with all those who share our goals and values, and are prepared to act in their support".[16] The strategic objectives and culture implicit in such assertions developed in the context of the EU's increasing engagement in Asia. Brussels has acknowledged that "the rise of Asia is dramatically changing the world [...] The establishment of a strong, coordinated presence in different regions of Asia will allow Europe at the beginning of the 21st century to ensure that its interests are taken fully into account there".[17] In this respect, the Strategic Partnership with India reflects the "focus on strengthening the EU's political and economic presence across Asia, and raising this to a level commensurate with the global weight of an enlarged EU".[18]

---

14 *Ibid.*, p. 30.

15 Baroowa, S., "The Emerging Strategic Partnership between India and the European Union: A Critical Appraisal," in *Europe, India and China: Strategic Partners in a Changing World*, Aix-en-Provence, Université Paul Cézanne Press, 2006, p. 3. For a different take on such transformations, see Kavalski, E., "The Peacock and the Bear in the Heartland: Central Asia and the Shifting Patterns of India's Relations with Russia," *Indian Journal of Asian Affairs*, Vol. 23, No. 1, 2010, pp. 1-20.

16 *European Security Strategy: A Secure Europe in a Better World*, Brussels, EUISS and European Commission, 2003, p. 14.

17 European Commission, *Towards a New Asia Strategy*, Brussels, COM(1994)314 final, p. 3.

18 European Commission, *Europe and Asia: A Strategic Framework for Enhanced Partnerships*, Brussels, COM(2001)469 final, p. 15.

In this context, the EU-India relationship had already begun its discursive alteration within the context of regularized annual high-level meetings, starting with the 2000 Lisbon Summit. Brussels declared that the summit was "a turning point" as it provided the foundations for "a coalition of interest in addressing global challenges".[19] It furthered the "enhanced partnership"[20] between India and the EU by providing a forum for the discussion and negotiation of differences. Chris Patten, the then External Relations Commissioner of the EU, proclaimed that the regular summit meetings opened "a new chapter in the EU-India relationship" premised on the appreciation that "just as we are changing fast, India herself is evolving".[21] Brussels has, thereby, acknowledged that "the EU has a very direct interest not only in what happens on its own borders but also in the situation in South Asia".[22]

Thus, the Strategic Partnership is promoted as "the starting point of a collective reflection on upgrading EU-India relations".[23] At the same time, by acknowledging that "the EU and India are increasingly seen as forces for global stability [and that] the focus of their relations has shifted from trade to wider political issues", Brussels intends "a strategic alliance for the promotion of an effective multilateral approach".[24] These assertions recognise that "the institutional architecture of EU-India relations defined by the 1994 Cooperation Agreement and the 2000 Lisbon Summit has created a complex structure of meetings at different levels in virtually all areas of interest and cooperation. It is now time to streamline and increase its effectiveness".[25] In this respect, the 2004 Strategic Partnership identifies five areas for the interactions between Brussels and New Delhi: (i) cooperation at international fora: on multilateralism, human trafficking and migration, conflict prevention and post-conflict reconstruction, non-proliferation of weapons of mass destructions, promotion of democracy and protection of human rights; (ii) economic cooperation: joint sectoral dialogues on regulatory and industrial policies; (iii) development cooperation; (iv) intellectual, scientific, and cultural cooperation; and (v) cooperation on the improvement of the institutional collaboration between India and the EU.[26]

---

19 *Ibid.*, p. 12.

20 European Commission, *EU-India Enhanced Partnership*, Brussels, COM(1996)275 final.

21 Patten, C., "The EU and India," *The Hindu*, 17 February 2004.

22 European Commission, *EU-India Enhanced Partnership, op. cit.*, p. 7.

23 European Commission, *EU-India Strategic Partnership*, Brussels, COM(2004) 430 final, p. 11.

24 *Ibid.*, p. 3.

25 *Ibid.*, p. 10.

26 *Ibid.*, pp. 3-10.

The implicit agenda of this "streamlining" is "to facilitate bridge-building" between Brussels and New Delhi by providing a framework for "continuous dialogue [...] especially, on implementation of [their] international obligations and commitments, and the strengthening of global governance".[27] However, just like the 1994 Cooperation Agreement, the 2004 Strategic Partnership reiterates the non-committal nature of Euro-Indian interactions. It plainly states that it is underwritten by the intention "to produce *non-binding* guidelines for a further deepening of EU-India relations".[28] Such replication of "*ad hoc*", "*non-binding*" discourses reflects the absence of strategic agreement – both on behalf of Brussels and of New Delhi – on a long term vision of their relations. This is made particularly conspicuous through a study of the grammars of their interactions.

Grammars of EU-India Relations

Traditionally, the public discourses of India and the EU accentuate the normative contiguity between the two polities. Thus, the intensification in the post-Cold War relationship between Brussels and New Delhi has been made possible by "the excellent relations and traditional links of friendship" between them.[29] Likewise, the premise of the 2004 Strategic Partnership is that India and the EU "already enjoy a close relationship, based on shared values and mutual respect".[30] In its policy-response, the Indian government also recognised that the enhancement of bilateral interactions "reveals a strong identity of views on the strategic priorities and issues of vital importance to both sides".[31] In this respect, the Indian Prime Minister Manmohan Singh declared at the 2006 Helsinki India-EU Summit that "India and the EU are *natural partners* as we share common values of democracy, pluralism and the rule of law".[32]

Thus, in their official articulations both Brussels and New Delhi tend to stress their normative similarity "as the largest democracies in the world that share common values and beliefs".[33] Despite such professed similarity of convictions, the narratives of EU-India interactions reflect

---

27 *Ibid.*, p. 4.

28 *Ibid.*, p. 11. Emphasis added.

29 European Commission, "Cooperation Agreement," *op. cit.*, p. 24.

30 European Commission, *EU-India Strategic Partnership*, *op. cit.*, p. 3.

31 Government of India, *India's Response to EU Communication Titled "EU-India Strategic Partnership,"* New Delhi, 2004, p. 3.

32 Government of India, "Prime Minister's Statement at the Press Conference at the 7th India-EU Summit," Helsinki, 13 October 2006. Emphasis added.

33 Government of India, "Political Declaration on the India-EU Strategic Partnership," New Delhi, 7 September 2005.

(at least) three distinct grammars, one shared and two specific to Brussels and New Delhi respectively: (i) focus on the untimely; (ii) the EU's proclivity towards international socialisation; and (iii) India's assertion of parity.

The emphasis on the untimely is probably the most conspicuous of the three grammars. Borrowing from a different context, the reference to the untimely here suggests that the EU-India relationship is "exapted"[34] not so much to present circumstances as to the future.[35] According to the 1994 Cooperation Agreement, Brussels and New Delhi "*will determine* together and to their mutual advantage the areas and priorities *to be covered* by concrete actions of economic cooperation".[36] The grammar of the untimely is also evident in the intention of "stimulating a wide discussion in order to establish priority areas for action to look at future challenges".[37] Likewise, the 2004 Strategic Partnership is infused with prescriptive proclamations that in their interactions India and the EU "*should seek to increase* cooperation," "*should devote* resources," "*should initiate* more concrete dialogue," and "*should work* together *to forge* an alliance".[38] Such discursive reliance on rhetoric of the future rather than the promotion of measures and mechanisms for adapting to its contingencies is also evidenced by the declarations of India-EU Summits. For instance, after the 2005 New Delhi Summit, the two sides agreed that they "*will strengthen* collaboration," "*will encourage* contacts," "*will hold* dialogues," "*will continue to work* closely together," and "*will increase* cooperation".[39] The suggestion here is that the grammar of the untimely is not only part and parcel of formal diplomatic discourse, but that it also intimates the particular attitudes that India and the EU hold about each other.

In this respect, the policy articulations of the EU suggest its educational vocation, in other words, its relations with India are targeted towards the *socialisation* of the country into (what Brussels perceives to be) appropriate patterns of both domestic and international behaviour

---

34 Exaptation is an evolutionary process in which a trait which previously served one purpose is co-opted to serve another, different purpose. A well-known example is feathers, which originally served as a heat-exchange mechanism, but latterly came to serve as a display mechanism and subsequently serve in bird flight.

35 Grosz, E., *The Nick of Time: Politics, Evolution, and the Untimely*, Durham, NC, Duke University Press, 2004, p. 11.

36 European Commission, "Cooperation Agreement," *op. cit.*, p. 27. Emphasis added.

37 European Commission, *EU-India Enhanced Partnership*, *op. cit.*, p. 13.

38 European Commission, *EU-India Strategic Partnership*, *op. cit.*, pp. 5-10. Emphasis added.

39 Government of India, "Political Declaration". Emphasis added.

under "an agenda of 'improved governance'".[40] The intention of this grammar is the projection of specific standards aimed at "building up its [India's] economic capabilities by way of provision of resources and technological assistance, in particular to improve the living conditions of the poorer sections of the population".[41] The focus on economic inequalities aims at "*imposing* an important human dimension" on Indian decision-makers.[42] Brussels also asserts that India's "'consumer class' [*is*] *not* on a par with Europe's middle class".[43] Reflecting the patronizing tone of such policy-attitude, the 1994 Cooperation Agreement has acknowledged that Brussels "is prepared in the course of its endeavours to take into account the interests of India".[44] Likewise, the 2004 Strategic Partnership suggests that "the EU must help India [to achieve] social and economic cohesion [because] poverty is still widespread, unemployment or under-employment is high and vast disparities persist".[45] The EU, therefore, has been intent on encouraging India "to achieve greater convergence" with international standards.[46] The socialising logic of Brussels' engagement is made apparent in its insistence on ensuring that "Asian leaders *are committed to* addressing global issues of common concern".[47]

At the same time, New Delhi seems to interpret its interactions with Brussels as a relationship of *parity*, in which both parties can (and have to) learn from each other. This grammar of implicit mutual socialisation reflects India's "own vision of fairness" in contemporary world affairs based on both equity of outcomes and legitimacy of process, i.e., the claim is that "equality of treatment is equitable only among equals".[48] For instance, the Indian government has made it explicit that "just like India [the EU] is one of the most important poles of a multi-polar world".[49] In this respect, New Delhi stresses that its own

[40] European Commission, "India: Country Strategy Paper," Brussels, 10 September 2002, p. 22.

[41] European Commission, "Cooperation Agreement," *op. cit.*, p. 25.

[42] European Commission, *EU-India Enhanced Partnership, op. cit.*, p. 15. Emphasis added.

[43] *Ibid.*, p. 4. Emphasis added.

[44] European Commission, "Cooperation Agreement," *op. cit.*, p. 11.

[45] European Commission, *EU-India Strategic Partnership, op. cit.*, p. 9.

[46] *Ibid.*, p. 7.

[47] European Commission, *The Social Dimension of Globalisation: The EU's Policy Contribution on Extending the Benefits to All*, Brussels, COM(2004)383 final, p. 12. Emphasis added.

[48] Narlikar, A., "Peculiar Chauvinism or Strategic Calculation? Explaining the Negotiating Strategy of a Rising India," *International Affairs*, Vol. 82, No. 1, 2006, pp. 63-65.

[49] Government of India, *India's Response, op. cit.*, p. 3.

international significance derives from its "rapidly growing consumer market, comprising over 250 million-strong middle class with increasing purchasing power".[50] Thus, from an Indian standpoint, the grammar of the interactions between Brussels and New Delhi reflects the dynamic parity between them. New Delhi insists that such partnership of "sovereign equality" can actually assist the EU in achieving "coherence among its expanding and increasingly diversifying population;" to that effect, India's experience "with the second-largest Muslim community in the world is a paradigm of Asia's syncretic culture and of how Islam can flourish in a plural, democratic and open society".[51] The implication from such assertions is that New Delhi can also *educate* Brussels into certain standards of appropriateness. The grammar of parity, thereby, intimates India's desire "to increase its ability to influence rule-making".[52] It has been suggested that the intention of this desire is "to counter the agenda-setting capabilities of the EU".[53]

These three grammars tend to pervade the narratives of EU-India interactions. The simultaneity of complementarity and of contradictions that underwrites their dynamics attests to the nascent complexity of world affairs. The claim here is that the interplay between these three grammars points to the discrepant perceptions that India and the EU hold both about themselves and each other. The following section details some of the contradictions reflected in the genealogy and grammars of EU-India interactions.

Contradictions of EU-India Relations

A number of contradictions underwrite the EU-India relationship. Some of them stem from the distinct points of departure of their policy approaches. Thus, while Brussels (and the capitals of other EU member states) "perceive India through the prism of British imperial lens,"[54] the perceptions of New Delhi's policy-elites towards the EU "continue to be essentially conditioned by the Anglo-Saxon media".[55] The starting premise of these viewpoints appears to prejudice the development of contextualised understanding of each other attuned to the complexities and nuances of policy making both in Brussels and in New Delhi.

---

50 *Ibid.*, p. 4.

51 *Ibid.*, pp. 4-10.

52 Lal, R., *Understanding China and India*, Westport, Praeger, 2006, p. 98.

53 Jain, R. K., "India, the EU, and Asian Regionalism," paper presented at the EUSA-AP conference, Tokyo, 8-10 December 2005, p. 11.

54 Dixit, J. N., "Cooperation with Europe," *Indian Express*, 10 July 2000.

55 Jain, R. K., "India, the EU, and Asian Regionalism," *op. cit.*, p. 7.

Another set of contradictions emanate from the EU's sluggish recognition of India's potential and significance. In fact, a senior European diplomat has acknowledged that the launch of the Strategic Partnership was intended to rectify this by "recognising that India is gaining in real importance for the EU. Before we looked more to China, and saw India rather as a leader of the developing world. Now it is an equal partner".[56] Yet, even when Brussels made such an acknowledgement, it insisted that its cooperation with India falls "within the framework of its programmes in Asian and Latin American countries".[57] In this respect, despite India's impressive development Brussels routinely circumscribes its achievements with the insistence that New Delhi still lags behind China "with a more modest rate of growth".[58] Such stance reflects the EU's struggles in coming to terms with Indian sensibilities. For instance, although Brussels did not take any punitive measures after the 1998 nuclear tests, its verbal denunciation tended to confirm Indian perception of the EU's "continued failure and reluctance to achieve a more pragmatic understanding of India's perspective".[59] Furthermore, the EU-India interactions are also marred by the seeming unwillingness of Brussels to discriminate between the positions of Pakistan and India through its "search for balance between the two competing neighbours".[60] At the same time, the EU has suggested that "for India in particular, the strengthening of bilateral cooperation on political, economic and social cooperation" is conditional on "enhanced partnership on global issues".[61] It seems, therefore, that the intensifying rhetoric of the EU's security identity remains unconcerned that it "impinges on India's interests".[62]

In this context, New Delhi interprets the "normative power" of the EU as a disguise for its lack of effective military capabilities.[63] Prominent Indian commentators assert that "Europe's self-perception of its post-modern orientation is in essence a convenient escape from confronting

---

56 Cited in U. S. Bava, "India-EU Relations," in R. Balme and B. Bridges (eds.), *Europe-Asia Relations*, Basingstoke, Palgrave, 2008, p. 248.

57 European Commission, "Cooperation Agreement," *op. cit.*, p. 30.

58 European Commission, *Europe and Asia*, *op. cit.*, p. 8.

59 Baroowa, S., "The Emerging Strategic Partnership," *op. cit.*, p. 8.

60 Ahmed, R., "EU Asks India to Ditch Narrow View of Pakistan," *The Times of India*, 10 October 2002.

61 European Commission, *Europe and Asia*, *op. cit.*, p. 21.

62 Baroowa, S., "The Emerging Strategic Partnership," *op. cit.*, p. 9.

63 For a detailed assessment, see Kavalski, E., "From the Western Balkans to the Greater Balkans Area: The External Conditioning of 'Awkward' and 'Integrated' States," *Mediterranean Quarterly*, Vol. 17, No. 3, 2006, pp. 86-100; and E. Kavalski, "Partnership or Rivalry between the EU, China and India in Central Asia," *European Law Journal*, Vol. 13, No. 6, 2007, pp. 839-856.

emerging challenges".[64] Thus, while Europe sees itself as heralding a unique model of global (and security) governance, such a stance provokes "disdain in India for the EU".[65] For instance, while Brussels "associates the concept of effective multilateralism with a strengthening of the UN […] India tends to pursue a selective form of multilateralism in order to assert its national interest".[66] Such discrepancy of visions underpins the contradictions in the international interactions between India and the EU. The narrative of assessment of their bilateral interactions intimates that what is often perceived as the very strength of the relationship between the two entities, i.e., that they "broadly share a common vision of world affairs", constrains the realisation of prospective gains and the fulfilment of the promise of partnership.[67] In this respect, some have declared that Indian discourses "on multilateralism and the need for a multi-polar world are a smokescreen designed in particular for European consumption".[68] This attitude reflects the pragmatism of India's forward foreign policy, which informs New Delhi's "jettisoning of *moralpolitik* in favour of *realpolitik*".[69] Such a departure from the European conceptualisation of normative power underwrites the claims of Indian commentators that Brussels "lacks consistency in its approach towards India".[70]

Given such a "mismatch of contexts, concerns and goals" most Indian commentators find it difficult to envisage a more substantial cooperation between the EU and India.[71] The misconceptions that decision-makers both in New Delhi and in Brussels seem to hold about each other's policy-making are intimately intertwined with and reflected by the genealogy and grammars of their relationship. In this respect, it is not surprising that the EU "hardly figures on the Indian 'radar screen'".[72] Instead, some have argued that Beijing has become "the measuring stick" for India's international agency,[73] while others aver that "apart from Washington,

64 Mohan, C. R., *Crossing the Rubicon: The Shaping of India's New Foreign Policy*, London, Palgrave, 2004, p. 76.

65 Jaffrelot, C., "India and the European Union: The Charade of a Strategic Partnership," *CERI-Focus*, 2006, p. 5.

66 Wagner, C., "India Moves into the Spotlight," *Deutschland Online*, 27 November 2006.

67 Cameron, F. *et al.*, *EU-India Relations*, *op. cit.*, p. 46.

68 Jaffrelot, C., "India and the European Union," *op. cit.*, p. 5.

69 Jain, R. K., "India, the EU," *op. cit.*, p. 2.

70 Duran, D., "The EU-India Strategic Partnership," *IPCS Article* 2222, 27 February 2007.

71 Jain, R. K., "India, the EU," *op. cit.*, p. 6.

72 Jaffrelot, C., "India and the European Union," *op. cit.*, p. 2.

73 Cohen, S., *India: Emerging Power*, Washington, D.C., Brookings, 2001, p. 266.

the rest of the world is more or less unimportant for New Delhi".[74] The following section traces the dominant representations of the EU when it *does* figure on the "radar screen" of India's policy-making.

Dominant Themes in India's Discourses on the EU

Several dominant themes in India's representation of the EU are evident in its public discourses: the economic significance of a single European market, Brussels management of dissimilar populations and the baffling complexity of the EU's bureaucracy. The following brief outline is intended as a suggestive rather than an exhaustive exploration of the narrations of these themes. In this respect, it is a sketch of the dominant Indian perceptions of the EU project.

The genealogy, grammars and contradictions of the EU-India relationship seem to confirm the suggestion that outsiders tend to perceive Brussels first and foremost as an economic actor. In this respect, although the EU is "both a key part of the multilateral structures of world politics and a player of growing resonance and influence in its own right," the weight and presence of its agency "seems to be consistently considered primarily in an economic context".[75] Thus, it is the commercial, trade, and aid capacities of the EU that underscore the perceptions of its status as a global actor. Likewise, India's reading of the EU gauges the agency of Brussels primarily from the script of its economic influence. In this respect, it is the economic imperatives that are "of paramount importance and [that] are bound to remain central to India's relations with the EU".[76] This perception is implicit in the appreciation and response both to the 1994 Cooperation Agreement and the 2004 Strategic Partnership, as well as the initiation of regularised India-EU Summits. R. K. Jain argues that it is the perception of the economic leverage of the European market that skews New Delhi's perception of "the EU not as one entity but as a conglomerate of states".[77]

At the same time, however, Indian narratives of the EU reflect a significant degree of fascination with its ability to bring together states and peoples with diverse (often conflictual) histories and cultures. As the Indian government has suggested, "the EU has become one of the most politically influential and economically powerful regional entities in the world [because] of its ability to synthesise the divergent approaches/goals of the

---

74 Jain, R. K., "India, the EU," *op. cit.*, p. 5.

75 Chaban, N., Elgström, O., and Holland, M., "The European Union as Others See It," *European Foreign Affairs Review*, Vol. 11, No. 2, 2006, p. 260.

76 Baroowa, S., "The Emerging Strategic Partnership," *op. cit.*, p. 3.

77 Jain, R. K., "India, the EU," *op. cit.*, p. 7.

Member-States into a coherent whole".[78] In this respect, the EU's ability to unite a restive continent through shared institutional arrangements is a significant incentive for New Delhi's collaboration with Brussels. As one Indian observer put it, "the distinctiveness of the EU lies in the flexibility to arrive at a decision mostly based on consensus. For [Indian] observers, it is understandably an experience to note the continuous compromise amongst 25-plus member nations on a daily basis in almost all aspects of European lives".[79]

The appeal of the EU as a symbol of "unity in diversity", however, is underwritten (if not undermined) by the (alleged) baffling complexity of its institutional arrangements. In spite of suggestions that India should be more understanding of European political structures (as the interactions between New Delhi and the various Indian states as well as "policy coherence" within the government administration are not so dissimilar to that of the EU), a number of Indian commentators have asserted that "the EU suffers from 'a lack of consensus'," which prevents New Delhi from "earning high points in Europe" because Brussels "has no strategic vision".[80] In particular, the bureaucratic structure of Brussels has turned the attempts "to reach consensus [into] 'a nightmare'".[81] Such a stance appears to validate the inference that the preoccupation of Brussels with internal processes prevents it from playing an effective global role. Thus, the perception of convoluted procedures impeding the process and practices of the EU tend to impact negatively on its "diplomatic power" and impairs its regard as "a cohesive force".[82] In this respect, Indian commentators have criticised the 2004 Strategic Partnership as an "empty rhetoric rather than a content driven strategy" owing to the "obstacles imposed by the EU institutional architecture, and decision-making mechanisms".[83] Thus, because of its "[structural] fuzziness," there is a real question "whether the EU is indeed a power".[84]

These themes seem to underwrite the contradictions emanating from the interplay between the genealogy and grammars of the EU-India relationship. Their dominant inkling is that the EU (although significant) is not central to the foreign policy aspirations of New Delhi. Capturing the popular and policy Indian mood of the interactions between Brussels

78 Government of India, *India's Response*, *op. cit.*, p. 4.

79 Mukhopadhyay, A., "The EU-India Helsinki Summit," *IDSA Strategic Comment*, 10 October 2006.

80 Jain, R. K., "India, the EU," *op. cit.*, p. 6.

81 *Ibid.*

82 Chaban, N. *et al.*, "The European Union," *op. cit.*, p. 255.

83 Duran, D., "EU-India," *op. cit.*

84 Mukhopadhyay, A., "EU-India," *op. cit.*

and New Delhi, Jain affirms that "Europe is like 'the dowdy old lady'," who does not only want to be "liked," but also yearns to be "loved;" thus, "Europe is disillusioned when it finds that India is not willing to reciprocate".[85]

Conclusion

The lacklustre EU-India relationship tends to eschew the limelight of media and scholarly attention. In an attempt to rectify this trend, this chapter brings together the divergent articulations on the interactions between Brussels and New Delhi in the post-Cold War period. Relying on a narrative assessment of key texts and proclamations of the nascent strategic partnership, the investigation identifies the distinct genealogy, specific grammars, and underlying contradictions of the EU-India relationship. The preceding analysis traces the discursive descent of the positions, perspectives, and perceptions animating the outlook of both Brussels and New Delhi and teases out the misconceptions that affect their policy choices.

At the same time, this chapter demonstrates, despite claims that the interactions between the EU and India form "the most 'natural' relationship,"[86] that it is increasingly obvious that there is little beyond commercial interests (at least for the time being) that brings the two *strategic* partners together. As one columnist put it: "To the extent that India is able to perceive an independent EU policy particularly involving India's critical security considerations, India would look to the EU for enhanced levels of cooperation in different fields".[87] Thus, while the EU asserts the global relevance of its normative power, India's forward foreign policy is framed by the emphasis on hard power capabilities. It is expected that such ideational discrepancy would continue to hinder the interactions between Brussels and New Delhi. As one observer noted, "despite shared values, the lack of shared interests on a number of issues will continue to limit cooperation".[88]

The Eurozone debt crisis did not seem to bode well for the development of a "truly strategic partnership"[89] between the EU and India either. In fact, the former Indian Finance Secretary, Ashok Chawla, suggested that the crisis would be good for India as it would attract global capital

85 Jain, R. K., "India, the EU," *op. cit.*, p. 6.

86 Cameron, F. *et al.*, *EU-India Relations*, *op. cit.*, p. 46.

87 "India Is Not Interested in a US Europe," *Asian Times*, 26 June 2006.

88 Jain, R. K., "India's Relations," *op. cit.*, p. 230.

89 European Commission, *EU-India Strategic Partnership*, *op. cit.*, p. 11.

looking for a "relatively safer haven".[90] Such statements reaffirm the "frenemy" pattern dominating the interactions between Brussels and New Delhi. In this respect, while the external agency of both the EU and India is framed by idiosyncratic constructions of proximity, the prospective pattern of relations between them seems to be dependent upon the discursive articulations of geographic and normative contiguity. It is hoped that the careful reading of EU-India interactions offered in this chapter will remind commentators that we do not know what differences can do; however, heeding the observation in the epigraph, the prospective patterns of interactions between the EU and India hinge on their "energy, perseverance," and, ultimately, mutual willingness to overcome "difficulties".

[90] "India Immune to Eurozone Debt Crisis," *The Hindu*, 10 May 2011.

The EU in the Asia-Pacific Region

Strategic Approach or Self-marginalization?

Gudrun WACKER

Asia Division, German Institute for International and Security Affairs (Stiftung Wissenschaft und Politik) Berlin

Introduction

Historically, Europe and Asia were connected through trade routes, and especially the Silk Road which brought goods from China through Central Asia to Europe. Relations between Europe and Asia became more intense as European powers began exploring the seas, establishing colonies, including in Asia. Despite this colonial past, Europe has not played a central role in the region since the end of the Second World War. Economic relations and interests have been dominating European goals in Asia (and vice versa).

The EU and its member states are interested in peace and stability, primarily because of their economic and trade links with East Asia, and in the last decade or so also because of their concern with challenges to global governance, namely the proliferation of weapons of mass destruction, international terrorism and climate change. With respect to "traditional" security in the region, however, the United States continues to be the most important external actor in the Asia Pacific. In terms of hard security, European powers and the European Union (EU) have been "free-riders" of the American security architecture in East Asia.[1] Thus, Europe's role in the region is limited.

---

1 In this chapter, "East Asia" is used for Northeast and Southeast Asia, basically the ten ASEAN member states plus China, Korea and Japan (Asean plus three). The Association of Southeast Asian Nations (ASEAN) was founded in 1967 by Thailand, Indonesia, Malaysia, Singapore and the Philippines. Brunei joined in the 1980s, Vietnam, Laos, Vietnam, Myanmar/Birma and Cambodia in the 1990s. See official website of the Asean Secretariat, http://www.aseansec.org/64.htm, accessed 20 August 2009.

The chapter will address the following questions: what characterizes the EU's interests in the Asia Pacific? What are Europe's ambitions and how does it pursue its goals? What internal and external factors limit a more proactive European role? How are Europe and the EU perceived in various East Asian countries? Finally, some options are discussed: how could the EU make its Asia policy more effective?

Most of the academic literature on European policy *vis-à-vis* Asia[2] comes to the conclusion that Europe has been mostly focused on trade relations and investment, that it has been punching below its weight and that it has been slow in realising the on-going global power shift. Therefore, it is argued that the EU has to become more proactive, more coherent and more strategic in its approach. However, considering the institutional

---

2 Most academic publications deal with EU-China relations and the Asia-Europe Meeting (ASEM). Moreover, there are quite a few works on China and transatlantic relations, many edited by David Shambaugh. See also Gill, B. and Murphy, M., *China-Europe Relations: Implications and Policy Response for the United States*, CSIS, May 2008; Gill, B. and Wacker, G. (eds.), *China's Rise: Diverging U.S.-EU Perceptions and Approaches*, Berlin, SWP August 2005, 66 pp., http://www.tfpd.org/publications.html, accessed July 5, 2009; Shambaugh, D. and Wacker, G. (eds.), *American and European Relations with China. Advancing Common Agendas*, SWP Research Paper 2008/RP 03, June 2008, 144 pp., http://www.swp-berlin.org/en/common/get_document.php?asset_id=5028, accessed 21 August 2009. Less research has been done on other bilateral relations like EU-Japan or EU-India. On the EU and Asia, see, for example, Gilson, J., "New Interregionalism? The EU and East Asia," in *European Integration*, Vol. 27, No. 3, September 2005, pp. 307-326; Aho, E. *et al.*, *Dragons, Elephants and Tigers: Adjusting to the New Global Reality*, Brussels, European Policy Centre, Sept. 2006 (Challenge Europe Issue 15), http://www.epc.eu/PDF/challenge2006.pdf, accessed 21 August, 2009; Wacker, G., "Europe in Asia: In search of a strategic approach," in N. S. Sisodia, and V. Krishnappa (eds.), *Global Power Shifts and Strategic Transition in Asia*, New Delhi, Academic Foundation, 2009, pp. 135-149; Murray, P., Berryman, A., and Matera, M., *Coherence, Effectiveness and Recognition in EU-East Asia Relations*, July 2008, Research Paper, The University of Melbourne and CERC; Gilson, J., "New Interregionalism? The EU and East Asia," *European Integration*, Vol. 27, No. 3, September 2005, pp. 307-326. On ASEM, see Dent, C., "The Asia-Europe Meeting (ASEM) process. Beyond the triadic political economy?," in H. Hänggi, R. Roloff and J. Rüland (eds.), *Interregionalism and International Relations*, London and New York, Routledge, 2005, pp. 113-127. On EU-Japan, see Soerensen C., "The EU's Approach toward Relations with Tokyo and Beijing," *China Brief*, Vol. 7, No. 9, 2 May 2007; Nabers, D., "Ohne Probleme, ohne Substanz? Die 'strategische Partnerschaft' zwischen der EU und Japan," in A. Bendiek and H. Kramer (eds.), *Globale Außenpolitik der Europäischen Union. Interregionale Beziehungen und 'strategische Partnerschaften'*, Baden-Baden, Nomos and SWP, 2009, pp. 128-149. On the EU and India, see Jaffrelot, C., *Indien und die EU: Die Scharade einer strategischen Partnerschaft*, *GIGA Focus*, Vol. 5, May 2006, 8 pp., http://www.giga-hamburg.de/dl/download.php?d=/content/publikationen/pdf/gf_asien_0605.pdf, accessed 21 August, 2009; Wagner, C., "Die Beziehungen zwischen Indien und der Europäischen Union," in A. Bendiek and H. Kramer (eds.), *Globale Außenpolitik der Europäischen* Union, *op. cit.*, pp. 115-127.

framework of the EU and the limitations of the European Common Foreign and Security Policy (CFSP), the question is how to achieve such goals and how to avoid the marginalization of Europe in the longer run.

Europe's Interests and Declared Goals *vis-à-vis* the Asia Pacific Region

Although first formal contacts between the European Community (EC) and East Asia were established in the 1970s and economic and trade relations intensified over the next decade, the EC/EU really (re)discovered the region in the 1990s when the Cold War was over and all signs pointed in the direction of a coming Pacific century. Before the 1990s, European states generally did not consider countries in Asia as equal political partners – with the exception of Japan, which was not only a highly industrialized country, but also considered as a member of the (political) West.

Broadly speaking, European interests in Asia (including South Asia) before the end of the Cold War were mainly focused on economic and trade relations on the one hand and developmental aid on the other hand. This latter aspect is still an important part of European policy *vis-à-vis* South Asia and economic interests still dominate and shape the agenda of Brussels and the European member states *vis-à-vis* Asia in general. However, the rapid *economic* development in Northeast and Southeast Asia (Japan and the four "tiger states") and later the emergence of China as an economic power house have made these countries relevant and attractive also as *political* partners for the EU. Due to its growing economic strength and political influence, China has taken centre stage for the member states as well as the European institutions (Council Secretariat, Commission and European Parliament): a summit meeting has been held between the EU and China on an annual basis since 1998 and high level visits (level of president, chancellor, prime minister) have become common. Over time, the EU and China have built an extensive web of dialogue mechanisms, among them more than twenty "sectoral dialogues" covering cooperation on a broad range of issues from agriculture over food safety to the information society.[3] In comparison to China, other countries in the region, especially member states of the Association of Southeast Asian Nations (ASEAN), have not been devoted the same degree of attention by Europe. Again, Japan is the exception, since it is a member of the G8, the informal club of the eight most important industrialized countries. Annual summit meetings are held not only with Japan and China, but also with India; summits with Korea are held biannually.

3 An overview over the sectoral dialogues including short descriptions can be found at: http://ec.europa.eu/external_relations/china/sectoraldialogue_en.htm, accessed 20 August 2009.

After the Treaty of Maastricht[4] had laid the foundation for a Common Foreign and Security Policy in 1992, the EU made a first attempt to formulate a comprehensive and balanced framework for Europe's relations with the entire Asian region. The EU published strategy papers (communications) on its relations with individual Asian countries, with the region and sub-regions. These communications were updated from time to time – most often with respect to China, since the partnership became more important, more complex and more difficult, given the fast pace of developments.[5] The documents cannot be taken as presenting the reality of relations. Rather, they represent, in a sense, the "common thinking" in the European Commission about a region or partner country. They also provide an overview of major areas for cooperation, of the direction in which Europe would like the relation to develop as well as problematic or critical points, as identified by the EU and its member states.

The first communication of the Commission on Asia was published in 1994 under the title "Towards a New Asia Strategy".[6] The document was motivated by the realization that the Asian region, and especially East Asia, had become one of the most dynamic regions in the world in terms of economic growth, and that Europe needed stronger relations with the region in order to safeguard its economic interests. The document listed four objectives for the EU to pursue in Asia: strengthen the EU's economic presence; contribute to stability in Asia; promote/assist the development of poor countries and sub-regions; and, lastly to contribute to the development of democracy, rule of law, respect for human rights and fundamental freedoms in Asia.

The Asia strategy paper of the European Union was completely updated in 2001.[7] The new document intended to provide a "comprehensive strategic framework" for European relations with Asia. It offered

4 "The Maastricht Treaty," 7 February 1992, http://www.eurotreaties.com/maastrichtec.pdf, accessed 3 January 2008.

5 On Japan COM(1995) 73 final, on Korea COM(1993) and COM(1998) 714 final, on China: (long-term relations) COM(1995) 279 final, ("comprehensive partnership") COM(1998) 181 final, (implementation of 1998) COM(2000) 552 final and COM(2001) 265, ("maturing partnership") COM(2003) 533 final, ("growing responsibility") COM(2006) 631 final; on Asia: ("new Asia strategy") COM(1994) 314 and ("enhanced partnership") COM(2001) 469 final; on Southeast Asia ("new partnership") COM(2003) 399/4.

6 COM(1994) 314, Brussels, 13 July 1994, http://eur-lex.europa.eu/LexUriServ/LexUriServ.do?uri=COM:1994:0314:FIN:EN:PDF, accessed 9 April 2010.

7 Commission of the European Communities, "Europe and Asia: A Strategic Framework for Enhanced Partnerships, Communication from the Commission," COM(2001) 469 final, Brussels, 4 September 2001, http://ec.europa.eu/development/icenter/repository/strategy_asia_2001_en.pdf, accessed 9 April 2010.

insights into the changes in the European perception of, and its approach to Asia at the beginning of the new century.

Four key sub-regions were identified in this strategy paper: North-East Asia, South-East Asia, South Asia, and Australasia. Australasia was included for the first time because of its ongoing close economic integration with the Asian region.[8]

The communication states that European presence is lagging in Asia in comparison to other regions in the world: "The degree of mutual awareness between the two regions remains insufficient" (p. 3). Consequently, the core objective for the EU's policy in Asia is defined as "[...] strengthening the EU's political and economic presence across the region, and raising this to a level commensurate with the growing global weight of an enlarged EU" (p. 3). Asia is described in this paper as "a crucial economic and political partner for Europe" (p. 4).

Six objectives are listed which the EU should try to achieve with respect to Asia in general (p. 15):

- Contribute to peace and security in the region and globally, through a broadening of our engagement with the region;
- Further strengthen our mutual trade and investment flows with the region;
- Promote the development of the less prosperous countries of the region, addressing the root causes of poverty;
- Contribute to the protection of human rights and to the spreading of democracy, good governance and the rule of law;
- Build global partnerships and alliances with Asian countries, in appropriate international fora, to help address both the challenges and the opportunities offered by globalisation and to strengthen our joint efforts on global environmental and security issues; and
- Help strengthen the awareness of Europe in Asia (and vice versa).

With the second last point the EU demonstrates the acknowledgement of the increased international importance and international weight of Asia.

Another important document for European relations with Asia was the first *European Security Strategy*, published in 2003 by the High

8 However, the five republics in Central Asia are from a European perspective considered as part of the post-Soviet space, and were therefore not addressed in this document. A new Central Asian strategy paper (Communication) by the EU was published under the German EU presidency in the first half of 2007. Cf. Council of the European Union: "The EU and Central Asia: Strategy for a New Partnership," 31 May 2007, http://register.consilium.europa.eu/pdf/en/07/st10/st10113.en07.pdf, accessed 3 January 2008.

Representative of the European Common Foreign and Security Policy, Javier Solana.[9] In this document, three Asian countries were singled out with which the EU planned to develop a "strategic partnership", namely Japan, China and India. While Japan and India, with their democratic systems have been considered "natural" partners of the EU, China has become the most important (albeit also most difficult) economic partner of the EU in the region and is perceived more and more as a challenge in terms of the global order.

Economic and Trade Relations

Economic interaction with Asian countries has been dominating European interests, and of course, economic and trade relations are also the field in which the Commission has a mandate to negotiate on behalf of the member states, i.e. in which the member states have given up sovereignty or "pooled" it on the supra-national level. The negotiations on China's accession to the World Trade Organization (WTO) were a good example of this authority.[10] The EU initiated a Free Trade Agreement with Korea which was finalised in late 2009 and entered into force in 2011.[11] Negotiations with ASEAN were also started in 2007 but did not go very far. Therefore, the EU has negotiated with two individual ASEAN states, namely Singapore and Vietnam. Singapore and the EU initialled the text of a comprehensive free trade agreement on 20 September 2013 and negotiations with Vietnam are ongoing.[12] Talks between the EU and India are also underway.

How have trade relations developed over the last two decades and where did they stand in 2008?

---

9 "A Secure Europe in a Better World. European Security Strategy," December 2003, http://www.consilium.europa.eu/uedocs/cmsUpload/78367.pdf, accessed 9 April 2010.

10 The WTO negotiations can also be seen as one of the reasons why China has taken the EU more seriously than other Asian countries – as GATT founding members, Japan, Korea nor indeed India had to go through such a process with the EC/EU.

11 For the entire text see the website "EU-Korea Free Trade Agreement online," http://trade.ec.europa.eu/doclib/press/index.cfm?id=443&serie=273&langId=en, accessed 9 April 2010; see also European Commission, Trade, Countries and Regions, South Korea, http://ec.europa.eu/trade/policy/countries-and-regions/countries/south-korea/, accessed 18 July 2014.

12 European Commission, Trade, Countries and Regions, Singapore, http://ec.europa.eu/trade/policy/countries-and-regions/countries/singapore/, accessed 18 July 2014.

Graph 1: *Development of trade EU27 with ASEAN plus 6*

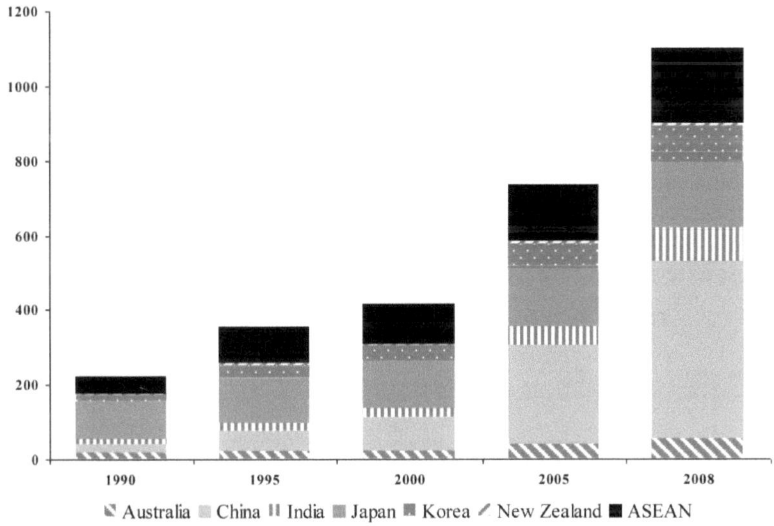

Source: IMF, Direction of Trade Statistics, April 2010, reporting countries EU27.

Graph 1 shows the more than five-fold increase in trade between the EU and ASEAN-plus-6 (China, Japan, Korea and India, Australia, New Zealand). It is also clear how dynamically trade relations with China have developed, especially since the year 2000.

Graph 2: *Relative shares of ASEAN plus 6 in trade with EU-27*

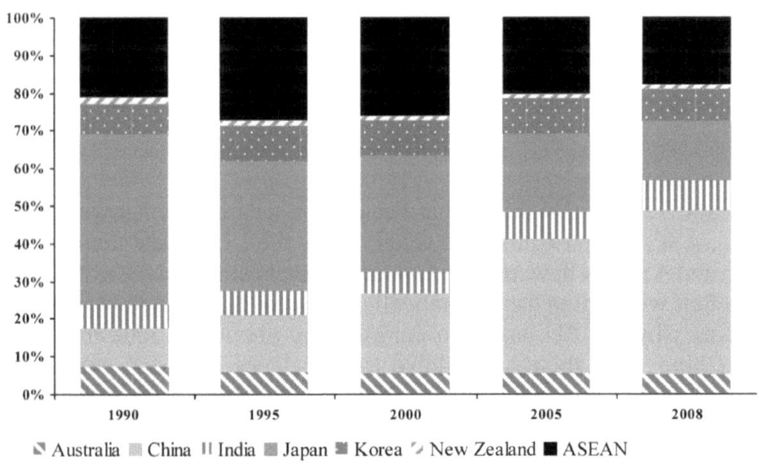

Source: IMF, Direction of Trade Statistics, April 2010, reporting countries EU-27; goods only.

Graph 2 shows the changes in trade flows that have taken place since 1990. While the share of trade with China has been rising steadily (accompanied by a growing trade deficit on the side of the EU), the percentage share of most other countries, especially Japan's, has shrunk. This reflects the changes in production chains within Asia: China has developed into the "workbench" of the world, absorbing raw materials and semi-finished products from the region. The goods are then assembled and finished in China and from there exported to the US and EU markets. Due to European enlargement and the rise of the euro, the EU in 2004 became the biggest trading partner of China, while China has become the second largest external trading partner of the EU.

Graph 3: *Trade balance of EU27 with ASEAN Plus Six*

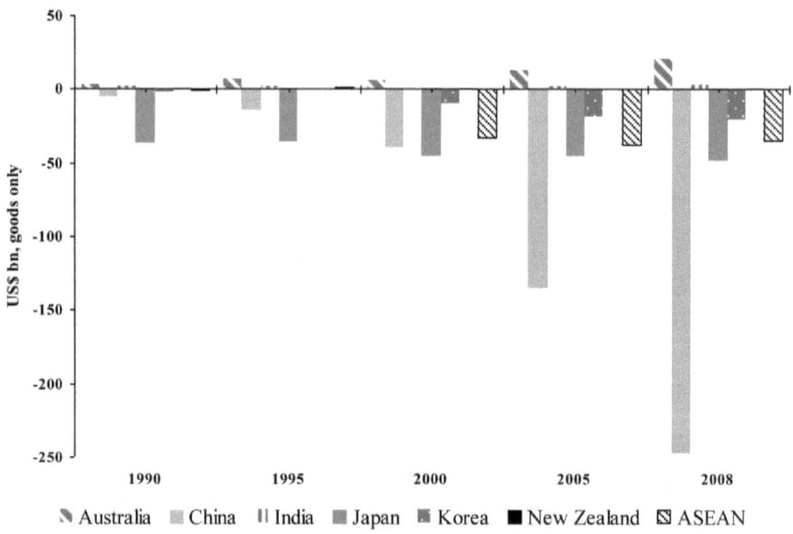

Source: IMF, Direction of Trade Statistics, April 2010, reporting countries EU27.

Graph 3 shows that the EU has been running a trade deficit with Japan, Korea, ASEAN and China. However, while the EU's trade deficits with Japan and ASEAN have remained comparatively stable in the last decade, the deficit with China has dramatically grown over the same period. This explains why the EU has been complaining about the trade imbalance with China, even though its global trade balance has been positive (in contrast to the US which has not only been running a trade deficit with China, but also a global deficit).

European direct investment in Asia has traditionally been strongest in ASEAN, Japan and Australia, and has been increasing continually with ASEAN (at least until the global economic and financial crisis). Investment in China and – from a lower base and at a slower pace – India have also been growing dynamically over the last years. It is noteworthy that direct investment by the EU in Korea, China and India has been higher than US investment in these countries.

In the opposite direction, Japan has played the dominating role as an investor in Europe, but investment flows from ASEAN and Australia have also been substantial. China and India have not yet become big investors in Europe. However, more activity can be expected in the future, especially if China continues on its growth path and tries to find productive ways to make use of its foreign reserves. Even though Chinese investment in European countries has been quite modest so far, the increased activity has already prompted some concerns and a discussion on the desirability of a stronger presence of Chinese companies, especially state-owned enterprises, has been under way in some EU member states.[13]

Political Relations and Security Engagement

Contacts and meetings between the member states of the EU and countries in East and Southeast Asia have not only been taking place on the national level between governments, but there have also been meetings between EC/EU and individual countries in Asia as well as between EC/EU and ASEAN.[14] In addition to this, there is the Asia-Europe Meeting (ASEM) process which now brings together 51 members.[15]

ASEM was not initiated by Europe, but can be traced back to an idea first floated by Singapore.[16] Its first summit was held in 1996 in Bangkok with fifteen European member states as well as ten East Asian states (ASEAN 7 plus Korea, Japan and China) attending this meeting. Through the participation of the three economic "heavyweights" Japan, China and Korea, the Asian component in this inter-regional dialogue mechanism was considerably strengthened.[17] ASEM was designed as a non-institutionalized dialogue framework based on three pillars, i.e. an economic, a political and

---

13 Okano Heimans, M. and van der Putten, F., "Europe needs to screen Chinese investment," *Financial Times*, 11 August, 2009.

14 A first summit was held between the EU and ASEAN in November 2007 in Singapore.

15 For a list of members see ASEMinfoboard, http://www.aseminfoboard.org/members.html, accessed 18 July 2014.

16 See, for example, Dent, C. M., "The Asia-Europe Meeting and Inter-Regionalism: Toward a Theory of Multilateral Utility," *Asian Survey*, Vol. 44, No. 2, March/April 2004, pp. 213-236 [215].

17 See also, Gilson, J., "New Interregionalism? The EU and East Asia," *European Integration*, Vol. 27, No. 3, September 2005, pp. 307-326 [313].

a socio-cultural pillar. Common challenges faced by European and Asian countries were included in the political agenda of ASEM: international terrorism, trans-national migration, environmental challenges and the impact of globalization (positive opportunities and negative effects).[18]

During the 1990s, Europe began to fear the economic competition coming from the dynamic region of Asia. In light of its own low economic growth rates and generally low birth rates, Europe was concerned that it would be marginalized as the most irrelevant part in the new global "economic triangle". The anticipation of a "Pacific Century" at that time was clearly focused on the other two poles, namely East Asia and North America: in the US-East Asia EU economic triad which started to develop after the end of the Cold War, the EU-East Asia link was clearly the weakest. Thus, in response to the launching of the Asia Pacific Economic Cooperation (APEC) forum in the early 1990s, Europe pursued its own dialogue process with Asian countries. For the Asian states participating in ASEM, this inter-regional dialogue presented an opportunity to diversify their external relations and to counter-balance Great Power influence in the region, especially that of the United States.[19] Moreover, ASEM "confirmed" East Asia as one of the three poles in the global "economic triad", thereby boosting its newly found self-confidence. From the European perspective, ASEM was intended to serve three purposes: the promotion of liberal internationalism, building of the EU's identity as a global actor and the promotion of the EU's power and competitiveness.[20] The second ASEM summit in London in 1998 was over-shadowed by the Asian financial crisis. The crisis came as a heavy blow to Asian states' self-confidence and optimism, and it rebutted or at least dampened expectations of a Pacific 21st century. From a European perspective, the crisis demonstrated growing global interdependencies, thereby showing that, under conditions of globalization, European countries could be negatively affected by instability in other parts of the world. Globalization and increased interaction with East Asia raised Europe's stakes in peace and stability in the Asia-Pacific region. ASEM has remained a forum for improving mutual understanding, but has been less successful in producing concrete results.

The EU would also like to get observer status at the East Asian Summit. This forum held its first meeting in December 2005, bringing

---

18 Casarini, N., "The Making of the EU's Strategy Towards Asia," in N. Casarini and C. Musu (eds.), *European Foreign Policy in an Evolving International System. The Road towards Convergence*, New York, Palgrave, 2007, pp. 209-225 [212].

19 See also, Dent, C., "The Asia-Europe Meeting (ASEM) process," *op. cit.*, p. 121.

20 See, Istenič, S., "The EU's Endeavors to Achieve a Discernible Political and Security Role in Asia in the Framework of ASEM: The Taiwan Issue," *Issues & Studies*, Vol. 43, No. 3, September 2007, pp. 53-96.

together the ten ASEAN states and China, Japan, Korea as well as India, Australia and New Zealand. As a precondition to become an observer, the EU had to accede to the Treaty of Amity and Cooperation (TAC).[21]

The EU or its member states do not have a significant military presence in the Asia Pacific. They are not involved in military alliances with any of the countries in the region, nor do they maintain permanent military bases. The United Kingdom is still a member of the Five Power Defence Arrangements,[22] and the bigger European member states have military relations and sometimes conduct joint military manoeuvres with countries in the region, for example with China. The EU has also been involved early on in the Asean Regional Forum, which was initiated in 1993 and established in 1994 as a forum to address security issues.

In a few cases, the EU became directly involved in security issues, usually under a UN mandate: Europeans participated in the UN mission in Cambodia in the early 1990s, as well as in KEDO, the Korean Peninsula Energy Development Organization which was established in 1995 to help implement the Agreed Framework's provisions (mainly by supplying heavy oil to North Korea).[23] The EU joined KEDO in 1997 and became a member of its executive board, but its main contribution was financial. It also sent a mission to Aceh. The Aceh Monitoring Mission (AMM) was conducted from September 2005 to December 2006 in cooperation with some ASEAN states.[24] It had three tasks: the decommissioning of weapons, monitoring the demilitarization of the Indonesian security forces and facilitation of the re-integration of ex-combatants into the Acehnese society.

---

21 ASEAN, Text of the Treaty of Amity and Cooperation in Southeast Asia and Related Information, March 2005, http://www.aseansec.org/TAC-KnowledgeKit.pdf, accessed 28 August 2009. The accession to TAC is a good example of the lack of coordination between EU member states. Since EU efforts proceeded very slowly, France and the UK planned to accede individually and France actually signed in 2007. The EU finally acceded in July 2009, the same day the US signed. While it took the US only six months between the announcement of US Secretary of State Hilary Clinton that the US would look into this matter to signing the TAC, it took the EU at least three years.

22 FPDA were established in 1971 and include the UK, Singapore, Malaysia, Australia and New Zealand. See Thayer, C., "The Five Powers Defence Arrangements: The Quiet Achiever," Paper presented at the 1st Berlin Conference on Asian Security (BCAS), September 2006, http://www.swp-berlin.org/common/get_document.php?asset_id=3563.

23 The Agreed Framework was signed in 1994 in Geneva for freezing and ultimately dismantling North Korea's nuclear programme.

24 For details, see Quigley, J., "Enhancing South-East Asia's Security: The Aceh Monitoring Mission," in S. Bersick, W. Stokhof and P. van der Velde (eds.), *Multiregionalism and Multilateralism. Asian-European Relations in a Global Context*, Amsterdam, Amsterdam University Press, 2006, pp. 61-81.

With respect to the regional "hot spots", namely Taiwan/cross-strait relations and the (revived) nuclear programme of North Korea, the European role has been very limited – the EU has not been directly involved in either issue and so has had to play the part of a bystander in unfolding developments.

The US has been legally obligated to help Taiwan defend itself under the provisions of the Taiwan Relations Act.[25] This Act was passed by Congress in 1979 after the US had switched recognition from the Republic of China to the People's Republic. No such commitment exists on the side of the EU or any of its member states. The EU's overriding interest concerning the situation in the Taiwan straits is the preservation of peace and stability, which in practical terms means supporting the status quo.[26] After Chen Shui-bian was elected president in Taiwan in 2000, the EU gradually became more outspoken on cross-strait relations – not, as one might have expected, in defending Taiwan's position *vis-à-vis* the PRC, but rather in appealing to both sides to refrain from activities challenging the status quo in cross-strait relations. Thus, the European Council's presidency made several public statements on behalf of the EU expressing concern about steps taken by Chen Shui-bian's government which could be interpreted as provocative by Beijing. Especially in the second term of Chen Shui-bian's presidency, Beijing managed quite successfully to "enlist" the Europeans (and Washington, for that matter) to support China's understanding of the status quo. On the other hand, the EU also reacted when the Chinese National People's Congress passed the so-called anti-secession law in spring 2005, which threatens Taiwan with the use of non-peaceful means, should all hopes for peaceful unification be lost.[27]

Since Europeans tend to believe that (economic) interdependence between countries lowers the risk of conflict escalation, it is only natural that they should welcome all developments that point to deeper interdependence between China and Taiwan. This also explains the positive reactions from the EU side when Ma Ying-jeou was elected president in Taiwan in March 2008. President Ma stood for a less confrontational approach and for a

---

25 "Taiwan Relations Act," United States Code Title 22 Chapter 48 Sections 3301-3316, enacted 10 April 1979, http://www.taiwandocuments.org/tra01.htm, accessed 25 August 2009.

26 Of course, the status quo is not stagnant, but continually in flux. "Status quo" therefore means that no side openly challenges the present state of de facto, but not de jure independence of Taiwan.

27 "Anti-Secession Law," adopted at the Third Session of the Tenth National People's Congress on 14 March 2005; full text at http://english.peopledaily.com.cn/200503/14/eng20050314_176746.html, accessed 28 August 2009. The passing of this law also provided the EU with a welcome excuse to refrain from lifting the arms embargo against China.

willingness to deepen cooperation with mainland China by opening direct communication and transport links and other measures. Since Ma took office in May 2008, developments between China and Taiwan have taken a course which has been welcomed by the EU, i.e., more dialogue and more practical cooperation. The EU also issued a statement applauding the decision of China's political leadership to allow Taiwan to be invited as an observer to the World Health Assembly in 2009.[28]

With respect to the North Korean nuclear problem, the EU was not invited to participate in the Six-Party Talks (6PT),[29] nor did it openly express a wish to join these negotiations. In light of the diversity of interests among the six parties to the discussions, the position of the EU as a bystander prepared to provide humanitarian aid to the people in North Korea seems prudent. It is doubtful whether the EU or the member states could have contributed anything substantial to the talks themselves.

Again, the EU generally favours a solution through negotiations and would be ready to provide material and technical assistance if such a solution is found. But it is certainly not prepared for any role in case of a military escalation.

Within the context of a more comprehensive security concept, the EU has made contributions to peace and stability in East Asia by supporting post-conflict reconstruction, nation-building, institution-building, security sector reform, and police training. These are the fields for which the EU and its members have provided assistance and funding. However, this approach has not been recognized as a welcome addition to the "classical" US approach to security in the region.

Despite all the dialogue forums and meetings between Europe and Asia, the profile of the EU and its member states in the region, and especially in Northeast Asia, is not very prominent.

Constraints to Europe's Role in East Asia: Gaps and Dilemmas

In order to understand the limitations in Europe's engagement beyond economic activities in East Asia and in Asia more generally, it is necessary to take a look at the institutional framework of the EU and what it means

28 Council of the European Union, "Declaration by the Presidency on behalf of the European Union on the occasion of the participation of Taiwan as an observer in the 62nd session of the World Health Assembly," 8 May 2009, 9486/09 (Presse 123), http://www.consilium.europa.eu/uedocs/cms_data/docs/pressdata/en/cfsp/107600.pdf, accessed 11 May 2009.

29 The 6PT were started in 2003 to address the nuclear issue; its members are South and North Korea, the United States, China, Japan and Russia.

for those competencies that have been transferred to Brussels. While the European Community had become accepted as an *economic* power by the end of the 1980s, the progress of European integration (Maastricht Treaty, CFSP, etc.) and its enlargement (made possible by the transformation of Eastern Europe and the end of Cold War) gave rise to expectations within and without Europe that the Community would develop into a relevant *political* actor on the international stage.

There are internal and external factors which limit the role of the EU and the member states in Asia. The internal factors stem from disagreements as to what sort of international actor the Union should be and what authority it should have. With the enlargement rounds in 2004, 2007 and 2013,[30] which increased membership from 15 to 28, the EU has not only become bigger in terms of population and territory; it has also become more diverse. The range of national interests, preferences, priorities and approaches has become broader and the different positions more complicated to reconcile. In the absence of profound institutional reform – the Constitutional Treaty failed to find favour with a majority of voters in two of the founding members of the EC (France and the Netherlands) – reaching agreement or a common position became difficult. The external factors stem from the actor constellation in East Asia, in which the United States plays a central role.

CFSP and ESDP: Work in Progress – Lack of Coherence

The Common Foreign and Security Policy of the EU was introduced as recently as 1998, so it looks back to hardly more than sixteen years of experience. While the EC/EU has been prominent in the daily lives of the people in Europe in many ways since sovereignty has been transferred by the member states to the European institutions, decisions on foreign and security policy still very much fall into the realm of the individual member states. These have different priorities and pursue different interests, often based on their respective geographical position,[31] but also on historical bonds (like a special interest in former colonies by particular countries). One could therefore argue that the EU is not as post-modern as it sometimes likes to pretend. When it comes to the field of foreign and

30 Ten countries joined the EU in 2004, namely the East European countries Czech Republic, Poland, Hungary, Slovakia, Slovenia and the three Baltic States (Estonia, Lithuania, Latvia), as well as the two Mediterranean islands Malta and Cyprus. This brought the total number of member states to 25. In 2007, two more countries, Bulgaria and Romania, joined. Croatia acceded in 2013, leaving Turkey as the only officially recognized candidate country. Five more countries have expressed their wish to join.

31 A good example for such geographically based interests was the initiative launched by France for a Mediterranean Union ("Club Med"), which was understandably not greeted with the same enthusiasm by all member states.

security policy, member states have been very reluctant to transfer sovereignty to the supra-national level.

Despite the fact that a broad majority of the public in EU member states have expressed strong support for CSFP and even the European Security and Defence Policy (ESDP),[32] the member states tend to pursue their own national interests and their own foreign policy, mostly on a bilateral basis, with countries outside the EU. There was a reluctance and even resistance to allow Javier Solana, High Representative for the Common Foreign and Security Policy and Secretary-General of the Council of the European Union, to speak on behalf of the EU. A sign of this was the resistance to having a European foreign minister, or rather, to calling the position "Foreign Minister".[33] With the Treaty of Lisbon[34] having entered into force on 1 December 2009 after a difficult ratification process, a foreign service ("European External Action Service") is being built up, but this by no means renders the national diplomatic missions redundant or obsolete.

All member states still pursue their own external relations, based on their perceived national interest, often without consulting the others. This would have changed, albeit not fundamentally, had the Constitutional Treaty been ratified. But as it is, even with the Treaty of Lisbon in force, this will not transform the EU into a single and unified (state-like) actor. If we look back at the last couple of years, we find ample proof for the lack of a unified European voice: the US invasion of Iraq (2003) showed a deep rift within the EU, a rift that was identified (perhaps too glibly) as dividing "old" and "new" Europe.[35] Such differences in the position of member states cannot only be seen with respect the United States, but also with respect to other important partners like Russia and China.

A study on European China policy conducted in 2008 by the European Council on Foreign Relations came to the conclusion that within the

32 See Eurobarometer, "Support for Common Foreign and Security Policy (CFSP) is reinforced," May 2003, http://ec.europa.eu/public_opinion/archives/notes/csf_pesc_papr03_en.pdf, accessed 25 August 2009. The only EU member state in which less than 50% of the interviewees expressed support for CFSP in this survey was the UK.

33 The position of a European foreign minister was part of the Constitutional Treaty, but in the Treaty of Lisbon, the position is called "High Representative of the Union for Foreign Affairs and Security Policy".

34 "Treaty of Lisbon amending the Treaty on European Union and the Treaty establishing the European Community, signed at Lisbon, 13 December 2007," 2007/C 306/01, *Official Journal of the European Union*, 50, 17 December 2007, http://eur-lex.europa.eu/JOHtml.do?uri=OJ:C:2007:306:SOM:EN:HTML, accessed 24 August 2009.

35 Actually, the UK can hardly be seen as "new" Europe. Moreover, the rift was mainly between the governments in Europe. The majority of the people all over Europe had a critical stance *vis-à-vis* the Iraq war.

European Union, four distinct approaches *vis-à-vis* China can be identified. Based on these differences, member states can be roughly divided in the following categories: "assertive industrialists" (Poland, Czech Republic and Germany under Chancellor Angela Merkel), "ideological free-traders" (Netherlands, Sweden, Denmark and UK), "accommodating mercantilists" (Slovenia, Finland, Bulgaria, Malta, Hungary, Portugal, Slovakia, Italy, Greece, Cyprus, Romania, Spain) and "European followers" (Belgium, Ireland, Austria, Luxemburg and the three Baltic States). Only France under President Sarkozy did not clearly fit into any of the four categories.[36] These differences between member states help to explain why a truly strategic and unified approach in European China policy will be hard to bring about. Even in the field of economic relations with China, EU member states have been competing with each other. And China has become quite adept at playing the Europeans off against each other.[37]

There might be fewer differences with respect to other Asian countries, simply because the relationship is not seen as important as the one with China. But in general, diverse positions within the EU exist on many issues and efforts to come to more coherent positions have rarely been made.

With respect to foreign policy and international relations, it seems that the member states (at least the bigger ones) want to have their cake and eat it. For example, they are not willing to give up their national seat and voting rights in international organizations in favour of a single seat and voice for the EU.[38] The big member states fear a loss of influence and room to manoeuvre on the national level, although there is a general recognition that Europeans bring more weight to the table if they agree on a common or position.

Concentric Circles: Substance versus Symbolic Policy

The EU and its member states have been very much focused on themselves and their immediate neighbourhood. Over the last two decades, most attention has been absorbed by the ongoing processes of integration and

[36] Fox, J. and Godement, F., *A Power Audit of EU-China Relations*, April 2009 (European Council on Foreign Relations), full text at http://ecfr.eu/page/-/documents/A_Power_Audit_of_EU_China_Relations.pdf, accessed 13 August 2009, p. 4.

[37] This can be illustrated by the different meetings of European leaders with the Dalai Lama and China's reaction to it. After French President Nicolas Sarkozy met the Dalai Lama in late 2008, Beijing not only "postponed" the EU-China summit, but Wen Jiabao travelled to Europe in January 2009, basically visiting the countries around France: Switzerland, Germany, Belgium and Spain. After this "tour de France," Paris issued a press statement acknowledging the status of Tibet as a part of China.

[38] See, for example, Germany's wish to have a permanent seat in the Security Council of the United Nations.

enlargement. Some people criticize the EU for its "navel gazing".[39] EU external relations – with perhaps the sole exception of the transatlantic partnership – seem to be structured in concentric circles around the EU as a centre: the greater the geographic distance, the more declaratory and symbolic the policy. This applies not only apply to East Asia, but also to other regions: for almost every part of the world, the EU has formulated lofty goals, but failed to set clear priorities or to define a roadmap for how to achieve them. Also lacking are any mechanisms to monitor in an effective way what has been achieved. Under these circumstances, it is hardly surprising that there has been no definition of what qualifies as the EU's strategic partnerships. Currently, the EU claims to maintain or to be in the process of building strategic partnerships with Japan, China, India and Korea.[40]

This focus on itself and its geographic neighbourhood constitutes a limiting factor to a stronger and more pro-active European role in other regions like Asia or Latin America. Even in the three big member states, Germany, France and the UK (the "EU-3"), the capacities and capabilities devoted to East Asia are limited.

However, the EU has a strong interest in global issues such as the international financial order, energy security, climate change and the proliferation of weapons of mass destruction (WMD). For addressing all these issues, cooperation, especially with the emerging Asian powers, is absolutely indispensable. Geographical distance is not relevant in this respect. Thus, a "strategic" dimension is introduced into the relations between the EU and (East) Asia from this global perspective.

External Constraints: A Dilemma for the EU

As mentioned in the introduction, the United States is the single most important external actor in Asia Pacific and the main provider of security. This role is mainly based on the "hub-and-spokes" security architecture centred around the US and consisting of five bilateral alliances with Japan, Korea, Australia, the Philippines and Thailand. In addition to these, the US also has military and security agreements with other countries in the region and substantial military bases, as in Guam.

---

39 See, for example: Okano-Heimans, M. and van der Putten, F., "Clinton opts for Asia, Europe for its navel," *European Voice*, 20 February 2009, http://www.clingendael.nl/cscp/publications/?id=7388, accessed 24 August 2009.

40 For a critical look at the EU's regional policies and strategic partnerships, see Bendiek, A. and Kramer, H., *Die EU als globaler Akteur. Unklare "Strategien," diffuses Leitbild*, Berlin, April 2009 (= SWP-Studie S 12), http://www.swp-berlin.org/common/get_document.php?asset_id=5898, accessed 24 August 2009; on CFSP, see Katsioulis, Ch., *European Foreign Policy on Trial: Global Actor in the Making?*, International Policy Analysis, Friedrich-Ebert-Stiftung, March 2009, http://library.fes.de/pdf-files/id/ipa/06157.pdf, accessed 14 August 2009.

The US is mainly focused on this alliance system in the Asia-Pacific region. Traditionally, Washington has not displayed particular interest in the activities of the EU in East Asia since the EU was not seen as a relevant political actor in the region. Conversely, the Europeans perceived the US mainly as an Atlantic power and neglected the fact that it is also (if not more so after the end of the Cold War) a relevant actor in the Pacific. At a minimum, the US expected from its European NATO (North Atlantic Treaty Organization) allies that they would not do anything in the Asia Pacific that goes against US strategic interests or jeopardizes US security or the security of her "allies and friends".

As long as the EU more or less follows the US lead in the region, it is largely irrelevant from Washington's perspective. The first time the US really took notice of European activities in East Asia was when in 2003 several EU member states, most prominently Germany and France, started to lobby for lifting the European arms embargo against China.[41] This move was widely seen in US political circles, and especially in the US Congress, as opportunistic, greedy and irresponsible behaviour of the Europeans who were apparently willing to compromise the safety of the US and their allies' troops for profits from arms sales.

On the "positive" side, the indifference of the United States implies that there are no high expectations as to what can be contributed from Europe. In case of a military escalation of one of the conflicts in East Asia, the United States will certainly turn to its military allies, first and foremost Japan, for support.[42] Europe could be indirectly affected if the US, in such a case, had to withdraw troops from other theatres and ask the EU or NATO partners to take over their tasks, at least temporarily.

It should also be noted that it is far from clear whether all countries in East Asia would welcome a more pronounced EU security profile. Like the United States, China, for its part, wants the EU to take a supportive stance on issues that it considers its "core national interests" (territorial integrity and sovereignty). The same applies to other states in the region. A stronger EU involvement is welcome as long as it is in line with their respective positions. Most Asian countries would welcome Europe in the

41 The European arms embargo against China was instituted in 1989. As a reaction to the events on Tiananmen Square in early June 1989, the member states of the European Community (EC) agreed at a summit meeting in Madrid on a list of sanctions against China. For the full text of the document, see "Declaration of European Council," Madrid, 27 June 1989, http://ec.europa.eu/external_relations/cfsp/sanctions/measures.htm#China, accessed 8 August, 2009. With the exception of the ban on arms sales, all sanctions were abolished during 1990.

42 Berger, B. and Gilmartin, H., "The Quiet Europeans? Appraising Europe's Commitment to East Asian Security," in H. Giessmann (ed.), *Emerging Powers in East Asia: China, Russia and India*, Baden-Baden, Nomos, 2008, pp. 211-239 [231].

region principally as a regional counterweight to the United States, as the origins of the ASEM process show. For such considerations, differences in strategic thinking also play a role. While (neo)realist and balance-of-power thinking is still quite dominant in Asia and the US, Europeans tend to think in liberal or even constructivist terms when it comes to international relations.

This situation poses a dilemma for the EU and its member states. On the one hand, it is only noticed (and consulted) by the United States as an actor in East Asia if it does something that, from Washington's perspective, is assessed as unacceptable and against US interests. On the other hand, it will be hard for the EU to raise its profile in the region if it just follows and supports the United States' positions to the letter.[43] How can the EU be accepted as a credible actor under such conditions? As Berger and Gilmore point out: "European states must find a balance between the reality of US regional influence and the necessity of acting independently for their own interests. Unfortunately, there are differing perspectives within Europe on the degree to which European policies should be coordinated with Washington".[44]

As direct results of the conflict over the Chinese arms embargo, the US and the EU established a regular transatlantic dialogue mechanism on security in East Asia, mainly addressing the rise of China and its implications. Moreover, under British presidency (second half of 2005) an EU document on security in East Asia was drafted, the "Guidelines for the EU's Foreign and Security Policy in East Asia". This document was updated and finally also published two years later. The special position of the US is explicitly acknowledged in this document:

> The US's security commitments to Japan, the Republic of Korea and Taiwan and the associated presence of US forces in the region give the US a distinct perspective on the region's security challenges. It is important that the EU is sensitive to this. Given the great importance of transatlantic relations, the EU has a strong interest in partnership and cooperation with the US on Foreign and Security policy challenges arising from East Asia.[45]

Since most European member states are also members of NATO, it is clear that the EU cannot simply ignore US security concerns, even if these are outside the "classical" NATO space. For this reason alone, the

---

[43] See Ward, A., "The Taiwan Issue and the Role of the European Union," in B. Gill and G. Wacker (eds.), *China's Rise. Diverging U.S.-EU Perceptions and Approaches*, Berlin, SWP, August 2005, http://www.swp-berlin.org/common/get_document.php?asset_id=2402, pp. 43-47 [47].

[44] Berger, B. and Gilmartin, H., "The Quiet Europeans?," *op. cit.*, p. 231.

[45] Council of the European Union, "Guidelines on the EU's Foreign and Security Policy in East Asia," undated, p. 3, http://www.consilium.europa.eu/ueDocs/cms_Data/docs/pressdata/en/misc/97842.pdf, accessed 4 March 2008.

expectation that the EU would develop into a counterweight of the United States on the regional level is therefore bound to be frustrated.

All factors listed above contribute to the limitations of a European role in East Asia.

Europe's Image in the Region

Public opinion polls and surveys have been conducted in recent years to find out how the EU is perceived in Asian countries. While some of these surveys were globally oriented and assessed the relevance and role of the EU within a broader context of global order,[46] there have also been specialized polls on the perception of the EU only.[47] Not all of the reports which are based on surveys funded by the European Commission were published.[48] In general, the results of these public opinion surveys have not been very flattering for Europe, especially in Asia.

In the perception of the public in China, India and Japan, the European Union is not, at present, a world power, and only a minority expects the EU to play a bigger international role in the future:

	World Power now?			**World Power in 2020?**		
	EU	**US**	**China**	**EU**	**US**	**China**
Average*	32	81	45	30	57	55
China	17	84	44	14	42	71
Japan	20	83	31	17	40	40
India	7	65	34	7	51	43
United States	24	81	51	24	66	54
UK	53	89	66	53	78	72
Germany	75	90	68	77	82 (-8)	79

Source: Bertelsmann Stiftung, *World Powers in the 21st Century*, pp. 13f., p. 16. *The survey was conducted in Brazil, China, France, Germany, India, Japan, Russia, the UK and the US from October to December 2005.

46 For example, Bertelsmann Stiftung, *World Powers in the 21st* Century, Berlin, 2 June 2006, http://www.bertelsmann-stiftung.de/bst/en/media/xcms_bst_dms_19189_19190_2.pdf, accessed 25 August 2009; Lucarelli, S., *The External Image of the European Union*, GARNET Working Paper 17/07, http://www.garnet-eu.org/fileadmin/documents/working_papers/1707.pdf, accessed 28 August 2009.

47 Holland, M., Ryan, P., Nowak, A. and Chaban, N. (eds.), *The EU through the Eyes of Asia. Media, Public and Elite Perceptions in China, Japan, Korea, Singapore and Thailand*, Singapore-Warsaw, University of Warsaw, 2007.

48 For example, there was a study on the visibility of the EU in China in 2004 which was not made publicly available.

It is noteworthy that it is not only the EU that is perceived as declining in its international status in the three Asian countries, but also the United States, albeit starting from a much higher level. The perception of the EU in Asia is strikingly different from the assessment in the European countries. Also remarkable is the fact that a bigger percentage of the interviewees in France, Germany and the UK see the EU as a world power rather than their own respective countries.

Another survey which was conducted in China, Hong Kong, Japan, Singapore, South Korea and Thailand among elites from business, politics, civil society and media circles comes to slightly different conclusions with respect to relevance of the EU as a foreign policy partner at present and in the future. In China, the EU now ranks second behind the United States and is even seen as the most important partner in the future. Japan and Singapore also expected the EU to gain importance (from rank 6 to 4 and from 6 to 5, respectively), while Hong Kong, Korea and Thailand did not expect such a change for the future.[49] It is also noteworthy that the "dominant image" associated with the EU is its common currency, the Euro.[50]

Conclusion: Strategic Approach or Marginalization?

The European Union is not the United States, nor will it become a unified actor in this sense for the foreseeable future. This sceptical perception of the EU is actually shared by many people within Europe. Despite the generally positive attitude with respect to the EU, many people in Europe see Brussels and the European institutions as a bureaucratic juggernaut, lacking efficiency, lacking coherence and lacking democratic legitimization.

If the European Union aspires to play a bigger political role in East Asia, it could do worse than to start with the following measures:

Less symbolic policy, more substance: The EU should be more realistic about what it can and cannot deliver and accomplish.

More honesty: The EU should be more explicit about European interests, and not pretend to pursue goals for altruistic reasons.

Improved public diplomacy: The EU should advertise and sell better how it has been supporting domestic transformation processes in Asia and what it has done to advance peace and security in the region.

Less "teaching": The EU should not lecture countries in Asia and instead be more self-critical (or aware of its own weaknesses, its shortcomings, and its history).

---

49 Holland, M., Ryan, P. *et al.*, *The EU Through the Eyes of Asia*, *op. cit.*, p. 239.

50 *Ibid.*, p. 243. However, only a part of the member states belong to the Euro-zone.

More research: Commission and member states should support independent academic expertise on Asia in Europe.

While the above list of recommendations should be possible to implement even under the present institutional and political constraints, other steps would require either additional efforts by the European Commission or some political initiative by all or, at a minimum, by a group of member states.

Such additional efforts would, for example, consist of a more thorough discussion among the member states and with EU institutions on the goals they want to pursue in East Asia. A strategic approach would require a clear idea of which goals have priority and which are less important. A regular and transparent mechanism to assess what progress has really been made should also be introduced. The discussions that have led to the "Security Guidelines" are a good example for a successful initiative, since this document – despite its non-binding character – can now serve as a frame of reference.

With CFSP a work-in-progress, other options also need to be explored. One would be for the EU-3 to work together more closely, agree on a joint position and coordinate their moves in political relations with Asia, especially with respect to China. For example, it should be possible to agree on a "standard procedure" for meeting with the Dalai Lama. This would certainly not prevent China from protesting, but if such a procedure existed it would be less easy to play the Europeans against each other, as has happened frequently in the past. The EU-3 could also try to come up with a plan to end gradually development aid in some Asian countries. It is important, however, that such initiatives are fed back to the member states and the European institutions, so that it will not undermine the EU and its concept of effective multilateralism.

If, however, the member states do not get their act together and constantly fail to live up to the expectations they have created themselves, they should not be surprised if marginalization is the most likely outcome.

The European Community's Policy towards the People's Republic of China

Establishing Diplomatic Relations (December 1973-May 1975)

Marie Julie CHENARD

The London School of Economics and Political Science

Introduction

On 14 December 1973 at the Copenhagen Summit, the foreign ministers of the nine member states of the European Community (EC), pledged in the Declaration of European Identity "to intensify their relations with the Chinese Government".[1] They also affirmed the cohesion of the Community in external relations. Thirteen months after the Copenhagen Summit, Sir Christopher Soames, Vice-President of the European Commission responsible for external relations, accepted the invitation by the Institute for Foreign Relations of the People's Republic of China (PRC) to visit China in an official capacity and in May 1975 he led a delegation to Beijing. At a meeting with the Chinese foreign minister, Chiao Kuan-hua on 6 May, the Chinese government declared its wish for official EC-PRC relations. Soames was quick to oblige. "Speaking for the Community as a whole as well as for the Commission", he stated with confidence that "the question of establishing diplomatic relations could be settled right away without any delay whatsoever".[2] It was this meeting that effectively sealed the establishment of EC-PRC diplomatic relations.[3]

1 Declaration of European Identity, *Bulletin of the European Communities*, No. 12, December 1973, pp. 118-122.

2 Churchill Archives Centre, Cambridge (henceforward CAC), The Papers of Baron Soames (henceforward SOAM) 42/1975/China, Record, Second Meeting between Sir Christopher Soames and the Chinese Foreign Minister, Mr Chiao Kuan-Hua, 6 May 1975.

3 *Ibid.*

This chapter investigates the evolution of the European Community's policy towards the PRC beginning with the publication of the Declaration on European Identity in December 1973 until the establishment of diplomatic relations in May 1975. Focusing on European efforts to "speak with one voice", it examines the development of the EC's response towards the PRC – a country associated with substantial economic potential and extremely delicate political links to the United States and the Soviet Union.

The research takes a multi-archival and multilateral approach and adopts a Community-centred perspective.[4] Hence it investigates how the interests of the nine EC member states (the Nine) and the interests of the EC intergovernmental and supranational actors came together in Strasbourg and Brussels to shape the Community's response to China. Concerning the role of individual member states, it focuses on the foreign policies of France, West Germany and Britain. This chapter will first trace the path of EC institutional decision-making with regard to China, between December 1973 and May 1975. Second, it will consider the perceived risks and benefits for the EC in engaging in official political relations with the PRC. Third, the chapter draws out how these issues played out within the Community institutions after the Copenhagen pledge.

Existing literature on the EC in the 1970s tends to dismiss the role of the European Parliament (EP) and the European Commission in the decision-making process, particularly in the area of external relations.[5] Moreover, the few accounts which consider the EC-PRC connection are concerned mainly with Chinese and Soviet foreign policy and as such, they overwhelmingly stress the external, geo-strategic factors for the EC to normalise relations with the PRC.[6] In contrast, this chapter emphasises

---

4 See Ludlow, N. P., *Dealing with Britain*, Cambridge, Cambridge University Press, 1997; *The European Community and the Crises of the 1960s*, London, Routledge, 2006. This chapter is based on the following archives: Council of Ministers Archives, Brussels (henceforward CMA); European Commission's Historical Archives, Brussels (henceforward ECHA); The National Archives, Kew (henceforward NA); Archives Nationales Contemporaines, Fontainebleau (henceforward ANF); Politisches Archiv des Auswärtigen Amts, Berlin (henceforward PAAA); CAC.

5 See for example Taylor, P. G., *The Limits of European Integration*, London, Croom Helm, 1983; Rosamond, B., *Theories of European Integration*, Hampshire and New York, Palgrave Macmillan, 2000, p. 98; Olivi, B. and Giacone, A., *L'Europe difficile*, Paris, Gallimard, 2001.

6 Kapur, H., *China and the European Economic Community*, Dordrecht, Martinus Nijhoff Publishers, 1986; Ebinger, P., "The Politics of Potential: The Relations of the People's Republic of China and the European Community and its Member-States France and Great Britain, 1969-1979," PhD thesis, Tufts University, 1988; Shambaugh, D., "China and Europe," *Annals of the American Academy of Political and Social Science*, Vol. 519, 1992, pp. 101-114; Chang, J. Y. P., "The History of Diplomatic

the importance of the internal workings of the Community and reconsiders the popular and long-held view of the 1970s as a decade of stagnation.[7] The period from December 1973 to May 1975 formed a significant evolution of the Community's joint decision-making and implementation capability in response to the PRC because the European Parliament urged action, and above all the Commission asserted itself in taking the lead to set up diplomatic relations with China.

China in the Decision-making Corridors of the Community

At the Copenhagen Summit in December 1973 the Nine committed themselves to intensifying their ties with the PRC. Therefore when the Commission established official relations with China in May 1975, it appears at first sight that the Commission merely carried out instructions of the member states. But taking a closer look, the issue proves more complicated.

After the Copenhagen commitment the Council did not press ahead to follow their words with Community action. Neither at the Council nor at the summit meetings did the EC-China relations feature in any meaningful manner. The other intergovernmental institutions, the European Political Cooperation (EPC) and the Permanent Representatives Committee (Coreper), were equally lax. The Nine had created the EPC in 1970 after the Hague Conference, which had marked a relaunch of European integration.[8] The member states had created the EPC for the very purpose of coordinating national foreign policies more closely, and it had provided important input for the Declaration on European Identity.[9] But even on the level of the EPC Asia Working Group, the EC-China connection did not lead to substantial discussion, let alone calls for action. Within Coreper, the crucial committee of ambassadors from the member states to

---

Relations between the Republic of China on Taiwan and the European Community and its Member States," PhD thesis, Cambridge University, 1997; Yahuda, M., "The Sino-European Encounter, Historical Influences on Contemporary Relations," in D. L. Shambaugh, E. Sandschneider and H. Zhou (eds.), *China-Europe Relations*, London, Routledge, 2008.

7 Griffiths, R., "A Dismal Decade? European Integration in the 1970s," in D. Dinan (ed.), *Origins and Evolution of the European Union*, Oxford, Oxford University Press, 2006, pp. 169-190; Ludlow N. P., "From Deadlock to Dynamism: The European Community in the 1980s," in *ibid.*; Gillingham J., *European Integration, 1950-2003: Superstate or New Market Economy?*, Cambridge, Cambridge University Press, 2003.

8 Harst, J. v. der, "The 1969 Hague Summit: a New Start for Europe?," *Journal of European Integration History*, Vol. 9, No. 2, 2003, pp. 5-10.

9 Ifestos, P., *European Political Cooperation: towards a Framework of Supranational Diplomacy?*, Avebury, Aldershot, 1987; Wallace, H., Wallace, W. and Pollack, M. A., *Policy-Making in the European Union*, Oxford, Oxford University Press, 2005, p. 433.

the EC which prepared all Council decisions, the case was similar. This is surprising since Coreper was the very institution which checked the diplomatic ambitions of the Commission.[10]

Strikingly, nor did the Commission assume at first an active political role. It adopted an attitude of "If the Chinese want something from the EC, they need to come to us". This is reflected particularly in Soames' stance.[11] Soames was a Conservative politician involved in the first British application for EC membership (1961-1963), serving until 1972 as ambassador to France and was the first British Commissioner responsible for external relations after Britain's accession to the EC in January 1973.[12] He wrote, for example, to former British Prime Minister Edward Heath in May 1974: "We are not panting for recognition by China. We are perfectly ready for them to work up their relationship with the Commission without going through the business of accrediting an Ambassador [...]".[13]

It is also revealing that the Commission's programme for 1974 did not treat China under the heading of Europe's external personality.[14] Moreover, a proposal by the Directorate General for External Relations on increasing the EC external representation in 1975 deemed representation in Peru and Canada more important than in China.[15]

It was the European Parliament (EP) which persisted in putting the Community's official ties with China on the Council and Commission agenda. Written questions illustrate how the EP repeatedly inquired which steps the Council and the Commission were taking to improve the relationship with the PRC.[16] Notably the Belgian Socialist Ernest Glinne demanded to know on 23 January 1975: "[...], whether the Council has taken any recent steps towards establishing direct bilateral diplomatic relations at a high level between the Community and the People's Republic

10 Ludlow, N. P., "The European Commission and the Rise of Coreper: a Controlled Experiment," in W. Kaiser, B. Leucht and M. Rasmussen (eds.), *The History of the European Union: Origins of a Trans- and Supranational Polity 1950-72*, Abingdon, Routledge, 2009, p. 191.

11 ECHA, BAC 48/1984/687, Schéma de Réponse à la Question Orale 30/72, DGXI B/5 to Soames, 7 February, 1973.

12 Dinan, D., *Europe Recast*, Basingstoke, Palgrave Macmillan, 2004, p. 127.

13 ECHA, BAC 136/1987/628, Soames to Heath, 17 May 1974.

14 European Commission *et al.*, *Seventh General Report on the Activities of the European Communities in 1973*, Brussels, 1974, p. 1.

15 ECHA, BAC 3/1978/1511, Note, Renforcement de la Représentation Extérieure en 1975, Soames to Members of the Commission, 18 July 1974.

16 For example: CMA, Intermediate Archive (henceforward IA), 040284, QO Dodds-Parker to Commission and QO Jahn to Commission, 9 Jul. 1974; ECHA, BAC 71/2004/92, QE No. 340/74 O'Hagan to Commission, 12 September 1974; ECHA, BAC 71/2004/92, QE No. 340/74 O'Hagan to Commission, 12 September 1974.

of China. What have been the results to date?"[17] Certainly, at this point the EP was devoid of significant power in the EC legislative processes. But it was the one Community institution which required the Council and the Commission to justify their lack of action and pushed the Community to improve the relationship with China.

It was only in March 1975 that Soames finally accepted the invitation to visit the PRC. It is important to note that the Chinese government left the Commission in complete darkness regarding the agenda of its delegation's visit.[18] Therefore, considering the Commission's initial reluctance to seek out China for official political relations, it is, then, ironic that its representative should have taken the lead in establishing these. After all, it was up to Soames to travel to Beijing and up to him to declare right at the beginning that he wished for official links.[19] Thus, it looked like the Commissioner was doing precisely what he had pledged not to do: bowing to the Chinese.

To understand this peculiar path which the China issue took within the EC institutions, it is therefore necessary to examine the deliberations behind the decision for the Community to set up diplomatic relations with the PRC.

Risks and Benefits of EC-PRC Diplomatic Relations

The Council and Commission were reluctant to implement the Copenhagen pledge, not only because China was hardly a priority on the Community agenda, but also because they were extremely aware of the economic and above all the political risks which any change in the Community's relations with the PRC entailed – both for the individual member states and for the EC as a whole.[20]

Official Community relations with China implied national economic disadvantages. Diplomatic relations could precede an EC-PRC trade agreement, which in turn meant that the Nine had to abrogate even more national control over trade negotiations with China to the Community level. The member states had already gone some way in this direction with the adoption of the EC common commercial policy (effective from 1 January 1973) but in the absence of an EC-PRC trade agreement, the

17 NA, FCO 21/1390, Draft Reply to Written Question No. 687/74, Council, 29 January 1975.

18 CAC, SOAM 42/1975/China, Schedule "Visit to China," April 1975.

19 CAC, SOAM 42/1975/China, Speech by Sir Christopher Soames at a Banquet given by Mr Ko Po-Nien, 4 May 1975.

20 European Commission *et al.*, *Eighth General Report on the Activities of the European Communities in 1974*, Brussels, 1975, p. 1; ANF, SGCI files, versement 19880514, art. 96-125, Conseil des Communautés européennes.

national governments still exercised significant leverage over autonomous trade arrangements.[21]

For the Community as a whole, economic risks prevailed too, especially for the already strained trade links with the Soviet Union. After the expiration of bilateral agreements on 1 January 1975 the Eastern bloc had made no attempt to revive trade with the EC.[22] This deadlock would not be helped if the Community set up diplomatic relations with the PRC, the Soviet's rival for leadership within the Communist bloc.[23]

Inextricably linked to the economic jeopardy of officially engaging with China were the political consequences. The Nine would have to consent to framing their foreign policies on a Community level, and these were not homogenous.[24] They risked sending an adverse signal to the Soviet Union, which touched directly upon national security concerns. Richard Mark Evans, Head of the Far East Department in the Foreign and Commonwealth Office, noted "[...] several of the Ministers showed concern about the likely reactions of the USSR to closer links between China and the EEC".[25] In the case of Germany, although Chancellor Willy Brandt had recognised the PRC at a diplomatic level in October 1972, a common European policy towards China could still jeopardise his *Ostpolitik*.[26] Revealingly, the German Council Presidency, which began precisely after the Copenhagen Summit, dropped China from the list of foreign policy issues to be coordinated.

Raising relations to an official level was fraught with difficulties for the Community – even more so, as it was unlikely to be an act of quiet

21 ECHA, BAC 136/1987, Note, "La Chine et les Matières Premières," DGI ID4 to Soames, 25 April 1975.

22 ECHA, BAC 259.80, PV 309, 2e partie, 24 Septembre 1974; European Commission *et al.*, *Ninth General Report on the Activities of the European Communities in 1975*, Brussels, 1976, p. xxviii; Yamamoto T., "Détente or Integration? EC Response to Soviet Policy Change towards the Common Market, 1970-75," *Cold War History*, Vol. 7, No. 1, 2007, pp. 75-94.

23 Kuisong, Y., "The Sino-Soviet Border Clash of 1969," *Cold War History*, Vol. 1, No. 1, August 2000.

24 NA, FCO 21/1097, The External Relations of the European Community: Relations with Non-European Communist Countries, Permanent Under-Secretary's Planning Committee, 8 March 1973.

25 NA, FCO 21/1097, Evans to Davies, April 1973.

26 Haftendorn, H., *Deutsche Aussenpolitik zwischen Selbstbeschränkung und Selbstbehauptung 1945-2000*, Stuttgart, Deutsche Verlags-Anstalt, 2001; Schaefer, B., "'*Ostpolitik*,' '*Fernostpolitik*,' and Sino-Soviet Rivalry," in C. Fink and B. Schaefer (eds.), *Ostpolitik, 1969-1974. European and Global Responses*, New York, Cambridge University Press, 2009, pp. 136-137, p. 146.

diplomacy as Soames correctly predicted.[27] The Community's political relations with the Soviet Union were particularly at stake. Considering the ongoing Conference on Security and Cooperation in Europe (CSCE), where a central objective of the EC was that the Soviet Union should recognise the EC as a political actor, it was a considerable risk for the EC to actively reach out to the PRC because it could nurture the Soviet fear of geo-strategic encirclement.[28] In any relations with China, the Soames *cabinet* kept a controlling eye on the other Commission services.[29]

Therefore, despite the Copenhagen pledge, it was far from self-evident that the Community would seek official ties with the PRC. Economic, and more importantly, political risks, prevailed on the national and Community levels. But what were the expected benefits of the EC engaging with China?

Diplomatic EC-China relations would offer the Nine a means of keeping an eye on the competition from the other EC members regarding their trade with China. This is demonstrated by the change in the attitude of the Foreign Office. Initially it opposed policy co-ordination at EC level but the growth of French and West German trade with the PRC risked displacing the previously privileged British position.[30] By March 1975 the Foreign Office favoured a Community approach to the Chinese.[31] Furthermore, if China increased its trade with the EC following the establishment of diplomatic relations, the member states could demonstrate that the Community was a useful and more effective vehicle for international economic competition. After all, following the end of the Chinese Cultural Revolution in 1969, none of the member states had yet established significant links with the PRC.

For the Community as a whole, formal engagement with China offered economic advantages, too. If the establishment of diplomatic relations was followed by a trade agreement, the EC would further demonstrate its capacity to act as a single unified economic actor. In the early 1970s this capacity had so far only been acknowledged within the GATT after the successful Kennedy Round.[32] The Nine and the Commission were

---

27 ECHA, BAC 136/1987/628, Soames to Heath, 17 May 1974; for a collection of press articles see CAC, SOAM 42/1975/China.

28 For an analysis of the Community objectives at the CSCE, see Romano, A., *From Détente in Europe to European Détente*, Bruxelles, P.I.E.-Peter Lang, 2009; on the Soviet fears of encirclement, see *ibid.*, pp. 83-88.

29 ECHA, BAC 48/1984/686, Hannay to Wellenstein, 11 October 1974.

30 NA, FCO 21/1097, Permanent Under-Secretary's Planning Committee, 8 March 1973.

31 NA, FCO 21/1390, Report "Indo-British Talks", 6 March 1975.

32 *Ibid.*, p. 96; Zeiler, T., *American Trade and Power in the 1960s*, New York, Columbia University, 1992, pp. 244-245; Coppolaro, L., "The European Economic Community

particularly keen to prove to the Soviet bloc that the EC was an actor with which business could be conducted, irrespective of ideological differences.[33]

More importantly, the Community could use official relations with China to address an internal priority, tackling the economic crisis. The break-down of the Bretton Woods system in 1973 and the first oil shocks had revealed global structural tensions, and recession in Europe led to protectionist tendencies and social unrest.[34] On the one hand, trade with China suited the EC's need for export markets and at the same time it also promised to address the EC's dependence on imports of raw materials.[35]

It is important to note, however, that the Community did not develop diplomatic relations with the PRC for the sole purpose of establishing better trade links. Although individual member states, the Council, the EP and the Commission all noted that official links held significant potential for economic growth, the expectations of the principal decision-making authorities remained sober: they based their analysis of the Chinese economy only on estimates because the PRC did not publish official data and such data as was available was unreliable. Chinese trade policy changed rapidly according to the PRC's needs leading the Chinese government to arbitrarily cut off supplies. Above all, China's fourth Five-Year Plan re-affirmed the aim of achieving autarky.[36] As Soames admitted to Heath in May 1974, "Chinese trade with Western Europe is, and is likely to

---

in the GATT Negotiations of the Kennedy Round (1964-1967)," in A. Varsori (ed.), *Inside the European Community. Actors and Policies in the European Integration 1957-1972*, Bruxelles, Nomos Bruylant, 2006; Bossuat, G. and Legendre, A., "The Commission's role in external relations," in M. Dumoulin (ed.) *et al.*, *The European Commission, 1958-72 – History and Memories*, Luxembourg, Office for Official Publications of the European Communities, 2007, pp. 355-362.

33 Romano, A., *From Détente in Europe to European Détente*, *op. cit.*, pp. 40-46.

34 Schulze, M.-S. (ed.), *Western Europe: Economic and Social Change since 1945*, London, Longman, 1999; Tsoukalis, L., *The New European Economy Revisited*, Oxford, Oxford University Press, 1997.

35 CMA, Historical Archive (henceforward HA) /CM2/CEE, CEA/2026/1974, Rapport des Conseillers Commerciaux (3e Rapport), 24 October 1974; PAAA, B37, Zwischenarchiv 100108, Fernschreiben No. 668, Sachs to Bonn AA, 16 February 1973.

36 CMA, HA/CM2/CEE, CEA/2026/1974, Rapport des Conseillers Commerciaux (2e Rapport), 26 March 1974; 3e Rapport; ECHA, BAC 136/1987/629, Rapport des Conseillers Commerciaux (4e Rapport), 3 April 1975; see, for example, PAAA, B201/411/433, Verhältnis EG-VR China, 411-423-CHN, 8 November 1973; ECHA, BAC 136/1987/628, Soames to Heath, 17 May 1974; ECHA, BAC 136/1987/624, Report "Interviews with Leading Companies in the China Trade," Maslen and Westerby, 30 April 1975; ECHA, BAC 136/1987, Note "La Chine et les Matières Premières," DGI ID4 to Soames, 25 April 1975.

remain, very limited".[37] Addressing the European Parliament on 18 June 1975 Soames again stressed that expectations for economic gains should not run too high.[38] Furthermore, the Chinese authorities had not given any guarantee that diplomatic relations would lead in the foreseeable future to a trade agreement.[39] As Emanuele Gazzo, Director of Agence Europe, noted, it was the Chinese who called the shots.[40] His analysis of Chinese policy was shared in European decision-making circles.[41] It is essential therefore to examine political deliberations more closely.

Official Community relations with China would provide member states with a vehicle to carry out their respective foreign policies more effectively. Their relations with developing countries serve as an example. The British government's practice in this regard is a case in point. For example, in August 1972 the British Embassy in Beijing sought a full briefing from the Far East Department on China's link to the so-called Third World. The aim was to use this information to steer future meetings between representatives of the EC member states in Beijing to British advantage.[42] In contrast, the West German government used the EC as a cloak for decisions that were unpopular in individual bilateral relations. Bilateral relations with China could jeopardise the *Ostpolitik*. Hence, official EC-PRC relations offered a useful channel to demonstrate to China Germany's interest in liaising, all the while sending a message to the Soviet Union that the decision was one taken by the Community.

For the Community, diplomatic relations with China also presented important political benefits. Official ties meant the implementation of its pledge to increase Europe's independence in international relations. In his "Year of Europe" speech in April 1973 American Secretary of State Henry Kissinger had riled European leaders, dismissing the European allies as holding only regional interests, as opposed to America's global responsibilities.[43] Indeed in conversation with Chinese Foreign Minister

---

37 ECHA, BAC 136/1987/628, Soames to Heath, 17 May 1974.

38 *Official Journal*, "Debates of the European Parliament," Sitting of Wednesday 18 June 1975.

39 ECHA, BAC 136/1987/628, Hannay to Soames, 27 November 1974; NA, FCO 21/1390, Note "Voyage en Chine," Klein, 8 April 1975; CAC, SOAM 42/1975/China, Record, Meeting between Soames and Chiao, 5 May 1975.

40 ECHA, BAC 136/1987/628, *Agence Europe*, No. 1432, Gazzo, 10 January 1974.

41 See, for example, FCO 21/1097, Permanent Under-Secretary's Planning Committee, 8 March 1973.

42 NA, FCO 21/979, Hum to Crompton, 8 August 1972.

43 Möckli, D., *European Foreign Policy during the Cold War*, New York, I. B. Tauris, 2009, p. 142; Hanhimäki, J., "Searching for a Balance: the American Perspective," in N. P. Ludlow (ed.), *European Integration and the Cold War*, London, Routledge, 2007, pp. 166-168.

Chiao, Soames sharply criticised Kissinger's "Atlantic Declaration".[44] Against this background, a Community approach to China demonstrated an ability to take a common European stance in some of the more delicate areas of world politics, something which EC member states had failed to do in the aftermath of the Middle East crisis in October 1973.[45] The speech of Xavier Ortoli, the President of the Commission, to the European Parliament in February 1975 shows how reaching out to China fitted into the Community's agenda. The "first objective must be to make Europe less dependent. […] Europe offers us an opportunity of exercising to the full the modicum of power allowed us in the new centres of decision. […] It holds good for international organisations and for our relations with our larger partners, notably the US".[46] Official relations with China meant that the Community linked up with a country whose government was outspoken in challenging the bi-polar world order.[47]

It is revealing that the Community established official relations with the PRC just before the CSCE Helsinki Summit in July 1975. Even if meaningful discussions or cooperation over security issues between the EC and the Chinese were highly unlikely, the mere act of establishing diplomatic relations demonstrated that the Community was active in external relations, had bridged its ideological differences, spoke "with one voice", and was not to be ignored. This was precisely the role the Community as a whole wanted to display during the CSCE.[48] Therefore, reaching out politically to the PRC in May 1975 set the tone for Helsinki.

However, this balance sheet of risks and benefits is not yet sufficient to fully understand the timing, the singular manner in which the EC established diplomatic relations with China, and the peculiar part which the European Parliament and the Commission took in the process. To this end, the internal workings of the Community need closer examination.

European Integration at Work

Evidence suggests that relations with China turned into a means for the European Parliament and the Commission to assert their role within the Community. The Treaties of Rome did not provide for the EP to behave as a national parliament on the wider Community level.[49]

44 CAC, SOAM 42/1975/China, Record, Meeting between Soames and Chiao, 5 May 1975.

45 Möckli, D., *European Foreign Policy during the Cold War*, *op. cit.*

46 ECHA, Discours Ortoli, 18 February 1975.

47 Soames was informed: ECHA, BAC 136/1987, China and the E.C., Ernst to Soames' *cabinet*, 4 April 1975.

48 See Möckli, D., *European Foreign Policy during the Cold War*, *op. cit.*, p. 99.

49 Dinan, D., *Ever Closer Union*, Basingstoke, Palgrave Macmillan, 2005, p. 259.

Compared to the Commission and the Council, the European Parliament lacked decision-making power. It also struggled in its claim to represent the European citizens, not least because until 1979 it was not directly elected.[50] Since its creation, however, the EP had sought to raise its political profile and institutional standing.[51] Establishing relations with China was one way to raise its visibility, as plans to organise a MEPs' visit to the PRC illustrated.[52] Such official visits received substantial attention from the press, and would show that the European Parliament took an active stance in international affairs. Furthermore, Community relations with the PRC proved one of the controversial issues which the EP took up in its debates and regular inquiries to the Council and the Commission.[53] The European Parliament might have been a "talking shop", but research shows that it was effective in keeping the issue of EC diplomatic relations with the PRC on the "to do list" of the two more powerful Community institutions.

As for the Commission, taking an active role in the China issue offered an opportunity for it to take an authoritative role in the European integration process – particularly with regard to the Community's external relations. The continuous struggle to assert itself in the 1970s is illustrated not least in the second enlargement negotiations from 1970 to 1973. The Six and the three applicant states insisted on bilateral negotiations rather than allowing the Commission to coordinate them, and the Council eventually did so.[54] Similarly, it was the EPC rather than the Commission that took on the coordination of the Community's external relations.[55] Furthermore, during a dinner preparing the next summit of the EC Heads of State and Government at the *Elysée* in September 1974, Wilson noted: "we would like the Council to do more work of

---

50 Lodge, J., *Direct Elections to the European Parliament 1984*, Basingstoke, Macmillan, 1986; Hix, S., Noury, A. and Roland, G., *Democratic Politics in the European Parliament*, Cambridge, Cambridge University Press, 2007.

51 Dinan, D., *Ever Closer Union*, *op. cit.*, pp. 259-280; Ludlow, N.P., *The European Community and the Crises of the 1960s. Negotiating the Gaullist Challenge*, *op. cit.*, p. 1.

52 CMA, IA/040284, *OJ*, No. 179/68, PV de la Séance du 9.7.1974, July 1974.

53 See, for example, ECHA, BAC 71/2004/92, QE No. 243/71, Berkhouwer to Council, 10 August 1971; PAAA, B37, Zwischenarchiv 100108, Sachs to Bonn AA, 16 February 1973; CMA, HA/CM2/CEE, CEA/1816 OQ No. 79/73, Dodds-Parker to Council, 19 September 1973; ECHA, BAC 71/2004/92, QE No. 152/73, 18 June 1973.

54 Harst, J. v. der, "Enlargement: the Commission Seeks a Role for Itself," in M. Dumoulin (ed.), *The European Commission 1958-1972, History and Memories*, *op. cit.*, pp. 533-556.

55 Ifestos, P., *European Political Cooperation: towards a Framework of Supranational Diplomacy?*, *op. cit.*; Möckli, D., *European Foreign Policy during the Cold War*, *op. cit.*, pp. 184-247.

this kind (cooperation over Cyprus), separate from the Commission".[56] Responding to such attacks, Ortoli asserted before the EP in February 1975: "In the next two years, the Commission's political mission will once again occupy a major place in its work".[57] Improving relations with China was one way for the Commission to pass from words to deeds.

One of the key reasons why the pressure of the European Parliament was effective, and why the Commission was able to act in the first place was that the Nine chose not to obstruct. France, Britain and West Germany had recognised the PRC by November 1972. And following Nixon's China visit in February 1972, which set important conditions for the Western European governments' willingness to normalise their relationship with the PRC, numerous European politicians had visited China.[58] In addition, all the member states had already accepted in principle official EC-PRC relations.[59] Yet none of the intergovernmental institutions exercised meaningful pressure to actually do so.

The timing of Soames scheduling his visit to China points to an important factor shaping the way the Community established official relations with the PRC. It was one month before the British referendum on EC membership. The referendum had the effect of provoking a debate beyond British borders about the value of the Community, and, as a result, discussions on the issue were of interest to the Commission's Directorate for External Relations.[60] Hence the Commission was more than happy to publicly assert its political role and to underline the significance of the EC. Considering the voluminous press coverage that foreign relations with China attracted, Soames' visit to Beijing represented just such an opportunity. It would show that the Commission spoke for a Community which actively addressed national economic concerns by reaching out

---

56 NA, PREM 16/78, Impressions of the Discussions at the Meeting of EEC Heads of State of Government, Wilson, 16 September 1974.

57 ECHA, Discours Ortoli, 18 February 1975.

58 ECHA, BAC 136/1987/628, Soames to Heath, 17 May 1974; see also Wilson D., "China and the European Community," *The China Quarterly*, No. 56, 1973, p. 648.

59 ECHA, BAC 136/1987/624, Meyer to Soames and Ortoli, 18 May 1973; European Commission *et al.*, *8th* Gen. Rep., p. 1; ANF, SGCI, versement 19880514, art. 96-125, Conseil des Communautés Européennes.

60 Young, J., "Europe," in A. Seldon and K. Hickson (eds.), *New Labour, Old Labour*, New York, Routledge, 2004; Young, J., *Britain and European Unity 1945-1999*, Basingstoke, Macmillan, 2000, pp. 111-120; see, for example, ECHA, Discours Soames, Speech by Sir Christopher Soames to the Conservative Political Centre Symposium on "Our First Year in Europe," The Royal Festival Hall, 26 January 1974; ECHA, Discours Ortoli, 18 February 1975; CAC, SOAM 42/1975/China, Record, Meeting between Soames and Chiao, 5 May 1975.

to a country widely associated with important economic potential.[61] The Commission would also prove that it implemented the advice of business circles, according to which official EC-PRC relations would help European trade.[62]

In the final analysis, however, it seems that it was the danger of the newly created European Council which was the decisive reason for the Commission to take the lead in establishing official relations with China in the spring of 1975. The timing of Soames' acceptance of the invitation to visit the PRC is an essential indication: 4 March 1975, just one week before the first meeting of the European Council in Dublin. The European Council, created at the Paris Summit in December 1974, represented a major institutional innovation because it essentially defined the Heads of State and Government as the ultimate decision-making body within the EC.[63] The European Council met regularly to provide leadership to the EC in times of economic and political crisis, and the mid-1970s provided ample opportunity for the new institution to flex its muscles.[64] The danger for the Commission was that this new body would encroach on its traditionally held position in the Community's external relations. Evidence of this challenge is exemplified when, in April 1973, the Nine had held that in principle the Presidency of the Council of Ministers, rather than the Commission, should reply to a Chinese inquiry about an accreditation to Brussels.[65] Further evidence of this wariness is to be seen in Ortoli's warning in front of the EP that the European Council might lead to "the low road of inter-governmental cooperation when we should be taking the high road of integration".[66]

Moreover, directly engaging with the Chinese government was an opportunity for the Commission to demonstrate that it could overcome its previous tendency to react in ineffective manner to crises in world affairs, such as the Yom Kippur War in October 1973 or the Turkish

---

61 See, for example, CAC, SOAM 42/1975/China, Bulletin d'Information No. 94, Commission des Communautés Européennes, Groupe du Porte-Parole, quoting Reuter-23.43, 7 May 1975.

62 ECHA, BAC 136/1987/624, Report "Interviews with Leading Companies in the China Trade," Maslen and Westerby, 30 April 1975.

63 Ifestos, P., *European Political Cooperation: towards a Framework of Supranational Diplomacy?*, *op. cit.*, p. 186; Ludlow, N. P., "From Deadlock to Dynamism: The European Community in the 1980s," *op. cit.*, p. 227.

64 Weinachter, M., "Le tandem Valéry Giscard d'Estaing – Helmut Schmidt et la gouvernance européenne," in W. Loth, (ed.), *La gouvernance supranationale dans la construction européenne*, Bruxelles, Bruylant, 2005, pp. 208-209.

65 NA, FCO 21/1097, Evans to Davies, April 1973.

66 ECHA, Discours Ortoli, 18 February 1975.

invasion of Cyprus in July 1974.[67] The act of diplomacy would show that the Commission had taken the initiative in international relations, thereby eschewing armed confrontation, relying rather on regular diplomatic exchanges. The EC-PRC relationship was generally characterised by the Chinese setting the pace, and the EC officials were conscious of this.[68] However, in this particular instance it was a Commissioner that took the initiative. Soames insisted that he would only accept an invitation to China on condition that his visit was treated as an official one.[69] The Chinese government proved very hesitant to take their interest in the EC further.[70] One week before his visit Soames confided in a personal letter to Murray MacLehose, British Governor of Hong Kong, "fascinating though it is going to be, I have seldom felt a greater sense of operating totally blind".[71]

The Nine allowed the Commission to act not just because they themselves had already recognised the PRC, or simply because they hoped some benefit could spring from official EC-PRC relations. In the 1970s the content of any Community policy towards China was more about symbolism than tangible results. Moreover, considering the unpredictability the Europeans experienced in their dealings with the Chinese authorities, it was not at all impossible that the Commission would fail to set up Community relations with China.[72] In that case, the Commission would take the blame. Yet, if the Commission were successful, the Nine would be proven capable of controlling the Commission's ambitions and even take over its role – if deemed necessary.

At an Opportune Time, an Effective Action on a Favourable Subject

The Commission's establishment of diplomatic EC-PRC relations on 6 May 1975 marked a decisive point in the Community's opening to

67 European Commission *et al.*, 7th *Gen. Rep.*, p. xvi; 8th *Gen. Rep.*, p. 249.

68 ECHA, BAC 136/1987/628, Agence Europe No. 1432, Gazzo, 10 January 1974; CMA, HA/CM2/CEE, CEA/2026/1974, 2e Rapport; 3e Rapport; ECHA, BAC 136/1987/629, 4e Rapport, 3 April, 1975; Compare: FCO 21/1097, Permanent Under-Secretary's Planning Committee, 8 March 1973.

69 ECHA, BAC 136/1987/628, Soames to Heath, 17 May 1974; CAC, SOAM 42/1975/China, Press Notice, Hannay, 18 March 1975; see also Kapur, H., *China and the European Economic Community*, *op. cit.*, pp. 31-33.

70 ECHA, BAC/1987/624, telex No. 358, Luyten to Soames *cabinet*, 4 December 1974; see also Kapur, H., *China and the European Economic Community*, *op. cit.*, p. 35; Schaefer, B., "'*Ostpolitik*,' '*Fernostpolitik*,' and Sino-Soviet Rivalry," *op. cit.*, pp. 145-146.

71 CAC, SOAM 42/1975/China, Soames to MacLehose, 28 April 1975.

72 FCO 21/1097, Permanent Under-Secretary's Planning Committee, 8 March 1973.

China. Despite the Copenhagen commitment by the Council of Ministers in December 1973 to intensify relations with China, this step was far from a foregone conclusion. It was not simply that the expected benefits for both the member states and the Community outweighed the costs which changed the initially reluctant stance of the Commission to send a delegation to Beijing and propose the establishment of diplomatic relations. The period under investigation was significant in the evolution of the EC's China policy because the European Parliament persisted in urging the Council of Ministers and the Commission to implement the Copenhagen pledge, and above all because the Commission asserted itself as the channel through which the Community conducted its relations with China.

The Commission's actions were undertaken with one eye on public opinion in the context of the impending British referendum on EC membership. However, foremost in the Commission's thoughts were the Council Presidency and the newly established European Council. Using the establishment of relations with China as an example, the Commission demonstrated that it assumed political responsibilities, and that the Community was more than just the sum of its member states. Ultimately, it was the institutional struggle over the definition of European integration that fundamentally shaped the EC's opening to China between December 1973 and May 1975. This opening posed questions regarding which external relations issues the EC should tackle, how the Community as a whole should tackle them and who should speak for the Community in international politics. Thus, the establishment of diplomatic relations between the EC and the PRC reveals a struggle for the Community's emancipation from the bipolar Cold War order as well as for the emancipation of political decision-making within the Community itself.

In the long term, official EC-PRC relations would most probably have come about in some way. After all, the Chinese government had shown interest, even if not in a consistent fashion and the national governments in principle had consented. But remarkably, as far as the Community was concerned, the Declaration on European Identity was not the immediate turning point for such a diplomatic act. The creation of the European Council instead proved to be more decisive for the Commission to take action.

A central question remains the relevance of China for the EC between 1973 and 1975. After all, geographically the PRC was far removed and exerted marginal influence on European citizens' everyday lives. Archival evidence also shows that the PRC did not feature as a priority on the member states' agenda in that period. However, although relations with China proved themselves to be different from any other of the Community's external relations, their significance was greater than this. EC relations with the PRC in that period are significant as they were linked to major issues on the agenda of the member states and the Community: tackling the economic crisis and seeking détente in Europe. Most revealingly, however, the establishment of official EC-PRC relations became intertwined with essential questions of membership.

From Trade Conflicts to "Global Partners"

Japan and the EEC 1970-1978

Dr Hitoshi SUZUKI

University of Niigata Prefecture

> Japan and Europe should widen, expand and increase the contacts between each other, not only between national governments, but also at the levels of academic, business, information exchange and public affairs. [...] My intention of visiting Europe was to search for a new cooperative relationship with an old friend of ours.[1]

Introduction[2]

What was the Japanese image of the European Community (EC)[3]? Was the role played by the European Commission influential during trade negotiations with Japan? The EC common commercial policy was launched in January 1970. Japan and the EC member states experienced trade conflicts during the 1970s and 1980s, however, especially after the first oil crisis. The European Commission, with the unanimous support of the Council of Ministers (Council), was responsible for negotiating foreign trade with the Ministry of Foreign Affairs of Japan (MOFA). Although finding difficulty in unifying the voices and claims among all the member states, the Commission was able to negotiate with Japan,

1 Speech by Foreign Minister Masayoshi Ohira, "After finishing top-level meetings (visit to the Soviet Union and Europe by Prime Minister Kakuei Tanaka and Foreign Minister Ohira)," Tokyo, 22 October 1973, The Diplomatic Record Office of the Ministry of Foreign Affairs of Japan (hereafter DRO-MOFA), 0120-2001–01539.

2 I would like to thank Pascaline Winand, Natalie Doyle, Jan Zielonka, Takashi Inoguchi, Kazuo Ogoura, Wilfried Loth, Federico Romero, Ken Endo, and Emmanuel Mourlon-Druol for their helpful comments, and the Suntory Foundation for their research funding. The usual disclaimer applies.

3 European integration started with the launch of the European Coal and Steel Community (ECSC) in 1952. In 1958 the European Economic Community (EEC) and European Atomic Energy Community were launched. From 1967 onwards the three Communities were collectively called EC.

not only with MOFA but also with other stakeholders: with the Ministry of International Trade and Industry (MITI) and the Japanese business lobby group, the *Keidanren*. Thanks to MOFA's cooperation, the Commission was able to persuade MITI and Japanese industry to make compromises, notably, to free the Japanese market for EC exports in order to ease the trade imbalance, and for Japanese firms to build factories in the EC instead of exporting from factories in Japan. What was the Commission's role in the negotiations?; to what extent was it influential, and what were the points of discussion during the negotiations? Who were the participants and actors of the negotiations, and what roles did they play? What was Japan's image of the EC and the Commission, and what changes did the trade negotiations bring to the attitudes of MOFA, MITI and *Keidanren*?

Academic research about European integration history has focused mainly on the internal dynamics among the EC member states, especially on national diplomacy, which had negotiated and shaped European policies since the launch of the European Coal and Steel Community (ECSC).[4] Currently the focus has shifted towards exploring supranational institutions of the European Economic Community (EEC),[5] such as the European Commission, the Council of Ministers,[6] and the European

---

4 One third of the articles (nearly 60 in number) of the *Journal of European Integration History* are studies based on diplomatic history. Seidel, K. "From Pioneer Work to Refinement: Publication Trends," in W. Kaiser and A. Varsori (eds.), *European Union History: Themes and Debates*, Basingstoke, Palgrave Macmillan, 2010, pp. 26-44.

5 Kaiser, W., Leucht, B. and Rasmussen, M. (eds.), *The History of the European Union. Origins of a Trans- and Supranational Polity 1950-72*, New York, Routledge, 2009; Mourlon-Druol, E., "Filling the EEC leadership vacuum? The creation of the European Council in 1974," *Cold War History*, Vol. 10, No. 3, 2010, pp. 315-339; Romano, A., *From Détente in Europe to European Détente. How the West Shaped the Helsinki CSCE*, Brussels, P.I.E.-Peter Lang, 2009; Dumoulin, M. (ed.) *et al.*, *La Commission européenne, 1958-1972, histoire et mémoires d'une institution*, Luxembourg, Office for Official Publications of the European Communities, 2007; Palayret, J.-M., Wallace, H. and Winand, P. (eds.), *Visions, Votes and Vetoes: The Empty Chair Crisis and the Luxembourg Compromise Forty Years On*, Brussels, P.I.E.-Peter Lang, 2006; Ludlow, N. P., *The European Community and the Crises of the 1960s. Negotiating the Gaullist Challenge*, Abingdon and New York, Routledge, 2006; Bitsch, M.-Th. (ed.), *Jalons pour une histoire du Conseil de l'Europe*, Brussels, P.I.E.-Peter Lang, Collection Euroclio, 1997.

6 Naurin, D. and Wallace, H. (eds.), *Unveiling the Council of the European Union: Games Governments Play in Brussels*, Basingstoke, Palgrave MacMillan, 2008; Thomson, R., "The Council Presidency in the European Union: Responsibility with Power," *Journal of Common Market Studies*, Vol. 46, No. 3, June 2008, pp. 593-617; Hayes-Renshaw, F. and Wallace, H., *The Council of Ministers* (2nd ed.), Basingstoke, Palgrave MacMillan, 2006; Tallberg, J., "The Agenda Setting Powers of the EU Council Presidency," *Journal of European Public Policy*, Vol. 10, Issue 1, February 2003, pp. 1-19.

Council, using multilateral and multi-levels of archives.[7] Such research has shown that while national governments play indispensable roles, the European institutions such as the European Commission have themselves also played significant roles in the policy-making of the EEC/EC. It is the aim of this chapter to use this methodology in analysing how the common commercial policy developed and was implemented in the case of Japan.[8] The archival materials I have used in the preparation of this chapter include the Historical Archives of the EU (HAEU, Florence), the German Federal Archives (BA, Koblenz), and MOFA (DRO-MOFA, Tokyo), together with secondary sources of MITI and *Keidanren*. Integrating Japanese archival evidence into the interpretation of European integration history will make it clear how Japan viewed the EC as a trade negotiator and clarify the priorities which Japanese diplomacy pursued during the negotiations, and to what extent these factors helped to shape the common foreign trade policy of the EC.

Why should we focus on the history and development of the EC/EU's "global" self-image and strategy? As in European countries, Japanese historians have increased their interest in European integration history in the 1960s and 1970s,[9] spurred on, in part, by the on-going release of

---

7 W. Kaiser and A. Varsori (eds.), *European Union History: Themes and Debates*, *op. cit.*; Kaiser, W., Leucht, B. and Rasmussen, M. (eds.), *The History of the European Union. Origins of a Trans- and Supranational Polity 1950-72*, *op. cit.*; Mourlon-Druol, E., "Filling the EEC leadership vacuum? The creation of the European Council in 1974," *op. cit.*; Romano, A., *From Détente in Europe to European Détente. How the West Shaped the Helsinki CSCE, Brussels*, *op. cit.*; Michel Dumoulin (ed.) *et al.*, *La Commission européenne, 1958-1972, histoire et mémoires d'une institution*, *op. cit.*; Palayret, J.-M., Wallace, H. and Winand, P. (eds.), *Visions, Votes and Vetoes: The Empty Chair Crisis and the Luxembourg Compromise Forty Years On*, *op. cit.*; Ludlow, N. P., *The European Community and the Crises of the 1960s. Negotiating the Gaullist Challenge*, *op. cit.*

8 Suzuki, H., "How Trade Conflicts against Japan Prompted Europeans to Launch and Continue the Summits," paper presented at the International Conference, *The Art of Chairing the G8 Summits: Lessons from the Past and Recent Trends of Multi-lateral Diplomacy*, 16 July 2010, Tokyo; Suzuki, H., "How the EU Emerged as a Global Actor by Solving the Trade War against Japan: A Historical and Japanese Perspective," paper presented at the EUSA Asia-Pacific Conference, *Connections and Dialogue: The European Union and the Asia Pacific. Perspectives, Perceptions and Policies*, 8 January 2010, New Delhi; Suzuki, H., "From Trade War Conflicts to Global Partners: A Japanese Perspective of the EU's Role and Presence," paper presented at the Global Conference of the Monash European and EU Centre, *The External Relations of the European Union: Historical and Contemporary Perspectives*, 24 September 2009, Melbourne.

9 Endo, K. (ed.), *A History of European Integration* (in Japanese), Nagoya, Nagoya University Press, 2008; Yamamoto, T., "Détente or Integration? EC Response to Soviet Policy Change towards the Common Market, 1970-75," *Cold War History*, Vol. 7, No. 1, 2007, pp. 75-94; Suzuki, H., *Digging for European Unity: the Role Played by the*

30-year-old archival materials. The second reason, which is more significant, is the ongoing change of international relations in the Asia-Pacific, especially since the end of the cold war. This thawing of hostilities stimulated Japan's interest in Europe. The end of the cold war wrought far-reaching changes in Japanese diplomacy, bringing it out of its heavy dependency on the bilateral relationship with the US. In the post-cold war era, the Japan-US alliance came to be looked upon, not only as a bilateral military alliance defending Japan but also as a cornerstone of the stabilization of the Asia-Pacific region.[10] Japan was asked to play a more "global role" by the US.[11] For pursuing such diplomacy, Japan "re-discovered" Europe as a partner in seeking a global role. The re-discovery of Europe's role and presence can be traced back to the early 1970s, when the then-EC took a vital step forward towards launching its common foreign trade policy. As mentioned at the beginning of this chapter, Japanese Foreign Minister Masayoshi Ohira opined in 1973 that Japan re-discovered Europe as "an old friend with a new role". Were the early 1970s the origin of both Japan and the EC seeing each other as "global actors"[12] with potential "global partnerships?"

This chapter consists of four sections. The first briefly reviews Japan's post-war reconstruction and its bilateral trade relations with the EEC member states. Japanese exports increased sharply during the 1960s, and both the member states and the European Commission came to see Japan as a potential threat in terms of trade. The second section looks into the launch of the common commercial policy of the EC. The European economy fell into stagnation in the 1970s and this was exacerbated by the first oil crisis. In an effort to recover from stagnation in its own economy, Japan had a policy of flooding the EC market with its exports, a policy that earned it harsh rebukes from EC member states. The European Commission, voicing no criticism, chose another tack, however. It instead concentrated its efforts on persuading Japan to open its market in order to expand EC's exports, thus easing the trade imbalance. This was a strategy

---

Trade Unions in the Schuman Plan and the European Coal and Steel Community from a German Perspective 1950-1955, Ph.D. thesis, European University Institute, Florence, 2007; Senoo, T., *Die Bedeutung der Konferenz über Sicherheit und Zusammenarbeit in Europa für die Ostpolitik Willy Brandts unter besonderer Berücksichtigung der gesamteuropäischen Konzeptionen Egon Bahrs und der Koordination des Vorgehens mit den westlichen Partnern 1969-1975*, Dissertation, Rheinische Friedrich-Wilhelms-Universität Bonn, 2008.

10 Ikenberry, J., Inoguchi, T. (eds.), *Reinventing the Alliance: U.S.-Japan Security Partnership in an Era of Change*, New York, Palgrave Macmillan, 2003.

11 Inoguchi, T., Bacon, P., "Japan's Emerging Role as a Global Ordinary Power," *International Relations of the Asia-Pacific*, Vol. 6, No. 1, 2006.

12 Bretherton, C., Vogler, J., *The European Union as a Global Actor*, Abington and New York, Routledge, 1999.

that found favour with MOFA, to a lesser extent with *Keidanren*, but MITI voiced strong resistance. The third section focuses on how MOFA and the European Commission found consensus on a joint trade issues communiqué. MITI and *Keidanren* started to change their attitudes and approach and initiated debates in Japan on sharing the burden of sustaining the world economy. This led MITI and *Keidanren* to discuss possibilities of building factories in the EC instead of exporting from Japan, thereby avoiding criticism that Japanese exports had caused mass unemployment in Europe. MOFA issued the Ushiba-Haferkamp Joint Communiqué in March 1978.

From Post-war Reconstruction to Trade Imbalance between Japan and the EEC/EC

Reconstruction of European countries took off after the Paris Treaty was ratified by the original six member states and the ECSC was established in August 1952. Japanese reconstruction had started earlier than in Europe. It took off shortly after the Korea War broke out in June 1950. Japan, whose industry had been forbidden by the American Occupying Authority from producing or maintaining military equipment, was suddenly urged to fix and repair American military vehicles, planes and guns. Thanks to this change, industrial production and investment in Japan rose rapidly, and the economic boom took off.

In parallel with the economic recovery, Japan joined a number of international organisations, namely the General Agreement on Tariffs and Trade (GATT) (September 1955), the United Nations (December 1956) and the Organisation for Economic Cooperation and Development (OECD) (April 1964). This last membership was seen in Japan as a historic symbol of the country's successful reconstruction: Japan joined the club of developed countries. After the OECD was launched in 1961, the US was keen to make Japan a member. Up to that point, the only formal connection Japan had with Western countries was its bilateral alliance with the US. Japan faced the danger of becoming the "isolated child of the free world". In order not to isolate Japan, the US was keen to see Japan join. Another question for the US was Japanese exports. Japan's economic growth was sustained by its exports to the US. The US started to feel that the EEC should also "share the burden" of opening its market to Japanese exports. European OECD members opposed letting Japan join. Whether Japan was a reliable trade country was still not certain, they maintained. The steady growth of the Japanese economy and its rapid increase of exports made Japan appear once more as a threat. Japan's economic growth showed a sustained year-on-year growth rate of 8% to 10% until 1973.

Objections to Japan's membership of the OECD can hardly be described as groundless. Before the Second World War, Japan had flooded the US and European markets with cheap and low quality exports to Europe and the US. Japan had also been accused of "social dumping" by the International Labor Organization (ILO).[13] The image of Japan as a threat was strong both in the US and in European countries. After the Second World War, Japan was once more emerging as an exporter, this time with improved quality products but still at a relatively low price. Japanese exports during the 1960s centred on clothes, steel products and ships, complemented in the 1970s by cars and electronic products.

After the Rome Treaties were signed by the six member states in March 1957, the EEC was launched in January 1958. During the early 1960s, when the EEC had not yet adopted a common commercial policy, trade with Japan was based on bilateral agreements with each member state. However, meetings and committees of the European Commission were used by the member state governments to discuss foreign trade issues and problems. Because Japan joined the GATT in 1955, Japan and the EEC member states were committed to implementing free trade without tariff or non-tariff barriers. Both Japan and the EEC member states, however, reserved exceptions on "sensitive items". The Benelux countries protected 42 items and also obtained bilateral safeguards against Japanese exports.[14] France, for its part, kept 42 items under protection with bilateral safeguards.[15] Italy and Germany protected 48 and 18 items respectively, without any bilateral safeguards.[16] Whether the member states would use safeguards or not on specific items was discussed at meetings, working groups and sub-committees under the European Commission. One example of this process was the case of the Japanese export of textiles in the 1960s.

Japanese export of textile products had increased rapidly and became alarming for some of the EEC member states. The Benelux countries claimed that Japanese textile products had damaged the income of their national industries, and that the member states should take a hard line against Japan.[17] The effect of this would be that Japan would self-restrict its textile export based on bilateral agreements with each member state. The Federal Republic of Germany struck a contrasting note, however:

---

13 Patterson, G., *Discrimination in International Trade, The Policy Issues, 1945-1965*, Princeton, NJ, Princeton University Press, 1966.

14 "EEC's Common Trade Policy towards Japan," *Keidanren Monthly (Keidanren Geppou)*, Vol. 19, No. 1, January 1971, pp. 48-51.

15 *Ibid.*

16 *Ibid.*

17 HAEU, BAC 1/1970, Generaldirektion Auswärtige Beziehung, *Niederschrift über die Konsultation am 4. März 1963 zwischen den Mitgliedstaaten und der Kommission über die gemeinsame Handelspolitik gegenüber Japan*, Brüssel, den 6. März 1963.

both the member states and the EEC should stand firmly with free trade, they argued.[18] Free trade was one of the core principles of the EEC. Italy and France stood in an intermediate position between Germany and the Benelux countries. Both countries had traditionally developed their textile industries, and Japanese exports had caused them considerable damage. Despite their initial reservations, Italy and France sided with Germany and decided not to restrict Japanese exports.[19] EEC member states were "generous" towards Japanese exports on this occasion as Japanese exports to the EEC were of very modest proportions, less than 4% of the total GDP of the EEC. The largest trade partners of the individual EEC member states were the other member states, with Japan occupying a position as a very minor trade partner.

The Japanese government, both MOFA and MITI, were accurate in their analysis of the situation, noting that Japanese exports were not a priority for the EEC and seeing Germany as a key partner.[20] The German government firmly supported free trade and did not refuse Japanese exports. But MOFA and MITI failed to understand that the claims among the various EEC member states differed considerably, in particular, in their understanding of what constituted "serious damage to their industry sectors" caused by Japanese exports. During the 1960s, thanks to the good performance of the European economy, the steady increase of Japanese exports was still not seen as an imminent threat to the largest EEC member state, namely Germany, but France and Italy could not allow themselves to be equally phlegmatic.

The EEC and its member states concentrated on the negotiations concerning agriculture and the Kennedy Round of the GATT in the 1960s.[21] This did not mean, however, that the European Commission did not see Japan as a threat in foreign trade. While the EEC was yet to launch a common commercial policy, the Commission analysed Japan's exports and the structural competitiveness of Japanese industry. The Directorate General (DG) of Social Policy carried out research in cooperation with the Foreign Relations DG in 1965.[22] The report compared working standards

---

18 *Ibid.*

19 *Ibid.*

20 "The implications of the launch of the enlarged EC and its future," *Keidanren Monthly*, Vol. 21, No. 1, January 1973, pp. 18-34; "EEC's Common Trade Policy towards Japan," *Keidanren Monthly*, Vol. 19, No. 1, January 1971, pp. 48-51.

21 HAEU, CES 1183, letter from Genton to Noël, 5 October 1964; HAEU, CES 1183, Dokumentation und ausgewählte Artikel "Initiative 1964," Vorlage der Kommission an der Rat und an die Regierung der Mitgliedstaaten, 9 October 1964.

22 HAEU, BAC 144/1992, No. 243, Salaires, coût de la main-d'oeuvre et autres conditions de travail dans l'industrie japonaise par comparaison aux conditions prévalent

of workers in Japan with those of EEC countries: population of workers, wages, working hours, labour productivity, trade unionism, education level of workers, and the ratification of ILO treaties. The report concluded that the production of large-scale Japanese producers was sustained by small- and middle-sized firms, and that workers employed in the latter suffered less favourable working conditions.[23] Although carefully avoiding using the term "social dumping", the report concluded that Japan's export competitiveness with low-price products was due, in large part, to the relatively poor working conditions in Japan.[24] The Commission had started to see Japan as a potential threat, with the view that the difference in working conditions between Japan and the EEC gave an advantage to Japanese exports.[25]

The Common Commercial Policy, the First Oil Shock and Trade Conflicts

After adopting the customs union in July 1968, the EC launched its common commercial policy on 1 January 1970. The Council decided on 26 May that the European Commission would propose "orderly marketing" to Japan.[26] This meant that Japanese exports would be controlled or restricted based on agreements between the Japanese government and the Commission. At this point, member states aimed to shape the common commercial policy by extending the bilateral safeguards put in place by France and the Benelux countries to a European common safeguard.[27]

The Japanese government resisted this move. MOFA claimed that both the EC and its member states were not respecting the free trade discipline of the GATT. It was especially MITI, representing Japanese economic and industrial interests, that took an uncompromising stance. MITI criticised the EC and its member states for discriminating against Japanese products.[28] On the other hand, MOFA carefully persuaded both

dans la CEE, note d'information diffusée sous l'autorité de M. Levi Sandri, 25 February 1965.

23 *Ibid.*

24 *Ibid.*

25 *Ibid.*

26 *Ibid.*

27 "Reviewing the Japan-German and Japan-French Joint Economic Committee," *Keidanren Monthly*, Vol. 18, No. 7, July 1970, pp. 54-57. The *Keidanren* assumed that the Commission would not be able to abolish national safeguards. See, "Report of the European Economic Mission," *Keidanren Monthly*, Vol. 19, No. 12, December 1971, pp. 26-42.

28 "Report of the European Economic Mission," *Keidanren Monthly, op. cit.*

MITI and *Keidanren* that the European Commission had ambitions as an international actor in trade issues,[29] and that it would be better in the longer perspective to take a more compromising attitude.[30] *Keidanren* was puzzled by the differing attitudes of MOFA and MITI. MITI was in charge of administering Japanese industry, while it was MOFA that would formally negotiate with the European Commission. *Keidanren* also found difficulty in reconciling the diverging claims of its member firms, each from different industry sectors. *Keidanren* disagreed with MITI, because some executives were prepared to countenance EC countries' temporary bilateral safeguards against Japanese exports, as long as this was a "necessary compromise" for persuading them to abolish their safeguards in the longer term.[31]

After the first oil crisis in late 1973, the trade negotiations turned from bad to worse and fell into open conflict. In October 1973, the six Middle East countries decided to increase the price of petroleum and reduce its production by 25%. This caused panic among the developed countries, whose economic growth depended heavily on oil supplies with low prices from the Middle East countries. Economic growth of the US, Japan and EC member states halted, prices soared, and workers lost their jobs. Protectionism seemed once more to be on the rise, as it had been during the 1930s.

The oil shock had a direct impact on the trade negotiations between MOFA and the European Commission. The EC member states warned that the trade negotiations were "in a state of crisis".[32] MOFA and MITI were surprised. They had hoped that, as in the 1960s, the marginal place occupied by Japanese exports to the EEC, coupled with a German government veto to any protectionist moves in the Council of Ministers, would insulate them from concerted action. The Japanese economy relied heavily on exports to the other developed countries and had no other choice:[33] Japan had few domestic energy resources of its own, neither petroleum, nor nuclear.

At the first G6 Summit held on 15 November 1975 at Rambouillet, French President Valéry Giscard d'Estaing stressed the importance of

---

29 "Japan-EEC Relations in a New Stage," *Keidanren Monthly*, Vol. 18, No. 1, January 1970, pp. 62-65.

30 *Ibid.*

31 "Report of the European Economic Mission," *Keidanren Monthly, op. cit.*

32 "Problems and Solutions for Trade Imbalance with Europe," *Keidanren Monthly*, December 1976, pp. 8-23.

33 "Talks with the British and German Industry Representatives," *Keidanren Monthly*, June 1976, pp. 32-37; "Opinion of the 9 Member Associations of the *Keidanren* on Economic Policies," *Keidanren Monthly*, January 1976, pp. 18-20.

orderly marketing. This was a careful but clear pressure for Japan to take a more cautious line in its "flood of exports".[34] Because the Summit created an informal and relaxed atmosphere, however, MOFA and MITI failed to sense the hostile tone. In February 1976, following up the statement of orderly marketing at Rambouillet, France and the UK proposed at the Council of the EC that they should adopt a "crisis declaration" in the trade negotiations with Japan.[35] France and the UK claimed that unemployment had increased due to Japanese exports. This proposal was rejected, thanks to the opposition of the Germans.[36] The German government was also reluctant to place any self-restriction on Japanese export.[37] Both MITI and *Keidanren* assumed that, thanks to the friendly Germans, the EC would not take a harder line. As in the 1960s, Japan failed to understand the criticisms and fears that were being marshalled against Japan by EC member states.

Japan's optimism was misplaced, however. Its only friend in the EC, Germany, also turned hostile against Japan shortly after. The European economy stagnated further in 1975, and Germany was no exception. MITI and *Keidanren* did not sense this change of tone until being invited to Europe by the French and German industry groups, the CNPF and the BDI.[38] The Commission Delegation in Tokyo also urged *Keidanren* to attend. The Doko Mission, led by the President of *Keidanren*, Toshio Doko, was sent to Britain, Germany, France, Belgium, Denmark and the European Commission in Brussels.[39] The Mission arrived in London on 16 October 1976. Executives of the *Keidanren* were surprised after their arrival that the European economy had turned from bad to worse, and that the Europeans were more hostile to Japan than they had estimated.[40] Even the German Ministry of the Economy had turned into sharp critics of what they saw as aggressive

---

34 "Problems and Solutions for Trade Imbalance with Europe," *op. cit.*; "Expectations for Future Development between *Keidanren* and the French business CNPF," *Keidanren Monthly*, April 1976, pp. 32-34; "Promoting Import from Europe: Visiting West Germany, France and Italy," *Keidanren Monthly*, December 1973, pp. 51-54.

35 "Achieving Trade Balance through Expansion," *Keidanren Monthly*, February 1976, pp. 14-33.

36 BA, B 136, 6258, Niederschrift über die deutsch-japanischen Wirtschaftsbesprechungen am 13 November 1973, Bonn.

37 *Ibid.*

38 "Expectations for Future development between Keidanren and the French business CNPF," *op. cit.*, pp. 32-34; "Talks with the British and German Industry Representatives," *Keidanren Monthly*, June 1976, pp. 32-37.

39 "Problems and solutions for trade imbalance with Europe," *op. cit.*; *European Community Newsletter*, No. 13, November 1976, p. 1.

40 "Problems and solutions for trade imbalance with Europe," *op. cit.*

Japanese export tactics which, in their view, had caused serious unemployment in Germany.[41]

Keidanren felt that MOFA and MITI should urgently make contact with the European Commission,[42] because the trade negotiations had fallen into conflict. Worse still, the Japanese government had not noticed this change before the Doko Mission was sent to Europe. MOFA and MITI had not been informed earlier that the European Council scheduled in the following November was to adopt a resolution that was critical for Japanese exports.[43] It fell to the European Commission to make a constructive proposal. When the Doko Mission was welcomed by Commission President François-Xavier Ortoli in Brussels both sides chose to emphasise the positive difference in opinion:[44] President Ortoli stressed that Japan and EC member states should solve the trade imbalance by mutual expansion of trade.[45] This meant to expand the EC's exports to Japan without reducing or controlling Japanese exports. The Commission at this point was reluctant to introduce safeguards against Japanese exports, and preferred to respect the strict definitions of the GATT for fear of accusing Japan of dumping.[46]

After returning to Japan, the Doko Mission reported to Prime Minister Takeo Fukuda, MOFA and MITI and warned that the trade negotiations with the EC were in crisis.[47] If Japan did not make concrete and immediate efforts to ease the trade imbalance, the issue would turn from a "mere trade issue" into a "social and political *problem*".[48] Japan had two ways to reduce its trade imbalance with the EC. The first was to restrict and reduce Japanese exports to the EC. This was difficult, because any such actions would be tantamount to establishing an export cartel, and thus violating German anti-cartel laws. The alternative solution was to increase European exports to Japan, in the hope that the trade imbalance

---

41 *Ibid.*

42 *Ibid.*

43 *Ibid.*

44 HAEU, BAC 3/1978, No. 1519, Elements of reply to the oral question of Mr Osborn, 28 September 1976; HAEU, BAC 3/1978, No. 1519, Note for the attention of Mr Gundelach, under cover of the Cabinet of Sir Christopher Soames, Relations with Japan, Commission meeting of 3 November and meeting with Coreper.

45 HAEU, BAC 28/1980, No. 881, Rapport des conseillers commerciaux des pays de la communauté économique européenne au Japon (1) 55e rapport, 26 février 1976.

46 HAEU, BAC 3/1978, No. 1519, Elements of reply to the oral question of Mr Osborn, 28 September 1976; HAEU, BAC 3/1978, No. 1519, Note for the attention of Mr Gundelach, *op. cit.*

47 "Discussing Japan-US-Europe's Cooperation and Japan's Position," *Keidanren Monthly*, March 1977, pp. 32-40.

48 *Ibid.*

could be eased by expanding free trade. The European Commission had been proposing the latter solution to MOFA and MITI, though it was not until the Doko Mission was sent to Europe that MITI started to accept this idea.[49] It gradually became a consensus in Japan that tariff and non-tariff barriers should be abolished step-by-step.

Thanks to the Doko Mission, MITI made decisions to improve the market access to the Japanese market. The items concerned were automobiles, electrical goods, chemical and medical products. MITI, based on the support and cooperation of *Keidanren*, also sent imports promotion missions to France and Italy, so that Japanese and European firms could discover possible export opportunities on the Japanese market.[50] France was especially enthusiastic at the prospect of selling Airbus planes to Japanese airlines.[51]

MITI's swift response caused a change of attitude among the EC member states. The Council held on 25 March 1977 formally approved of Japan's efforts to reduce the trade imbalance. Member state governments conceded that European firms needed to redouble their efforts to export to Japan, and that they should learn the techniques and know-how of Japanese industry.[52] The change was not entirely one-sided, however: executives of *Keidanren* also conceded that Japanese industry had to adopt new business practices, and to develop an awareness of sensitivities to perceived dumping activity.[53]

At the London G7 Summit held in April 1977, arguments that the US, Germany and Japan should act as the motor of recovering economic growth were put forward. Facing debates referring to Japan's responsibilities in the world economy, not only MOFA but also MITI and *Keidanren* started to claim that Japan should "pay the necessary costs for sustaining the world economy".[54] The rationale behind Japan's diplomatic efforts had started to change, due in no small part to the trade negotiations with the European Commission.

---

49 "Debates about Japan-Europe Trade Conflict and the Keidanren's Correspondents," *Keidanren Monthly*, July 1977, pp. 28-31; "Considering Japan and Europe's economic relations: visits to Europe," *Keidanren Monthly*, June 1978, pp. 10-30.

50 "Japanese Import Promoting Mission to France," *Keidanren Monthly*, May 1977, pp. 32-36.

51 *Ibid.*

52 *Ibid.*

53 "Discussing Japan-US-Europe Cooperation and Japan's Position," *Keidanren Monthly*, March 1977, pp. 32-40.

54 *Ibid.*

The Ushiba-Haferkamp Joint Communiqué

Through the trade negotiations, Japan had gradually become aware of the criticism of its aggressive export policies, and had started to take concrete action in order to ease their trade imbalance. Japan's awareness of acting as a major power urged not only MOFA but also MITI and *Keidanren* to take on the costs of stability and growth of the world economy. Although this change of heart was a significant step, it was not matched by success in reducing the trade imbalance. The EC and Japan had agreed after the Doko Mission's visit that the trade imbalance would be solved by increasing the EC's exports to Japan. While MITI and *Keidanren* made efforts to abolish tariff and non-tariff barriers in Japan, the EC's exports to Japan only increased by very modest amounts.

In January 1977, Roy Jenkins became the new President of the European Commission. The new Commission adopted a harder line against Japan than before. Wilhelm Haferkamp was named Vice-President of the Commission and accepted the foreign relations portfolio. Before joining the Jenkins Commission, Haferkamp had been a German trade union specialist on energy resources and the economy. He became a member of the Economic and Social Committee (ECOSOC) in 1967 and joined the Commission in 1973. Under Ortoli's presidency, the Commission had carefully refrained from criticising Japanese export policy which would have incensed MOFA and MITI. While certain member state governments criticised Japan's exports for causing mass unemployment, the Commission itself did not adopt this line of criticism until the end of 1976.[55] After Haferkamp became responsible for foreign relations, the Commission adopted this viewpoint in negotiations and the rhetoric changed to one based on "unemployment in Europe and Japan's understanding of the matter".[56]

Haferkamp visited Tokyo on 19 and 20 May 1977 in order to persuade the Japanese government and *Keidanren* to make progress on their stated strategy. He met Prime Minister Fukuda, Foreign Minister Iichirō Hatoyama, Minister of MITI Tatsuo Tanaka, and Chairman of the *Keidanren* Toshio Doko, not to mention Japanese trade union leaders.[57] Haferkamp once more stressed that the trade imbalance should be solved, not by restricting Japanese exports to the EC but by increasing EC exports

---

55 HAEU, BAC 28/1980, No. 881, Rapport des conseillers commerciaux des pays de la communauté économique européenne au Japon (1) 55e rapport, 26 février 1976; HAEU, BAC 3/1978, No. 1519, Note for the attention of Mr Gundelach, *op.cit.*

56 HAEU, BAC 28/1980, No. 885, Rapport des conseillers commerciaux des pays de la communauté économique européenne au Japon (1) 56e rapport, 24 mars 1977.

57 *European Community Newsletter*, No. 20, June 1977, p. 1.

to Japan.[58] Haferkamp emphasised that unemployment in the EC member states had worsened, and that Japan must come up with results rather than making mere promises.[59] MOFA agreed, while MITI was less wholehearted in its assent. *Keidanren* suggested that Japanese producers should build factories in the EC and create employment in those countries,[60] rather than producing cars in Japan and being accused of "exporting unemployment to Europe".[61]

When Haferkamp took on the external relations portfolio, the Japanese government also changed its personnel and named a temporary Minister of State for Special Missions, with special responsibility for negotiations involving trade conflict with the US and the EC. On 28 November 1977, Prime Minister Fukuda named Nobuhiko Ushiba as the Minister of State for External Economic Relations. Ushiba was a long-serving diplomat and was fluent in English and German, having served in Britain and Germany. He became Japanese Ambassador to the US from 1970-1974, and negotiated the reversion of the Island of Okinawa to Japan and the Japan-US textile agreement. Fukuda, who personally trusted Ushiba, asked him to accept the Ministerial post "during the current situation of emergency".[62] Minister Ushiba's office was situated in MOFA and his staff of three were all MOFA employees.[63] Ushiba's primary task was to negotiate with the US in order to ease the trade conflict.[64] He achieved a notable success with the signing of the Ushiba-Strauss Agreement on 13 January 1978. Shortly after this, Ushiba turned to negotiate with the European Commission.

Ushiba's strategy for dealing with the EEC, shared by the members of the Fukuda cabinet, was to propose an agreement drawn up on the same lines as the Ushiba-Strauss Agreement between Japan and the US. The Japan-US statement foresaw the gradual freeing up of trade. Ushiba explained that the Agreement was of a global nature and that it would be "applied globally".[65] Because Japan and the US had reached agreement, while the EC had achieved no agreement with Japan at that point, Ushiba

[58] *Ibid.*

[59] HAEU, BAC 28/1980, No. 881, Rapport des conseillers commerciaux des pays de la communauté économique européenne au Japon (1) 55e rapport, 26 février 1976; HAEU, BAC 3/1978, No. 1519, Note for the attention of Mr Gundelach, *op. cit.*

[60] "Thinking about the debates of responsibility," *Keidanren Monthly*, September 1977, pp. 6-20.

[61] *Ibid.*

[62] Press briefing by Minister Ushiba, 28 November 1977, DRO-MOFA, 2009-0620.

[63] *Ibid.*

[64] *Ibid.*

[65] Press briefing for foreign press by Minister Ushiba at the Foreign Correspondents' Club, 27 February 1978, DRO-MOFA, 2009-0620.

faced the criticism during his visit to Europe that Japan and the US had intentionally excluded the EC in agreeing upon trade issues.[66] On 28 January, President Jenkins urged Minister Ushiba and Japan to make further concrete efforts to open the Japanese market, and more specifically, he urged Japan to purchase Airbus aircraft.[67] In MOFA's view, represented by Minister Ushiba, "global application" meant first to reach agreement with the US and only subsequently to apply it to the EC. Although he offered assurances that Japan had no intention of excluding the EC nor of taking advantage of such actions,[68] Minister Ushiba felt that the EC was not fair in the negotiations,[69] nor did he feel that the negotiations had enough substance.[70] His tactic of "global application" was a reluctant and passive one.[71] Furthermore, Ushiba made a number of bold statements criticising the EC and its member states:

> The country which is the largest exporter to France is Germany, and not Japan. Why is it that exports from Germany are not a problem and ours are? [...] The argument about trade imbalance is unfair.[72]

> The EEC, the Council, and so on [...] it is difficult to understand their institutions. They are trying to telescope the negotiations [by the complication].[73]

> The US seems to have warned the Europeans not to put political pressure on Japan. We are bearing that pressure. That is why we are well thought of in America.[74]

Still, Minister Ushiba realised nonetheless that the Japanese government had to reach an agreement with the European Commission on the trade issue, and he persuaded Prime Minister Fukuda to make decisions.[75] Ushiba was helped in his negotiations by the Chairman of the Council of the Foreign Ministers, Danish Foreign Minister Knud Børge Andersen.

66 Minister Ushiba's remarks during his press briefing at the Foreign Correspondents' Club, 27 February 1978, DRO-MOFA, 2009-0620.

67 *European Community Newsletter*, No. 29, March 1978, p. 1.

68 *Ibid.*

69 Minister Ushiba recalls that the European Commission had not officially explained to MOFA what mandate the Commission was given by the Council of Foreign Ministers. Press briefing by Minister Ushiba, 2 March 1978, DRO-MOFA, 2009-0620.

70 Press briefing by Minister Ushiba, 15 February 1978, DRO-MOFA, 2009-0620.

71 *European Community Newsletter*, No. 29, *op. cit.*

72 Press briefing by Minister Ushiba after the cabinet meeting, 14 March 1978, DRO-MOFA, 2009-0620.

73 Press briefing by Minister Ushiba, 2 March 1978, DRO-MOFA, 2009-0620.

74 Informal briefing with the Japanese press by Minister Ushiba, 2 March 1978, DRO-MOFA, 2009-0620.

75 Press briefing by Minister Ushiba, 24 February 1978, DRO-MOFA, 2009-0620.

Minister Andersen's visit to Tokyo from 27 February to 1 March 1978 was decisive for establishing formal negotiations between Minister Ushiba and Vice-President Haferkamp. It was Minister Andersen, as Chairman of the Council, who informed Minister Ushiba that the deadline to conclude an agreement with the EC would be 7 and 8 April 1978,[76] when the European Council would be held. Andersen explained that the Commission would send Haferkamp to Tokyo in March, and that the Commission wished to conclude the negotiations by issuing a joint communiqué at the end.[77] He emphasised the seriousness of the Japan-EC trade conflict and stressed the political significance of the negotiations.[78] Andersen assured Ushiba that the EC would strive to refute claims of protectionism, but only on condition that Japan reached agreement with the Commission.[79] Ushiba agreed to this, but bluntly replied that the joint communiqué should be fair to both sides, and that the contents would not be dramatic or new.[80] Andersen agreed to this.[81]

Andersen's trip to Japan was undertaken outside of the usual round of diplomatic visits,[82] the significance of which was far from clear to the Japanese public.[83] Minister Ushiba understood the visit of such a high-ranking representative as an indication that both the EC and its member states considered the issue to be of the utmost importance.[84]

Haferkamp once more arrived in Tokyo on 22 March 1978. On 24 March, after a one-day extension, Haferkamp and Ushiba concluded their talks and issued a joint communiqué, in which the guidelines for reducing the trade imbalance between Japan and the EC were laid out.[85] The communiqué stated that the trade imbalance should be reduced by efforts made by both Japan and the EC: European firms would make further efforts to export to Japan, which would be supported by MITI and *Keidanren*. In response, Japan would make further efforts to improve accessibility to the

76 Press briefing by Minister Ushiba, 3 March 1978, DRO-MOFA, 2009-0620.

77 *Ibid.*

78 *Ibid.*

79 *Ibid.*

80 *Ibid.*

81 *Ibid.*

82 Press briefing by Minister Ushiba, 28 February 1978, DRO-MOFA, 2009-0620.

83 Press briefing by Minister Ushiba, 3 March 1978, *op. cit.*

84 Informal briefing with the Japanese press by Minister Ushiba, 15 February 1978, DRO-MOFA, 2009-0620. This was confirmed by Minister Andersen during his visit in Tokyo. Press briefing by Minister Ushiba, 3 March 1978, *op. cit.*

85 "Considering Japan and Europe's economic relations: visits to Europe," *Keidanren Monthly*, June 1978, pp. 10-30; "Report of Keidanren's mission sent to Europe," *Keidanren Monthly*, June 1978, pp. 31-37.

Japanese market.[86] The communiqué clarified the basic guidelines on how both the Japanese government and the Commission should solve the trade conflict. Haferkamp and Ushiba agreed that the guidelines shown in the communiqué would prevent an increase in unemployment and the rise of protectionism.[87]

Although the Joint Communiqué was not a panacea and could not be expected to solve the trade conflict, MOFA and *Keidanren* saw it as a positive sign that the tensions of trade conflict had been eased, if only temporarily.[88] The European Council adopted a resolution supporting the Joint Communiqué the following April.[89] The Commission was, however, not as optimistic as MOFA and *Keidanren* were. Haferkamp described the Joint Communiqué as a "mere start-line for solving the imbalance".[90] Haferkamp was disappointed by the limited progress made during the negotiations, complaining that he was tired of repeating the same claims to the Japanese over and over again.[91] The trade imbalance remained unchanged throughout the 1970s, with the conflict continuing into the 1980s. The solution to the trade imbalance was Japanese firms constructing factories in the EC during the 1980s and 1990s. This change had the effect of reducing exports from Japan, with production being carried out closer to the market. A considerable increase in the EC's exports to Japan was also decisive in improving the imbalance.

Conclusion

This chapter has looked at the process of how the common foreign trade policy of the EC was launched and implemented in the case of Japan. One of the core objectives of the EC was free trade. Economic stagnation in the 1970s, and Japan's aggressive export strategy led to EC member states calling for orderly marketing and seeking to restrict Japanese exports. The European Commission took a different approach and proposed that the trade imbalance should be reduced by expanding EC exports to Japan. The Commission found difficulty in unifying the voices among the member states, as each country differed in its definition of how much damage Japanese export had caused. The Commission was, however, able to negotiate and persuade MOFA, and to a lesser

86 *European Community Newsletter*, No. 30, April 1978, pp. 1-3.

87 *Ibid.*

88 "Considering Japan and Europe's economic relations: visits to Europe," *op. cit.*; "Report of Keidanren's mission sent to Europe," *op. cit.*

89 *Ibid.*

90 "Report of Keidanren's mission sent to Europe," *op. cit.*

91 MITI, "Japanese-French economic relations in consideration," *Tsusan Journal*, June 1979, p. 59.

extent MITI and *Keidanren*, to reach agreement with the EC based on the Commission's proposed solution. The Ushiba-Haferkamp Joint Communiqué, issued in March 1978, was the agreed stance that laid out the basic guidelines designed to improve the trade imbalance. Danish Foreign Minister Andersen, as Chairman of the Council of Foreign Ministers, played a significant role in issuing the Joint Communiqué, helping the Commission arrange its negotiation in Tokyo.

The Japanese government, especially MOFA and Minister Ushiba, saw the agreement between Japan and the EC as a "global application" of trade rules which had "global nature". What did this mean? "Global", in this context, was defined by Japan as meaning Tokyo would first reach agreement with the US on trade issues, and only subsequently apply the same provisions to other countries and regions. Although Japan retained a certain reluctance to open its markets and displayed passive attitudes, Japan's trade negotiations with the EC opened the way for Japan to agree on trade on a multilateral basis. The Commission was successful in persuading Japan to pursue a more open trade policy and to reach agreement with the EC. The limits to this approach were also made evident, however. The Commission was not able to negotiate with MOFA, MITI and *Keidanren* on its own, but had to accept simultaneous bilateral negotiations conducted by member states. Each member state differed in its preferences regarding its trade with Japan, so that the common commercial policy was not able to define a clear and unified trade policy with Japan. Bilateral safeguards remained until the 1990s. Moreover, no Free Trade Agreement between Japan and the EU has yet been agreed although negotiations are on their way.

Besides the formal negotiations, informal negotiations and contacts also played indispensable roles. The Commission made regular contact not only with its formal negotiation partner MOFA, but also with MITI and *Keidanren*. In this way, the Commission was able to attenuate MITI's and *Keidanren*'s policy of resisting the EC's claims and change their thinking, thereby allowing both parties to cooperate in the world economy. This led to Japanese producers building factories in the European Community during the 1980s and 1990s instead of exporting from factories in Japan. This solution contributed to creating employment in Europe rather than having Japanese industry being criticised for exporting unemployment to Europe, therefore removing one of the core criticisms of Japan in the EC.

Part III

The EU, the United States and Latin America

Containing Chaos

American Social Sciences and Perceptions of a United Europe in the 1940s and 1950s

Flora ANDERSON[1]

Monash University

Introduction

The European Union (EU) presents the era from 1945-1958 as a turning point in European history, when European elites bravely established a new tradition of trans-national cooperation to restore the continent to the path of modernity and Enlightenment. Whilst the EU acknowledged the help of the United States (US) in helping to fund these endeavours, the intellectual influence of the American social sciences is rarely recognised. Transnational cooperation in Europe was a huge project that relied on a transatlantic network of elites to make it possible: business leaders, cultural leaders, policy- and decision-makers all played central roles. Traditionally, academic research into the influence of this network since the 1950s has focused on the question of the "real" role played by the US policymakers in the development of post-war European cooperation. Two broad arguments have emerged, one arguing that European elites established the institutions of European integration to serve their national interests; the other that American policymakers forced European cooperation as precondition for aid. Recently, researchers have begun to look at the role played by various parts of the wider transatlantic network.[2] What has emerged is that

1 The author would like to acknowledge the post-doctoral grant from the Monash European and EU Centre that made this chapter possible.

2 A very good example of this is Aubourg, V., "Organizing Atlanticism: The Bilderberg Group and the Atlantic Institute, 1952-1963," in G. Scott-Smith, and H. Krabbendam (eds.), *The Cultural Cold War in Western Europe, 1945-1960*, London, Frank Cass Publishers, 2003; see also Boel, B., *The European Productivity Agency and Transatlantic Relations 1953-1961*, Copenhagen, Museum Tusculanum Press, 2003; Scott-Smith, G., *Network of Empires: The US State Department's Foreign Leader*

Americans had an influence over the intellectual basis on which unity was sought; that is, they had an influence over the *vision* of a united Europe that emerged in Europe in the 1950s, as well as the policies pursued by European elites. The vision of a cooperative Europe, freed from ethnic tensions, peaceful, prosperous, and safe for democracy, was something on which the Americans and the Europeans could agree, and thus laid the foundation for on-going cooperation across the Atlantic ocean.

This chapter focuses on the role played by two academics in the US, Talcott Parsons and Karl W. Deutsch, working in the relatively new discipline of the social sciences, in order to add more to this story of the transatlantic networks. These individuals had close ties to the State Department and during the Second World War they were involved in the Department's research into the causes of European fascism and how to stabilise and secure Europe and Germany after the end of the conflict. After the war, their academic work continued to be very concerned with how the US could best ensure stability and cohesion on the continent. Understanding the work of these men helps the researcher to develop a much more nuanced understanding of what role the American policymakers had in post-war Europe. This chapter makes use of primary evidence gathered by the author at the Harvard University Archives in November 2009.

This chapter will focus on connecting the theorisations of the social scientists to the American policy towards Europe that emphasised the idea of elite dominated institutional change. It is this narrative or vision that this chapter is concerned with; how it was developed in academia, and how we can see it operating in the Marshall Plan and the European Coal and Steel Community. This chapter will thus challenge the EU's own myth of its origins as purely European, and show how the projects of European integration can be understood as part of a much wider post-war American project of strengthening the liberal democratic alliance.

The Fable of Post-War European Unity

The official fable of the origins of the EU is well known, and reproduced in nearly every EU publication; it holds that the dream of a united Europe has existed for as long as there were forward-thinking intellectuals and philosophers who desired peace and harmony in a continent divided by war and conflict. This history of internal violence came to a head in 1933, when a racist, nationalist psychopath was sworn in as the

Program in the Netherlands, France, and Britain, 1950-1970, Brussels, P.I.E.- Peter Lang, 2008.

German Chancellor. Hitler spent the next twelve years turning Europe into a hell of war, destruction and violence, based on the barbaric and false idea of ethno-nationalism. He rejected the republicanism, democracy and rule of law that characterised European civilisation; he was, in fact, un-European. This was a moment in which the far-sighted European philosophers, intellectual descendents of Immanuel Kant, had to fight for the very survival of Europe. As Churchill put it, although "large tracts of Europe and many old and famous States have fallen or may fall into the grip of the Gestapo and all the odious apparatus of Nazi rule, we shall not flag or fail".[3]

In the ruins of post-war Europe a belief in the possibility of a better, peaceful Europe was strong. A network of enlightened decision makers, from the academic, political and business communities, came together across national and political lines, and proposed the European Coal and Steel Community (ECSC) to bind French and German destiny together through economic cooperation. As an official EU publication, written by a former assistant to Jean Monnet, tells it in 2006;

> People who had resisted totalitarianism during the war were determined to put an end to international hatred and rivalry in Europe and create to conditions for lasting peace. Between 1945 and 1950, a handful of courageous statesmen [...] set about persuading their peoples to enter a new era [...] [i]n a practical but also richly symbolic way, the raw materials of war were being turned into instruments of reconciliation and peace.[4]

The ECSC was so successful that the political and intellectual elites of Europe increased the areas of, and states involved in, such cooperation. As the people of Europe saw prices go down, wages and employment go up, and peace begin to spread, they, too, welcomed the changes. Economics was the justification; but the ECSC was fuelled by a traditional, European intellectual and philosophical devotion to peace, unity and the rebuilding of Western civilisation. Over the sixty years since then, the EU as it is today has developed as an institution of political, social and economic cooperation that has seen prosperity and peace throughout Europe, and, has led to Europe becoming a serious player on the international stage.

This is the foundational narrative of today's EU; the story of the rise of the spirit of peace and unity against the dark forces of ethno-nationalism, born out of the pain of war, and accomplished by Europeans, for Europeans. There is, of course, a level of somewhat understandable, and perhaps forgivable, idealisation in any new institution or political

3 Churchill, Winston, "We Shall Fight on the Beaches," House of Commons, London, 4 June 1940.

4 Fontaine, P., *Europe in 12 Lessons*, Brussels, Office for Official Publications of the European Commission, 2006, p. 5.

organisation, and, of course, this account of the EU's origins is a caricature – that it appears throughout the EU's own literature does not mean that this is a particularly popularly accepted version of events in the member states.[5] But the official articulation of a myth gives the researcher a clue as to how legitimacy and history is understood within a community; and leads to the question of how it emerged, and what, if anything, it missed. In the case of this chapter: was Europe itself the originator of ideas of transnational European cooperation?

The Academic Origins of Post-War US Policy towards European Integration: The "Vision Thing"

Given their involvement in post-war Europe, the US policymakers exercised great influence over the organisation of Europe in the 1940s and 1950s. US policymakers felt a strong sense of responsibility for Europe's recovery after the war. In a purely pragmatic view, a strong, rebuilt Western Europe would be the US's subordinate ally in the new Cold War world, and be very useful to the US in the ongoing engagement in Asia and the third world. Immediate post-war Europe was, of course, in no condition to provide any kind of significant help, continuing to rely heavily on the US's economic, military and political support and guidance. But the US was increasingly preoccupied with the situation in the Pacific, as the war with Japan continued, and as it became increasingly clear that the pre-war configurations in Asia, based on the colonial empires of European nations, would not return. An integrated, peaceful, and stable Western Europe, which did not require quite so much American attention, seemed a much better option than allowing Europe to succumb to post-war chaos, and would deter the Soviets from any ideas about extending their influence beyond their side of the continent.

Accompanying these policy goals was a narrative of what America was trying to create in the Western alliance; a vision of European unity, and of the role that the United States would play in the post-war world. That is, the vision of liberal democracy that was the defining ideology of the West against the Communist East. The project of European integration was a microcosm of the wider American and Western goal of making the world safe for democracy. This chapter will turn to the question of where this vision came from, and argue that the social sciences in American academic institutions at this time provide us with at least one source of

[5] Eurobarometer, the EU's statistical service, shows that when asked about the "meaning of the EU" in May 2001, 39% of respondents felt it meant "the ability to go wherever I want in Europe" rather than "guaranteed lasting peace in Europe" with only 23%, "Meaning of the EU," *Eurobarometer*, 30 August 2009, http://www.ec.europa.eu/public_opinion/cf/nationoutput_en.cfm.

this, along with the vast transnational network.[6] These social scientists contributed to the liberal democratic narrative by giving structure and scientific understanding to the processes that had led Germany and Europe to totalitarianism, and how American policy could fix it. Having outlined the visions of European unity that came from the American social scientists, this chapter will then show how the major projects of European integration both used, and were made to fit into this narrative.

This chapter will focus on the work of Talcott Parsons (1902-1979) and Karl W. Deutsch (1912-1922), both of whom worked at Harvard and were involved in American policymaking during the war. The work of these men reveals the basic contours of the vision of a united Europe in the post-war American social sciences; Nazism as a corrupted form of modernisation that appealed to the irrational, overly-nationalistic masses; and that the elite had to take the lead by establishing the institutions of cooperation and unity that would teach the masses to be correctly modern (where modern means, among other things, peaceful). There is no evidence that Parsons and Deutsch worked closely together: rather, they were part of a network of professors and students at Harvard who were determined to help America win the war, and restructure German – and European – society to avoid future conflict.

Parsons is well known as the father of structural functionalism in the American social sciences. Born in 1902, he earned his PhD in Sociology and Economics from the University of Heidelberg, and became a Professor at Harvard University in 1927 where he remained until his retirement in 1973. Parsons' reputation is as an "irredeemable theorist", focusing on his largely abstract theoretical elaboration of human society.[7] As a result, his work on Germany stands out due to his engagement directly with the question of a specific social system and how

6 Though by no means the only one. American history is so often understood as a story of ever-increasing freedom that the Cold War seemed to be the fight that America was created for. Economists, academics, policymakers, politicians, soldiers, ordinary individuals – the idea of America as the leader of the liberal democracies arose from nearly ever aspect of American life. For a masterly investigation of this "American creed," see Lieven, A., *America Right or Wrong: An Anatomy of American Nationalism*, Oxford, Oxford University Press, 2004, especially chapter five.

7 Parson's role in policy has only recently become clear, as the archival work of Uta Gerhardt has revealed. Gerhard, U., *Talcott Parsons: An Intellectual Biography*, Cambridge, Cambridge University Press, 2002; *Talcott Parsons on National Socialism*, New York, Walter de Gruyter, 1993; "Scholarship, not Scandal," *Sociological Forum*, Vol. 11, No. 4, December 1996, pp. 623-630; and "Talcott Parsons and the Transformation of German Society at the End of World War II," *Sociological Review*, Vol. 12, No. 3, December 1996, pp. 303-325. Gerhardt's investigations are augmented by the author's own time in Parsons' and Deutsch's papers at the Harvard University archives in November 2009.

policymakers could best go about changing Germany from a state of violent ethno-nationalism, to a fully modern, western liberal democracy. His work on this topic was communicated directly to policymakers, and though he did write a proposal for a book on the German social system, it was never published.[8]

Parsons aimed to explain why the German people had been susceptible to Nazism; whilst he also believed that European unification would help to solve it. He left the details of this European-wide solution to other academics such as Deutsch to articulate more fully, and concentrated on diagnosing the problems of Germany. From 1943-1945, Parsons devoted his teaching time at Harvard to instructing the government and military officers who would be responsible for Germany after the war, where he was able to communicate his theories on the cause of, and solution to, German fascism.[9] He took a position with the Federal Economic Administration in Washington, and communicated his theories directly to Phillip Kaiser at the State Department in Washington, and to Henry H. Fowler with the High Commission and State Department in Germany. Both men appear to have regularly sought Parson's thoughts on proposed policies in the Department.

Deutsch, an outspoken anti-Nazi activist from Czechoslovakia, fled Germany in 1939 as the German army invaded the Sudetenland. He

8 Parsons, T., "Outline of a Book Proposal on German Social Structure," undated but appears to be around 1944 or 1945, Parsons papers, HUG (FP) 15.2, Box 11, Harvard University Archives, Pusey Library, Cambridge. In particular through his part-time work with the Foreign Economic Administration (FEA), where Parsons communicated directly with Henry Fowler and Phillip Kaiser in the State Department. See Memo, Parsons to Henry H. Fowler, "The Need for Further Social and Economic Research on Problems of Policy toward Occupied Countries," 11 October 1945, Parsons papers, HUG (FP) 15.2, Box 10, Harvard University Archives, Pusey Library, Cambridge; Memo, Parsons to Philip Kaiser, "Separation of Western Territories from Germany," August 1947, Parsons papers, HUG (FP) 15.2, Box 10, Harvard University Archives, Pusey Library, Cambridge.

9 There is a wealth of material in Parsons' archives dealing with this. Parsons, Talcott, letter to Carl J. Friedrich, "Decisions of Planning Committee for Balance of Third Term," December 1943 Parsons papers, HUG (FP) 15.2, Box 10, Harvard University Archives, Pusey Library, Cambridge; "Program for General Area Studies," 1943, Parsons papers, HUG (FP) 15.2, Box 10, Harvard University Archives, Pusey Library, Cambridge; and a draft of a lecture Parsons was to give, "Draft of Ideology," September 1943, Parsons papers, HUG (FP) 15.2, Box 10, Harvard University Archives, Pusey Library, Cambridge. Gerhardt, U., "Talcott Parsons and the Transformation of German Society at the End of World War II," *op. cit.*, pp. 303-325 and p. 310. The details of what Parsons presented are preserved in his archives, including "Full Report on Conference on Germany after the War," Parsons papers, September 1945, HUG (FP) 15.2, Box 11, Harvard University Archives, Pusey Library, Cambridge, where Parsons emphasised that the US had a responsibility to not just destroy the Nazis, but build a democratic spirit.

received a scholarship for refugees from Nazism to Harvard to undertake his PhD on nationalism and he then worked at the Massachusetts Institute of Technology (MIT) and Harvard University. This scholarship was for refugees from Nazism, and was funded by Harvard students who sought to help talented students escape the Nazi regime.[10] It resulted in a Master of Arts in 1941.[11] He spoke many times in favour of the US joining the war against Hitler, and was active with the American Defence Group – Harvard before the war along with Parsons. The Defence group agitated for the US to make a greater war effort; after this, they continued to gather support for the war and to work closely with the State Department disseminating information to the American people. After Pearl Harbour, Deutsch worked for the US government. Deutsch and Parsons had both worked as consultants for the Biographical Records Committee of the Defence Group. In June 1943 the OSS asked this committee to form to study the elites in enemy states and their occupied territories.[12] From 1942 – 1944 he led a research group in the Office of Secret Services (the war time antecedent of the CIA) and continued working in the State Department until 1946.[13] After the war ended, Deutsch returned to academia at Harvard and MIT.

Parsons and Deutsch: Integration and the Future of Europe

The work of Parsons and Deutsch covers two distinct areas; Parsons focused on diagnosing what had allowed the emergence of fascism and totalitarianism in Europe, while Deutsch used this understanding to formulate a plan to block its reoccurrence. Parsons thought European unity would be the outcome of successfully reorienting Germany culture away from fascism, but it was the next generation of theorists who engaged directly with the debates of post-war Europe, drawing on Parsons' work. Deutsch transformed Parsonian theory into proposals for the future of Western Europe, a fully modernised Europe that could eradicate the threat of anti-modernisation violence, in the form of fascism or communist totalitarianism, and create a great and powerful Western Alliance. This

10 Merritt, R. L., Russett, B. M. and Dahl, R. A., *Karl Wolfgang Deutsch, 1912-1992. A Biographical Memoir*, Vol. 80, Biographical Memoirs, Washington, D.C., The National Academy Press, 2001, pp. 59-60.

11 Letter, David T. Page to Deutsch, "Draft Bibliography for Yale Banner," date unknown but after 1960, Deutsch Papers, HUG (FP) 141.6, Box 2, Harvard University Archives, Pusey Library, Cambridge.

12 Deutsch, K., letter to Ralph Barton Perry accepting position as consultant, 23 September 1943, HUD 3139, Box 47, Harvard University Archives, Pusey Library, Cambridge.

13 Personal Communication, Page, David T., to Karl Deutsch, date unknown, HUG (FP) 141.6, Box 2, Harvard University Archives, Pusey Library, Cambridge.

section will offer a brief overview of Parsons' thoughts before concentrating on how Deutsch used these ideas to formulate the basic outlines of his European integration theories.[14]

Talcott Parsons argued German fascism was a result of a "cultural lag",[15] a reaction to the fast pace of technological and social change that societies experience when undergoing modernisation. The German social system had remained too old-fashioned to cope with the rapid pace of change in the modern world. Instead of developing a liberal-democratic social system (the most ideal to deal with the modern condition), after the First World War, the German social system developed an economy that was permanently in a state of wartime mobilization, and a family structure that valued a strong, authoritarian father figure.[16] Given the situation of prolonged economic and social crisis that existed in Germany in the 1920s and 1930s, for Parsons it was relatively simple for the Nazis to come to power "with the help of certain physiological mechanisms, latent possibilities or orientations of the German people which are understandable in terms of the strains involved in its institutional and social situation".[17] For these reasons, defeating the Nazis was only the first step for America; that, in itself, would not eliminate the German social system that had given rise to it.

Parsons argued that rendering Germany peaceful and no longer a threat to her European neighbours relied on institutionally-based democratisation and social change in German society. In a memo to the Chief of the Planning Staff of the Foreign Economic Administration, Philip Kaiser, in 1945, Parsons argued that for Germany

> [...] the most important thing would be the creation of a focal centre for the development of a liberal-democratic society among the German population. So long as the moral-psychological situation is good, a favourable situation for

---

14 For a deeper investigation of Parsons' thoughts on German fascism, see the author's work in Anderson, F., "Una Cierta Idea de la sociedad. Talcott Parsons, Carl J. Friedrich, y el Plan de Integración de las Ciencias Sociales de América de la década de 1940," http://www.ba.unibo.it/NR/rdonlyres/475B2D6B-14FF-4667-AF59-3EB4F0AEFE04/238147/6_anderson.pdf, accessed 6 May 2013.

15 Gerhardt, U., "Talcott Parsons and the Transformation of German Society at the End of World War II," *op. cit.*, p. 320. Gerhardt also correctly notes that that idea of cultural lag comes from the 1920s, the work of William F. Ogburn.

16 Parsons, T., memo to Henry H. Fowler, "The Need for Further Social and Economic Research on Problems of Policy toward Occupied Countries," 11 October 1945, Parsons papers, HUG (FP) 15.2, Box 10, Harvard University Archives, Pusey Library, Cambridge. Gerhardt, U., *Talcott Parsons on National Socialism*, *op. cit.*, p. 44.

17 Parsons, T., "Outline of a Book Proposal on German Social Structure," undated but appears to be around 1944 or 1945, Parsons papers, HUG (FP) 15.2, Box 11, Harvard University Archives, Pusey Library, Cambridge.

relative economic prosperity and an expanding field of economic opportunity should work in that direction.[18]

For Parsons, institutional patterns modify the behaviour of those within them; sufficiently modern institutions could "teach" the German people to be correspondingly modern, in the same way that the Nazis had taught the Germans to be violent and aggressive.[19] Given his understanding of the role of the economy and family, Parsons argued that the most important institutions to focus on would be the economy, and the family; if these social institutions could be made modern, then it would have a spillover effect, teaching the German people modern values and culture.[20] The increased prosperity would also be very beneficial: for Parsons, "an expanding field of economic opportunity, even though the rate be very gradual, is one of the most fundamental conditions of a type of institutional change which would reduce the emphasis on authoritarianism".[21] In 1945, Parsons envisaged the emergence of a Germany that pursued a "policy of cosmopolitan interchanges with all neighbouring areas […] [that would redefine German cultural] values as supra-national".[22] That is, in eliminating the potential for fascism, a united Europe would emerge almost automatically.

Where Parsons focused on diagnosing the causes of German fascism, Deutsch took up the challenge to use the modern social sciences to create a united Europe, and a peaceful, modern world.[23] Deutsch understood

---

18 Parsons, T., memo to Philip Kaiser, "Separation of Western Territories from Germany," August 1947, Parsons papers, HUG (FP) 15.2, Box 10, Harvard University Archives, Pusey Library, Cambridge.

19 Gerhardt, U., "Talcott Parsons and the Transformation of German Society at the End of World War II," *op. cit.*, p. 311.

20 Parsons was particularly optimistic about the role of the family in stabilizing and modernizing Germany. In 1945, in a memo to Henry Fowler, he suggested that the reunification of families might be one of the few ways to impart a sense of stability and security to the German masses. He was very concerned that the four powers in Germany would not do enough to try and reunite those separated by the war. Giving German institutions responsibility for reuniting families was a particularly good way to start the process of controlled institutional change. Parsons, Talcott, memo to Henry H. Fowler, 2 July 1945, Parsons papers, HUG (FP) 15.2, Box 10, Harvard University Archives, Pusey Library, Cambridge.

21 Parsons, T., memo to Henry H. Fowler, "The Need for Further Social and Economic Research on Problems of Policy toward Occupied Countries," 11 October 1945, Parsons papers, HUG (FP) 15.2, Box 10, Harvard University Archives, Pusey Library, Cambridge.

22 Parsons, T., memo to Philip Kaiser, "Separation of Western Territories from Germany," August 1947, Parsons papers, HUG (FP) 15.2, Box 10, Harvard University Archives, Pusey Library, Cambridge.

23 Deutsch, K., *Political Community and the North Atlantic Area; International Organisation in the Light of Historic Experience*, New York, Greenwood Press Publishers, 1957, p. vii.

fascism much as Parsons did, as primarily a response to economic depression and the failure of any strongly democratic leadership to institute the social changes needed to deal with it. The worldwide depression hit Germany hard, her citizens felt, harder than the rest of the world. Deutsch found such poverty dangerous, for it was poverty and inaction surrounded by plenty of workers, equipment, and technology that seemed to promise wealth and productivity. Idleness led to frustration, a sense of hopelessness and bitterness among the unemployed. If the state could not find some way to deal with this, a social malaise or "anomie" (as Parsons qualified it) would emerge.[24] "Frustration leads to fear and insecurity. These lead to hate, and they all together lead to aggression".[25] That is, the kind of frustration engendered by the failure of the state to institute social change to match and adapt to technological and industrial progress sowed the seeds of violent and reactive ideologies.

If the modern west is "to understand our opportunities to achieve a stable world order", Deutsch wrote, "we shall depend in large part on the ability of the social sciences to suggest answers".[26] In his view, social scientists could help to find the replacement for nationalism, something that would bind societies together, help them to achieve stability and cohesion, until peace throughout the West and eventually, throughout the globe was achieved. Integration would be facilitated by institutions and technologies that eliminated national boundaries, and helped all individuals feel loyalty to their brothers beyond the nation-state boundaries. It is difficult to overestimate the importance that Deutsch attached to the role of the social sciences in encouraging integration: "On [our] victory depends the course of human evolution, the hopes of the living and the dead. In the history of mankind as well as in the history of religion our final victory over fascism and poverty and war will not be an end but the greatest beginning".[27]

Integration in Deutsch's work can be defined almost as the march of peace – the end of the possibility of war, and the creation of a sense of shared destiny and brotherhood with other regions. Integration meant that a territory had attained a "sense of community" through the establishment of institutions and practices, which were strong enough and wide-spread

---

[24] Deutsch, K., "Faith for Our Generation: A Study Unit on Youth and Religion," 1943, published by American Unitarian Youth, Massachusetts, HUG (BD) 322.72, Box 1, Harvard University Archives, Pusey Library, Cambridge.

[25] *Ibid.*, p. 43.

[26] Deutsch, K., "Nationalism and the Social Sciences," presented at Eleventh Conference on Science, Philosophy and Religion, Columbia University, September 1950, Deutsch Papers, HUG (FP) 141.77, Box 1, Harvard University Archives, Pusey Library, Cambridge.

[27] *Ibid.*, p. 62.

enough to allow an assumption of "peaceful change" among its population.[28] Integration carried many benefits, but the clearest and most important for Deutsch was that it rendered the idea of war between participating units abhorrent – an unthinkable act of "fratricide".[29] Deutsch argued that history provided many examples that integration, helped along by technological and institutional changes, had led to peace, most importantly in the US. Integration emerged as a symptom of the elimination of war and the development of brotherly feelings over an extended area. Importantly, for structural functionalists such as Parsons and Deutsch, the logic ran the other way, too. Establish well-functioning institutions of integration, and this would eliminate war and cause the development of brotherly feeling. Parsons had investigated what had caused the emergence of fascism and total war; Deutsch saw the chance to develop an institutional organisation in Europe that would prevent it ever occurring again.

Deutsch agreed with Parsons that defeat of Nazism was no guarantee that Germany – and Europe – would never return to such violence. According to Deutsch, history showed that the German people were inclined towards "extremes"; in rebuilding German society, this tendency needed to be guarded against.[30] Deutsch considered the best way to achieve this was by ensuring that the German elites were committed to a culture of democracy, human rights, and good relations with their neighbours; these values would be communicated to the German masses through the institutions they established and ran. The task in Germany then was not to convert the whole of the German population into modern liberal democrats overnight. So long as the elites and the political institutions of Germany could be made assuredly democratic and peaceful, the masses would eventually, gradually, adopt a modern culture. That is, in establishing a democratic, modern elite, Germany could overcome the cultural lag that Parsons diagnosed.

Deutsch argued in 1950 that most German elites were already ready to embrace these western liberal democratic traditions; and, considering that political elites traditionally had a high level of power and influence in German society, post-war Germany was ripe for the kind of institutional cultural modification Parsons envisaged. Deutsch made it more explicit that it was the German elites who must guide this change. German elites "did not have to be open or explicit [about their aims]; they should not bother the voters with the burden of decision".[31] Such a statement appears rather shocking to contemporary sensibility in that it appears to deny the

---

28 Deutsch, K., *Political Community and the North Atlantic Area*, *op. cit.*, p. 5.

29 *Ibid.*, p. 73.

30 *Ibid.*, p. 18.

31 *Ibid.*, p. 47.

traditional sense of the democratic nation-state: the sovereignty of the people. However, Deutsch used a definition of "elite" that suggests his justification of this term. In Parsonian structural functionalism, the elite in any group, or any social system, were those in the population who were better informed about policy, and had greater influence on decision-makers. Thus, if one was an elite member of society in the position to make a decision on government policy, then one was already assumed to be the best person to make that decision.[32] Moreover, Deutsch constantly revealed a suspicion that the masses would be resistant to change until it was inevitable; they could be swayed by rational argument, they must be taught through the kind of institutionally-controlled change that Parsons advocated. Deutsch concluded optimistically that the elite, free from the direct interference of the German people, could be taught by the elite-constructed and implemented institutions the kind of modern values that would encourage the pursuit of stability, a resistance to ideology, and an emphasis on the private life. This would be the basis for a newly established German national social system; and, indeed, a European social system.[33]

Deutsch's work reveals a deep sense of the necessity of restoring Germany to a position of a fully-fledged member of western civilisation as a prerequisite to European integration (that is, peace on the continent). He argued that Germany had deeply democratic roots, and the recovery of her moral and political alliance with the West was essential to peace in Europe, and the world. The German state must be recreated so that it could be a good ally, a strong part of the newly emerging integrated Europe. Only in this way could Germany achieve "redemption for the sins committed by the Nazis in their name".[34] In other words, to atone for the sin of having promoted irrational violence, disintegration and war, Germany must show she was dedicated to the cause of progress and modernisation by becoming a leading light of the new Europe: "membership in a European integration scheme for a German state both wealthier and more populous than any other Continental state holds out the prospect not

32 *Ibid.*, p. 60.

33 *Ibid.*, pp. 192-193.

34 Deutsch's enthusiasm for Germany's rehabilitation should not be taken as a kind of sentimental desire for a return to the great past by an escapee from the Nazi regime. Rather, Deutsch sees the possibility of Germany becoming a fully European nation; which would lead to progress, peace and stability in Europe on a previously unimagined scale. Deutsch writes to reassert his separation from Germany, in no way acknowledging his own ethnic origin; but it seems plausible that what he had in mind was that in re-establishing her international "credit," Germany must also seek redemption in the eyes of the refugees from Nazism scattered around the world – including Deutsch himself. Deutsch, K., *Political Community and the North Atlantic Area*, *op. cit.*, pp. 152, 156.

only of equality for the Federal Republic in such a union, but potential leadership of the democratic nations of continental Europe".[35]

In coming through this experience of disintegration, collapse and horror, Germany would gain the strength and insight to create peace in Western Europe. Out of the chaos of the Second World War, peace and harmony could be established.

From Vision to Policy: Social Science in Action

The remainder of this chapter will detail the main practical policies of the US in regards to European integration in the 1950s – the Marshall Plan, and the European Coal and Steel Community – and the ways in which the American position reflects the influence of the American social sciences.[36] This section will demonstrate how these institutions were fuelled by an underlying vision of an integrated Europe on the part of American policymakers. Parsons and Deutsch certainly had the ear of the US policymakers; but this did not in itself guarantee that their ideas and theories would be taken seriously. But as we shall see, the policies pursued by the Americans in Europe are very similar to the plans suggested by Parsons and Deutsch. Beyond what can legitimately be criticised as perhaps mere rhetoric surrounding the Marshall Plan and the ECSC, there is clear evidence that the vision of a Europe united in peace permeated the American policymakers and followed the contours of structural functionalist thought. John Foster Dulles argued that as the United States seemed to continually become entangled in the wars on the continent, that is, as the United States kept getting called on to play the role of saviour, they had the right to some control over the post-war contours of Europe. As Dulles put it, "[f]rom a purely selfish standpoint, any American program for peace must include a federated continental Europe".[37]

---

35 *Ibid.*, p. 153.

36 For a history of the Marshall Plan, see Behrman, G., *The Most Noble Adventure: The Marshall Plan and the Time When American Helped Save Europe*, New York, Free Press, 2007; Lundestad, G., *"Empire" by Integration: The United States and European Integration 1945-1997*, Oxford, Oxford University Press, 1998. For a history of the European Coal and Steel Community, see Diebold, W., *The Schuman Plan: A Study in Economic Cooperation 1950-1959*, New York, Frederick A. Praeger, 1959 or Gillingham, J., *Coal, Steel and the Rebirth of Europe, 1945-1955. The Germans and French from Ruhr Conflict to Economic Community*, Cambridge, Cambridge University Press, 1991; or Milward, A. S., *The European Rescue of the Nation State*, London and New York, Routledge, 2000.

37 Quoted from the Dulles archives in Garvin, V., "Power through Europe? The Case of the European Defence Community in France (1950-1954)," *French History*, Vol. 23, No. 1, January 2009, pp. 69-87, p. 71.

The Marshall Plan

Through the Marshall Plan, the US sought to foster European cooperation by placing the responsibility for the initial formulation of economic projects of reconstruction onto European shoulders; it created institutions of economic cooperation that would foster elite collaboration and eventual European unity. The Marshall Plan distributed around 13 billion US dollars between 1948 and 1951, and was an incredibly successful contribution to heaving Western Europe out of post-war chaos, starvation and stagnation.[38] This image of success might come from the sense that the Marshall Plan achieved two aims – firstly, the reconstruction of Europe through economic institutions; but secondly, and more importantly, the perception that it laid the foundations of European integration.

It made clear sense for the USA to encourage Europe to act as a single unit when it came to distributing aid; most continental states faced similar problems with destroyed infrastructure, post-war starvation and so on.[39] Moreover, money could be more effectively deployed if the European elites were cooperating with one another.[40] The Marshall Plan established the Organisation for European Economic Co-operation (OEEC) to administer the aid, initially used mainly to shore up the Europeans dollar-balance deficit.[41] In 1949, the US informed the OEEC that they felt the aid money was not being used to sufficiently promote freer inter-European trade, that is, the kind of economic cooperation that Parsons encouraged as a way to bind the European states together. The final two years of aid would be provided on condition of trade liberalisation. The Europeans agreed to fifty per cent of private trade being free of import duties. In 1950 the OEEC created the European Payments Union, and in June of that year the chairman put forward a plan for European economic integration; it seemed that the Europeans were open to the idea that economic cooperation would be key to European unity. The relevance of the OEEC declined markedly with the end of the Marshall Plan, and the creation of NATO in 1949. However by its end, the Marshall Plan had served its

---

38 Behrman, G., *The Most Noble Adventure: The Marshall Plan and the Time When American Helped Save Europe*, *op. cit.*, p. 339.

39 For a detailed survey of the post-war damage, and the costs of fixing it, see Robinson, N., "Problems of European Reconstruction," *The Quarterly Journal of Economics*, Vol. 60, No. 1, 1945, pp. 1-55.

40 Chollet, D. and Goldgeier, J. M., "The Faulty Premises of the Next Marshall Plan," *The Washington Quarterly*, Vol. 29, No. 1, 2005, pp. 7-19.

41 The State Department estimated that France required 100 million dollars a month of food, coal and "basic supplies". The income for exports was 10 million a month. Italy required between 85 and 95 million dollars of resources a month; exports were worth 20 million. "The Immediate Need for Emergency Aid to Europe," 29 September 1947, President's Secretary's Files, Truman Papers, accessed 23 November 2009.

purpose; Western Europe was back on its feet, and was beginning to move towards economic cooperation.

It would be wrong to consider the Marshall Plan as merely a policy driven by only the most functional and practical of concerns; there was always a greater vision among the American policymakers that underlay the policies pursued. And like Parsons, these policymakers felt that the establishment of a modern economic system would be fundamental to any chance of recovery or future integration of the continent. Marshall justified his plan as supremely pragmatic, protecting vital American interests and ensuring stability; but we can see how a modern economic system is seen as vital to the formation of a strong Western alliance.

> It is logical that the United States should do whatever it is able to do to assist in the return of normal economic health in the world, without which there can be no political stability and no assured peace [...] [the purpose of this aid] should be the revival of a working economy in the world so as to permit the emergence of political and social conditions in which free institutions can exist.[42]

Even documents not intended for public consumption reflected concern beyond simple economics or politics.[43] The State Department's summary position on the Marshall Plan suggested that a communist Europe would be an existential threat to the American way of life. "The sacrifices would not simply be material. With a totalitarian Europe which would have no regard for individual freedoms, our spiritual loss would be incalculable".[44] It is also worth noting that for many American policymakers, Europe appeared totally incapable or rebuilding without their help in the post-war world. George Kennan, for example, felt that "Europe's pathetic weakness, and European consciousness of that weakness", meant it would never be able to rebuild itself alone; it needed a strong leader to weld it together and America had to fulfil that role.[45]

---

42 Secretary Marshall, G. "Commencement Address at Harvard University Cambridge, Massachusetts, 5 June 1947," USAID, http://transition.usaid.gov/multimedia/video/marshall/marshallspeech.html, accessed 6 May 2013.

43 Kennan, G., "The Long Telegram," 22 February 1946, Harry S Truman Administration Files, Elsesy Papers, Truman Library, http://www.trumanlibrary.org/whistlestop/study_collections/coldwar/documents/pdf/6-6.pdf, accessed 6 May 2013.

44 "The Immediate Need for Emergency Aid to Europe," 29 September 1947, President's Secretary's Files, Truman Papers, accessed 23 November 2009.

45 Quoted in Harper, J. L., *American Visions of Europe: Franklin D. Roosevelt, George F. Kennan, and Dean G. Acheson*, Cambridge, Cambridge University Press, 1996, p. 201.

Coal and Steel

The Schuman Declaration in May 1950 was a concrete step towards European unity taken by the Europeans rather than the Americans; yet it clearly reflected the ideas of the American social scientists. Schuman suggested that French and German coal and steel industries be administered together under a common, transnational authority. Schuman's stated aim was to make "war not only unthinkable but materially impossible" through economic institutions, and it met the interests of all the participant powers. The Schuman Declaration called for the pooling of French and German coal and steel resources, along with those of any other nation which wished to join.[46] The practicalities were not elaborated on in the declaration – rather Schuman's speech was an articulation of the vision that underlay his position; a way of uniting Europe to avoid war. The Treaty of Paris went into much greater detail, about the supranational authority that would oversee the practical requirements of harmonising production across the member states. It defined the task of the Community in Article 2 as of ensuring economic expansion, and a rising standard of living; once again the modern economy was seen as the basis of developing a modern social system on the continent.[47]

The US had an important role in ensuring the passage of the Coal and Steel agreement. Despite the success of the Marshall Plan, the American policymakers still felt there was a lot of work to do. As the American Ambassador to France David Bruce put it, less than two months before Schuman's Declaration, "Western Europe today is [in the position that] without extraordinary assistance from the United States free nations there could not survive in their present form by their own efforts".[48] They feared that the economic troubles of Western Europe would lead to a leftward swing in politics, potentially opening the door to Soviet influence. The Schuman Declaration seemed to offer a solution by fulfilling the interests of all participants. The Americans wanted more economic integration between France and Germany. France needed access to German coal. Adenauer by all accounts immediately saw the Schuman Plan as the best chance Western Germany was likely to get to rejoin Europe. In the immediate aftermath of Schuman's declaration, elites on both sides of

---

46 Schuman, R., "Declaration of 9 May 1950," EUROPA, 17 December 2010, http://europa.eu/abc/symbols/9-may/decl_en.htm, accessed 15 December 2010.

47 EUROPA, "Treaty Establishing the European Coal and Steel Community," *Summaries of European Legislation* 2nd September 2009, http://europa.eu/legislation_summaries/institutional_affairs/treaties/treaties_ecsc_en.htm, accessed 1 December 2010.

48 Report "Meeting of United States Ambassadors at Rome, March 22-24, 1950," 24 March 1950, *Foreign Relations of the United States*, Vol. 3, Department of State, Washington, D.C., Government Printing Office, 1950, pp. 796-824.

the Atlantic were incredibly optimistic about the prospects of the project, and the Europeans certainly enthusiastically embraced it, at least early on. The initial negotiation period in mid-1950 required little input from the Americans, though two men from the State Department, Robert Bowie and William Tomlinson, seemed to have been a constant presence at the Europeans' negotiations.[49] That being said, the Americans exerted a huge influence over this European plan since its inception; Schuman came out with his declaration after much urging from the US that France devise a plan that would bring Western Germany back into the fold. More significantly, negotiations among the Europeans stalled in late 1950, and it was the High Commissioner to Germany, John McCloy, who finally broke the deadlock and allowed the Europeans to produce the Treaty of Paris.[50] President Truman welcomed the Declaration as "opening a new outlook for Europe" but took no ownership of the project, preferring to suggest that it was a wholly European invention.[51] Truman's statement reflects this in the subdued, unemotional language that it uses – in contrast to the Marshall Plan, which was accompanied by much visionary language. The ECSC seemed to be a genuinely European project, and so the Americans were keen to avoid being seen as its underwriters. A genuinely European project was thought to have more chance of success. In considering the influence of the structural functionalists, the idea of the US now dealing with the Community on matters of coal and steel is particularly interesting; it can be read as straightforward political support, but may also reflect something of that structural functionalist belief that economic institutions will lead to a change in the social systems of Europe.

Conclusion

It is of course possible to come back at the language and public statements quoted above and suggest that they are not evidence of a structural functionalist influence, but are rather the rhetoric and pronunciations of politicians who tend towards overblown speechifying when they are seeking to justify spending billions of taxpayer dollars overseas. Yet such pronunciations do point the researcher towards the kind of philosophies and beliefs that fuel foreign policy; and they help us in an attempt to reconstruct precisely why particular decisions are made, and what the intended outcome might have been. They help us to understand the image of Western Europe the Americans had, and, the concept of their own role.

49 Lovett, A. W., "The United States and the Schuman Plan: A Study in French Diplomacy 1950-1952," *The Historical Journal*, Vol. 39, No. 2, 1996, pp. 425-455, p. 449.

50 Lovett provides a detailed recount of this involvement in *Ibid.*, pp. 425-455.

51 "Official Statement by Harry Truman" ENA (18 May 1950), 13 August 2009, http://www.ena.lu/, accessed 7 December 2010.

This is where an understanding of the Parsonian structural functionalism can fill a gap by providing an insight into the vision of the Europe that underpinned the American policies in the post-war world.

But academic investigations of this nature must also guard against the temptation to identify a single reason that the institutions of European integration emerged as they did. Post-war European cooperation, and the visions of what it could achieve, emerged from a truly transatlantic network, which included American academics, American policymakers, and European policymakers; but also included the business communities, philanthropic organisations, and cultural practitioners (artists, writers etc.) on both sides of the ocean. This chapter has looked at one part of this network and suggested ways in which its influence was felt in Europe and America, and suggested that a greater understanding of the influences of the American social sciences might challenge the way the EU understands its origins today. It does not argue that these social scientists "created" Europe, or European cooperation; merely that they were one voice among many who, at the end of the Second World War, saw the possibility for a peaceful and free Europe, and did everything they could to use their own specialities to make that reality.

The US Perception of EC Enlargement

Cold War Constraints and Empire-building, 1962-73

Max GUDERZO

CIMA – University of Florence

Enlightened Self-Interest

In May 2005, Javier Solana, High Representative for the Common Foreign and Security Policy (CFSP) of the EU, remarked:

> Foreign and security policy was not part of the original package. Quite the contrary. The European Community had adopted a posture of self-denial in matters of security and diplomacy. These were the preserve of NATO and the transatlantic link. Of course, the 1950s and 1960s were not short of bold initiatives, such as the Pleven Plan or the Fouchet Plan. All were brave attempts. All sank without trace.[1]

The European Defence Community (EDC) Treaty, promoted by the Pleven Plan and signed on 27 May 1952, contained the important Article 38, calling for durable engagements that might grant the new Community a strong – possibly proto-federal – institutional structure.[2] This perspective was in line with what had just been achieved on the supranational level by France, the Federal Republic of Germany, Italy and the Benelux countries with the creation of the European Coal and Steel Community (ECSC), an outcome that was even more important

---

1 Speech by Javier Solana, EU High Representative for the CFSP, Man of the Year 2005 Award, Gazeta Wyborcza, Warsaw, 11 May 2005, p. 2, www.consilium.europa.eu/uedocs/cms_data/docs/pressdata/en/discours/84823.pdf. For an overall analysis see Kramer, E., *Europäisches oder atlantisches Europa? Kontinuität und Wandel in den Verhandlungen über eine politische Union, 1958-1970*, Baden-Baden, Nomos, 2003.

2 See the pioneering books by Preda, D., *Storia di una speranza. La battaglia per la CED e la Federazione europea*, Milano, Jaca Book, 1990; *Idem*, *Sulla soglia dell'Unione. La vicenda della Comunità Politica Europea*, Milano, Jaca Book, 1993, esp. pp. 53-54. For more recent contributions, see, for example, Dumoulin, M. (ed.), *La Communauté européenne de défense, leçons pour demain?*, Bruxelles, PIE-Peter Lang, 2000.

from the political, rather than just the economic or technical point of view. Narrow-minded politicians and national economic establishments could confine their appreciation or neglect of the ECSC to the latter aspects. Jean Monnet and the strong network of his American friends and institutional supporters[3] knew, on the contrary, that a great step forward had been taken. This advance was, at once, of political significance and of importance in the decision-making process. The High Authority of the Community had been given the powers of a supranational executive body with a freedom to operate that has not been surpassed in the ensuing six decades. For the first time, this power went beyond the juxtaposition of national interests on two key European economic matters. Dealing with the control of coal and steel was dealing with an aspect of European history – the access to, and the use of, resources – that had meant, and could still mean, war or peace. A supranational approach to the multiple and complex issues involved by that control meant trying to overcome once and for all the problem of rivalry for the paramount position in Europe.[4] It meant transforming the border between Germany and France, which had cost so much European blood, into a regional, "domestic" border within a widened, supranational concept of economic security. And this implied a new dimension of "European" foreign policy that the US gradually came to support in the dual perspective, or even expectation, of enlargement and deepening of the Community "experiment".

The EDC, therefore, was the logical consequence of that conceptual extension. It was the result of an immediate need – controlling the rearmament of the Federal Republic of Germany – and a long-term objective – creating a European army that could block any old or new temptation of national militarism and work for the supranational defence of the West and its values. It was no surprise that the US, after

3 On Monnet and the American Europeanists, see Duchêne, F., *Jean Monnet. The First Statesman of Interdependence*, New York-London, Norton, 1994, esp. pp. 330 ff.; Hackett, C. P. (ed.), *Monnet and the Americans. The Father of a United Europe and His U.S. Supporters*, Washington, D.C., Jean Monnet Council, 1995; DiLeo, D. L., "George Ball and the Europeanists in the State Department, 1961-1963," in D. Brinkley, and R. T. Griffiths (eds.), *John F. Kennedy and Europe*, Baton Rouge, Louisiana State Univ. Press, 1999, pp. 263-280; Wells, S. B., *Jean Monnet. Unconventional Statesman*, Boulder (Col.), Lynne Rienner, 2011, esp. pp. 127-184. On the ECSC, see also Poidevin, R., "La Haute Autorité de la CECA et les Etats-Unis (1950-1967)," in G. Müller (ed.), *Deutschland und der Westen. Internationale Beziehungen im 20. Jahrhundert. Festschrift für Klaus Schwabe zum 65. Geburtstag*, Stuttgart, Steiner, 1998, pp. 262-269.

4 See the enlightening pages by Dehio, L., *Gleichgewicht oder Hegemonie*, Krefeld, Scherpe, 1948 (English translation: New York, Knopf, 1962).

some hesitation at the very beginning, sponsored the idea.[5] But the EDC had its enemies, too. Given the cold war backdrop, the Soviet Union was obviously against, which meant that political parties and societal movements that were inspired by Moscow in Western Europe did not like it either. Equally, those forces in the West that did not accept the very concept of a supranational level of politics, such as the Gaullists in France, were ready to fight to bring it down. Exceptional circumstances – the apex of the cold war – allowed the treaty to be signed. More normal circumstances, when Stalin died and détente signals came from the East, killed it in August 1954.

The failure of the EDC seemed to block the whole integration mechanism for a while. Less than three years later, however, the Rome treaties were signed in March 1957, giving birth to two new Communities, one devoted to coordinate the research programmes of the Six for the peaceful use of nuclear energy (the European Atomic Energy Community, or Euratom) and the other to create a general common market (the European Economic Community, or EEC). When the treaties entered into force in January 1958, it seemed that a new critical step from integration to construction had been made, paving the way to increasing forms of institutionalisation of the supranational pattern chosen by the six member states. The executive power of the EEC Commission, representing the common interest and thereby the innovative core of that Community (immediately perceived as the most important of the three, including the ECSC), was limited by the Council of Ministers, made up of representatives of the six governments and vested with decision-making powers. But the objectives and the ambitious scope of the new Community seemed to make the general framework satisfactory, with specific reference to the fact that important decisions, after a transitory period, would have to be taken by majority instead of unanimity rule. Security and foreign policies obviously were not – deliberately, after the EDC experience – the main focus of the EEC treaty, but the articles concerning the association of other states and territories had foreign policy implications, and it was clear to everybody that building a European common market had political and security, not just economic, implications. Furthermore, the basic idea of an open Community implied the concepts of enlargement and an extension of activity into the area of foreign relations.

The strong interest of the US in this wide-ranging political dimension of European integration and Washington's support for the enlargement drive of a new European "foreign policy" that would rapidly include

5 See, for example, Lundestad, G., *The United States and Western Europe since 1945. From "Empire" by Invitation to Transatlantic Drift*, Oxford and New York, Oxford University Press, 2003.

also the British partners was clearly stated by President Kennedy in his Philadelphia speech on 4 July 1962:

> The nations of Western Europe, long divided by feuds far more bitter than any which existed among the 13 colonies, are today joining together, seeking, as our forefathers sought, to find freedom in diversity and in unity, strength. The United States looks on this vast new enterprise with hope and admiration. We do not regard a strong and united Europe as a rival but as a partner. To aid its progress has been the basic object of our foreign policy for 17 years. We believe that a united Europe will be capable of playing a greater role in the common defense, of responding more generously to the needs of poorer nations, of joining with the United States and others in lowering trade barriers, resolving problems of commerce, commodities, and currency, and developing coordinated policies in all economic, political, and diplomatic areas. We see in such a Europe a partner with whom we can deal on a basis of full equality in all the great and burdensome tasks of building and defending a community of free nations.

Kennedy specified that the US was "ready for a Declaration of Interdependence" and "prepared to discuss with a united Europe the ways and means of forming a concrete Atlantic partnership, a mutually beneficial partnership between the new union" taking shape in Europe and the "old American Union". This partnership – added the President – was to constitute "a nucleus for the eventual union of all free men".[6]

Taking up John Kennedy's legacy, Lyndon Johnson and his collaborators regularly proposed integration as a key goal to European partners. Both in public and private meetings the members of the administration did not conceal, unless for tactical reasons, their support for European progress towards unification and the enlargement of the EEC. From time to time, often unintentionally, they confused the game, confusing distinct concepts such as integration and institutional construction, unity and unification, community, confederation and federation. But most American policy-makers were convinced that Europe's future, after the Second World War, should emerge from the sum of its enormous energies, which, in turn, had to be tightly linked to a transatlantic common management of the Western bloc.[7]

---

6 *Public Papers of the Presidents of the United States* (hereafter, PPP), *John F. Kennedy, 1962*, pp. 537-539. See also Winand, P., *Eisenhower, Kennedy, and the United States of Europe*, New York, St. Martin's Press, 1993; Brinkley, D. and Griffiths, R. (eds.), *John F. Kennedy and Europe*, *op. cit.*; Devuyst, Y., "Is Washington Ready for the 'Equal Partnership'? Kennedy's Legacy for Transatlantic Relations," *Studia Diplomatica*, Vol. 61, No. 3, 2008, pp. 91-109, and quoted literature.

7 See Winand, P., "American Attitudes toward European Unity from the Rome Treaties to the Kennedy Administration," in É. Remacle, and P. Winand (eds.), *America, Europe, Africa / L'Amérique, l'Europe, L'Afrique / 1945-1973*, Bruxelles, P.I.E.- Peter Lang,

It was taken for granted that the US was the leader of the bloc and the American offer had to be interpreted in terms of enlightened self-interest. It was no accident that Charles Bohlen once used exactly this expression to describe US support for European unification:

> It was largely because we wished to find an approximately equal partner in Western Europe which would contain all the necessary impersonal ingredients which could look forward to a partnership that we have consistently favored European unification. A unified Western Europe would be sufficiently near equality in population, resources and economic power to afford a solid basis for a continuing relationship between the United States on the one hand and a unified Europe on the other. It is obvious, and has always been obvious to us, that the process of unification will take a very long time, but for reasons of our enlightened self-interest [it] is what we support and will continue to support and the only method whereby the interdependence and association of the United States and Western Europe can be put on a solid foundation.[8]

The proposed objective was common responsibility and participation in the organisation of the "Free World", as Kennedy had proposed in Philadelphia and again, during his European tour, at the Paulskirche in Frankfurt, on 24 June 1963. It was also clear, however, that US national interest had the priority and was, within the trammels of US national interest, intertwined with European integration and with the enlargement of the European Communities. Nonetheless, in the background, an inclination to consider a single European pole the best junior partner to lead a hegemonic power system based on respect for complexity and diversity still prevailed in Washington from 1963 to 1968.

In those years, especially in 1966-67, the American perception of transatlantic relations was particularly influenced by the new British bid to enter the European Community, since this could stimulate the confluence of the two main streams of European policy the US had developed

---

2009, pp. 115-144; "L'administration Johnson, l'intégration européenne et les relations transatlantiques," *ibid.*, pp. 144-164; "L'administration Johnson, les Communautés européennes et le Partenariat atlantique," *Relations Internationales*, No. 119, 2004, pp. 381-398. See also Guderzo, M., "Johnson and European Integration: A Missed Chance for Transatlantic Power," *Cold War History*, Vol. 4, No. 2, 2004, pp. 89-114; *Idem*, "Gli Stati Uniti e il primo allargamento della Comunità Europea," in A. Landuyt and D. Pasquinucci (eds.), *Gli allargamenti della CEE/UE, 1961-2004*, Bologna, Il Mulino, 2005, Vol. 2, pp. 1129-1160; Winand, P., "Le réseau Monnet et le premier processus d'élargissement des Communautés européennes: vers l'adhésion de la Grande-Bretagne," *ibid.*, Vol. 1, pp. 181-205.

8 Lyndon B. Johnson Presidential Library, Austin, Tex. (hereafter, LBJL), National Security File (NSF), Files of McGeorge Bundy, Box 16, Correspondence with Ambassadors, No. 2n, Bohlen to Bundy, 12 June 1963. On the concept roots see, among other classic readings, Tocqueville, A. de, *Democracy in America*, New York, Vintage Books, 1990.

to contain the Soviet threat during the previous twenty years. The British Government was trying to get closer to the continent, but did not wish to completely lose its function and ambitions of global co-responsibility; and the EC, having survived the empty-chair crisis in 1965, seemed to be working again in a satisfactory way. Important sectors of the Johnson administration, however, had serious doubts about the future. On 3 May 1967, for instance, in a meeting of the National Security Council devoted to European issues, Secretary of the Treasury Henry Fowler wondered whether the US should really support a further strengthening of the EEC through enlargement and technological progress. If the administration still wished to encourage European integration, he declared, Washington should probably require clear evidence of "maturity" from the Six. According to Fowler, they had at least to commit themselves to a more equitable sharing of the foreign exchange costs of common defence. In short, the Atlantic political and military partnership should be enriched with a full-scale financial dimension.[9]

From a very different perspective, five days later, the American Ambassador to the UK, David Bruce, reported to the Department of State that he had talked with Monnet, fully convinced that the British initiative marked "a famous moment in European history". Bruce, too, strongly supported the idea that the US, "far from being injured by the existence of a cohesive and united Europe", would derive "massive and fortunate benefits from it". Since the Anglo-American special relationship had become "little more than sentimental terminology", the UK entry into the European Community would only strengthen American relations with it and its new partners.[10] This favourable approach to the matter still mirrored general opinion at the Department of State, even if prudence was the priority for Secretary Dean Rusk and the main officials dealing with European affairs.

When de Gaulle officially stated French opposition to the British application for membership in the Community, on 27 November 1967, the British asked for direct American help. On 12 December, in Brussels, UK Foreign Secretary George Brown told Rusk that France would prove

9 *Foreign Relations of the United States. Diplomatic Papers* (hereafter, FRUS), *1964-68*, Vol. 13, doc. 251, *Summary Notes of the 569th Meeting of the NSC*, Smith, 3 May 1967, top secret, sensitive, for the President only. See also LBJL, NSF, National Security Council Meetings File (NSCMF), Box 2, Vol. 4, tab 51, No. 7.

10 LBJL, NSF, Country File (CF), UK, Box 211, Vol. 11 (memos), Nos. 93-93a, Rostow to Johnson, 8 May 1967, secret, and encl. tel. 9217, Bruce to Rusk, London 8 May 1967, secret, copy. On the special relationship, see, among others, Danchev, A., "Special Pleading," in K. Burk and M. Stokes (eds.), *The United States and the European Alliance since 1945*, Oxford-New York, Berg, 1999, pp. 271-288. On Monnet's action in the 1960s and 1970s, see Wells, S., *Jean Monnet*, *op. cit.*, pp. 221-241.

susceptible to combined pressure from its five EC partners. Brown asked him to support this line in his bilateral conversations with the EC member states. Rusk, however, thought that old errors should "not be repeated again" and declared that it would be much better to let time keep playing in Britain's hands, having the FRG, Italy, and the Benelux countries choose whatever course they deemed best.[11] Thus, the British manoeuvre culminated in an explicit request for US help, but the Americans preferred to maintain their non-interventionist position, not to make the situation worse, calculating that little worked better than nothing, as their reaction to the Luxembourg Compromise in 1966 had shown.

Realpolitik

The United States did not neglect Europe in the Johnson years, but a clear analysis of European developments gradually fostered doubts in important sectors of the administration about the wisdom of supporting its allies' policies, for higher strategic reasons, even when they could directly damage the national interest of the US. European integration and institutional construction, as well as the enlargement of the EEC to include Britain, Ireland and Denmark, were among those policies. When Nixon entered the White House, US foreign policy soon went through a period of change and general reassessment, also because of those doubts. This change, therefore, was not exceptional or unforeseeable, but logically linked to the perception of European developments and choices in the 1960s. The American attitude towards Western Europe, strongly influenced by the new President and his National Security Adviser, Henry Kissinger, gradually implemented the consequences of the disillusionment *vis-à-vis* the hypotheses of effective co-responsibility and common management of global affairs which had clearly emerged in the NSC meeting held in May 1967. During the period 1969-72, for instance, Washington grew suspicious of EC initiatives in the association policy developed with post-colonial Africa under the second Yaoundé Agreement. That policy, according to the American view, might become an impediment to the full implementation of US global interests in the trade and financial sectors.

Although important initiatives were taken to improve relations with the allies in Western Europe, troubles soon emerged. As noted in a report

[11] FRUS, *1964-68*, Vol. 13, doc. 280, tel. 1011, Rusk to Department of State (DS), Bruxelles 13 December 1967, secret. On the possibility of an American intervention, see LBJL, NSF, CF, UK, Box 211, Vol. 12 (memos), No. 147, memo of conversation (D. Rusk, *et al.*; [censored names]), Cheslaw, 9 December 1967, secret; and, above all, No. 148, memo of conversation (D. Rusk, *et al.*; [censored names]), Cheslaw, 6 December 1967, secret. In the latter document, in particular, Rusk remarked that creating a structure of bilateral talks on France might prove quite dangerous.

prepared by the Central Intelligence Agency in collaboration with the National Security Agency and the intelligence sections of the State and Defence Departments on 4 December 1969, the prosperity achieved by the six EC members thanks to economic integration had weakened the momentum towards new forms of cooperation in the political sector, notwithstanding the enlargement perspectives.

> Despite [...] economic achievements, confidence in the future of the Community as a political entity is at a low ebb. [...] One of the most pressing problems the Community faces concerns the entry of new members. [...] The UK would contribute significantly to the economic resources, military strength, and political influence necessary to make the EC at least potentially equivalent in power to the US. [...] But for a long time to come this Community is likely to resemble the confederation de Gaulle had in mind more than the supranational government envisaged by Monnet. [...] Enlarged or not, the EC will be no more than an economic union for some years to come, with its members pursuing foreign policies based largely upon national interest.[12]

Because of "Europe's greater economic strength and independence, its reduced sense of danger" and other issues, according to the report, "the US probably will find it increasingly troublesome to satisfy its allies and speak for the West on issues affecting European interests: an era of tougher negotiation and greater compromise *within* the Alliance probably has begun".

In fact, the following years would see the development of the New Economic Policy, destined to mark the kind of "tougher negotiation" the report had foreseen in 1969. A White House secret memorandum submitted to Kissinger on 14 January 1970 implicitly referred to the enlargement issue, highlighting that:

> [t]he issue of how Europe will be organized politically and economically, although subject to our influence, is largely beyond our power to decide. Indeed, earlier efforts to exert a major influence led to unforeseen and disastrous results. An active US role would probably bring the same results again. Whatever we decide we cannot force the French to go against what they see as their own vital interests. On the other hand, it can be argued that the pure Gaullist vision of Europe is receding. The main tendency among Europeans is toward greater collaboration, even if not on the federal model advocated by some. American influence could be decisive, if exerted in the

[12] National Security Archives, Soviet Estimates, microfiche 440, National Intelligence Estimate No. 20-1–69, *Europe, the US, and the USSR*, Director of Central Intelligence, 4 December 1969, secret. See also Guasconi, M. E., *L'Europa tra continuità e cambiamento. Il vertice dell'Aja del 1969 e il rilancio della costruzione europea*, Firenze, Polistampa, 2004; Poggiolini, H., *Alle origini dell'Europa allargata. La Gran Bretagna e l'adesione alla CEE (1972-1973)*, Pavia, Unicopli, 2004; Guderzo, M., "Gli Stati Uniti e il primo allargamento," *op. cit.*, pp. 1150-1160.

> right way at the right moment. In any case, a clear-cut American position is necessary, lest it be assumed that in fact we oppose European unity for narrow national motives.[13]

As for the British accession to the Common Market, the report remarked that US support "was on political rather than economic grounds; indeed, the US must anticipate some economic discrimination from an enhanced Common Market". The issue thus was: "Should we make the expansion of the EEC the objective of our foreign policy? If so, should we attempt to influence the outcome in such a way as to serve broader objectives of promoting political cohesion among the EEC members?" Three possible American policy options were open: (a) low posture, "taking the position that the composition and terms of the EEC relationship were entirely up to the Europeans but expressing beneficent approval of any move toward European unity that the European might undertake"; (b) active support of UK accession, "taking the position that we are interested in it as a condition for getting on with the construction of a European grouping to which we can devolve some of our responsibility for defence, and indicating that we would be prepared to make economic concessions in terms of our special interests in order to promote this construction"; and (c) free-trade statement of position "we refrain from expressing any view of the outcome of the UK accession issue but discreetly make it clear that our special interests and our general interest in free trade would compel us to oppose European preferential tariffs either by retaliation or proposing another Kennedy Round or both".[14]

The report – prepared by Helmut Sonnenfeldt, member of the National Security Council Operations Staff for Europe, incorporating the short notes that Kissinger had added to a first draft – discussed the three options, underlining from the very beginning the paramountcy of political considerations:

> The main arguments against our support of the UK entry are that we will suffer economically from the expansion of the EEC and that in the end the organization will become diluted so that no major political benefits will accrue [...] However, to improve the chances that a more cohesive Europe will be the end result, we might want to oppose association of other states with the EEC, especially neutrals, which could lead to little more than a customs union. [...] We also might want to soften any economic demands we intend to raise, until the outcome of the British entry is clearer.

13 National Archives, College Park, Maryland (hereafter, NA), Nixon Presidential Materials Staff (NPMS), National Security Council Files (NSCF), Country Files (CO) Europe, Box 667, Europe General, memo, *A Review of United States Policy Toward Europe*, Sonnenfeldt to Kissinger, 14 January 1970, secret.

14 *Ibid.*

> In any case, if the administration were to decide to support British entry, it would be important to obtain a firm commitment from the UK government that they would not back out, especially if we intend to attempt to influence the French decision on the terms of entry. Further, we might want to indicate to the British the potentially dangerous consequences of trying to play the Germans against the French on this issue. Indeed, one of our main aims may be to prevent the development of new alignments between the British and the Germans versus the French.[15]

The conclusion of the section devoted to the enlargement of the EEC mentioned the fact that

> [...] if a high value were placed on moving toward an enhanced Western Europe, as opposed to simply making the present relationship more acceptable psychologically, this would logically dictate subordinating the protection of American economic interests to an overriding interest in promoting the economic and political foundation of a European defense community.[16]

But this more "political" point of view would not prevail at the White House during the following years.

In October 1970, the foreign ministers of the Six approved the Davignon Report, which aimed to achieve progress towards the political unification of Europe. The text emphasised a direct link between this goal and cooperation in the field of foreign policy, focusing on two main objectives: "(a) to ensure greater mutual understanding with respect to the major issues of international politics, by exchanging information and consulting regularly; and, (b) to increase their solidarity by working for a harmonization of views, concertation of attitudes and joint action when it appears feasible and desirable".[17] The report triggered a lively debate at the highest levels of the European Commission[18] and within the political commission of the European Parliament.[19]

---

15 *Ibid.*

16 *Ibid.*

17 "Davignon Report" (Luxembourg, 27 October 1970), Bulletin of the European Communities, November 1970, No. 11, pp. 9-14. See the "Étienne Davignon Interview," 11 December 2007 and 14 January 2008, www.ena.lu, esp. the three sections devoted to the report.

18 See, for example, Historical Archives of the European Union (hereafter, HAEU), Fonds Franco Maria Malfatti (FMM), 37, *Communication du Président Malfatti concernant les implications sur le fonctionnement de la communauté de la coopération en matière d'union politique*; Projet de note établie par Albonetti au nom de Spinelli portant sur la construction progressive d'une Communauté politique européenne. See also Fonds Emile Noël (EN), 386, 387, 388.

19 HAEU, Fonds Klaus Meyer (KM), 26, *Compte-rendu de la réunion de la Commission politique du Parlement européen du 24-25 septembre 1970*, Bruxelles.

A few months later, in March 1971, writing to Peter Peterson – Assistant to the President for International Economic Affairs and Executive Director of the Council for International Economic Policy (CIEP) – Secretary of the Treasury John Connally singled out the key issue of the new American globalism: according to the Nixon Doctrine, other countries had to take up their own share of responsibilities. The problem was how to reach this goal without paving the way to an international clash. The US, therefore, should aim (a) to transform the EC in a really outward-looking partner, i.e. ready to adopt economic and trade policies coherent with US needs, and (b) to foster initiatives effectively supporting that objective, fundamental for the future of the world economic community.[20] This attitude prepared the decisions taken by the US in the summer, which dismantled the Bretton Woods system and fostered growing distrust among the European partners *vis-à-vis* the American partners.[21] The transatlantic gap would become even deeper when Kissinger, in April 1973, proclaimed the so-called "Year of Europe".[22]

Against such a controversial backdrop, the issue of EC enlargement, with particular reference to the UK, remained nonetheless associated on the American agenda with an attitude of benign encouragement, since Washington thought that, even in the case of a change of the American attitude towards Western Europe – as emerged after the 1971 decisions – Britain's accession to the EC would strengthen the outward-looking inclinations of the new enlarged Community. This theme, marking the paramountcy of economic worries for the definition of a political comprehensive attitude towards the perspectives of the enlargement, had emerged very clearly during the UK-EC negotiations and again, during a meeting of President Nixon and Prime Minister Edward Heath, in January

20 Declassified Documents Research System, 1999, 373, memo, *CIEP Study Memorandum No. 1, March 8, 1971*, Connally to Peterson, 29 March 1971, confidential. See also NA, NPMS, White House Special Files (WHSF), Subject Files (SF), Confidential Files (CF), 1969-74, Oversize Attachments (OA) 121, Box 7, memo, Peterson to Rogers *et al.*, 30 June 1971, confidential, and encl. memo, *The United States in the Changing World Economy*, Peterson, April 1971, confidential draft.

21 NA, Record Group (RG) 59, General Records of the Department of State (GRDS), Subject-Numeric File (SNF), 1970-73, Pol Def, POL EUR-US, Box 2262, memo, *Tensions in U.S. Relations with Europe*, Hillenbrand to Rogers, 15 November 1971, secret. See also FRUS, *1969-76*, Vols. 3-4, also in www.state.gov/r/pa/ho/frus/nixon; Basosi, D., "Il crollo di Bretton Woods tra teoria economica e *Realpolitik*," *Storia delle relazioni internazionali*, Vol. 14, No. 2, 1999.

22 See Winand, P., "Loaded Words and Disputed Meanings. The Year of Europe Speech and its Genesis from an American Perspective," in J. van der Harst (ed.), *Beyond the Customs Union: The European Community's Quest for Deepening, Widening and Completion, 1969-1975*, Bruxelles/Baden-Baden, Bruylant/ Nomos, 2007, pp. 297-315; Bentivoglio, G., *La relazione necessaria. La Gran Bretagna del governo Heath e gli Stati Uniti (1970-1974)*, Milano, FrancoAngeli, 2011, pp. 105-147.

1973.[23] The Office of the Special Representative for Trade Negotiations prepared a memorandum urging Nixon to underline that:

> The US has, and continues to have, support for the European Community's movement toward European enlargement and unity. This support covers those matters necessary for such unity, but not policies which are neither essential for such integration nor for a sound well-functioning world economy. 1) Specific issues illustrating our support are: a) three new European entrants; b) financial and technical assistance to LDCs; c) monetary unity in EC, consistent with the world system; d) generalized preferences; e) internal EC preferences. 2) Specific policies that we do not believe necessary to EC unity or sound policies are: a) reverse preferences; b) purely commercial preferences in non-European association agreements; c) transfer of domestic problems to trading partners, i.e., export subsidies [...]; d) association agreements without taking into account the trade distortions they may cause to third nations.
>
> [...] the US desires to support a more effective and increased US-EC dialogue and consultation on substantive issues for dealing with the totality of our political, security and economic relationships in all their interrelated aspects.[24]

As for the issue "Support of EC integration", the report stated that "the firmness of US support for European integration can hardly be subject to the question. Issues arise, however, over the interpretation the US gives to that support and how the US reconciles it with other guiding principles of US foreign policy".[25]

As Secretary of State Rogers had told EC Commission President Sicco Mansholt on 6 December 1972: "We recognize that the US and the EC are competitive in many areas but we welcome this competition". The objective was reconciling US support for European integration with the American desire that integration should take into due account US economic interests and the burden-sharing pattern in world responsibilities.

On the specific issue of enlargement and the examination by the GATT Contracting Parties of the treaty providing for the accession to the EC of Denmark, Ireland, and the UK, the report defined Washington's point of view as follows:

> The world trading system needs the assurance that the fundamental changes resulting from UK accession to the EC are being cooperatively examined and considered by the world community. Actions impeding an informed

23 See Bentivoglio, G., La relazione necessaria, *op. cit.*, pp. 110-111.

24 NA, NPMS, WHSF, SF, CF, CO 160 UK (1971-74), Box 9, memo, *Economic Issues for President Nixon and Prime Minister Heath*, Eberle to Flanigan, 18 January 1973, confidential.

25 *Ibid.*

examination do violence to the need for a broad and fair study of effects of enlargement.[26]

These were important difficulties that had been partly foreseen by the "European Policy Paper" prepared by Sonnenfeldt for Kissinger in 1970. Specific problems in the economic and trade dimension of transatlantic relations, as well as in the political and security realms, would continue to worry the Nixon and Ford administrations along the policy framework described in the quoted documents. On 23 July 1973, three weeks after the beginning of the Helsinki Conference on Security and Cooperation in Europe (CSCE), the foreign ministers of the Nine officially approved the second report on European political cooperation on foreign policy, the Copenhagen Report. Great expectations were raised by the ambitious concept of the document:

> Europe now needs to establish its position in the world as a distinct entity, especially in international negotiations which are likely to have a decisive influence on the international equilibrium and on the future of the European Community. In the light of this it is essential that, in the spirit of the conclusions of the [1972] Paris Summit Conference, co-operation among the Nine on foreign policy should be such as to enable Europe to make an original contribution to the international equilibrium. Europe has the will to do this, in accordance with its traditionally outward-looking mission and its interest in progress, peace and co-operation. It will do so, loyal to its traditional friends and to the alliances of its Member States, in the spirit of good neighbourliness which must exist between all the countries of Europe both to the east and the west, and responding to the expectations of all the developing countries.[27]

Four months later, after the Yom Kippur war, the Nine tried a first exercise by adopting a common declaration that called for a peaceful solution in the Middle East, on 6 November 1973.[28] In the following years, the intergovernmental nature of their cooperation would help the EC member states to effectively coordinate their action not only towards the Arab-Israeli conflict and other problems but especially on pan-European issues

---

26 NA, NPMS, WHSF, SF, CF, CO 160 UK (1971-74), Box 9, memo, *Economic Issues for President Nixon and Prime Minister Heath*, Eberle to Flanigan, 18 January 1973, confidential.

27 "Second Report on European Political Cooperation on Foreign Policy," *Bulletin of the European Communities*, September 1973, No. 9, pp. 14-21. See HAEU, KM-26, Déclaration des chefs d'État et de gouvernement suite à la conférence des 19-21/10/1972 à Paris. 2e rapport sur la Coopération politique européenne en matière de politique étrangère, 23 July 1973; and Meyer's notes, KM-60. See Bentivoglio, G., *La relazione necessaria*, *op. cit.*, pp. 96-103.

28 Bentivoglio, G., *La relazione necessaria*, *op. cit.*, pp. 176-186.

during the CSCE working phase in Geneva, in 1973-75.[29] In Javier Solana's view, speaking at thirty years' remove from these events, European political cooperation was just "an attempt to exert a degree of collective influence on international events. But, if truth be told, our critics had a point: EPC was too reactive, too long on process and too short on substance".[30] A kind of supranational spirit tinged the new mechanism, however. The overall effect was that it appeared "less than supranational, but more than intergovernmental".[31]

American policies towards the European allies had to be adjusted to this slow beginning of a new co-operative pattern on the other side of the Atlantic, gradually opening the way to the CFSP, governed by Title V of the Treaty on the European Union. Specific concepts and initiatives were developed to face the following enlargement waves in the 1980s and 1990s, while Washington also had to develop adequate reactions to the important changes in the international system marked by the renewal of tension from 1979 onwards and, after 1985, by the great détente allowed by Mikhail Gorbachev's new course in the Soviet Union. In many respects, however, the oscillations between worry and encouragement *vis-à-vis* the "foreign policy" and enlargement moves of the European Communities (and later, the EU) mirrored the changing perceptions and attitudes taken by American policymakers in the 1960s and 1970s.

---

29 See Romano, A., *From* Détente *in Europe to European* Détente. *How the West Shaped the Helsinki CSCE*, Bruxelles, P.I.E.-Peter Lang, 2009; also Romano, A., "La Comunità Europea e il blocco sovietico negli anni Settanta," in A. Bitumi, G. D'Ottavio, and G. Laschi (eds.), *La Comunità europea e le relazioni esterne, 1957-1992*, Bologna, Clueb, 2008, pp. 107-131.

30 "Speech by Javier Solana," 11 May 2005, *op. cit.*, p. 2.

31 Wessels, W., "European Political Cooperation: A New Approach to Foreign Policy," in D. Allen, R. Rummel, and W. Wessels (eds.), *European Political Cooperation towards a Foreign Policy for Western Europe*, London, Butterworths, 1982, p. 13; see also Zampoli, D., "Verso una politica estera comune: problemi di coordinamento tra i lavori della Cooperazione Politica e della Comunità negli anni Settanta," in A. Bitumi, G. D'Ottavio and G. Laschi (eds.), *La Comunità europea, op. cit.*, pp. 41-63: 44. See also the abundant literature on the EPC cited in *ibid.*, p. 43, note No. 43.

An Ever Closer Alliance?

Transforming the EU-NATO Partnership

Dr Rémy DAVISON

Monash University

Introduction

Every major regional and multilateral security institution has been forced to reappraise and re-evaluate its approach to terrorism since 9/11. Military alliances, such as the North Atlantic Treaty Organization (NATO), have been compelled to reassess their regional and global security strategies, as asymmetrical threats, rather than conventional conflicts, have emerged as the dominant security concern. September 11 brought a new urgency and dynamism to countering terrorism, exemplified by NATO's Terrorism Defence Concept (2002) and the NATO Response Force (2002). The invocation of Article V of the North Atlantic Treaty following the 9/11 attacks presaged a new debate on NATO's role in the 21st century. By 2001, NATO's downsizing in the wake of the collapse of the Warsaw Pact was already over a decade old. Concomitantly, the 1990s had seen the emergence of new EU initiatives, which appeared ready to replace NATO's functions in the post-Cold War era: the Common Foreign and Security Policy (CFSP); the European Security and Defence Policy (ESDP) and the "Berlin Plus" agreements (1996), which permitted EU forces to utilize NATO assets under the Combined Joint Task Forces (CJTF) agreements. A raft of analyses prophesised the death of NATO, arguing that the alliance would decline due to "Cold War deprivation syndrome" and become a mere talking shop, akin to the Organisation for Security and Co-operation in Europe (OSCE).[1] As recently as 2002, one commentator predicted that Kosovo would be "NATO's first and last war".[2] In short, the majority of analysts assumed that

1 See Van Ham, P., "Security and Culture, or, Why NATO Won't Last," *Security Dialogue*, Vol. 32, No. 4, 2001, pp. 393-406.

2 Hamilton, D. and Garden, T., "Should NATO's new function be counter-terrorism?," *NATO Review*, Summer, 2002, p. 17.

the EU would usurp NATO's political and military roles with an EU rapid reaction force, EU politico-military command structures, and EU defence industries gradually displacing the alliance and reducing Europe's dependence upon the shield of US military power, despite Madeleine Albright's admonition that EU security and defence policies should produce "no duplication, no discrimination and no decoupling".[3]

In the 1990s, and particularly after 9/11, NATO defied its critics and redefined its mission. Washington, in particular, declared that NATO had to move "out of area" or go "out of business". Self-evidently, this shift in focus was driven by the collapse of the USSR and the diminution of the Russian threat. Throughout the Cold War, NATO's traditional strength was two-pronged: hard power and deterrence. As a deterrent force, NATO forces were responsible for the defence of Western Europe and North America; the alliance was not designed to adopt a counter-terrorist role, fight asymmetrical conflicts, or undertake policing missions. Indeed, a number of the most senior former alliance leaders continue to view NATO's role in largely traditional security terms, despite some acknowledgement of the very different challenges posed by asymmetrical warfare, religious fundamentalism and terrorism. In a widely-criticized report, co-authored by five former NATO defence chiefs in 2007,[4] the maintenance of NATO's nuclear first-strike capability was described as an "indispensable instrument", while the report devoted little space to NATO's lack of non-military capabilities, despite recognizing that the alliance needs to develop these. Conversely, analyses of counter-terrorism strategies in Europe increasingly emphasize the growth and development of counter-terrorism (CT) "networks" since 9/11,[5] comprising "vertical" organizations, such as Europol and Eurojust, and "horizontal" institutions, such as the G6.[6] By default, "vertical" institutions, such as NATO, have been compelled to address CT issues in recognition of the need for the alliance to develop beyond its original mission of military deterrence, and in addition to its present role as peace-enforcer and peace-keeper. Structural

---

3 Jenkin (2002) argues that EU policies such as ESDP merely "dilute" NATO and divert political leaders from concentrating upon developing and achieving NATO's common objectives. See Jenkin, B., "The War against Terrorism, The EU's Response, and the Future of NATO," The Heritage Foundation, Lecture #735, 2002, http://www.heritage.org/Research/Europe/HL735.cfm, accessed 15 August 2009.

4 See Naumann, K., Shalikashvili, J., Inge, P., Lanxade, J. and van den Breemen, H., *Towards a Grand Strategy for an Uncertain World: Renewing the Transatlantic Partnership*, Lunteren, The Noaber Foundation, 2007.

5 See Den Boer, M., Hillebrand, C. and Nölke, A., "Legitimacy under Pressure: The European Web of Counter-Terrorism Networks," *Journal of Common Market Studies*, Vol. 46, No. 1, 2008, pp. 101-24; and Yost, D., "NATO's evolving purposes and the next Strategic Concept," *International Affairs*, Vol. 86, No. 2, 2010, pp. 489-522.

6 Comprising France, Germany, Italy, Poland, Spain and the UK.

realists point to the imbalance in military capabilities and power projection between the US and Europe,[7] which has meant the maintenance of American bases and military assets in Europe, even in the absence of a Soviet threat. Realists have traditionally stressed NATO's military dimension, evidenced by its role in Gulf War I, Bosnia, Kosovo, Afghanistan and Libya; conversely, neoliberal institutionalists argue that institutional linkages increasingly provide a governance framework capable of meeting the challenge of CT effectively.[8] The extensive literature that provides a critical comparison of NATO and EU capabilities asserts that NATO remains the most efficacious institutional means of meeting the terrorist threat in emergency situations, given that the EU has no specific mandate to deploy military resources across EU borders, or within member states' territories.[9] Both realists and neoconservatives in the Clinton and Bush II administrations, respectively, tolerated EU attempts to develop a notionally "independent" security and defence policy, combined with a European military force, but both administrations were sceptical about the willingness of the EU to act in an independent or joint capacity when confronted with international crises, as well as its ability to fight terrorists abroad. Moreover, the US has demonstrated little need to draw upon NATO's military assets to fight wars, although these have proven helpful, if not essential, in theatres such as Afghanistan and Libya. Consequently, the US has continued to employ the NATO framework as a "toolbox" around which coalitions may be built for *ad hoc* international security operations, such as Kosovo, Afghanistan and Libya, while simultaneously transforming NATO into a CT military force. Nevertheless, US administrations tend to work more effectively bilaterally with NATO countries with which they have interoperability, and whose force strengths are complementary with those of the US military. Iraq demonstrated the difficulty of building a multilateral consensus within NATO on the need to destroy Iraq's potential as a terrorist threat; thus, Washington has tended to turn to its traditional transatlantic allies (Britain) as well as the "New European" members of NATO.

This chapter provides a brief survey of a number of NATO-centric initiatives that have sought to transform the alliance from a military deterrent force, to a proactive, "global NATO", which now has responsibilities and operations well beyond the "homeland" theatre. The first section provides an overview of NATO's transformation in the 1990s

7 See Mearsheimer, J., *The Tragedy of Great Power Politics*, New York, W.W. Norton, 2000.

8 Hess, M., "The EAPC/PfP as an instrument to combat global terrorism," *The Quarterly Journal*, Vol. 2, No. 3, 2003, pp. 99-108.

9 Keohane, D., "The Absent Friend: EU Foreign Policy and Counter-Terrorism," *Journal of Common Market Studies*, Vol. 46. No. 1, 2008, pp. 125-46.

into an "out-of-area" offensive military force. The second section examines the NATO Military Concept introduced at the Prague Summit. This is followed by a discussion of the key elements of the Terrorism Defence Concept (TDC) and its counter-terrorism components, including the NATO Response Force (NRF). Section four turns to the Euro-Atlantic Partnership Council, which has broadened participation in NATO activities and initiatives by increasingly involving Partnership for Peace (PfP) countries, as well as Mediterranean Dialogue members in a range of NATO programs. Section five continues this discussion with its examination of the Partnership Action Plans on Terrorism (PAP-T). Section six examines the major challenges identified by NATO even before 9/11: counter-proliferation and ensuring Weapons of Mass Destruction (WMD) capabilities do not become available to terrorist organizations; this has formed the centrepiece of a number of the alliance's strategic plans. NATO-EU collaboration and competition is the subject of section seven, followed by a brief discussion of the transatlantic divisions that have placed obstacles in the path of an increased multilateral consensus within NATO. Finally, the concluding section assesses some of the challenges the alliance faces as it undergoes a period of profound transformation.

From the Gulf War to Prague: Out-of-Area Missions

Gulf War I altered perceptions of NATO's utility dramatically. The war against Saddam Hussein amply demonstrated NATO's offensive capabilities in an out-of-area conflict.[10] The Gulf War illustrated that the alliance needed to be ready and willing to respond to conflicts on NATO's periphery. However, it was not until 1995 that NATO belatedly employed its offensive capabilities in the Bosnian war, in the wake of the failure of both the EU and the alliance to take any decisive action following eruption of the conflict in 1991. The air strikes upon Serbian forces in Bosnia and Kosovo, as well as the alliance's subsequent peace-keeping role in the Balkans, transformed its mission from deterrence to out-of-area conflicts.[11] Since 1999, it has undertaken major peace-keeping roles in the

10 As an *institution*, NATO did not have a direct role in the first Gulf War.

11 A strictly legalistic interpretation of NATO Article VI restricted alliance operations to NATO's borders until 1999, although US officials have routinely argued that NATO's defence strategy throughout the Cold War always presupposed an out-of-area role in order to defend alliance territory in the event of a Warsaw Pact offensive. The NAC in 1998-99 determined that the conflict in Yugoslavia was "in area". The 2002 NATO Reykjavik summit conclusively ended debate on the "in-area/out-of-area" issue concerning the alliance's theatres of operation, by determining that the alliance would meet Article V threats, irrespective of their location. See Metreveli, M. (2003), "Legal Aspects of NATO's Involvement in the Out-of-Area Peace Support Operations,"

Balkans, and member countries also participate in logistics, policing, security, training and in-area combat zone missions (the Mediterranean) and out-of-area operations, such as Sudan, Congo, Afghanistan, Iraq and Lebanon. As Richard Lugar argues

> In a world in which terrorist attacks on our countries can be planned in Germany, financed in Asia, and carried out in the United States, old distinctions between "in" and "out of area" become meaningless [...]. If "Article 5" threats to our security can come from beyond Europe, NATO must be able to act beyond Europe to meet them if it is going to fulfil its classic mission today.[12]

The 2002 Prague summit demonstrated the seriousness with which NATO now approached its new role. Prague sought to ensure that the alliance would not only operate out-of-area, but would also possess global force projection capabilities, evidenced by the Afghanistan and Iraq operations. September 11 and the Prague summit revealed the two-pronged strategy the alliance adopted: fighting terrorism abroad via military means; and enhancing its capabilities to prevent and respond to terrorist threats within both NATO's borders, and those of its Partners.

The US objective at Prague was not only to convince Europeans to increase defence spending, but also to invest in new resources to enable the alliance to implement effective CT strategies. Problematically, EU states have already made substantial investments in the Rapid Reaction Force (RRF), and NATO commitments consume resources and slow progress of the EU's own defence capabilities, further widening the "capabilities-expectations" gap, whilst permitting the EU's dependence upon NATO's military and non-military assets to persist. More importantly, Washington viewed the adoption of a comprehensive CT strategy as integral to the alliance's core objectives, particularly as much of the planning for the 9/11 strikes had taken place in al-Qaeda's Hamburg cell. Thus, 9/11 compelled NATO to consider incorporating civil defence into alliance doctrine, and to recognize that defence of a "NATO homeland" was an integral facet of its *raison d'être*. NATO member countries have experienced major terrorist attacks since September 11, including the Istanbul, Madrid, London and Athens bombings. However, a number of potentially serious strikes planned by terrorists in Europe have been thwarted, largely as a result of more rigorous policing and security measures throughout the continent.

NATO-EAPC Research Fellowship 2001-2003, Final Report, Tblisi, http://www.nato.int/acad/fellow/01-03/metreveli.pdf, accessed 20 May 2008.

12 Lugar, R., "Redefining NATO's Mission: WMD Terrorism," *The Washington Quarterly*, Vol. 25, No. 3, 2002, pp. 7-13.

The 2010 NATO Lisbon summit produced the alliance's first Strategic Concept (SC) document since 1999.[13] Although the SC was widely criticised as a tepid statement,[14] it effectively reiterated the Reykjavik doctrine of responding to out-of-area Article V threats under the rubric of crisis management and collective security via international and regional partnerships. This doctrine was tested as early as March 2011, following the UN Security Council's adoption of Resolution 1973, which authorised the protection of civilians in Libya. By lending military assistance to Libyan rebel forces, NATO acted under the rubric of Article 20 of the SC, as the SC does not contain an explicit endorsement of the UN General Assembly's "Responsibility to protect" (R2P) concept. However, a central aspect of the 2010 SC reiterates the counterterrorism strategies articulated at the 2002 Prague Summit, such as Terrorism Defence Concept.[15]

The NATO Military Concept for Defence Against Terrorism

The 2002 Prague summit, which produced the NATO Military Concept (NMC) threat assessment, identified religious extremism, socio-economic and political forces and emerging ideologies as NATO's main challenges. It also argued that although conventional weapons remained the predominant form of terrorist attack, terrorists were also likely to seek to acquire weapons of mass destruction. Furthermore, the NMC viewed states that harboured terrorists as likely to afford individuals and groups considerable resources. This redefinition of NATO's mission to place counter-terrorism operations at the forefront of the organization's agenda was made explicit by one alliance official in 2003: "if it's not terrorism, it's not relevant".[16] US officials also make this point explicit, noting that NATO activities are now virtually all geared towards fighting terrorism.[17] Consequently, NATO's assumption of command of allied operations in Afghanistan in 2003 has been presented not only as a peace support operation (PSO), but also as a CT mission. The NRF is a core component of this CT strategy, in addition to NATO's role in conducting peace support operations.

---

[13] NATO, "Strategic Concept for the Defence and Security of the Members of the North Atlantic Treaty Organisation," press release, 2010, p. 2.

[14] Arms Control Association, "Experts Call NATO Strategic Concept 'Missed Opportunity to Reduce Role of Obsolete Tactical Nukes from Europe'," 19 November 2010.

[15] See NATO, Articles 10-12, 19 and 34.

[16] Quoted in Ellis, B., "'If it's not terrorism, it's not relevant': evaluating NATO's potential to contribute to the campaign against terrorism," *Journal of Military and Strategic Studies*, Vol. 7, No. 1, 2004, p. 3.

[17] Nevers, R., "NATO's international security role in the terrorist era," *International Security*, Vol. 31, No. 4, Spring 2007, p. 37.

The Terrorism Defence Concept

The 9/11 attacks fundamentally altered NATO planners' perspectives upon both out-of-area military missions and PSOs, as well as the alliance's internal security role. As early as 1999, NATO developed its "Strategic Concept", which sought to transform the alliance from a Cold War deterrent to a flexible force designed to combat a multiplicity of security threats. In December 2001, NATO defence ministers sought to develop a "Military Concept" to combat terrorism, defining it as the pre-eminent threat to members' security. This found expression in the 2002 Prague summit, which produced the Terrorism Defence Concept (TDC).[18] The TDC defines its counter-terrorism doctrine as "offensive military capabilities designed to reduce terrorists' capabilities".[19] This "four-pillared" approach comprises (i) anti-terrorism; (ii) consequence management; (iii) counter-terrorism;[20] and, (iv) military cooperation with civilian authorities. Ensuring the implementation of each of these four pillars requires NATO to develop sufficient military capabilities, including rapid force deployment, improved civil-military relations, and effective surveillance and intelligence activities.

NATO's role in CT operations is flexible under the TDC. For example, NATO may undertake missions either in support of an international coalition, or in a secondary role with other NATO or EU member states. These roles have both a military and political dimension. Examples of NATO's military CT role include the deployment of NATO forces to Afghanistan; surveillance and policing in the Mediterranean; and basing and overflight rights (as occurred during the 2003 Iraq war). NATO also provides political support for partners who face potential or actual terrorist threats, exemplified by the invocation of Article V in 2001.

The TDS' CT component specifically advocates the development of "more specialized anti-terrorist forces".[21] The NATO Response Force (NRF) was one of the initiatives that emerged as part of the TDS CT strategy. The NRF is expected to be deployable anywhere in the world within

---

18 NATO Press Release, Prague Summit Declaration, 21 November 2002, http://www.nato.int/docu/pr/2002/p02-127e.htm, accessed 15 August 2009.

19 NATO Issues, "Military Concept for Defence against Terrorism," http://www.nato.int/ims/docu/terrorism.htm, accessed 15 August 2009.

20 See Federal Republic of Germany, *White Paper German Security Policy and the Future of the Bundeswehr*, Berlin, Federal Defence Ministry, 2006, pp. 66-68 and Davison, R., *Foreign Policies of the Great and Emerging Powers*, Frenchs Forest, NSW, Prentice Hall, 2008, p. 193.

21 *NATO Issues*, "Military Concept for Defence against Terrorism," http://www.nato.int/ims/docu/terrorism.htm, accessed 15 August 2009.

7-30 days. The total force strength required is 63,000.[22] One pronounced shift in NATO's post-9/11 CT strategies has been the rapid transformation from defensive to offensive capabilities. This largely correlates with the US *National Security Strategy* (NSS) documents of 2002, 2006 and 2010,[23] together with the US *National Strategy for Combating Terrorism* (2006). The latter identifies four main CT operational areas: preventing rogue states and terrorists from acquiring WMD; preventing terrorists from securing bases in states to use to plan and launch operations; preventing terrorist acts before they occur; and, preventing terrorists from claiming refuge in, or support from, rogue states.[24]

These policies have largely shaped "NATO in the lead" and "NATO in support" policies under the TDC to prevent terrorist attacks being carried out upon the territories of NATO member and Partner countries. The TDC recognizes that the alliance may be compelled to adopt offensive strategies, including out-of-area deployments, in order to implement CT missions effectively. Afghanistan represents one example of the "NATO in the lead" concept, with NATO's assumption of responsibility for ISAF.

The Euro-Atlantic Partnership Council

A number of multilateral institutions and bilateral treaties facilitate CT strategies, including NATO's specialized committees and partnerships, including the Euro-Atlantic Partnership Council (EAPC), the NATO Special Committee and the Partnerships for Peace (PfP), as well as the Club of Berne, Europol's Counter-Terrorism Task Force, the Financial Action Task Force (FATF),[25] the Kilowatt Group and the UKUSA agreement. Under the auspices of the EAPC,[26] NATO adopted a range of measures in response to 9/11, and the subsequent invocation of Article V. In September 2001, 39 EAPC member countries offered disaster relief to the US.[27] NATO has also employed the Mediterranean Dialogue and the

---

22 De Wijk, R., "European Military Reform for a Global Partnership," *The Washington Quarterly*, Vol. 27, No. 1, 2003, p. 207.

23 The 2010 NSS issued by the Obama administration has not rescinded or resiled from these objectives. See *National Security Strategy of the United States*, Washington, D.C., May 2010, http://www.whitehouse.gov/sites/default/files/rss_viewer/national_security_strategy.pdf, accessed 31 May 2010.

24 See *National Strategy for Combating Terrorism*, September 2006, http://georgewbush-whitehouse.archives.gov/nsc/nsct/2006/, accessed 15 February 2007.

25 Davison, R., "'Soft law' regimes and European organizations fight against terrorism and money laundering," in L. T. Holmes (ed.), *Terrorism, Organized Crime and Corruption: Networks and Linkages*, Northampton, MA, Elgar, 2007, pp. 60-85.

26 The EAPC comprises the 28 NATO members, plus 22 Partner countries.

27 See NATO Parliamentary Assembly, 2006 Annual Session, http://www.nato-pa.int/Default.asp?SHORTCUT=995, accessed 15 August 2009.

NATO-Russia Council as vehicles for the expansion of terrorism-related intelligence exchange. Nevertheless, intelligence sharing remains a sensitive issue in both intra-NATO and intra-EU politics. The Echelon program, shared by the US, UK, Canada, Australia and New Zealand, is restricted to the "Anglosphere", which Washington also employs to assist its corporations in commercial competition with EU firms to gain Third World contracts. Neither the US nor Britain share any Echelon material with EU states. In an effort to reduce dependency upon US intelligence sources, France, Italy and Spain employ the Hellios satellite system. Both groups have refused to countenance the establishment of an EU agency, comparable with the CIA, due to a reluctance to engage in EU-wide intelligence sharing.[28] The sensitivity of intelligence means that both Alliance and Partner countries regard the issue as an essentially national matter, and this is one area that has not altered markedly in either the post-Cold War or post-9/11 eras.

Via the EAPC, NATO has also made incremental, but nevertheless significant, steps towards improving cooperation across borders, particularly in the area of humanitarian crisis or disaster assistance, including biological, chemical, radiological or nuclear incidents. The 2004 Istanbul summit approved border security cooperation, and training to improve counter-terrorism capacity building projects. By July 2010, 13 states had ratified the Memorandum of Understanding (MoU) on the facilitation of Vital Civil Cross Border Transport.

In a number of respects, EAPC is a more important forum than the NAC. For example, its membership is wider,[29] incorporating states from Central Asia, such as Pakistan, a territory rife with terrorist activity. The Prague summit adopted the Partnership Action Plan which permits individual action plans (IPAPs) to be structured according to individual national circumstances. For example, the IPAP negotiated with Kazakhstan provides for cooperation in fighting corruption; promoting human rights; supporting democracy; ensuring the supremacy of law, and a number of other areas.[30] Moreover, the *political* context of the EAPC is of particular importance, as it provides the means for cooperation in military and political activities in an area – Central Asia – where Islamist terrorism possesses some of its strongest supporters and significant assets, by incorporating states such as the Kyrghyz Republic, Tajikistan, Turkmenistan

---

[28] Nomikos, J. M., "A European Union Intelligence Service for Confronting Terrorism," *International Journal of Intelligence and Counter-Intelligence*, Vol. 18, No. 2, 2005, p. 192.

[29] Fifty members, including the NATO-28.

[30] McDermott, R. N., "Kazakhstan's partnership with NATO: Strengths, limits and prognosis," *China and Eurasia Forum Quarterly*, Vol. 5, No. 1, 2007, p. 15.

and Uzbekistan into NATO's network of global partnerships.[31] It would not have been possible to launch Operation Enduring Freedom successfully without the cooperation of Russia and Kazakhstan. Similarly, the EAPC makes peace support operations (PSOs) possible, such as ISAF in Afghanistan, which involves non-NATO troops, such as those from Azerbaijan, Jordan and Ukraine. Nevertheless, the EAPC is limited insofar as IPAPs are concerned, leaving much of the content and implementation of the plans to partner countries. One significant weakness is that important regional actors – such as Pakistan – are not members.[32] Moreover, no Middle East state is a signatory to a PfP agreement, despite the region's proximity to NATO's periphery, together with its importance as the world's major source of oil supplies, and its position as a locus of terrorist activity. A much weaker, non-binding Mediterranean Dialogue process has been the main forum for NATO-Middle East consultation since 1994, and Egypt and Jordan, long-time US allies, and the only states in the region maintaining diplomatic relations with Israel, have joined as Middle East participants in the Dialogue process.

The Partnership Action Plan

The EAPC introduced Action Plans for 1998-2000 and 2000-2002. In 2002, at the Prague Summit, all NATO members and 27 Partner countries agreed upon a new two-year Partnership Action Plan on Terrorism (PAP-T), which included: provisions to improve intelligence sharing; intensifying consultations and information sharing; enhancing preparedness to combat terrorism; impeding the support of terrorist groups; enhancing capabilities to contribute to consequence management; assisting partners' efforts against terrorism; and, a long-term program for consultation and cooperation.[33]

The PAP-T sought to integrate new and acceding NATO countries, and, increasingly, Partner countries, including Mediterranean Dialogue countries, into a counter-terrorism framework. Under the PAP-T, the EAPC/PfP Intelligence Liaison Unit (ILU) was established to facilitate information exchanges on potential terrorist threats. To date, the ILU describes intelligence information exchange as "reasonable". ILU activities were restricted initially to PfP countries, but in 2003 they were expanded to

---

31 Davison, R., "Russia and India in the Asia Pacific," in Connors, M., Davison, R. and Dosch, J., *The New Global Politics of the Asia Pacific*, 2nd ed., New York, Routledge, 2011, pp. 90-91.

32 The US has employed its bilateral alliance with Pakistan, rather than NATO, as the basis for joint cooperation in the war on terror.

33 See NATO, "Euro-Atlantic Partnership Council (EAPC) Action Plan 2002-2004," 7 December 2001, http://www.nato.int/docu/pr/2001/p01-165e.htm, accessed 1 November 2011.

include members of the Mediterranean Dialogue. The ILU also incorporates a Terrorist Threat Intelligence Unit, which became operational in 2004. Under the PAP-T, Mediterranean Dialogue countries have been incorporated into the ILU on a case-by-case basis, providing they have signed a NATO Security Agreement. Joint meetings of NATO's Political Committee and the Political-Military Steering Committee on Partnership for Peace (PMSC/PfP) are the main platforms for the implementation of the PAP-T and debates concerning the Action Plan. A major element of the PAP-T is reviewing the Political-Military Framework for NATO-led PfP Operations, and implementing the Operational Capabilities Concept for NATO-led PfP Operations. However, Clarke and McCaffrey argue the PAP-T has not been particularly effective, due partly to the diverse nature of the Partnership countries, and the divergence and complexity of the individual action plans.[34]

Countering Weapons of Mass Destruction

The WMD issue created significant divisions between the North Atlantic allies, particularly France and the US. French foreign minister Hubert Védrine's assessment of the threat capabilities of "rogue states" was that they were "not very serious", and that the threats themselves were "theoretical".[35] French defence plans stressed the importance of Theatre Missile Defence (TMD) utilizing short and medium-range missiles, with French defence budget papers including provision for the development of a TMD system in their spending through and beyond 2005. French policy makers view this as a useful means of defending NATO's southern flank, although TMD does not provide a "shield" capacity in the way the NMD is designed to. President Chirac argued against the concept of NMD, stating that where there was a "struggle between sword and shield, there is no instance in which the shield has won".[36] Rather than pursuing NMD, Chirac persistently called for more active support for non-proliferation efforts, forming what he labelled a "virtuous circle of the non-proliferation of weapons and disarmament" under the CTBT.

Following 9/11, the US cited Iraq, Iran and North Korea as state sponsors of terrorism and potential WMD threats. The Bush II administration

34 Clarke. R. A. and McCaffrey, B. R., "NATO's Role in Confronting International Terrorism," *Atlantic Council Policy Paper*, June 2004, p. viii.

35 Ministry of Foreign Affairs, France, "Entretien du Ministre des Affaires Étrangères. M. Hubert Védrine avec la Revue Trimestrielle Politique Internationale," press release, November 2000.

36 Joint press conference by President Chirac, Prime Minister Blair and Prime Minister Jospin during the Franco-British summit at Cahors, press release, 9 February 2001.

was also widely viewed as damaging WMD non-proliferation efforts by abandoning the ABM Treaty in 2002, which also released Russia from its ABM obligations. The failure of coalition forces to find any operational WMD in Iraq also damaged the credibility of US intelligence assessments of the WMD threat considerably. Nevertheless, even prior to the Iraq invasion, Richard Lugar argued that the US's Cooperative Threat Reduction Program (CTR), introduced in 1991 to assist in the destruction of Soviet-era missiles, required NATO political and military cooperation to address and isolate states that act as sponsors of WMD, or harbour terrorists.[37] Lugar further asserted that the world faced a "vertex of evil – an intersection of WMD and terrorism".

Even prior to 9/11, NATO recognized that WMD proliferation posed a serious threat, not only from state-based, but also non-state-based actors. The 1999 WMD Initiative established a WMD Centre located at NATO headquarters, with a brief to implement an alliance battalion explicitly designed to combat and manage chemical and biological threats. The battalion became operational in 2004. In addition, NATO endorsed the Comprehensive Political Guidance (CPG) of the NAC at the 2006 Riga summit, although this has not introduced any new initiatives beyond those already implemented.

NATO and the EU

NATO members – the majority of which are also EU member states – are extremely unlikely to propose and implement policies that are at significant variance with the formal positions they adopt at the EU level. Consequently, since the early 1990s, despite the EU's development of security and defence policies discrete from NATO's, the reality is that in the realm of counter-terrorism, the EU and NATO have produced a great deal of policy convergence, particularly since 9/11. This has been evidenced by NATO expansion (alliance membership being a virtual precondition for EU membership); EU-NATO logistical cooperation at African Union headquarters; EU Commission funding for aid, administrative and legal activities in Afghanistan; and EU-NATO joint participation in the UN negotiations on the final status of Kosovo.[38] In addition, the NATO Prague Capabilities Commitments (PCC) were explicitly aligned with the objectives of the European Capabilities Action Plan (ECAP), citing mutual reinforcement, role specialisation and additional financial resources a key goals.

---

[37] Lugar, R., "Redefining NATO's Mission: WMD Terrorism," *The Washington Quarterly*, Vol. 25, No. 3, 2002, pp. 10-11.

[38] Keohane, D., "An insecure future for NATO," *E-Sharp*, November-December 2006, pp. 53-55.

NATO, as a military alliance, has few powers to make decisions concerning the implementation of national counter-terrorist initiatives; these powers fall within the purview of the area of freedom, security and justice (AFSJ) of the Lisbon Treaty (Title V), which superseded the intergovernmental Justice and Home Affairs pillar of the Maastricht Treaty. Lisbon (Art. 3(2)) provides for power sharing between the Council, Commission and Parliament in the AFSJ, while the European Court of Justice (EJC) gained new competences over the AFSJ in 2014. However, the emergence of the "Quint",[39] comprising the four largest EU states plus the US, arguably enhances and accelerates transatlantic decision making by circumventing the formal institutional confines and strictures imposed by both the EU and NATO.

EU counter-terrorism initiatives were enhanced considerably by the decision of the British, French, Italian, German and Spanish governments in 2003 to combine their intelligence efforts, with Poland joining the group (the "G6") in 2006. Its initiatives to this point include: Multilateral police support teams to counter terrorist strikes; a common database of suspected terrorist cells and individuals; transborder investigation teams; and, information sharing on weapons or explosives theft.[40]

EU CT action has included the finalisation of the text of an EU arrest warrant, in order to coordinate EU-wide information sharing on suspected terrorists. The development of a European arrest warrant was agreed at the September 2001 EU ministerial meeting. President Chirac called for the rapid establishment of a common judicial area.[41] Proponents of EU integration pointed to this as evidence of the EU's unity of purpose. However, it was quickly clear that nation-states, not the EU, would take the lead in security policy making after September 11. Chirac, Blair and Schröder did not attempt to coordinate their policy responses, despite their three-way meeting at the Ghent European Council on 19 October 2001, which produced a public façade of unity, which was not supported by the triumvirate's subsequent actions.[42]

---

39 See Gegout, C., "The Quint: Acknowledging the existence of a Big Four-US *Directoire* at the heart of the European Union's foreign policy decision-making process," *Journal of Common Market Studies*, Vol. 40, No. 2, 2002, pp. 331-344.

40 Lavenex, S. and Wallace, W., "Justice and Home Affairs: Towards a European Public Order?," in H. Wallace, W. Wallace, and M. Pollack (eds.), *Policy-Making in the European Union*, Oxford, Oxford University Press, 2005, p. 466.

41 Chirac, J., speech to Future of Europe Regional Forum, Montpellier, 4 October 2001.

42 Heibourg, F., "Europe and the Transformation of World Order," *Survival*, Vol. 43, No. 4, Winter 2001/2002, pp. 143-148, 2001, p. 146. It was to be another nine years before the EU established the post of Commissioner for Justice, Fundamental Rights and Citizenship, and divided DG Justice, Liberty and Security into two separate DGs: DG Home and DG Justice. See, Schroeder, U. C., *The Organization of European*

Important differences persist between the US and its European allies over the optimum use of NATO and EU resources. This gulf is particularly apparent in relation to France and the US; Washington argues that NATO provides the most effective means of consequence management, while Paris believes that NATO should remain a military instrument, leaving consequence management to EU agencies.[43] These divisions resurfaced during March 2011; Nicolas Sarkozy argued for a Franco-British command of military operations in Libya, while the US and Turkey pressed for NATO control of the mission. Subsequently, the latter view prevailed, although both Britain and France reserved the right to strike ground targets without being bound by NATO's rules of engagement.[44]

Transatlantic Divisions

Divisions between the transatlantic allies over NATO's counter-terrorism role emerged even as alliance forces entered Afghanistan. France and Germany opposed the transformation of NATO into a counter-terrorism force, believing this would dilute the alliance's military role. Moreover, the UK, Spain and Turkey – which supported US efforts in the Global War on Terrorism (GWOT) – effectively vetoed a US proposal that would have given NATO an explicit role to play in counter-terrorism efforts. Following 9/11, the US and France instead agreed that NATO's Strategic Concept could include counter-terrorism as a "core" component, given domestic and transnational threats to allies' national security.[45]

Problems have also plagued interoperability amongst the NATO and EU allies, particular in relation to the export of US arms technology. These include Congressional blocks on ITAR-waivers, complex and lengthy bureaucratic procedures and compromised outcomes.[46] For example, Italy was unable to secure Air-Sea Rescue flares for the NATO airforce operating during the Kosovo crisis; and the Joint Surveillance and Targeting System (J-STARS), which gives military commanders early warning of enemy movements and cues weapons systems, remains

---

Security Governance, Internal and External Security in Transition, Abington, Oxon; New York, Routledge, 2011, p. 71.

43 Bensahel, N., *Cooperation with Europe, NATO, and the European Union: The Counterterror Coalitions*, Santa Monica, RAND, 2003, p. 52.

44 *Time*, "Libya: NATO Takes Charge, but Will Europe Take the Lead?," 25 March 2011.

45 Bensahel, N., *Cooperation with Europe, NATO, and the European Union: The Counterterror Coalitions*, *op. cit.*, pp. 22-23.

46 Davison, R., "Arm in Arm? The European Security and Defence Policy and the EU Armaments Industry," in A. Arranz, N. Doyle, and P. Winand (eds.), *New Europe, New World?*, Brussels, P.I.E.-Peter Lang, 2010, pp. 191-212.

largely within the control of US commanders. For example, US decision makers may choose to filter or withhold data from NATO allies.[47]

US preventive war and pre-emptive strike doctrines under the Bush II administration ran counter to the European NATO partners' preference for soft power and containment solutions. "National caveats" also place restrictions upon the use of forces in combat operations; for example, the German Bundestag restricts the number, duration and the types of roles carried out by Federal troops; French air force pilots refused some targets in Afghanistan in 2001, on the basis that civilians would be endangered;[48] some countries restricted the use of their troops to daylight hours; France, Germany and Belgium launched an abortive attempt to prevent NATO guaranteeing the defence of Turkey before the 2003 Iraq war in the event of strikes from Baghdad;[49] only one third of NATO's troops in Kosovo in 2004 were available for use in riot control; France blocked the use of the NRF in Lebanon in 2006;[50] and Germany abstained on the UNSC vote to intervene in Libya in 2011. The diplomatic challenge for the US has been to shift the focus of NATO's European members from consequence management and defensive measures, to war-fighting and, possibly, pre-emptive action to counter asymmetrical threats.[51] The acrimonious debate surrounding the Iraq war made it clear that a minority of the European NATO allies were unwilling to countenance such a radical policy shift, a position bolstered by the departure of Spanish and Italian personnel from the Iraq theatre following changes of government. Although subject to a myriad of legal interpretations, Article V does appear to grant the NAC and NATO the right to conduct offensive operations in self-defence, including CT operations. UNSCR 1373/01 also grants the right "to combat by all means, in accordance with the Charter of the United Nations Charter of the United Nations [UNC], threats to international peace and security caused by terrorist acts", providing these are within the ambit

---

47 Bialos, J. and Koehl, S., "The NATO Response Force: facilitating coalition warfare through technology transfer and information sharing," Centre for Transatlantic Relations, National Defence University, Singapore, 2005, pp. 51-2.

48 Davison, R., "French security after 9/11: Franco-American discord," in P. Shearman, and M. Sussex (eds.), *European Security After 9/11*, Brookfield, VT, Ashgate, 2004, p. 75.

49 Only sustained US diplomatic pressure upon Germany and Belgium in the NAC forced them to reverse their stance, leaving the French government isolated on the issue.

50 Archick, K. and Gallis, P., "NATO and the European Union," Washington D.C., Congressional Research Service, 2006, pp. 10-11.

51 Faber outlines a case for NATO undertaking a serious debate to consider the adoption of a preemption doctrine. See Faber, P., "Countering Terrorism – Today and Tomorrow," NATO Defence College paper, 2002.

of Article 51 of the UNC.[52] Nevertheless, a significant number of the European NATO allies believe that "pre-emptive defence" and "preventative war" remain outside the mandate provided by UNSCR 1373/2004,[53] UNC Article 51 and NATO Article V.

Conclusion

NATO has produced a significant number of policy renovations as it has undergone the transformation from a static, defensive alliance to an offensive, counter-terrorism organization. However, it is difficult to gauge how effective these initiatives – such as the PAP-T and the Mediterranean Dialogue – have been in combating threats. Clearly, NATO has a strategic interest in combating terrorism, organized crime, WMD proliferation and smuggling, and it can only address these challenges through cooperation on border security, improving civil-military emergency responses, and resolving out-of-area and NATO-periphery conflicts. The transformation of NATO into an effective CT alliance still has a considerable way to go, but its achievements – such as responsibility for ISAF in Afghanistan – could not have been envisaged during the 1990s. Nevertheless, the US maintains a disproportionate share of the burden for both defence spending and military combat roles in out-of-area operations. In Afghanistan, which has experienced a deteriorating security situation recently, non-NATO countries, such as Australia, have a greater commitment and responsibility for combat operations than many alliance members.[54] If NATO members are serious about implementing effective CT measures outside NATO's "homeland", alliance countries need to contribute more to operations – particularly combat operations – such as ISAF, in financial, military and non-military terms.

In instances where national policy preferences diverge from those of the majority – such as France and Germany's rejection of Georgian and Ukrainian membership of NATO at the 2008 Bucharest NATO summit – new security initiatives are also likely to find obstacles in their path at the EU level. Moreover, there are certain security issues, whether related to countering terrorism or arms control, which have failed to achieve con-

52 Ayliffe mounts a convincing argument that both the UN and NATO grant sufficient legal authority for the alliance to undertake offensive CT measures. See Ayliffe, D., "NATO counterterrorism and Article 5: Hammer of the North Atlantic or paper tiger?," Paper 635, *BePress Legal Series*, University of California, Berkeley, 2005, pp. 40-46.

53 Davison, R., "'Soft law' regimes and European organizations fight against terrorism and money laundering," *op. cit.*, pp. 71-2.

54 Of the 43 countries' personnel present in Afghanistan, 15% of troops were from non-NATO countries.

sensual outcomes at either the NATO or EU levels, including the Iraq war and the lifting of the EU arms embargo on China.[55]

One of the most critical policy areas in which Americans and Europeans disagree relates to combating terrorism within NATO's homeland and abroad. Most of NATO's European allies believe that terrorism should be addressed through traditional crime-fighting procedures, whereas Washington views the development of military doctrines and training as appropriate to countering terrorist threats. With few exceptions, European governments are sceptical about military solutions to the problem of terrorism. The EU, for example, has worked to improve common CT doctrines for border areas, interior ministries and police. However, NATO covers a much larger number of states than the EU; European countries cannot counter terrorist threats effectively acting alone or even via EU regional CT initiatives. Consequently, it appears reasonable to argue that NATO should remain the core mechanism through which alliance countries, PfP members, and the Mediterranean Dialogue countries develop and implement their integrated responses to terrorist threats to both homeland and international security.

[55] Davison, R., "French security after 9/11: Franco-American discord," *op. cit.*, p. 76.

A Two-Way Mirror

Latin-American Perceptions of European Integration

Edward MOXON-BROWNE

University of Limerick

Introduction

It is almost a truism nowadays to describe the EU as a "global actor". The rhetoric of the EU itself certainly makes this assumption; and the role is assumed to carry with it burdens, responsibilities, opportunities and rewards. In the *European Security Strategy* document, for example, published in 2003, it is clearly stated that the EU is "a global actor: it should be ready to share in the responsibility for global security [...] the development of a stronger international society, well functioning international institutions and a rule-based international order".[1] Alongside these security preoccupations, the EU is unquestionably a major economic actor whose commercial interests span the globe, and whose development aid policies affect economic and democratic progress in dozens of the planet's most disadvantaged nations. Likewise, the EU interacts with other major actors such as the World Trade Organization (WTO), G8 summits, the United Nations (UN) and regional trade blocs like the Association of Southeast Asian Nations (ASEAN) and the Common Market of the South (MERCOSUR). Debate on the role of the "EU as a global actor" has not centred on whether the concept is plausible: it is widely assumed to be accurate and verifiable. What is debated is how we should interpret this role. At one extreme, the role of the EU has been portrayed as overwhelmingly altruistic. Originating in the concept of Europe as a "civilian power"[2] today's writers have labelled the EU as a "normative power", one that has the capacity to determine what passes for normal in the world.

1 *A Secure Europe in a Better World: European Security Strategy*, Brussels, December, 2003.

2 Duchêne, F., "Europe's Role in World Peace," in R. Mayne (ed.), *Europe Tomorrow: Sixteen Europeans Look Ahead*, London, Fontana, 1972.

The principal exponent of this view[3] argues that the normative power of the EU is expressed not in what it does, or what it says, but what *it is*. This viewpoint implies that the *sui generis* model of interstate relations exemplified by the EU offers a desirable post-Westphalian template for interstate relations in other parts of the world. This view, suggesting that the EU mission in the world is somehow morally and self-evidently superior to the foreign policies of existing nation states, has been challenged. Hyde-Price, for example, has argued that "the EU serves as an instrument of collective hegemony, shaping its external milieu through using power in a variety of forms: political partnership or ostracism; economic carrots and sticks; the promise of membership or the threat of exclusion".[4] Moreover, the claims of the EU to be an "ethical" international actor sound hollow when one recalls the remark of a former Australian Trade Minister who wryly commented that a "typical cow in the EU receives a subsidy of $2.20 per day, more than what 1.2 billion of the world's poorest live on each day".[5] In similar vein, Youngs has pointed out that the EU concern for human rights abuses is highly dependent on context: in the case of Ukraine, EU concern became most vocal, and hints of accession to the EU most overt, when "repression became acute".[6]

Analysis of how EU external relations are viewed by the rest of the world would go a long way towards resolving the tension between those who view EU policies as essentially self-interested (albeit disguised in the rhetoric of altruism), and those who view the EU as an essentially moral actor (although conceding a certain self-regard where the interests of the EU and the international community are deemed to coincide). A significant *lacuna* in discussions of EU external relations is any serious consideration of these from a non-European perspective. Almost all academic analysis of the EU as a global actor reflects the belief of many Europeans that the EU is the "world's leading moral authority"[7] and "[i]n its relations with the wider world, the Union [should] uphold its values and interests".[8] A Eurocentric approach to external relations where it is assumed that what is good for Europe must be good for

---

3 Manners, I., "Normative Power Europe: A Contradiction in Terms?," *Journal of Common Market Studies*, Vol. 40, No. 2, 2002, pp. 235-58.

4 Hyde-Price, A., "Normative Power Europe: a Realist Critique," *Journal of European Public Policy*, Vol. 13, No. 2, 2006, p. 227.

5 Hyde-Price, A., "'Tragic Actor'? Realist Perspective on 'Ethical Power Europe'," *International Affairs*, Vol. 8, No. 1, January, 2008, pp. 29-44.

6 Youngs, R., "Normative Dynamics and Strategic Interests in the EU's External Identity," *Journal of Common Market Studies*, Vol. 42, No. 2, 2004, p. 426.

7 Mayer, H. and Vogt, H. (eds.), *A Responsible Europe? Ethical Foundations of European External Affairs*, Basingstoke, Palgrave Macmillan, 2006, p. 3.

8 *Draft Treaty Establishing a Constitution for Europe* (Article I-3-4).

the world, needs to be replaced by a global perspective where what is good for the world is perceived as being good for Europe.[9] The interplay between the international system and the intricacy of EU external relations needs, in any case, to be redefined so as to express more fully the idea that the two are constantly moulding each other: the EU as a global actor is partly the creation of external perceptions just as the international system responds in various ways to the "presence" or "footprint" of the EU on the global stage. This process of mutual definition is captured by a recent study of the EU as global actor[10] where the full complexity of the international identity of the EU is illuminated by reference to other actors in the international system. A focus on the perceptions and expectations of third parties who interact with the EU permits the reader to gain a much more accurate, if less flattering, picture of the EU identity as an international actor. The interaction of *presence* (the ability to exert influence and shape perceptions and expectations of others), *opportunity* (changes in the external environment which are conducive to increased EU involvement in external policy) and *capability* (the capacity to respond to external opportunities and expectations) collectively illustrate how the role of the EU as an international actor is constructed. As the authors remark:

> The subsequent evolution of (the EU's) external roles reflects a similar dynamic – with the added dimension that the Union's emergence as an international actor itself contributed to the evolution of the meanings and practices which constitute intersubjective international structures. The EU's contribution in this respect has been a function not only of intentional decisions or purposive actions but also of its existence, or presence, as a new form of international actor which has defied categorisation.[11]

So, while an increasing amount of research has been devoted to trying to describe the "nature of the beast", remarkably little has been done to assess how the EU *as a global actor* is perceived in the rest of the world. This is presumably important since the EU not only allocates considerable resources to projecting a favourable image of itself abroad, but member state governments have a propensity to internalise this image and assist in promoting the Union's international identity in third countries. Yet, the success of this endeavour can be measured only in terms of how the EU is perceived by those who are the objects of its attention. Likewise, EU citizens' appreciation of their own identity, and of the Union's legitimacy

9 Mayer, H. and Vogt, H., *A Responsible Europe? Ethical Foundations of European External Affairs*, *op. cit.*, p. 5.

10 Bretherton, C. and Vogler, J., *The European Union as a Global Actor*, Abington, Routledge, 1999.

11 *Ibid.*, p. 22.

in their own eyes, must depend, in part at least, on how the Union is perceived beyond its borders, and in other regions.

This chapter tries to go some way towards remedying the deficit outlined above by evaluating Latin American perceptions of the European integration process. A number of caveats need to be mentioned at the outset. Firstly, there is no single Latin American "voice". Indeed, one of the recurrent problems facing Latin American integration projects is the uneven and asymmetrical levels of economic development achieved in the hemisphere, and an emotional attachment to national sovereignty that renders anything more than rhetorical commitments to supranational projects problematic. Secondly, because we discuss Central America as well as South America, this uneven response to external developments is even more marked. Thirdly, although our focus is the Latin American reaction to European integration, it is impossible to do this without some reference to the rival attraction of economic integration with North America. In the decades since the Second World War, Latin American perceptions of Europe have been generally affected by two competing imperatives: on the one hand, the historical, cultural, linguistic and demographic links between the two continents has provided a channel of communication along which ideas have flowed freely. On the other hand, political and economic forces have dictated a North-South orientation that has seen a powerful attraction exerted by the United States over the entire continent to its south. Although these two imperatives have not always been in direct confrontation, they have offered alternative visions or, more accurately, alternative facets of one vision of how the Latin American world could adapt to the internationalisation of trade that followed 1945, and then the more pervasive pressures of globalisation that ensued in the late 19th, an early 21st centuries. Fourthly, as there are significant differences between sub-regions within Latin America it is necessary to treat any generalisations with caution. Attitudes towards the EU in Latin America are not, on average, significantly different from attitudes in southern Africa or the Middle East. For example, 43 per cent of Brazilians and 42 per cent of South Africans, respectively, "have heard enough about the EU to have an opinion about it".[12] However, there can be significant differences on some issues between the sub-regions (e.g. southern cone; Andean, Caribbean, Central America) of which Latin America is composed). For example, while 62 per cent of Uruguayans claim to have "read or heard something about the EU", only 34 per cent of Mexicans could claim the same.[13]

12 Fioramonti, L. and Poletti, A., "Facing the Giant: Southern Perspectives on the European Union," *Third World Quarterly*, 2008, p. 169.

13 Poletti, A., "Country Report on Brazil," in S. Lucarelli (ed.), *The External Image of the European Union*, Florence, Forum on the Problems of Peace and War and Forlì, University of Bologna, Garnet Working Paper No. 17/07, 2005, p. 83.

Public Opinion

As a starting point, we consider the extent to which Latin Americans were aware of the EU between 1995 and 2000. Our hypothesis is that a high degree of awareness would be positively correlated with a favourable image. Overall, we see that 48 per cent of Latin American respondents reported that they had "read or heard" something about the EU. However, there are significant variations between sub-regions in Latin America: In Chile, 58 per cent reported awareness of the EU, in MERCOSUR countries it was 54 per cent, in Central America 47 per cent, in the Andean Group 44 per cent, and in Mexico only 34 per cent.[14] What this suggests is that levels of knowledge in the MERCOSUR group are generally higher than elsewhere on the sub-continent (two MERCOSUR members, Uruguay and Argentina, scoring 62 per cent and 57 per cent) respectively. Closer scrutiny of the data reveals also that higher levels of education are positively correlated with greater awareness of the EU: for example, those with third level education were twice as likely to be aware of the EU as those with only primary education (68 per cent compared to 32 per cent).[15] A more stringent test of the image of the EU in Latin America is to set it in a comparative context: respondents can also be asked if they have "heard or read" anything about other organisations (e.g. the North American Free Trade Agreement (NAFTA), MERCOSUR, the UN and the WTO). Here the results imply that the EU competes for attention in Latin America with other regional and global organisations. What is clear is that the United Nations is the organisation best known to Latin Americans generally (68 per cent saying they are aware of it). Next comes NAFTA (51 per cent) and as we have seen, the EU (48 per cent). Within MERCOSUR countries, however, the EU is slightly more familiar to respondents than NAFTA due, undoubtedly, to the greater level of interaction between MERCOSUR and the EU. As is often hypothesised, greater knowledge of the EU is correlated with more favourable attitudes towards it. When asked how they rate the EU, 44 per cent rate it as "good" or "very good" in the period 1996-8, rising to 58 per cent in 2000-2004. However, opinion was generally more favourable towards the United States (rising from 48 per cent in the earlier period to 67 per cent in the later period). Moreover there is a clear correlation between favourable attitudes towards the EU and awareness of it in countries like Nicaragua and El Salvador, for example. Similarly, there appeared to be a link between low awareness of the EU and a low rating in Mexico, for example, where 31 per cent answered "good" or "very good" and only 34 per cent claimed to have heard, or read, something about the

14 Poletti, A., "Country Report on Brazil," *op. cit.*, p. 83.

15 *Ibid.*, p. 91.

EU, both scores being the lowest in Latin America.[16] While the United States is more familiar to, and enjoys a higher rating than the EU among Latin American respondents, it is also true that positive evaluations of the EU are likely to increase as awareness of it becomes more widespread. In the opinion surveys cited here, around 30 per cent of respondents felt unable to express any opinion on the EU, but only 10 per cent were unable to evaluate the USA.[17] The clear implication is that the EU can enlarge its presence in Latin America and that this can feed back positively into its own identity formation. This finding is reinforced by another survey item where respondents were asked to give an opinion on how good they thought relations were between their own country and the EU. To place these opinions in some sort of context, Japan, the United States and "other countries in Latin America" were added as objects of comparison. Here again, the proportion of respondents feeling unable to express any opinion on relations with the EU was higher than for the United States. Due to its multidimensional presence in Latin America (cultural, economic, political) the United States clearly has a more distinctive profile (albeit an ambivalent one) in the public mind than the EU whose identity is inevitably more distant and less well-defined. Thus, the finding that the EU came lowest (i.e. for respondents saying relations were "good" or "very good"), after Japan, the USA, and other Latin American countries, suggests that the EU has some way to go to raise its profile in Latin America.

By inviting respondents to nominate a country as a "best friend in the world" the intention is to measure "closeness" between peoples. By and large, when faced with a triple choice between "the United States", a "European country" or "Japan", Latin Americans opt overwhelmingly for the United States, with Europe coming second by a long stretch (11 per cent to 29 per cent).[18] There are, however, striking variations within Latin America, with Argentina, for example, standing out as the most European (26 per cent) and the least friendly towards the United States (11 per cent). Another batch of questions in the 2004 *Latinobarometro* is especially pertinent to our purpose here: perceptions of the EU's relative contribution as a global actor in four discrete fields (democracy, free trade, peace, and development cooperation) are assessed in comparison to the United States. In all four areas, the United States is perceived as making a greater contribution than the EU. For free trade and development, the divergence between the EU and the USA is most marked, whereas for democracy and peace, differences are much smaller. Brazilians, representing about half

16 *Ibid.*

17 *Ibid.*

18 Poletti, A., "Country Report on Brazil," *op. cit.*, p. 13, but note that 49 per cent did not name *any* country as "best friend".

the population of Latin America, are generally more supportive of the EU contribution than the rest of Latin America and, in the case of "peace in the world', most Brazilians believe that the EU is the major contributor rather than the United States.[19] However, on all these four issues, the educational level of respondents is very significant. Respondents with a university education are much more appreciative of the EU contribution (in fact, for democracy, peace, and development, and in Brazil for free trade as well, a majority see the EU has having made a bigger contribution than the United States).[20] The fact that more educated cohorts in the Latin American public seem to have a more favourable image of the EU as a global actor again suggests that the EU needs to sell itself better by providing more information about its role in the world.

European Integration as a "Model" for Latin America

An important aspect of Latin American perceptions of the EU relates to the latter's suitability as a model for integration in Latin America. Ever since the 1960s, regional attempts at integration have left behind a legacy of schemes that have often achieved much less than their initial rhetoric had promised. The "alphabet soup" (CACM (Central American Common Market), CARICOM (Caribbean Community), LAFTA (Latin American Free Trade Association), CAN (Andean Community of Nations), MERCOSUR, to name but four) of regional organisations in Latin America is also a reminder of the extent to which Europe has provided templates for Latin American integration: more often than not, however, the adoption of institutional models from Europe has revealed the sad truth that the political context in Latin America is so different that the seeds of integration have failed to germinate amidst the rocky outcrops of national chauvinism and presidential power.

The extent to which Europe has provided a model for Latin American regionalism varies considerably. In general, countries of the extreme "southern cone" have been more attached to European models than have the smaller states of Central America whose geographical proximity to the United States tended to determine their external allegiances. However, opinion surveys suggest a strong connection between support for the EU and support for regional integration in Latin America.[21] This correlation is, however, pragmatic: if regional integration projects fail or falter, the alternative model(s) offered by the United States may appear more attractive. A more encouraging development in Latin America is that the

---

[19] Poletti, A., "Country Report on Brazil," *op. cit.*, p. 14.

[20] *Ibid.*

[21] Seligson, M., "Popular Support for Regional Economic Integration in Latin America," *Journal of Latin American Studies*, Vol. 31, No. 1, p. 145.

embedding of democracy at the same time as regional integration projects are attracting increased support. Are the two processes linked? At first sight, the European experience seems to suggest a linkage between integration and democratisation: Spain, Portugal, Greece and the countries of eastern and central Europe all saw their membership of the EU as the best way to preserve and enhance their transition to liberal democracy. There is some evidence that this European phenomenon has made an impact on Latin American political consciousness. In recent *Latinobarometro* polls, there is a convincing correlation between respondents who believe democracy "works well" in their own country, and those who are "willing to defend democracy if it became threatened", with supporters of regional integration in Latin America.[22] In sum, therefore, we can say that Latin Americans pay attention to Europe. The better educated and the better informed are knowledgeable about, and supportive of, the EU. Moreover, the more favourable the opinions are of the EU, the more robust the support for regional integration in Latin America.

It is not only the principle of European integration that is being applied in Latin America but also the practice. In particular, features of the recent evolution of the EU are being assumed to be relevant to the Latin American experience. For example, citizens of the members of the CAN can travel without a passport in each others' territory, thus providing a vital element of a single market: the free movement of people. A common passport, meeting the latest international standards, has been adopted by all the CAN countries. Likewise, in MERCOSUR, in January 2007, a tranche of US$100 million has been approved for social, health and infrastructure projects for Paraguay and Uruguay through the MERCOSUR Structural Convergence Fund (FOCEM).[23] These two examples mirror analogous innovations in the EU: on the one hand, the continuing improvement of the Schengen agreement allowing passport-free travel throughout most of the EU and, on the other, the Structural and Cohesion Funds of the EU which have, for thirty years, attempted to mitigate the regional inequalities between and within member states on the understanding that this will promote a more dynamic single market and a greater sense of political solidarity across the 28 member states of the EU.

Most recently, programmes for the promotion of "good governance" in the EU are being borrowed, or copied by the institutions of Latin American regional integration. The ambitious target of these programmes, often partly-financed by the EU, is to nurture civil society in

[22] *Ibid.*, p. 146.

[23] Kanner, A., "Governance in South American Integration: Insights and Encouragement from the European Union," *Jean Monnet Papers*, Vol. 7, No. 5, University of Miami, 2007, p. 6.

countries where democracy has only recently taken root. In CAN, through the European Commission's 2004-2006 Regional Indicative Programme for the Andean Community, supported by €4 million, the intention of the EU is to transfer:

> European know-how relating to the participation of civil society in political processes [...] particularly to minorities such as indigenous peoples and to other social groups such as women and trade unionists, who have traditionally been neither consulted about political initiatives nor involved in their implementation or whose vital interests are threatened by such initiatives.[24]

Concrete outcomes from these programmes include the creation and support of consultative councils. A Business Advisory Council and a Labour Advisory Council have been in existence since 1998. More recently, and more significant, perhaps, was the creation of an Andean Indigenous Board in 2002 with representation from Andean indigenous organisations, government spokespersons, ombudsmen and technical experts. The purpose is to advocate policy changes that help to reduce poverty, social inequities, and discrimination among indigenous communities. In MERCOSUR, similar institutions have been created: the principal consultative body is the Economic and Social Consultative Forum (FCES) which was established in 1994 and modelled on the EU's European Economic and Social Committee (EESC). In addition to performing the same functions as the EESC, the FCES has prime responsibility for including civil society in the MERCOSUR integration process. As an adjunct to the FCES, a Women's Forum (FM) was set up in 1995 as a completely non-governmental group representing women's issues to the FCES and other MERCOSUR institutions. The main focus of the FM is the reduction of poverty and unemployment among women and the promotion of gender equality. It is too early to say how effective these groups are but their mere existence provides a new forum for debate, and helps to raise the level of legitimate expectation in Andean and "southern cone" societies. They also provide a clear reflection of the notion that Latin Americans perceive European representative mechanisms as appropriate for transplantation to the southern hemisphere.

It is fair to point out, however, that perceptions of EU policies in Latin America may not always be as benign as the progenitors of these policies hope or expect. As we indicated at the outset of this chapter, EU policies in Latin America are part of a broader projection of the EU's own normative mission as a global actor. The policies themselves are embedded in a stratum of implicit values: public participation, the rule of law, social inclusion, human rights, environmental protection, sustainable development,

---

[24] http://ec.europa.eu/comm/external_relations/andean/rsp.rip_0406.pdf, accessed 2 November 2012.

and gender equality. The unspoken assumption on the part of the EU is that Latin American society is not sufficiently different from European society for basic values, or political concepts such as citizenship, to require "translation" into the local political vernacular. These unspoken assumptions are reciprocated by Latin American elites for whom acceptance of EU financial support may be preferable to any real interrogation of the values or assumptions on which the support is based. So, while the EU may earn praise in some quarters for its policies of "modernisation" and "democratisation", it may not be able to escape accusations that it is self-interested, that its policies do not travel well; and that it is, in effect, perpetuating a benign imperialism dating back, *mutatis mutandis* to the 19th century, and involving the same power asymmetries as in the past.[25] In a similar vein, but attributing mistaken assumptions rather than neo-imperialism to EU Commission policies towards MERCOSUR, Grugel[26] has argued that a study of EU policies to promote "social citizenship" as part of democratic consolidation reveals a situation where the impact of these policies is suffused with the concept of "social citizenship" and has simply got "lost in translation". Grugel's analysis suggests three important conclusions. Firstly, the introduction of social citizenship into MERCOSUR societies is ambitious and difficult and is likely to challenge the interests and power of local elites. These elites find it relatively easy to avoid or dilute the policy changes that the EU is attempting. As another writer has remarked, norm diffusion from Europe to the "third world" leads to a mimicry of these norms, but not a real shift in policy.[27] Secondly, social citizenship has much more radical implications in Latin America than it does in Europe. In Latin America its introduction would require a re-writing of the contract between state and society, not a few isolated reform measures as the EU seems to suggest. This explains why EU initiatives are perceived very differently by different sectors of Latin American society. Thirdly, the assumption in Brussels that MERCOSUR is intrinsically similar to the EU is mistaken and needs to be challenged. More EU resources need to be diverted towards civil society actors if the task is to achieve state transformation and compel recalcitrant national elites to support it.

---

25 Meunier, S. and Nicolaidis, K., "The European Union as a Trade Power," in C. Hill and M. Smith, *The International Relations of the European Union*, 2nd ed., Oxford, Oxford University Press, 2005, p. 266.

26 Grugel, J., "Democratisation and Ideational Diffusion Europe, Mercosur and Social Citizenship," *Journal of Common Market Studies*, Vol. 45, No. 1, pp. 43-68.

27 Meyer, J. *et al.*, "World Society and the Nation State," *American Journal of Sociology*, Vol. 103, No. 1, 1997, pp. 144-181.

MERCOSUR as a Two-Way Mirror for the EU?

In the light of the foregoing comments on how the EU is perceived within the context of MERCOSUR, we now turn to a discussion of how MERCOSUR acts as a "two-way mirror" for the EU in Latin America. The EU perceives MERCOSUR as a reflection of itself. Latin Americans react to this reflection by behaving as if MERCOSUR countries were, indeed, susceptible to the same policy instruments that have proved effective in European integration. It is a game played by both sides for divergent reasons. The United States dimension also needs to be taken into account here because MERCOSUR is seen in Brussels as a means of resisting US domination in Latin America, just as support of MERCOSUR by its members is interpreted as a means of limiting US influence as far as possible from the hemisphere.

The temptation to portray MERCOSUR simply as a reflection of the EU in Latin America needs to be challenged. The advent of the so-called "new regionalism" in political science and international relations deliberately plays down the idea of the EU providing a template for regional projects outside Europe. Instead of the legalism, elaborate institutional framework, and distinctive supranational characteristics of the EU, "new regionalism" posits a broader range of modalities, largely setting aside the neo-functional and neo-realist theoretical canons of European integration. In particular, as the EU has become more preoccupied with questions concerning its own governance, and popular legitimation of its institutions, the gap between itself and analogous regional integration projects in the rest of the world has widened. Leaving the EU to one side, most other regional projects can claim an institutional structure that is still vestigial: and, therefore, any concerns about "constitutionalising" their systems of regional governance would be premature. Likewise, mass public opinion is only dimly aware of the existence of regional projects such as MERCOSUR; and, therefore, problems of alienation, accountability and legitimacy simply have not (yet) arisen.

Yet, however much we may distinguish between the EU experience of integration and the more recent experiments with regionalisation in other parts of the world, and however much we subscribe to the *sui generis* nature of the EU, the fact remains that similarities tend to be exaggerated by policy-makers in Brussels and elites in MERCOSUR, each for their own purposes. The blurring of European and non-European models of integration is further confused by the fact that regional organisations such as MERCOSUR have adopted or adapted the nomenclature of EU institutions. MERCOSUR includes institutions that mimic the European Parliament, and the EESC, of the EU. Similar, or identical, nomenclature for these regional institutions not only invites comparison, but legitimises it. The outcome of such comparison inevitably raises questions around the validity of comparing apples with oranges, as opposed to two species of apple.

This underlying Eurocentrism, promoted as actively by Latin American elites as by Brussels, tends to stifle the development of other paradigms that could more usefully relate regionalisation to globalisation. Indeed, globalisation may provide the crucial discriminating factor between the EU and other more recent regionalisation projects such as MERCOSUR. It can be argued that whereas these recent projects merely react to globalisation, the EU has been a "filter for globalisation". Its structural characteristics, consisting of a high degree of institutionalisation and the wealth and social stability of its member states, distinguish it sharply from the rest of the world. While new regional organisations are concerned with how to integrate, the EU is coming to terms with the degree of integration it has already achieved. Therefore, the literature and theoretical concerns emanating now from the European experience have, perhaps, less relevance for scholars analysing the process outside of Europe.[28] Our concern here is more immediately the role of the EU as a global and normative actor. In this latter sense, one of the key characteristics of the EU's global influence is its ability to "induce" regional integration schemes in other parts of the world with which it then pursues an interlocutory relationship. As we suggested at the outset, this "power by example" is arguably a core component of the civilianising role of the EU in a global context. Part of this process sees regional integration projects such as MERCOSUR "borrowing" institutional templates from the EU and applying them in very different economic and political contexts. Since imitation is the sincerest form of flattery the outcome of these experiments with institutional transplants matters little: if the experiment is successful, the EU can reap the credit; if the experiment fails, blame can be laid at the door of local incompetence or inhospitable "background conditions". In reality, MERCOSUR in particular, and Latin American integration projects more generally, now share with the EU a common exposure to the forces of globalisation. National political systems interact with their external environment and exogenous factors clearly have an impact on domestic politics. Tectonic shifts in the global strategic environment and global monetary crises create new fault-lines across the party political landscape of national polities. Neither the EU nor MERCOSUR are immune to these pressures: the debate as to whether regionalisation is a response to, or a product of, globalisation applies equally to the EU as it does to MERCOSUR. Although it may be hypothesised that both regional

28 Sbragia, A., "Comparative Regionalism: What might it be?," *Journal of Common Market Studies*, Vol. 46, 2008, pp. 34-35.

groupings owed their origins and evolution to a globalising international environment, the reasons for their rather different rates of progress may lie in a number of endogenous factors as varied as asymmetrical commitments to integration, political orientation, economic interests, and leadership deficits. On the other hand, we can detect themes that are shared between MERCOSUR and the EU which help to explain a similar commitment to the regional project: for example, the rationale for integration being the stabilisation and copper-fastening of democracy among the participating member states.

Creating institutions that resemble those of the EU is relatively easy: what matters is the political significance attached to these institutions and the role they are called upon to play. In MERCOSUR, institutions have sometimes been created according to a successful European template, but the anticipated osmosis whereby these new institutions might be imbued with significance comparable to their EU analogues does not materialise. The EU template is perhaps misleading in another respect: in an attempt to kick-start or revive a flagging integration process, institutions were sometimes prematurely created or deadlines arbitrarily designated, in the expectation that their underlying purposes would be fulfilled. The transformation of the European Assembly into a European Parliament, the "1992" programme and its ensuing Single European Market, the overly ambitious 1980 deadline for "monetary union", the introduction of "European citizenship" in 1992, and the adoption of the euro in 2002, are all examples of a method of "forced incubation" that has worked reasonably well in the European politico-historical environment. Similar tactics in a Latin American context have been much less successful. The difference can, perhaps, be explained by what integration theorists refer to as "background conditions". What is clear is that identically-named institutions in two different regional settings rarely, if ever, produce identical outcomes. In MERCOSUR, there is a distinct lack of the background conditions that have made political integration possible in the EU.

The underlying principle for all decision-making in MERCOSUR is unanimity. It is a strictly intergovernmental organisation with no autonomous bureaucracy where an accretion of "institutional memory" might pose as even a modest counterweight to overtly national policy preferences. This intergovernmentalism was consciously adopted at the outset in order to avoid the experiences of previous experiments in Latin America where "integration bureaucracies", remote from national policy implementation, often made commitments that were unlikely to be translated into legislation. The merit, such as it is, of MERCOSUR's structures, is that those who make the commitments at the regional level are closely associated, sometimes overlapping, with officials charged with implementation in the member states. The principal characteristics of MERCOSUR have been, therefore, its strongly intergovernmental character, the need for consensus, and the lack of any supranational judicial body to resolve disputes. The lack of a dense network of institutions such as that seen in the EU policy-making system, may not be a disadvantage in itself if there is sufficient political will to make the system work.

In his critical analysis of MERCOSUR as representing a divergence between "rising rhetoric and declining achievement", Malamud[29] alludes to a number of proposals that have been made to strengthen it, based on precedents already established by the EU. By dismissing each of these in turn he highlights some of the crucial differences between the two nascent "polities". The EU has consistently opted for the Monnet method, whereby integration processes are anchored in concrete projects whose rationale is clearly beneficial to the participating actors and whose potential to "spill over" to cognate sectors provides a basis for further integration. In MERCOSUR, by contrast, rhetoric appears to have run ahead of realities and the degree of interdependence between actors that lies at the heart of European regional integration is much less pronounced. MERCOSUR can boast no more than one-eighth of the EU level of intra-regional trade, for example. Ultimately, what distinguishes MERCOSUR from the EU as a project of regional integration is the lack of viable supranational institutions in the former.

This raises the question of asymmetry within MERCOSUR. Brazil's geographic size and dominance in terms of wealth and population risk turning the whole enterprise into a decidedly one-sided affair. Brazil's policies towards the EU and towards MERCOSUR are mutually reinforcing and reflect its self-image as the giant power in the region, and an aspirant for great power status on the global stage. Brazilian preferences dominate MERCOSUR and cause irritation to both a would-be rival Argentina, and the much smaller economies of Uruguay and Paraguay which run chronic trade deficits with their larger MERCOSUR partners. Successive Brazilian governments regard the EU as a significant trade partner in global terms and one on which Brazil's continuing economic development depends. There are, however, some cross-currents in Brazilian elite opinion: the EU is viewed in some quarters as a "protectionist" power that maintains high tariffs, and subsidises exports; this is particularly resented with regard to the Common Agricultural Policy which is seen as contradicting EU claims to favour free and fair trade with the Third World. The EU is nevertheless reckoned to be an important market for MERCOSUR exports, and a major source of foreign direct investment.

29 Malamud, A., "Mercosur Turns 15: Between Rising Rhetoric and Declining Achievement," *Cambridge Review of International Affairs*, Vol. 18, No. 3, 2005, pp. 421-436.

In the context of the overall schism that exists in Latin America between US plans for a Free Trade Area of the Americas (FTAA), and the EU favoured project of MERCOSUR, Brazil's position is clear. It favours MERCOSUR, partly on its own merits, but also because it thwarts what are seen as US neo-imperialist pretensions in the region. In an international political context, the EU is seen as a force upholding multilateralism, and a guarantor of a more multipolar international system. Brazil's aspirations for a seat on the UN Security Council reflect its ambition to be part of a "new world order" where the hegemony of one superpower is replaced by a more centrifugal pattern of international relations. The role of the EU in helping to achieve this is seen as indispensable. When President Lula (of Brazil) was quoted as stating that "the EU is not just a partner but a source of inspiration [...] we admire the determination to shape a new pole of development and civilisation,"[30] he was speaking for many governments in Latin America, but especially in MERCOSUR, for which the image of reconciliation and democratisation in Europe represents an important political and economic precedent.

Concluding Reflections

The application of models of European integration to new settings has preoccupied students of integration for three decades. Haas identified early three levels of conflict resolution between nation states that reflect differing degrees of integration: Firstly, that of accommodation by lowest common denominator; secondly, that of splitting the difference; and thirdly that of consciously, or implicitly, upgrading the common interests of the parties involved in the regional grouping.[31] Reflecting on the European experience we can say that the intensity of political integration is positively correlated with industrialisation and economic diversification. Processes which yield optimal progress towards the goal of political community at the European level simply cannot be reproduced in other contexts because the necessary preconditions exist to a much lesser degree. If regional integration proceeds in other parts of the world it is likely that it will proceed as a result of factors indigenous to those regions; and this is how it should be. It is a uniquely Eurocentric assumption to expect models developed in a "contextually specific" process in Western Europe to be appropriate for other regions of the world. Nevertheless, borrowing

30 Lula da Silva, L.I., Discurso do Senhor Presidente da República na Assembléia da República de Portugal, Lisboa, Assembléia da República de Portugal , 11 July 2003, www.mre.gov.br.

31 Haas, E., "International Integration: the European and the Universal Process," *International Organisation*, Vol. 15, No. 3, Summer 1961, pp. 366-392.

concepts or labels from the European experience sometimes gives the impression that such transferability is not only possible, but desirable.

Our analysis of Latin American perceptions of European integration permits a number of concluding reflections. Firstly, we argued that the role of the EU as a global actor cannot be fully appreciated without some reference to how that role is perceived by actors with which the EU interacts. Secondly, our summary of opinion poll data in Latin America suggests that the United States enjoys more well-defined profiles in public opinion than the EU. Thirdly, however, elites and more educated strata in Latin American societies are aware of the nuances of EU policies in Latin America and in the world more broadly, especially in the context of upholding peace and providing international stability. Fourthly, MERCOSUR, as the most developed of the regional projects in Latin America, is perceived by the EU as an interlocutor with whom it can do business and for whom it provides flattering recognition of its institutional framework which, in turn, has been deliberately modelled on European templates. Finally, the EU's self-image as a global normative actor needs to be considerably modified in the light of how it is reflected in the "mirror" of external perceptions.

Part IV

The European Communities and ACP Countries: The Post-Colonial Heritage in EU External Relations

A Matter of Preference

Commonwealth Africa, Britain and the EEC Association System, 1957-75

Ferdinand LEIKAM

PhD, Ludwig-Maximilians-Universität Munich

Introduction

In March 1957, European Integration took a major step forward: six countries formed the European Economic Community (EEC), which was based on a common market among its members. The foundation of this community fundamentally altered the political and economic relationships within western Europe.[1] The EEC members also established an "association" – a close relationship – between their colonies in Africa and the Community.[2] This had consequences also for those countries which were not (yet) part of this arrangement, namely the United Kingdom and the African Commonwealth members. So, the foundation of the EEC had ramifications beyond Europe.

Nevertheless, historiography of European integration tends to be rather introspective and Eurocentric. Only recently has the African dimension of European integration attracted substantial interest from historians.[3]

1 Bitsch, M.-Th., *Histoire de la construction européenne de 1945 à nos jours*, Brussels, Éd. Complexe, 2004; Milward, A. S., *The European Rescue of the Nation State*, Berkeley, University of California Press, 1992.

2 Chikeka, C. O., *Africa and the European Economic Community 1957-1992*, Lewiston, Edwin Mellen Press, 1993, pp. 25-31; Migani, G., "L'association des TOM au Marché commun: histoire d'un accord européen entre cultures économiques différentes et idéaux politiques communs, 1955-1957," in M.-Th. Bitsch and G. Bossuat (eds.), *L'Europe unie et l'Afrique. De l'Idée d'Eurafrique à la Convention de Lomé I*, Brussels/Paris/Baden-Baden, Bruylant, 2005, pp. 233-52.

3 See, for example, Bitsch, M.-Th. and Bossuat, G., *L'Europe unie et l'Afrique*, *op. cit.*; Milward, A. S., *Politics and Economics in the History of the European Union*, London, Routledge, 2005; Moser, T., *Europäische Integration, Dekolonisation, Eurafrika. Eine historische Analyse über Entstehungsbedingungen der Eurafrikanischen Gemeinschaft*

However, most historical research on the relations between Europe and Africa focuses on the (former) French colonies, whereas the relationship between Commonwealth Africa and the EEC remains neglected. Former British colonies in Africa are, typically, only dealt with from the 1970s onwards, that is, from the time after Britain's entry into the Community.[4]

This chapter tries to narrow this gap. It analyses the relations between Commonwealth Africa and the EEC between 1957 and 1975. More precisely, it examines the problems the EEC association system created for the newly independent African Commonwealth countries; it discusses the position of these countries *vis-à-vis* the association system, and it details the role of London's policy on Europe. In doing so, this contribution not only sheds light on an important, but neglected, aspect of Euro-African relations; it also allows a look at EEC policies from "outside", namely from the viewpoint of countries which originally were not part of the association arrangements.

The chapter is divided into four parts: The first deals with the founding of the EEC and the establishment of the association system, as well as with the consequences of these decisions for the British colonies in Africa which were soon to become independent states. The second part examines Britain's first attempt to become a member of the EEC between 1961 and 1963, London's decision to include Commonwealth Africa in the association system and the reaction of the newly independent African Commonwealth countries to this proposal. The third part focuses on the decision of some African Commonwealth countries to seek closer trade links with the EEC, the subsequent negotiations over association agreements in the 1960s and the problems which appeared during these discussions. The last part deals with Britain's accession to the EEC in the early 1970s, the deliberations within the Community and Africa about their future relationship and the subsequent negotiations on an association agreement which was to include the African Commonwealth members.

The chapter is based mainly on archival sources from Britain, which means that the position of the African Commonwealth countries is, to some extent, filtered by British interests and priorities. Nevertheless, a focus on statements, letters and memoranda from African Commonwealth countries, completed by African newspapers and accounts of African diplomats, allows us also to set out the position of these countries and minimizes the danger of limiting the analysis to a British perception of the topic.

---

von der Weltwirtschaftskrise bis zum Jaunde-Vertrag, 1929-1963, Baden-Baden, Nomos, 2000.

4 This is especially true for the works of Bitsch, M.-Th. and Bossuat, G. and Moser, T., cited above.

The Creation of the EEC Association System

The foundation of the EEC in March 1957 not only meant the introduction of a common market in Europe, but also the establishment of an association between the EEC members' colonies and the Community. This association envisaged a very close relationship, especially in economic terms: it was decided that the tariffs between the Six and the associated territories would gradually be removed. Eventually, the associated colonies should be allowed to export duty-free not only to the market of their respective colonial powers, but to the whole EEC market. In addition, not only the respective colonial powers, but all EEC members should be allowed duty-free access to the markets of the associated colonies. However, the associated colonies were to be allowed to impose quotas or to raise protective duties in order to protect the development of their economies.[5] The association system also envisaged the creation of an Overseas Development Fund to support the associated colonies. All EEC members, including those without colonial possessions, were obliged to contribute to this fund. The introduction of the fund can therefore be interpreted as a tool created by colonial powers to secure additional funding for economic development in Africa, as they found it increasingly difficult to finance colonial development projects themselves.[6]

The foundation of the EEC and the association of the French and Belgian colonies with the EEC were to have far-reaching repercussions for the British colonies and Commonwealth countries in Africa. The Six intended to form a common tariff against imports from third countries; the associated francophone colonies, however, were allowed to export duty-free into the EEC. Consequently, British colonies and Commonwealth countries in Africa would face increased tariffs on their exports to Europe and, moreover, be at a competitive disadvantage compared to those colonies which were part of the association system.

This serious threat to Commonwealth Africa's trade interests had consequences for Britain's European policy, which, in 1957, concentrated on the creation of a Free Trade Area for industrial products, covering Britain and the EEC members, but no overseas territories.[7] Officials suggested

---

5 National Archives (NA), Kew Gardens, FO 371/122039, Brussels to FO, 19.11.56, and T 234/223, Goldschlag (Canada House) to Crawley (CRO), 06.12.56.

6 Migani, G., "L'association des TOM au Marché commun: histoire d'un accord européen entre cultures économiques différentes et idéaux politiques communs, 1955-1957," *op. cit.*; Grilli, E., *The European Community and the Developing Countries*, Cambridge, Cambridge University Press, 1993, pp. 7-14.

7 Ellison, J., *Threatening Europe. Britain and the Creation of the European Community, 1955-58*, Basingstoke, Macmillan, 2000; Schenk, C. R., "Decolonization and European

two alternative solutions: on the one hand, Britain could stick to the industrial Free Trade Area as it was and seek additional adjustments to mitigate the damage the association system caused to the exports of its colonies and the Commonwealth countries. On the other hand, Britain could revise its Free Trade Area project to protect these countries' exporting interests. Concerning the latter option, British officials discussed a proposal to create an economic unit which was to include the EEC members and their colonies as well as Britain and its former and remaining colonies in Africa. But serious concerns against this proposal were raised: since Africa's most important export items were tropical goods, any scheme which included African members implied the inclusion of agricultural products. This would be a major departure from London's original concept of a Free Trade Area, however, which was confined to industrial goods and, thus, was not consistent with the overall economic interests of the United Kingdom. It was also argued that African countries would not be willing to take part in a scheme which included Europe and Africa; it could not be expected "that a project inspired from Europe (as this would be) would command much political support".[8] Consequently, the Cabinet concluded that the concept of a Free Trade Area for industrial goods, excluding all overseas territories, should not be changed. The British Cabinet additionally decided to negotiate arrangements with the EEC to safeguard the exporting interests of the colonies and Commonwealth countries. Britain should seek either a reduction of the EEC's common tariff on tropical goods from British colonies and Commonwealth countries or quotas for duty-free or preferential imports.[9]

The decision to stick to the industrial Free Trade Area confined to Europe was accepted by the British colonies and Commonwealth countries in Africa. The vast majority of the colonial governments in Africa acquiesced to the solution favoured by London. An important reason for this can be seen in the fact that the British government presented the alternative solutions in a very unfavourable light. It obviously wanted to avoid a situation in which its colonies would regard the EEC association as the model for the relationship between Europe and Africa in general.[10] London succeeded with its strategy: most colonial governments accepted

Economic Integration: The Free Trade Area Negotiations, 1956-58," *Journal of Imperial and Commonwealth History*, Vol. 24, No. 3, 1996, pp. 444-63.

8 NA, CAB 134/1835, E.S. (57) 9 (Revise), Association of Overseas Territories with the European Customs and Economic Union and the Industrial Free Trade Area. Report by the Economic Steering Committee, 22.03.57.

9 NA, CAB 128/31, CC 29 (57) 3, 03.04.57.

10 Leikam, F., *Empire, Entwicklung und Europa. Die Europapolitik Großbritanniens und die Entwicklungsländer im Commonwealth, 1945-75*, Augsburg, Wißner, 2011, pp. 63f.

Britain's decision.[11] Only Kenya demanded major changes and sought permission to associate with the Free Trade Area, which was to cover also tropical goods. This solution would allow Kenya to export to the EEC on the same terms as the associated French and Belgian colonies and to raise duties to protect their economic development.[12] In effect, Kenya proposed that London's Free Trade Area project should be modelled on the EEC's association system.

But the British government was not willing to change its policy and insisted on its decision to create a Free Trade Area for industrial goods and to seek additional arrangements to safeguard the trade interests of the British colonies and Commonwealth countries in Africa.[13] However, it soon became clear that it was far from easy to reach an agreement with the Six. The discussions with the EEC on concessions quickly hit the buffers over technical details and in the end, failed, as did Britain's Free Trade Area project, which was ultimately stopped by a French veto in late 1958.[14]

The First British EEC Entry Bid and Commonwealth Africa

In 1961, the association system was again intensively studied by Britain and the African Commonwealth countries, whose number was rapidly increasing in the early 1960s, when most British colonies in Africa became sovereign states. The reason for the renewed interest was the first British application for EEC membership. London concluded that Britain's economic and strategic interests required membership of the EEC. Because of the political and economic rise of the Community it was regarded as dangerous to remain outside the nascent power bloc.[15] At the same time, Britain's entry should not damage its relations with the Commonwealth, which was still seen as an "important buttress of our position as a Power with world-wide interests and influence".[16] This

---

11 NA, CAB 134/1858, E.S. (E.I.) (57) 95, Meeting with Colonial Representatives, March 27th-April 2nd, 04.04.57.

12 See NA, CAB 134/1855, E.S. (E.I.) 15th Meeting, 26.03.57.

13 NA, CAB 128/31, CC 38 (57) 5, 06.05.57, and CAB 129/87, C (57) 107, The Commonwealth, the Colonies and the Customs Union, 30.04.57; Schenk, C., "Decolonization and European Economic Integration: The Free Trade Area Negotiations, 1956-58," *op. cit.*, p. 458.

14 For the negotiations on a mitigation, see NA, CO 852/1730-32.

15 Kaiser, W., *Using Europe, Abusing the Europeans. Britain and European Integration*, 1945-63, Basingstoke, Macmillan, 1999, pp. 108-51; Milward, A. S., *The Rise and Fall of a National Strategy, 1945-1963*, London, Frank Cass, 2002, pp. 310-40.

16 NA, CAB 129/102, C (60) 107, Association with the European Economic Community, 06.07.60.

meant that special solutions had to be found: If the UK were to become a member of the EEC without any arrangements for the Commonwealth, it would be forced to apply the EEC Common External Tariff against imports from these countries.

By April 1961, the government departments agreed that Britain's relations with its former and remaining colonies in Africa could best be safeguarded if they were associated with the EEC.[17] Officials pointed at the advantages the EEC association system would offer to the African colonies and Commonwealth countries: "The association confers great benefits on the 'associated overseas territories' for their [importing] products into the whole of the Common Market (not merely into the market of the ex-Metropolitan country) and access to a substantial Development Fund, half of the Capital provided by Germany". Therefore, they suggested: "If we decide to join the Six, we shall seek to secure that the Commonwealth benefits from the arrangements".[18] London concluded that an inclusion of the British colonies and the newly independent African Commonwealth members would have two advantages: firstly, an association would make sure that the African colonies and Commonwealth countries could continue to enjoy free access to the British market. Secondly, British colonies and Commonwealth countries in Africa would be allowed to export into the EEC under the same rules as the associated former French colonies. So, inclusion in the EEC association system would end the discrimination against the exports of these countries.[19]

Meanwhile, the majority of Britain's African colonies had become independent states. These young nations aimed at economic development, African unity and a non-aligned position in the struggle between West and East. This had consequences for their position *vis-à-vis* the association system. It soon became apparent that the majority of the African Commonwealth countries were not willing to become associated with the EEC. Ghana and Nigeria, notably, rejected the association system both on economic and political grounds. They feared that they would not be allowed to raise duties against imports from EEC members, which would increase competition and impede their countries' economic

[17] NA, CAB 130/176, GEN 732/7 Revise, The Implications of Signing the Treaty of Rome. Associated Overseas Territories, 21.04.61.

[18] NA, T 229/126, Owen to Lee, Brief on E.Q. (61) 8, 05.05.61; see also Leikam, F., "A Strategy that Failed. Great Britain, Commonwealth Africa and EEC Association Policy, 1957-1963," in M. Rasmussen and A.-C. L. Knudsen (eds.), *The Road to a United Europe. Interpretations of the Process of European Integration*, Brussels, P.I.E.-Peter Lang, 2009, pp. 101-18.

[19] See NA, CAB 134/1511, CMN (61) 2, Brief on the Commonwealth and the Common Market, 04.09.61.

development. Moreover, they expected that the associated states would be requested to discriminate against imports from other African states in favour of imports from the EEC, which was regarded as a threat to the aim of further economic cooperation within Africa.[20] Besides these economic reasons, President Nkrumah of Ghana also expressed serious political concerns. He criticised the association as a manifestation of "political inequality" between Europe and Africa and as an attempt to keep the newly independent African countries closely aligned with the West.[21] Nkrumah also publicly criticized the association system, when he, in July 1961, informed Ghana's National Assembly that "we [the Government of Ghana] are most decidedly and strongly opposed to any arrangement which uses the unification of Europe as a cloak for perpetuating colonial privileges in Africa".[22]

However, not all African Commonwealth countries were as implacably opposed to an association as Nigeria and Ghana. Some countries indicated that they would study the provisions of the association system, without prejudice. Consequently, the British government departments were optimistic that their reservations could be overcome. The British representatives tried to convince the governments of the African Commonwealth countries that their main fears were unfounded. London stated that the associated states were free to raise duties in order to protect their development and were allowed to establish free trade area relations with other African countries.[23] But London was not able to alter the position of the African Commonwealth states. In September 1962, it became clear that most of the newly independent Commonwealth countries in Africa still refused to countenance an association. At the Commonwealth Prime Ministers' Conference the representatives from most African Commonwealth countries declared that they would not seek association. They stated that a better access to the EEC market was of vital importance, but that they did not want to be included in the association system.[24]

Refusing association, the African Commonwealth countries caused a stir within the British government. London developed alternative

[20] NA, FO 371/158322, Record of Consultations between John Hare and the Nigerian Government on 30 June 1961.

[21] NA, DO 165/55, Accra to CRO, 29.06.61; Nkrumah, K., *Africa Must Unite*, London, Heinemann, 1963, pp. 173-93.

[22] Parliamentary Debates of Ghana, First Series, Vol. 24, National Assembly, Official Report, Session 1961-62, 4 July-3 August 1961, Col. 8.

[23] NA, FO 371/158321, Sanders to Bottomley, 31.07.61.

[24] NA, DO 161/196, PMM (62) 5th Meeting, 11.09.62.

arrangements to safeguard the trade interests of these countries.[25] These deliberations came to an immediate end when, in January 1963, the accession negotiations between Britain and the EEC failed. This was not an end to all discussions on trade relations between Commonwealth Africa and the EEC, however. On the contrary, the African Commonwealth countries themselves made sure that the question on how best to organise these relations remained on the agenda.

Negotiations between Commonwealth Africa and the EEC

Already during the negotiations between London and the EEC, the idea to establish direct contacts with the Community became increasingly popular among the governments of some African Commonwealth countries. One major reason for this development was London's insistence on an association. In August 1962, George Kahama, Trade Minister of Tanganyika, complained that "for the African Commonwealth it was association or nothing, whilst for the older Commonwealth countries, such as Canada and New Zealand, some special form of treaty relationship was envisaged".[26] In September 1962, Nigeria's Prime Minister Sir Abubakar Balewa stated that he was unwilling to accept that "African countries should be offered only association while others were free to enter into direct negotiations".[27]

But even though the African Commonwealth countries rejected an association, they realized that it was essential to find an arrangement which would allow a better access to the EEC market – even if Britain did not join the EEC – and end the privileged status of the associated francophone colonies. The latter aim became even more important when the association system was continued after the independence of the French and Belgian colonies. Nigeria and the East African Commonwealth members in particular, which had close trade links with EEC countries, considered it vital to improve their access to the European market.[28] So, these countries aimed at direct contacts with the EEC to find an arrangement which would give them more favourable terms short of requiring their association. In October 1962, Kenya, Uganda and Tanganyika decided to send a delegation to Brussels.[29] In March 1963, a group of East African Ministers and officials discussed trade matters with members of the

25 NA, FO 371/164829, Draft speaking notes for the Lord Privy Seal at a Restricted Session on Association, [10/62].

26 NA, FO 371/164828, Carter (Dar-es-Salaam) to Preston (CRO), 09.08.62.

27 NA, DO 161/196, PMM (62) 6th Meeting, 12.09.62.

28 "The Common Market Question: Association or what?," *Daily Times* (Lagos), 12.09.62, pp. 7 and 11; NA, CO 852/2124, Adu (EACSO) to Garner (CRO), 22.10.62.

29 "E. Africa to send mission for 'Six'," *East African Standard* (Nairobi), 12.10.62, p. 1.

European Commission. The EEC tried to convince the African delegates that an association would be the best option for their countries – a proposal which found a reserved reception.[30]

But in the first half of 1963, the idea of an association with the EEC became more and more popular with Commonwealth Africa, mainly because of the new association treaty, the Yaoundé Convention. Contrary to the original treaty, this agreement was the result of negotiations between sovereign African states and the Community. So, for the African Commonwealth countries the association system lost some of its "neo-colonial" sheen. By 1961, Nigeria's leading newspaper had argued that "it is hard to believe that an economic association, with which these 16 African countries wish to continue, although originally it was formed only by the decision of France herself, is neo-colonialism".[31] The fact that the institutions of the new association system were adjusted to create more equality between Africa and Europe pointed in the same direction. Consequently, the African Commonwealth countries, despite their original antipathy, increasingly focused on association as the way forward.

In April 1963, the EEC made a major step towards an expansion of its association system. On Dutch insistence, the Council of Ministers decided that association should also be open to former colonies of countries which were not (yet) members of the EEC. These countries were allowed to either become part of the Yaoundé arrangements or to conclude separate association agreements with the EEC. The latter option was eventually taken by Nigeria and the East African Commonwealth countries.[32]

Nevertheless, the new association system rested on a principle which was deeply unpopular with the African Commonwealth members. The EEC demanded that the associated countries, in exchange for trade preferences in the European market, should provide the EEC members with preferential treatment in their markets – the so-called principle of reverse preferences or reciprocity. In the early 1960s, this rule was at the centre of a debate about how to organise trade relations between industrialized

---

30 "Aim is non-political link with Market," *East African Standard* (Nairobi), 23.03.63, p. 3; Historical Archives of the European Commission (HAEC), BAC 4/1969/8, S/01209/63, Compte rendu, 15.04.63.

31 "Report on Strasbourg Conference. Africa and the Common Market," *Daily Times* (Lagos), 06.07.61, p. 5; see also "Sapping African Economy," *Daily Times* (Lagos), 04.01.63, p. 4, and Mazrui, A. A., "African Attitudes to the European Economic Community," *International Affairs*, Vol. 39, No. 1, 1963, pp. 24-36.

32 NA, FO 371/171456, EER (63) 26, Tropical Products and the Convention of Association between the E.E.C. and the Associated Overseas Territories, 01.04.63; Zartman, W., *The Politics of Trade Negotiations between Africa and the European Economic Community. The Weak Confront the Strong*, Princeton, Princeton University Press, 1971, p. 78f.

and "third world" (to use the term of the times) countries. This discussion intensified with the first United Nations Conference on Trade and Development (UNCTAD) in 1964. The developing countries demanded improved access – without having to grant reverse concessions – to the markets of the industrialized countries.[33]

These activities influenced the discussions between Commonwealth Africa and the EEC, which proceeded in autumn 1963. After exploratory talks, Nigeria and the EEC decided to start formal negotiations.[34] So, Nigeria overtook the East African Commonwealth countries, while the EEC, for its part, gave priority to talks with the largest African country. This does not, however, mean that the negotiations went smoothly. On the contrary, in April 1964, the EEC members were still discussing whether the European Commission should be granted a mandate for negotiations. France demanded an examination of the consequences of an association of Commonwealth countries for the current associates. Only after completion of this study – which did not bring very obvious results – did the Council of Ministers, in June 1964, agree on a mandate for the negotiations.[35]

In July 1964, the first round of negotiations took place. The Commission made it clear that any arrangement was to be based on the principle of "reciprocity"; Nigeria was expected to grant preferences for imports from Europe in exchange for more favourable conditions in the European market.[36] At first, Lagos objected to this request, but quickly developed a new strategy, formally accepting the principle of reciprocity, but trying to avoid substantial concessions to the EEC.[37] This shows that, for Nigeria, better access to the EEC market was more important than standing on principle.

Nigeria offered to grant preferences on less important products or on goods whose main supplier was the EEC. The Community decided not to offer free entry, but duty-free quotas for imports from Nigeria, because especially France insisted on safeguards for the francophone associates. However, it was agreed within the EEC that these quotas should be

---

33 Okigbo, P., *Africa and the Common Market*, Evanston, Northwestern University Press, 1967, p. 120-22; on UNCTAD, see Prebisch, R., *Towards a New Trade Policy for Development*, New York, United Nations, 1964.

34 "Nigeria – ECM talks open in full swing," *Daily Times* (Lagos), p. 5.

35 Zartman, W., *The Politics of Trade Negotiations between Africa and the European Economic Community*, *op. cit.*, p. 82f.

36 HAEC, BAC 4/1969/5, 9880/VIII/64-F, Compte Rendu Analytique de la deuxième Session de Négociations avec le Nigéria 14-17 juillet 1964, n.d.; Zartman, W., *The Politics of Trade Negotiations between Africa and the European Economic Community*, *op. cit.*, p. 83.

37 NA, DO 162/31, Brussels to FO, 23.07.64.

increased annually by a certain margin.[38] In June 1965, Nigeria and the EEC reached a compromise: The EEC would enjoy fewer preferences on the Nigerian market than it had originally demanded. In turn, the quotas for imports from Nigeria to the EEC would be increased less quickly than Nigeria had demanded.[39] After some deferral, mainly because of the "empty chair crisis", in July 1966, the association treaty between Nigeria and the EEC, the "Lagos Convention", was signed.

Although the negotiations between Nigeria and the EEC ended successfully, the discussions between East Africa and the European Commission were still far from any major breakthrough. The first exploratory talks did not take place before February 1964, and the Council of Ministers did not supply the Commission with a mandate for negotiations before October 1964.[40] The negotiations were postponed until March 1965, since the EEC wanted to bring the talks with Nigeria close to a conclusion. During the first negotiating round, the East African delegation stated that it was unwilling to grant any preferences to the EEC, but the Community – as with Nigeria – demanded reverse preferences, since the association system "implied a minimum of give and take".[41] Unlike Nigeria, East Africa insisted on the principle of non-reciprocity. Since the parties were unable to reach a compromise, the negotiations were stopped. They did not resume before November 1966, when once again, the East African delegation asked the EEC to drop its demand for preferences, but without success.[42]

But in March 1967, the East African countries submitted to the will of the EEC and declared that they were in principle ready to grant preferences.[43] Nevertheless, it took the EEC a full year to agree on what concessions it wanted to demand from East Africa, since France aimed

38 "Our EEC hope fading. Culled from 'West Africa'," *Daily Times* (Lagos), 27.04.65, p. 10; Zartman, W., *The Politics of Trade Negotiations between Africa and the European Economic Community*, *op. cit.*, p. 86f.

39 HAEC, BAC 4/1969/1, 9578/VIII/65-F, Rapport sur les Résultats des Négociations (29 juin-8 juillet 1965) entre la Commission et une délégation du Gouvernement du Nigéria, 14.07.65; Okigbo, P., *Africa and the Common Market*, *op. cit.*, pp. 130-36; Zartman, W., *The Politics of Trade Negotiations between Africa and the European Economic Community*, *op. cit.*, p. 88-90.

40 "East Africa to seek special trade terms from 'Six'," *East African Standard* (Nairobi), 07.02.64, p. 4.

41 "Embassy to E.E.C. may open," *East African Standard* (Nairobi), 26 May 1965, p. 2.

42 "East African talks with the 'Six' end in deadlock. Ideas unacceptable," *East African Standard* (Nairobi), 19 November 1966, p. 2; Zartman, W., *The Politics of Trade Negotiations between Africa and the European Economic Community*, *op. cit.*, pp. 100-03.

43 "Brighter Hopes of E.E.C. link," *East African Standard* (Nairobi), 6 April 67, p. 1; Zartman, W., *The Politics of Trade Negotiations between Africa and the European Economic Community*, *op. cit.*, p. 103.

at more concessions than most of the other members did. When the talks resumed in April 1968, the East African countries offered very small preferences on no more than a handful of products, but soon had to increase their offer. The EEC in turn improved its proposal for duty-free quotas for products vital to the East African countries, especially for coffee.[44] In June 1968, a compromise solution was found, and in July the association agreement between Kenya, Uganda, and Tanzania – the "Arusha Convention" – was signed in the capital of Tanzania.

The preferences for the EEC had consequences for Britain: since they were granted exclusively by the Commonwealth countries, they meant discrimination for British exports. Not surprisingly, London was worried about these developments – not so much for economic, but for political reasons. Some African Commonwealth members seemed to regard an improved access to the European market as being more important than safeguarding their trade links with Britain. London warned that it might reconsider these countries' preferences in Britain, but ultimately decided against any form of retaliation in order not to offend the governments of these countries and thus weaken British links with Commonwealth Africa.[45]

The association agreements between Commonwealth Africa and the EEC were a new departure. For the first time, some former British colonies signed major commercial treaties with the EEC. Nevertheless, there was no full turning of Commonwealth Africa towards the Community. Most African Commonwealth countries did not seek closer trade links with the EEC. But when London was set to become a member of the EEC, these countries also had to deal with the future relationship between Africa and the enlarged Community.

British EEC Membership and the Lomé Convention

In the early 1970s, the question of an association with the EEC received renewed interest in Commonwealth Africa. This was due to the entry negotiations between Great Britain and the EEC, which were conducted between 1970 and 1972. As during the first entry bid in 1961, the British government decided that all African Commonwealth countries should be offered the possibility to associate with the EEC. London concluded – as it had in 1961 – that an association would be the best way to secure these countries' access to the British market as well as to improve their access to the European market. Since the current association agreement was to

---

44 Zartman, W., *The Politics of Trade Negotiations between Africa and the European Economic Community*, *op. cit.*, pp. 104-07.

45 The deliberations within the British government and the discussions between London and Commonwealth Africa are analysed in Leikam, F., *Empire*, *op. cit.*, pp. 160-204.

expire in early 1975, London and the Community decided that the African Commonwealth countries should be allowed to take part in the negotiations on the successor arrangement.[46]

The reaction of the Commonwealth countries to this proposal was much more welcoming than it had been in 1961, although there was still some scepticism. The main reason for this was again the principle of reciprocity. When, in early 1972, the preparation for the negotiations began, many African Commonwealth members voiced concerns about an association. The Nigerian government, in particular, was reluctant to commit itself to this option, also because the EEC had never ratified the "Lagos Convention" after the outbreak of the Biafra War, a secession war within Nigeria. Nigeria also criticized the fact that associated countries were forced to grant preferences to the EEC. Nigeria was not alone in its position, as became evident in April 1972, when the 20 Commonwealth members that were potentially candidates for associate status met and rejected the principle of reciprocity.[47]

The British government was against reciprocity, because it realized that it would have little to gain from the introduction of reverse preferences. But it decided not to make this position public in advance of the negotiations in order to avoid muddying the waters with France.[48] Britain tried to convince the African Commonwealth countries to at least take part in the talks, which were to start in 1973. These negotiations would be the best opportunity, London argued, to voice demands and to work for changes.[49]

In early 1973, it became increasingly clear that the African Commonwealth members were at least willing to take part in the talks about the arrangement. This development was caused not so much by London's arguments, but by developments within Africa. The Organisation of African Unity (OAU) managed to establish close links between the francophone associates and the anglophone "associables". The OAU aimed at a common negotiating position for all African countries – francophone

46 Milward, A. S., *Politics and Economics in the History of the European Union, op. cit.*, p. 87.

47 NA, CAB 170/11, FCO to Ottawa *et al.*, EEC Association for certain Developing Commonwealth Countries, 08.04.72. See also Akinrinade, O., "Associates and Associables: The Failure of Commonwealth Bridge-Building, 1971-3," *The Journal of Modern African Studies*, Vol. 27, No. 2, 1989, pp. 177-99.

48 NA, CAB 134/3504, EUO (72) 38, The Associable Commonwealth – Reverse Preferences, 21.09.72; Palayret, J.-M., "Mondialisme contre régionalisme: CEE et ACP dans les négociations de la convention de Lomé 1970-75," in A. Varsori (ed.), *Inside the European Community: Actors and Policies in the European Integration, 1957-1972*, Baden-Baden, Nomos, 2006, pp. 369-97, here pp. 372-75.

49 NA, FCO 30/1819, Duff (Nairobi) to Lynch (ODA), 10.01.73.

as well as anglophone.[50] This task was far from easy since some francophone African countries – especially Senegal – supported the principle of reciprocity. They argued that a treaty among equals implied concessions on both sides, whereas concessions given by Europe only implied an inferior status of the African countries. But during the first half of 1973 Senegal's position slowly changed. In May 1973, the OAU members agreed on a common negotiation position *vis-à-vis* the EEC: The African states demanded free access to the EEC market for their exports without having to grant preferences to the EEC. In addition, they stated that this should moreover apply to some agricultural products which were also produced within the EEC and covered by the Community's Common Agricultural Policy (CAP). The African countries also sought a scheme for the stabilization of their export revenues. Because of the volatile prices for agricultural goods and raw materials, they regarded better market access alone as insufficient. They also tried to secure minimum prices for certain export goods.[51]

The position of the African countries on reciprocity was reinforced by the European Commission: In April 1973, the so-called Deniau Memorandum on the future association system stated that reverse preferences could, but did not have to be, part of the future association convention.[52] Even though this document only reflected the opinion of the Commission and not of all member states, it was indicative of new thinking within the EEC. These developments – the creation of a common African negotiation position and a positive signal from within Europe – ultimately convinced all associable Commonwealth countries to take part in the negotiations.

In June 1973, the discussions between the EEC and the associated and associable countries – the so-called "ACP countries" (African, Caribbean and Pacific) – commenced. On behalf of the African group, Wenike Biggs, Nigeria's Trade Minister declared that the African countries insisted on the "principle of non-reciprocity in trade and tariff concessions".[53] Moreover, Biggs demanded that a scheme for the stabilization of export earnings should be part of the new arrangement. Whereas the EEC

[50] Chikeka, C. O., *Africa and the European Economic Community 1957-1992, op. cit.*, pp. 118f.

[51] Brown, W., *The European Union and Africa. The Restructuring of North-South Relations*, London/New York, Tauris, 2002, pp. 54-56; Milward, A. S., *Politics and Economics in the History of the European Union, op. cit.*, p. 100.

[52] Brown, W., *The European Union and Africa, op. cit.*, pp. 52-54.

[53] NA, FCO 69/470, Brussels to FCO, 26.07.73; Mailafia, O., *Europe and Economic Reform in Africa. Structural Adjustment and Economic Diplomacy*, London, Routledge, 1997, pp. 65f.; Palayret, J.-M., "Mondialisme contre régionalisme: CEE et ACP dans les négociations de la convention de Lomé 1970-75," *op. cit.*, p. 381.

members were willing to introduce measures to secure minimum levels of export earning, opinions on reciprocity were divided. France asserted that the principle of reciprocity should be upheld. According to Paris, the associated countries should give something in return, since the EEC was not the "demandeur" (supplicant).[54] The EEC could not agree on a common position on reciprocity and as a result, the negotiations started very slowly. Several negotiating rounds, conducted between November 1973 and February 1974, brought only results on secondary points.[55]

When the African countries, in February 1974, met to take stock of the first round of negotiations, they expressed deep dissatisfaction. Against this background of the slow progress, the ACP countries took the initiative: they invited the EEC members to attend a special high-level conference in July 1974 in Kingston, the capital of Jamaica.[56] The Community went along with this proposal and started preparations for this meeting. Only at the very last minute did the EEC members agree on their negotiating position on reverse preferences: France finally agreed that the Community should not ask for preferences in exchange for a better access to the EEC market.[57]

This allowed the Kingston conference to make a major breakthrough: the EEC and the ACP states agreed on the central principles of their future trade relationship. The details were to be settled later. The Community accepted that improved trade conditions for the associates should not be balanced by reverse preferences for EEC members. Both sides found a solution for the products which were covered by the CAP. The EEC members made it clear that they were not willing to grant free access for products which were part of the CAP, as had been suggested by the ACP states. The Community offered quotas for certain CAP products, and these were accepted by the ACP delegations.[58]

The Kingston meeting was a major success for Commonwealth Africa: the EEC finally accepted the position of the ACP countries on reverse preferences. Consequently, all African Commonwealth states could be

---

54 NA, FCO 30/1697, Miers (Paris) to FCO, 02.08.73.

55 NA, FCO 30/2129, CEE-ACP/1/73/E, Summary of Conclusions arising from the Meetings of the Plenary Committee of Ambassadors and Plenipotentiaries during the first Negotiation Phase – 21 November 1973-14 December 1973, 14.12.73; Chikeka, C. O., *Africa and the European Economic Community 1957-1992*, *op. cit.*, pp. 122f.

56 NA, FCO 30/2166, Brussels to FCO, 14.01.74; see also "Sanu's plea to Brussels. Market talks are a drag," *East African Standard* (Nairobi), 1 July 1974, p. 4.

57 NA, FCO 30/2135, Brussels to FCO, 22.07.74.

58 NA, FCO 30/2136, Kingston to FCO, 25 and 27 July 1974; Palayret, J.-M., "Mondialisme contre régionalisme: CEE et ACP dans les négociations de la convention de Lomé 1970-75," *op. cit.*, pp. 386-90; see also "Jamaica sets stage for big E.E.C. talks," *East African Standard* (Nairobi), 29 July 74, p. 6.

expected to take part in the new arrangement. This breakthrough, however, meant that in other fields the EEC was less willing to abandon its original negotiating position. This was true for the mechanism for stabilising export earnings and the amount of development aid granted by the EEC. Concerning the former, the EEC members stated that payments would not start automatically as soon as the price of a certain product fell below a certain point, as the ACP states had requested. Instead, the consequences of the drop in export prices for the general economic situation of the respective country should be examined first.[59] To reach a compromise on the size of the Development Fund turned out to be more difficult. Whereas the ACP countries demanded 8 billion units of account, the EEC intended to supply no more than 3 billion. This question was settled only in late January 1975 during the final negotiating round. The EEC and the ACP countries agreed that the Development Fund would be supplied with 3.4 billion units of account.[60] The convention was signed in Lomé, capital city of Togo, in February 1975.

Contemporary analyses, as well as historical accounts, lead to the conclusion that the outcome was a success for Commonwealth Africa. Even though the ACP countries were forced to adjust some of their demands, they nevertheless managed to include a scheme for the stabilization of export earnings and avoided reverse preferences. The main reason for the positive outcome was the fact that the ACP and especially the African countries succeeded in finding and keeping a common negotiating position *vis-à-vis* the EEC. This especially paid off in fields – as in the question of reciprocity – where the EEC was split.[61] Besides, London's entry into the EEC changed the balance in favour of countries which did not insist on – or were even opposed to – the principle of reciprocity. The result of the negotiations finally made the African Commonwealth countries full members of the EEC association system.

Conclusion

This chapter has shown that the foundation of the EEC and the creation of the association system in 1957 had far-reaching consequences for Commonwealth Africa. The association was a central issue in the relations

[59] NA, FCO 30/2136, Kingston to FCO, 27.07.74.

[60] Chikeka, C. O., *Africa and the European Economic Community 1957-1992*, *op. cit.*, p. 124; Palayret, J.-M., "Mondialisme contre régionalisme: CEE et ACP dans les négociations de la convention de Lomé 1970-75," *op. cit.*, pp. 390-92.

[61] See NA, FCO 30/2631, Braithwaite: The End of Protocol 22, [03.02.75]; Lister, M., *The European Community and the Developing World. The Role of the Lomé Convention*, Aldershot, Avebury, 1988, p. 75; and Milward, A. S., *Politics and Economics in the History of the European Union*, *op. cit.*, p. 102.

between the African Commonwealth members and the Community. The position of the African Commonwealth states on the association system – from the time they gained independence to the conclusion of the Lomé Convention – can be divided into three phases: during the first phase, covering the late 1950s and early 1960s, the African Commonwealth countries vigorously criticized the system. They regarded the arrangement as a "neo-colonial" tool to perpetuate Africa's role as supplier of raw materials and tropical products, to keep the newly independent states closely aligned with the West, and to sabotage political and economic cooperation within Africa. Consequently, they did not want to become associated with the EEC, a move which had been suggested by Britain during its negotiations on EEC membership.

Around 1963, the attitude of Commonwealth Africa to the association system changed. The second phase was therefore characterized by a gradual coming around of African Commonwealth members to an association with the EEC. Some of these countries pursued association agreements with the Community to improve their access to the European market. As the association system was changed and opened, it lost much of its "neo-colonial" image in the eyes of Commonwealth Africa. Nevertheless, the relationship remained vexed, since the EEC insisted on reverse preferences, whereas the African Commonwealth countries were opposed to the principle of reciprocity. Further, the appeal of a closer relationship with the Community was limited to a small number of former British colonies: only those states which had close trade links with the EEC approached the Community. This, however, changed in the early 1970s.

The fact that the UK was to become a member of the EEC caused a renewed and intensified involvement of Commonwealth Africa with the association system. Britain's entry into the Community therefore marks the beginning of the third phase, in which Commonwealth Africa eventually became a full member of the association system. In order to safeguard their trade relationship with Britain and to gain better access to the EEC market, the African Commonwealth countries decided to join the negotiations on the new association system. Once again, the principle of reciprocity was the central obstacle in the talks but the EEC dropped its demand for reverse preferences, mainly as a reaction on the formation of a common negotiation front of all African countries. The conclusion of the Lomé Convention in 1975 thus marked the end of separate trade agreements between African countries and the EEC and the introduction of a comprehensive association agreement between Europe and all sub-Saharan Africa.

An analysis of the relationship between Commonwealth Africa and the EEC demonstrates the political and economic power of the EEC as well as the far-reaching consequences of its decisions. The association system served as a model for the organisation of the relations between Europe and Africa in general. All discussions on closer trade links between Commonwealth Africa and the EEC took the association as their starting point. Until 1975, the EEC was also able to lay down the fundamental rules of the association, as was apparent in the question of reverse preferences. In the 1960s, the African Commonwealth countries eventually had to submit to the will of the EEC. Not before 1975 were the African Commonwealth countries able to reject this principle – and even then only after they had joined forces with the francophone associates and after Britain had become a member of the EEC. The creation of the association system not only strongly affected countries which remained outside the arrangements in the beginning – it also served as a framework for the relations between Europe and Africa until 1975 and well beyond.

Linking Europe and Empire

Making Strategic Choices on the Eve of the Treaty of Rome

Laura KOTTOS

University of Reading

On the eve of the Treaty of Rome, between April 1955 and March 1957, major political events came to influence the European integration process. In April 1955, countries which had obtained their independence after the war met at the Bandung Conference and proclaimed their opposition to colonialism. Two months later, at another historic conference in Messina, a number of European countries embarked on negotiations which would lead to the creation of the European Economic Community (EEC). Following the declaration of independence by a number of former Asian colonies, some African countries (Sudan, Morocco, Tunisia and Ghana) freed themselves from colonial rule in 1956-1957. The decline of France and the United Kingdom as imperial powers was underlined by their retreat from the Suez Canal in 1956, all this within a context in which the two great post-war powers – the United States and the Soviet Union – were highly critical of European imperialism. Whilst colonialism was under threat in this way, the Treaty of Rome establishing the EEC was signed in March 1957, containing a section which explicitly stipulated that the overseas territories of the Six would be associated with this new community.

This chapter will argue that the European integration process is indeed closely linked to this imperial context. Through a comparative analysis of three imperial powers – France, Belgium and the United Kingdom (UK) – the study will show that despite making different final choices, these three imperial countries were in fact pursuing the same objective: in order to maintain their interests in their overseas territories they were ready to adapt themselves to the new colonial context and to modernise their imperial system. For France and Belgium, the EEC could boost this process of modernisation. For the UK, Europe could restrain the transformation of its colonies. As part of the overall discussion on how Europe and

Empire could be linked, various colonial models were to be evaluated: the British and Belgian colonial situations, but also Dutch decolonisation, were closely analysed by the three imperial powers. From these comparisons there emerged a truly European policy: the European Policy for Aid and Development was the result of the association of overseas territories with the EEC in 1957.

While recent scholarship has shown an interest in the study of relations between the European Community and its overseas territories before the Treaty of Rome, scholars have often focused solely on one country,[1] whereas a comparative study of three major imperialist countries may be a more European approach to this essentially European topic, and provide an opportunity to draw new conclusions. When authors have gone beyond the "one-state" analysis, they have generally confined themselves to the period after the Treaty of Rome because they could then use European official sources from the EEC institutions. Whilst most works have analysed European integration and the colonial context through European official reports, this study will seek to add a new perspective by analysing the work of national and European pressure groups which sought to link Europe and Empire.[2] As Andrew Knapp and Vincent Wright put it, "It was characteristic, moreover, of much of the first half-century of European integration, that the initiatives and debates were carried out chiefly at elite level rather than being brought into the hurly-burly of democratic policies".[3]

Europe and Empire: The Choice of France and Belgium

Except for anti-colonialist communists and anti-European imperial conservatives, the French and Belgians tended to be favourable both to

1 Montarsolo, Y., *L'Eurafrique, Contrepoint de l'idée d'Europe. Le cas français de la fin de la deuxième guerre mondiale aux négociations des traités de Rome*, Aix-en-Provence, Publications de l'Université de Provence, 2010; Deschamps, E., "La Belgique et l'Association des Pays et Territoires d'Outre-mer (PTOM) au Marché Commun (1956-1957)," in M. Dumoulin, G. Duchenne and A. Van Laer (eds.), *La Belgique, les petits états et la construction européenne. Actes du colloque de clôture de la VIIe Chaire Glaverbel d'études européennes 2001-2002*, Bruxelles, P.I.E.-Peter Lang, 2003, pp. 119-146; Deschamps, E., "L'Afrique belge et le projet de Communauté politique européenne (1952-1954)," in E. Remacle and P. Winand (eds.), *America, Europe, Africa (1945-1973)*, Bruxelles, P.I.E. Peter Lang, 2009, pp. 307-323.

2 Palayret, J.-M., "Les Mouvements pro-européens et la question de l'Eurafrique, du Congrès de la Haye à la Convention de Yaoundé (1948-1963)," in M.-T. Bitsch, and G. Bossuat (eds.), *L'Europe Unie et l'Afrique. De l'idée d'Eurafrique à la convention de Lomé I. Actes du colloque international de Paris, 1er au 2e avril 2004, Groupe de liaison des historiens auprès des Communautés*, Bruxelles, Bruylant, 2005, pp. 185-229.

3 Knapp, A. and Wright, V., *The Government and Politics of France*, Abingdon and New York, Routledge, 2006, pp. 30-31.

European integration and to Empire. Indeed, from different perspectives, many influential lobbies campaigned to combine the advantages of these two entities. For some pressure groups, such as the Eurafrican lobby and the Socialist Movement for the United States of Europe (SMUSE), the African continent was seen as the natural extension of Europe. Unlike Asia, Africa was almost entirely administered by Europeans and, as a producer of raw materials, the continent was essential to European economies. For other pressure groups, such as the European League for Economic Cooperation (ELEC), Europe was seen as a means of getting rid of the whole imperial preferential system and of modernising the colonial economic system. These groups promoting the idea of linking Europe and Empire expressed what appears to have been a general consensus within French and Belgian public opinion.

People with strong interests in colonial territories were largely against European integration because it was seen as a threat to the imperial equilibrium. Proud of their work in the overseas territories, they strongly disapproved of a community where national sovereignty would be shared and where non-colonial partners could intervene in colonial administration. For French colonial settlers, the European integration process threatened the autarchic economy that served so many of their interests, while Belgian settlers feared that other European members of the Community would force harmful changes on their way of colonising. For a minority of them, however, European integration was welcomed because it fitted their ideal of one community which included Europe and Africa in one sole territory: Eurafrica.[4] Some colonialists saw the Eurafrican continent as a third force standing between Soviet and American blocs. One member of the French Academy of Colonial Sciences, General Meynier, created the eponymous journal *Eurafriqu*e. His aim was to bring Eurafrican thinkers into contact with each other, and to organise tourist tours and car rallies in Africa in order to encourage connections between Europeans and Africans. In the Belgian Congo, it was mainly the middle-class Congolese Federation (Fedacol) that pushed for the Congo-Europe rapprochement. For the white settlers, Eurafrica was often imagined as a broader form of colonisation over the South Mediterranean continent (often with France having supremacy at the head of the community). The SMUSE on the other hand envisaged Eurafrica as a community of equal African and European citizens.[5] Some of the SMUSE members believed in a Europe that would replace colonialism by a true economic

4 Scheurs, R., "L'Eurafrique dans les négociations du Traité de Rome, 1956-1957," *Politique Africaine*, No. 49, March 1993, pp. 82-92.

5 Palayret, J.-M., "Les Mouvements pro-européens et la question de l'Eurafrique, du Congrès de la Haye à la Convention de Yaoundé (1948-1963)," in M.-T. Bitsch, and G. Bossuat (eds.), *L'Europe Unie et l'Afrique. op. cit.*, pp. 185-229.

association with independent African countries. After all, they argued, an independent Africa would always be a relative concept in a global world with interdependent economies. André Philip, a socialist and economist who had already participated in the creation of the General Agreement on Tariffs and Trade (GATT), argued that giving independence to the Philippines allowed the USA nonetheless to maintain control on the territories, due to monetary and customs unions.[6] He wanted to do the same with Europe and its overseas territories, and thus to present a new Europe as an attractive and friendly partner released from its past reputation as an exploiter of African resources. For André Philip, this kind of Eurafrican community was the only way to ensure a long-term exchange between two complementary economies, one which supplied the raw materials and the other which supplied the capital for industrial projects. Along with influential members such as Paul Alduy (President of the French Section of the Workers' International in the French Union Assembly) and Michel Cépède (Professor of Colonial Agronomy), the SMUSE campaigned for the creation of a special Commission within the Council of Europe to consider the further integration of overseas territories. The French Minister of Colonies, Gaston Defferre, was close to the SMUSE and a strong supporter of the idea of linking Europe and Empire. It was under his initiative that the overseas territories were associated with the Treaty of Rome.[7] Indeed, in 1956, he declared that France would not join the EEC if its colonial territories were not associated with the community.

Some liberal economists also wanted to link Europe and Empire, although there was less unanimity between them. Since the 19th century, liberal economists had argued that colonisation would not benefit the mother country.[8] During the interwar period, but especially in the aftermath of the Second World War and with events in the Dutch Empire, many people continued to believe that colonies were a financial burden. The Dutch, for example, had faced a dramatic decolonisation in Indonesia, but were still experiencing a real economic boom, a process that was later to be known as the Dutch Complex. This has led some historians like Paul Biarnès and Jacques Marseille, and more recently Pieter Lagrou, to argue that colonial countries in fact wanted to give up their declining overseas

6 Philip, A., "L'Europe et les pays sous-développés, compte rendu de la conférence donnée le 19 février 1957 dans l'auditoire de la Fondation universitaire," *Comptes rendus de la société royale d'économie politique*, Bruxelles, February 1957, p. 20.

7 Ollivier, A.-L., "Entre Europe et Afrique: Gaston Defferre et les débuts de la construction européenne," *Terrains & Travaux*, No. 8, 2005, pp. 14-33.

8 Stengers, J., *L'Anticolonialisme libéral du XIXe siècle et son influence en Belgique, Expansion belge sous Léopold Ier (1861-1865)*, Bruxelles, Académie Royale des Sciences d'Outre-Mer, 1965, pp. 481-521.

Empires.[9] The liberal and integrated market envisaged for Europe seemed to be a more attractive system than the autarchic and non-competitive structure inherent in the French exploitation of Africa. This argument, however, needs to be qualified. A comparison with the Belgian experience suggests that rather than a withdrawal from Empire, the economic elite wanted to liberalise trade between Europe and European colonial territories. Indeed, Belgium followed a policy of colonial trade liberalisation[10] and, in 1956, the Belgian Congo was so prosperous that Brussels had little desire to withdraw from its Empire. This prosperity was a product of the unique context of Belgian colonisation: at the 1885 Berlin Conference, the Great Powers had agreed to recognise the Belgian Congo on condition that the region would always keep the door open to foreign investments. This open-door policy proved to be very efficient.[11] In comparison with the Dutch Complex argument, this economic policy could be described as the "Belgian Complex", and this Belgian model even attracted some of the French colonial settlers. Even though the nascent European market was perceived as a threat to various French colonial industries – but also to several clandestine operations in favour of Belgian manufacturing – some influential colonial capitalists were still in favour of the EEC. While many colonial industries were favoured by protectionist measures, large mechanical and electrical industries found it difficult to export outside the French Empire. For some French employers, Europe could thus be an unexpected opportunity to change the economic system and increase their profits.

In her study of decolonisation, Catherine Hodeir examines French colonial big-business strategies in the face of decolonisation and touches upon some of the leaders who were to become influential activists in European pressure groups.[12] One of these groups, the ELEC[13] wanted, among other objectives, to raise the whole issue of the integration of overseas territories

---

9 Biarnès, P., *Les Français en Afrique noire de Richelieu à Mitterrand*, Paris, Armand Colin, 1987; Marseille, J., *Empire colonial et capitalisme français. Histoire d'un divorce*, Paris, Albin Michel, 1984; Lagrou, P., "Europe in the World: Imperial Legacies," in M. Telo (ed.), *The European Union and Global Governance*, London, Routledge, 2009, pp. 306-326.

10 Deschamps, E., "La Belgique et l'Association des Pays et Territoires d'Outre-mer (PTOM) au Marché Commun (1956-1957)," *op. cit.*, p. 129.

11 Buelens, F. and S. Marysse, "Returns on Investments during the Colonial Era: the Case of the Belgian Congo," *Economic History Review*, Vol. 62, S1, 2009, pp. 135-166.

12 Hodeir, C., *Stratégies d'Empire. Le grand patronat colonial face à la décolonisation*, Paris, Belin, 2003.

13 Dumoulin, M., "La Ligue Européenne de Coopération Economique (1946-1954)," in M. Dumoulin, R. Girault and G. Trausch (eds.), *L'Europe du patronat. De la guerre froide aux années soixante. Actes du colloque de Louvain la Neuve des 10 et 11 mai 1990*, Berne, Euroclio P.I.E.-Peter Lang, 1993, pp. 207-212.

within the future European Community. The League was run by Edmond Giscard d'Estaing,[14] an important spokesman of the French employers' association Conseil National du Patronat Français (CNPF), and president of a colonial financial company (the *Société Financière pour la France et les pays d'Outre-mer: SOFFO*). He was aided by Luc Durand-Reville, another SOFFO associate, who was also Senator for Gabon and a member of the overseas commission in the French Upper House.[15] The League was additionally strengthened by the presence of Robert Lemaignen, president of an important commercial company (*Société Commerciale des Ports Africains*: SOCOPAO) in French West Africa, and Chairman of the Committee on International Economic Relations of the National Council of French Employers (CNPF) and by Henri Cangardel, at that time head of the shipping society *Compagnie Générale Transatlantique.*[16] These businessmen needed a strong European market open to overseas territories so that their firms would be free to trade in a non-protectionist market. But they also wanted to protect themselves from the presumed harmful political intervention of non-French European partners.[17] With the formula of economic association of overseas territories with Europe, France and Belgium kept their political power in their Empires and only linked their overseas territories to Europe economically. Thus both countries enjoyed the two-fold benefits of membership of the European Community, all the while keeping their status as imperial powers.

The French and Belgian governments were also able to adopt this policy because they enjoyed the general support of public opinion. Opinion polls can provide a useful window on the mood of the population, and reveal the non-institutionalised views of the public which were a contributing factor in political decision-making. It is important to note, however, that 1950s European polls can be unreliable sources. The American scientific polling method was implemented slowly in Europe and the results vary greatly from one study to another. However, the broad conclusions are fairly close and are good indicators of the general atmosphere on the eve of the Treaty of Rome, and of attitudes towards both European integration and Empire.

Jacques-René Rabier has said that the few European polls that existed before he launched the Euro-barometer public opinion survey in 1973

---

14 Father of Valéry Giscard d'Estaing, French President from 1974 to 1981.

15 Palayret, J.-M., "Les Mouvements pro-européens et la question de l'Eurafrique, du Congrès de la Haye à la Convention de Yaoundé (1948-1963)," *op. cit.*, pp. 193-194.

16 Comité National du Patronat Français, "L'inclusion des Territoires d'Outre-mer dans le Marché Commun," *Bulletin Mensuel du CNPF*, No. 157, February 1957, pp. 90-91.

17 Hodeir, C., *Stratégies d'Empire. Le grand patronat colonial face à la décolonisation, op. cit.*, pp. 280-281.

were essentially instigated by serious American institutes such as Gallup International or the United States Information Agency (USIA).[18] These polls, widely divergent in time and place, however, focused mainly on bigger countries such as France, Germany or the United Kingdom, and ignored the Belgian position.[19] Only an unpublished survey in 1950, carried out by the Eric Stern Public Opinion Research Institute, gives us a glimpse of Belgian public opinion during the period in question. This reported that 57% of Belgians were in favour of European integration. Other surveys appeared in the immediate aftermath of the Rome treaty and showed that between 65.7% (USIA) and 80% (Cologne Unesco Institute for Social Science) of Belgians approved of Europe. The gap between such results demonstrates the limitations of these first polls. French statistics are enhanced by subsequent surveys directed by the national *Institut Français d'Opinion Publique (IFOP).*[20] These polls show that during the negotiations of the Treaty of Rome a majority of French people supported European integration. In fact, there was a sharp upward trend in the months leading up to the signing of the treaty: in December 1955, 45% were in favour, 53% in April 1956, and 67% in September 1956.[21] However, even this seeming support was less than wildly enthusiastic and had more than a whiff of resigned acceptance about it.[22] A significant proportion of the population either had no opinion about Europe or was simply not interested in the issue at all.[23]

As a result of several years of colonial propaganda, Empire was still a popular idea both in France and Belgium. However, whilst colonial belief had been shaken in France after the Asian decolonisations and the upheavals in Africa, the Belgian Congolese colony remained quite peaceful. A majority of Belgians were convinced of the legitimacy of their presence in Africa: a survey conducted in 1956 by a Belgian University

18 Rabier, J.-R., "L'opinion publique et l'intégration de l'Europe dans les Années 50," in E. Serra (ed.), *La relance européenne et les traités de Rome*, Bruxelles, Bruylant, 1989, pp. 363-364.

19 Rabier, J.-R., *L'Information des Européens et l'intégration de l'Europe, comptes rendus de la XXXIe semaine coloniale universitaire*, Bruxelles, Université libre de Bruxelles, February 1965.

20 Bissery, J., *L'Opinion des Français sur le Marché Commun et l'unification européenne de 1950 à 1968*, Paris, IFOP, October 1968.

21 Merrit, R.-L. and Puchala, D.-J., *Western European Perspectives on International Affairs*, New York, Praeger, 1968, pp. 283-284.

22 Dulphy, A. and Manigand, C., "L'Opinion française vers l'euroconscience et le désenchantement," in A. Dulphy and C. Manigand (eds.), *Les opinions publiques face à l'Europe communautaire. Entre cultures nationales et horizon européen*, Bruxelles, P.I.E. Peter Lang, 2004, pp. 23-62.

23 Bissery, J., *L'Opinion des Français sur le Marché Commun et l'unification européenne de 1950 à 1968*, *op. cit.*, p. 49.

Institute (*Institut Universitaire d'Information Sociale et Économique – INSOC*) reported that 80.5% of the population thought that their presence in Congo was justified, whilst 86.3% were convinced that the colony was useful for Belgium.[24]

The situation in France, however, was different. The country had just withdrawn from Indochina, and Morocco and Tunisia were in the middle of gaining independence in 1956. These independence movements were to be overshadowed by events in Algeria, which quickly became one of the main national concerns. Algeria was a French *département* at the time, so the war that broke out in November 1954 was considered to be a matter of civil unrest, leading the government to declare a state of emergency. Given this context, the French were certainly more realistic about the future of colonialism. According to a 1956 IFOP survey, 25% of those polled said that Algeria would no longer belong to France within ten years, while 31% said the opposite.[25] This scepticism about the durability of Empire was sometimes expressed in open criticism of the imperial project, not only from communists but also from nationalists. As the future of colonialism was for the first time questioned, a famous French magazine argued that the Empire was in fact a major financial burden. Raymond Cartier, journalist at *Paris Match* – a popular weekly with a circulation of two million copies[26] – claimed that France was spending too much money overseas, and that these public funds would be better invested in France.[27] Such reservations may have been accentuated by the fall-out from the Suez affair, where France had been criticised by the United Nations for its role, alongside the UK, in trying to prevent Nasser from nationalising the Suez Canal in October 1956. Along with the news from Algeria, the autumn of 1956 was perhaps the moment when the Empire ceased to be unconditionally supported in France. Even if a majority of French people were moved by patriotic feelings and remained attached to their overseas territories, it was becoming obvious that the cost to France in safeguarding its prestige was now too high.

[24] Jacquemyns, G., *Le Congo Belge devant l'opinion publique*, Bruxelles, Institut Universitaire d'Information Sociale et Économique, 1956.

[25] Ensenhans, H., "Les transformations de la solution intermédiaire (1954-1962)," *Colloque du 20-22 juin 2006. Pour une histoire critique et citoyenne. Le cas de l'histoire franco-algérienne*, Lyon, ENS LSH, 2007.

[26] Omgba, R.-L., *La littérature anticolonialiste en France de 1914 à 1960. Formes d'expression et fondements théoriques*, Paris, L'Harmattan, 2004.

[27] Cartier, R., "En France noire avec Raymond Cartier," *Paris-Match*, No. 386, 1 September 1956, pp. 39-41.

Empire, not Europe: The Choice of the United Kingdom

For the United Kingdom, the EEC and the Commonwealth were mutually exclusive entities. Was the choice for Empire a product of British public opinion? Or was it the result of conservative pressure groups which refused to modernise the Empire? In reality, the United Kingdom was already engaged in the process of modernising its Empire and this policy was incompatible with a European community.

Contrary to what one might think, the British were not anti-European. In fact, USIA opinion polls conducted between 1948 and 1957 showed that the British were as European as their continental counterparts. During discussions over the integrated European Defence Community (EDC), 42% of the British who had heard about the subject were in favour of British participation (along with 42% of Italians, 45% of French, and 48% of Germans).[28] However, the British were generally less well informed about Europe because their country was not a party to the discussions. A survey on the EDC issue reported that eight out of ten French people had heard about the EDC against four out of ten Britons.[29] In 1957, an international poll showed the same trend: 61% of the British surveyed professed ignorance about the Common Market (compared to 38% of Germans, 36% of French and 33% of Italians).[30] According to Wendy Webster, whilst most British people knew nothing about the Common Market "a large proportion of those who had [heard about the EEC] believed that Britain was a member".[31] Despite these trends, some British personalities participated in important European lobbies such as Britain in Europe and the Federal Union.[32] Many others joined European organisations such as the SMUSE and the ELEC. The British decision therefore does not reflect an anti-European society but rather the fact that the British elite had failed to convince their population.[33]

---

28 Rabier, J.-R., "L'opinion publique et l'intégration de l'Europe dans les années 50," in E. Serra (ed.), *La Relance européenne et les traités de Rome*, *op. cit.*, p. 572.

29 *Ibid.*, p. 571.

30 *Ibid.*, p. 576.

31 Webster, W., *Englishness and Empire 1939-1965*, Oxford and New York, Oxford University Press, 2005, p. 174.

32 May, A., *L'Angleterre avec cette immense escorte; The Commonwealth and Britain's First Application to Join the EEC, 1961-1963*, London, South Bank University European Papers, 1995.

33 Foster, A., *Euroscepticism in Contemporary British Politics. Opposition to Europe in the British Conservative and Labour Parties since 1945*, London and New York, Routledge, 2002, p. 11.

British public opinion was no more attached to its Empire than the Belgian or French and, in reality, "domestic criticism of empire in France was much weaker than it was in Great Britain, and support for empire was much stronger".[34] According to British historians, British public opinion was either indifferent to Commonwealth issues,[35] or confident that the Empire was not in decline, but in transition.[36] In both cases, popular attachment to the Empire does not explain why the Commonwealth prevailed over European integration in Britain. Rather, three geopolitical arguments are at the root of the choice the UK would make.

First, if most liberals wanted to liberalise economic relations with European partners, the EEC, as a customs union with common external tariffs, was seen as yet another protectionist market.[37] The government feared that the United States would condemn a preferential market that would discriminate against American products, and contravene the General Agreement on Tariff and Trade (GATT). The United Kingdom also feared that the independent Commonwealth countries would condemn intra-European trade liberalisation since the measure would challenge their policy of protecting their vulnerable industries. In the 1950s, The *status quo* that prevailed in the 1950s was advantageous to Britain: the United States tolerated the preferential tariffs within the Commonwealth which had been granted before the signing of the GATT but criticised any increase in these preferential tariffs. If the United Kingdom were to join the Common Market, its special relationship with the US would be endangered, as would US support for the Commonwealth. The links with the Commonwealth would thus be challenged, especially since the independent Commonwealth countries also opposed the EEC. This would be in opposition to Britain's post-war policy, a strategy that followed the Churchill theory of Britain as being at the centre of three circles: the British Commonwealth and Empire, the English speaking world, and Europe. Within the ELEC, British members supported the idea of economic intergovernmental cooperation between the Commonwealth and Europe but did not want to be part

34 Philpott, D., *Revolutions in Sovereignty. How Ideas Shaped Modern International Relations*, Princeton, Princeton University Press, 2001, p. 232.

35 Ward, S. (ed.), *British Culture and the End of Empire*, Manchester and New York, Manchester University Press, 2001; Webster, W., *Englishness and Empire 1939-1965*, Oxford, Oxford University Press, 2004; Porter, B., *The Absent-Minded Imperialists. Empire, Society and Culture in Britain*, Oxford, Oxford University Press, 2004.

36 Ward, S. (ed.), *British Culture and the End of Empire*, *op. cit.*; MacKenzie, J. M., *Propaganda and Empire, the Manipulation of British Public Opinion 1880-1960*, Manchester and Dover, Manchester University Press, 1984.

37 Clarke, S. and J. Curtice, "The Liberal Democrats and European Integration," in D. Baker and D. Seawright (eds.), *Britain For or Against Europe. British Politics and the Question of European Integration*, Oxford, Clarendon Press, 1998, p. 15.

of a community with common external tariffs. Indeed, it was not the association of overseas territories with Europe but rather, the economic integration of the Six into a Customs Union, which worried the United Kingdom. The British members of the League feared that by losing their sovereignty over external tariffs, they would lose the preferential deal Britain had obtained with independent Commonwealth countries and the United States. France and Belgium, on the other hand, only had links with dependent raw-material producers and needed industrial economic partners in Europe in order to grow economically. The special relationship of the United Kingdom with the Commonwealth and the US also mattered for the British Eurafrican supporters. Even though the SMUSE defended a federal Europe, the British leader of the organisation, Fenner Brockway, explained that Labour members were too divided over the European question to add new complications by adding a Eurafrican debate to the discussions.[38]

If the British members of European pressure groups were reluctant to publicly support a Europe/Empire association, the colonial protectionist groups were more homogeneous and powerful than their Belgian and French counterparts. A handful of Tories within the Suez Group were briefly seduced by the prospect of an imperial association with France, but these hopes ended with the Franco-British military retreat from Egypt.[39] Within Britain's most influential industrial lobby, the Federation of British Industries (FBI), members were divided on the European question and the Commonwealth economic issue, notably on the question of whether the imperial preferential system was profitable to the country. The group's ideological divisions on these issues lessened its impact in comparison with the homogeneous colonial lobbies which were unanimous in their condemnation of Europe. Indeed, the Empire lobby, "placed Britain at the manufacturing centre of a united Empire that supplied raw materials, had implications on Britain's economy, society, diplomacy, imperial policy and role in the world and it was this vision that the Empire lobby sought to defend in opposing British participation in European integration".[40] Whereas in France, many influential colonial businessmen

38 Palayret, J.-M., "Les Mouvements pro-européens et la question de l'Eurafrique, du Congrès de la Haye à la Convention de Yaoundé (1948-1963)," *op. cit.*, p. 191.

39 Wilkes, G., "The Commonwealth in British European Policy: Politics and Sentiment, 1956-1963," in A. May (ed.), *Britain, the Commonwealth and Europe. The Commonwealth and Britain's Application to Join the European Communities*, Basingstoke, Palgrave, 2001, p. 55.

40 Bromund, T. R., *The Wave of the Future: the Defenders of the Empire Confront European Integration, 1956-1963, Paper Presented at the Biannual Meeting of the EUSA, Austin, Texas, 31 March-2 April 2005*, Austin, European Union Studies Association, 2005, pp. 1-2.

wanted colonial trade liberalisation within Europe, British colonial businessmen were organised within the Empire Industries Association (EIA) to defend the imperial preference. The idea of a mutually exclusive choice between Europe and Empire was popular among the conservative majority in parliament but also among less traditionalist spheres which thought that Commonwealth partners would feel betrayed and less privileged if Britain were to participate in another community. Diplomatic tensions with present and former colonies needed to be avoided in the troubled imperial context.

Finally, the choice Britain made was also influenced by the colonial policy which the country had adopted. During the African governors' conference of 1947, and in line with American policy, Britain agreed to grant autonomy to all its colonies within twenty or thirty years. In so doing, the country did not entirely give up its Empire but replaced old colonial relations with a modern community, the "Commonwealth of Nations" which would bring together the colonies which had gained independence.[41] While creating more acceptable links with its dominions and former territories, Britain could rely on an historical community comprised of economic powers and political partners such as Australia, New Zealand, South Africa and Canada which had grown stronger, both financially and militarily, during the war.[42] From this perspective, Britain did not need Europe in the same way that France and Belgium did. The country's special links with the United States and the Commonwealth were a guarantee of Britain's world-power status and this international position was not to be jeopardised by an association with countries like France and Belgium whose colonial policies were not directed towards giving full colonial independence.

France and Belgium, for their part, understood that many things could be learned from the English way of handling colonial troubles. On the continent, "Eurafrica" supporters closely followed Commonwealth developments. In 1954, the French general Octave Meynier clearly stated that France had to learn from the example of the Commonwealth and its association with economic powers such as Australia and New-Zealand.[43] According to Meynier, France could also be at the centre of its own Commonwealth in association with European countries if the Empire were to be integrated into the European community. In the Eurafrica community of General Meynier, the African continent would not be independent.

---

41 Fluchard, C. and Salifou, A., *L'Europe et l'Afrique du XVe siècle aux indépendances*, Bruxelles, De Boek Université, 1987, p. 207.

42 Wilson, H. S., *African Decolonisation*, London, Edward Arnold, 1994, p. 73.

43 Meynier, O., "L'Idée eurafricaine en marche," *Eurafrique*, Vol. 27, No. 13, April 1954, p. 13.

However, ten years after the British African Governors' conference and one month after he demanded that French overseas territories be associated with the EEC, Gaston Defferre finally introduced a law which provided for progressive steps towards autonomy of the colonies so that the "[...] 1956 Framework Law [...] aligned late colonial French rule in Africa more closely with its British equivalents".[44] When this measure was proposed in June 1956, however, the negotiations on the EEC were reaching their conclusion. The United Kingdom had already stated that it would not participate.

The Association of Overseas Territories in the Treaty of Rome: A Colonial Policy Inspired by the Belgian and British Model?

The French and Belgian decision to link Europe to Empire was not as opposed to British colonial policy as it might initially seem. Moreover, their choices were influenced by the political context in the United Kingdom. When, in May 1956, Gaston Defferre declared that France would not join the EEC if its overseas territories were not associated with the community, the French minister was probably inspired by both the British Commonwealth policy and the Belgian colonial model of trade liberalisation. He wanted to modernise the *Union française* (Uf) (French Union) and had been observing the colonial achievements of its neighbours.

In 1946, the Fourth Republic inaugurated the French Union, a community that replaced the French Empire. With the advent of the new organisation, the former colonies now became known as "overseas territories" (territoires d'outre-mer). As with the Commonwealth, the French Union aimed to conform to the principles of the United Nations Universal Declaration of Human Rights launched in December 1948 with its anti-colonialist effort to replace domination by relations which would be based on liberty and individual rights.[45] However, compared to the British Commonwealth, the French project encountered major difficulties. With protectionism and the post-war establishment of social laws for indigenous employment, large sectors of private investment deserted the colonies. The French government had two options. One option was to increase the prosperity of its overseas territories in order to strengthen economic relations between France and its colonies and thereby discourage colonial secession. This option would have required a major financial commitment,

[44] Shipway, M., *Decolonization and its Impact. A Comparative Approach to the End of the Colonial Empires*, Maden, Oxford and Carlton, Blackwell Publishing, 2008, p. 185.

[45] Deschamps, H., *La Fin des Empires Coloniaux*, Paris, Presses Universitaires de France, 1959.

and post-war national reconstruction and the conflict in Indochina were draining the national budget. Thus, the government would have to rely on private investment to achieve these aims. By opening colonial markets to its European partners, France could draw on European private investments and thus achieve the sort of economic growth seen in the Belgian Congo. The second option was to strengthen the political and historical ties with the colonies in the manner of the British model, where territories which gained their independence were included in the prosperous Commonwealth. For France to be a sufficiently attractive partner to its former colonies, it would have to show that it still had the status of a world power and could be a useful future economic partner. France's leading role in Europe and the assurance that overseas territories would benefit economically from European integration might then strengthen the links between the mother country and its colonial territories.

For some historians and contemporary observers, the association of Europe and overseas territories was a means of withdrawing from Empire. The French government followed the Dutch model: turning away from an expensive Empire in order to focus on European economic opportunities. Writing in 1956 in the journal *L'Express*, Georges Boris (a journalist and influential socialist politician, who had introduced Keynesian ideas in France in 1926, and was associated with major French leaders such as Léon Blum, de Gaulle and Pierre Mendès France)[46] inveighed against what he perceived to be an imperial withdrawal. According to Boris, the expansion of French colonial markets to the rest of Europe would ruin the economic ties between France and its Empire. Once France had divested itself of its economic links with its Empire, it could easily rid itself of its expensive political administration of these territories.[47] It is certainly true that Defferre's Framework Law provided for France granting autonomy to the colonies. However, the Minister of French Overseas Territories argued that he did not want a French withdrawal from Empire. He was aware that the Europe/Empire association challenged French political links with its colonies but he explained that these political ties were nonetheless already challenged by colonised populations and that France's influence in its Empire could only be strengthened by the economic advantages that overseas territories would gain by their association with Europe.[48] Whilst Defferre appeared to be preparing France for

46 Boris, G., *Servir la République. Textes et Témoignages. Présentation Pierre Mendès-France*, Paris, R. Julliard, 1963.

47 Boris, G., "Mirages de l'Eurafrique," *L'Express*, No. 288, 26 December 1956.

48 Letter from Gaston Defferre to Guy Mollet, "Problèmes posés pour la France d'Outre-mer par le projet de marché commun européen," 17 May 1956, in G. Bossuat, *D'Alger à Rome (1943-1957), Choix de documents*, Louvain-la-Neuve, Ciaco, 1989, pp. 167-177.

withdrawal from Empire, he was actually thinking of a worst-case scenario. His support for French association with the Treaty of Rome aimed to safeguard France's dominant role in the region. First, the country had no other choice than an association since it could not face the necessary developments overseas and the competition of foreign economies within the liberalised Common Market. If France wanted to join Europe without losing its empire, Defferre had to incorporate the Empire into Europe. Second, the association option anticipated the likely emancipation of the colonies as was the case with Britain and the Commonwealth. France lacked funds and independent overseas partners to attract the colonies through the French Union. If France had to grant autonomy to its overseas territories, Europe could be an economically appealing community. Yet, in return for opening its colonial markets, the government asked the European members to participate financially in the development of the French Union. Combined with a planned increase in private investment from Europe/Empire liberalisation, the public aid to be brought by the European Development Fund (EDF) established within the Treaty of Rome would allow France to finance her colonies and provide incentives for the territories to stay within the French Union. Finally, France would continue to maintain a dominant role both in Europe and in the French Union. By proposing association – instead of mere integration – Paris positioned itself as the necessary connection between the French Union and the European Community. This policy was to give the country a leading position in the EEC, particularly with regard to the resurgent economy in Germany.[49] The exclusive economic context of European integration thus allowed France to keep its entire sovereignty and prestige overseas while enjoying a unique opportunity to strengthen its colonial links.[50]

Belgian support for the association of overseas territories with Europe is evidence that the policy was not one of a withdrawal from Empire. Because the Belgian Congo was prosperous and relatively free from social agitation, Brussels was not inclined to support the Dutch model. Instead, the country sought to strengthen its economic power. At first glance, Belgian support seemed to be a two-fold desire to comply with the French ultimatum and achieve European integration. However, the country was also concerned about the small number of Belgian troops stationed in the Congo, and felt itself to be under US and UN anti-colonial pressure. It was therefore difficult for Belgium to dissociate itself

[49] Migani, G., "L'Association des TOM au Marché commun: histoire d'un accord européen entre cultures économiques différentes et idéaux politiques communs 1955-1957," in M.-Th. Bitsch and G. Bossuat (eds.), *L'Europe Unie et l'Afrique, op. cit.*, p. 237.

[50] Scheurs, R., "L'Eurafrique dans les négociations du Traité de Rome, 1956-1957," *op. cit.*, p. 85.

from France as an imperial ally. Nevertheless, the most important factor was France's promise to open its colonial markets to European partners because the Belgian Congo shared many borders with French colonial territories. The liberalisation of the French colonial economy explains why Belgium was ready to contribute very considerable sums to the EDF even though these funds would not directly benefit the Belgian Congo. In Belgian colonial circles, this measure was criticised as a gift of millions of dollars to French colonies[51] and the Minister of Foreign Affairs, Paul-Henri Spaak, was accused of having sold off the Congo to obtain the signing of the Treaty of Rome. Although dissatisfied by the huge Belgian contribution to the EDF, the Belgian Minister of Finance, Jean-Charles Snoy et d'Oppuers, backed the decision. He justified himself by proudly reminding everyone that a social fund is always disadvantageous to the richest partners, in this case the flourishing Belgian Congo.[52]

Finally, the association of overseas territories satisfied major pressure groups in France and Belgium. In fact, nearly all the Eurafrican intellectuals welcomed the Treaty of Rome as the first path to a Eurafrican Community, while colonial businessmen supported the liberalisation of the colonial market, now satisfied that their financial interests were being protected. The decision to link colonial territories to the EEC did not face stiff opposition because it was in line with mainstream public opinion. A few years later, when the colonies gained their independence, this resolution would be the basis for the modern European policy towards Africa.

Conclusion: Towards an African Policy in the European Community

When the Treaty of Rome was signed on 25 March 1957, the idea of further autonomy for colonial territories was generally accepted by France and the United Kingdom, although much less so by Belgium. New relationships with dependencies were expected to follow but nobody knew what their structures would be nor exactly when they would replace the old colonial model. To counter possible developments, many observers argued for bringing national forces together in order to maintain their influence over territories rich in raw materials. Surrounded by the American and Soviet blocs, imperialist countries had to find a solution through advanced regional communities. While Britain turned to a modernising Commonwealth, negotiations on a European Economic Community were the opportunity for France and Belgium to give some concrete form to

51 Gayet, G., *La Belgique et le Marché Commun en Afrique, Compte rendu des séances de l'Académie des Sciences d'Outre-Mer*, Paris, ARSOM, May 1957, p. 179.

52 Snoy et D'Oppuers, J.-C., "Les projets de Marché Commun, d'Euratom et d'Association des Territoires d'Outre-mer," *Eurafrica*, Vol. 1, No. 2, December 1957, p. 19.

these ideas. Contrary to the conclusions of previous studies in this area, it appears that in both these cases imperialists were, in fact, trying to perpetuate their leading position in the southern hemisphere.

It is in part because France lacked funds to legitimise its presence in its colonial countries that it turned for help to its European partners, hoping that the aid would be strong enough to persuade its dominions to stay within the French sphere of influence. Nonetheless, if the countries opted for independence, France would continue to have a role within the European Community through its extensive experience on the ground. As it turned out, the colonies opted for independence, but France nevertheless made every effort to hold on to its central position in European relations with Africa for the next twenty years. When French Guinea gained its independence in 1958, France made sure that the EEC did not propose a separate association for the country, a fact which was for Arnold Rivkin clear evidence that the association was aiming to maintain its domination in Africa.[53] Thereafter, European external policies with newly independent territories came under the ambit of the fourth part of the Treaty of Rome where association was established for five years, with an option of renewal. Despite the fact that decolonisation was almost completed by 1961, European members waited until the end of this agreement to launch the new five-year Yaoundé Convention confirming the economic association of Europe and independent African countries in 1963. Moreover, the convention, which accorded free trade commercial advantages and social aid, was limited to the eighteen former francophone colonies, called *Etats Africains et Malgaches Associés* (EAMEA).[54] Within the European Commission itself, France made sure that it was a French Commissioner who was put in charge of these territories until 1975.[55] The first person to hold this position in the DG Development was Robert Lemaignen, a central figure in the ELEC. His appointment revealed the influence of the League's ideas and the way in which their European project had developed. During his mandate, and in collaboration with other former colonial administrators, Robert Lemaignen established the European Development Aid Policy.[56] The conclusions of the pressure groups on European and colonial issues and the creation of the EDF had opened the

[53] Rivkin, A., *Africa and the West. Elements of Free-World Policy*, New York, Frederick A. Praeger, 1962.

[54] Palayret, J.-M., "Mondialisme contre régionalisme: CEE et ACP dans les négociations de la convention de Lomé 1970-75," *op. cit.*, pp. 369-398.

[55] Dimier, V., "Institutionnalisation et bureaucratisation de la Commission européenne: le cas de la DG DEV," *Politique Européenne*, No. 11, 2003, pp. 99-121.

[56] Dimier, V., "Négocier avec les rois nègres: l'Influence des administrateurs coloniaux français sur la politique européenne de développement," in M.-T. Bitsch and G. Bossuat (eds.), *L'Europe Unie et l'Afrique, op. cit.*, p. 395.

way to a modern development policy even though the term was not used in 1957. In conclusion, it seems reasonable to suggest that the history of European integration should be seen as closely linked to the history of decolonisation at this time if either process is to be fully and properly understood.

Part V

The EU and International Organizations: Conflict and Crisis Management

Global Governance and the Reform of the International Legal Order

Some Insights from the European Union

Rostam J. NEUWIRTH[1]

Associate Professor, University of Macau, Faculty of Law

Introduction

Both today's international legal order and the European Union legal order have their origin in the aftermath of the Second World War and were drafted in a similar spirit. Initially, the European Communities were created under international law. Later developments, however, set the European Communities and the European Union (EU) as their successor further apart from the international legal system. Nonetheless, their points of mutual contact and scope for reciprocal interaction remain numerous and are possibly converging in view of the increasing global interdependence and interconnectedness. Particularly, the challenges that they face in the governance of their respective affairs are quite similar, being different perhaps only in terms of scope and gravity. With regard to governance, the principal challenge they both face is primarily conceptual, as thoughts usually precede actions while their underlying ideas proceed towards their realisation. The conceptual difficulty with global governance is, first of all, reflected in the "mystery" that surrounds the concept itself.[2] By and large, global governance has been outlined as a series of questions that can be reduced to pondering how, and by whom we are currently governed, and by whom, and how we plan to be governed in the future. For the time being, these questions merely form the beginning of a debate as we, paradoxically,

1 The author would like to thank Marialaura Fino, Martina Spernbauer, Robert Schütze and Iris Eisenberger for their useful comments on earlier drafts of this chapter. The usual disclaimer applies.

2 See Kennedy, D., "The Mystery of Global Governance," *Ohio Northern University Law Review*, Vol. 34, 2008, p. 827.

lack both a common language and a common institutional platform for such deliberations to take place.[3] For this reason, the challenges for the debate about global governance have been aptly described by James N. Rosenau as follows:

> To anticipate the prospects for global governance in the decades ahead is to discern powerful tensions, profound contradictions, and perplexing paradoxes. It is to search for order in disorder, for coherence in contradiction, and for continuity in change. It is to confront processes that mask both growth and decay. It is to look for authorities that are obscure, boundaries that are in flux, and systems of rule that are emergent. And it is to experience hope embedded in despair.[4]

Against the backdrop of these manifold challenges, this chapter highlights some of the major flaws inherent in the architecture of today's international legal order. To this end, it builds upon the debate focusing on the complex relationship between international law and European law.[5] This debate has various aspects. A first aspect covers the question of whether European law is still part of international law, or whether, after half a century of continuous development, it can still be classified as a branch of international law.[6] Another aspect involves the attempt to assess the general quality of the relationship between European and international law.[7] Such is also the interest in the process of a "Europeanisation of international law" which tries to cast some light on the complex mutual influences between international law, European law and domestic law.[8] In sum, the different aspects of this debate are of great significance as there are many important questions of direct practical relevance linked to it. Prominent examples include questions about the legal status or

---

[3] See also Halpin, A. and Roeben, V. (eds.), *Theorising the Global Legal Order*, Oxford, Hart, 2009, p. 6 and Neuwirth, R. J., "A Constitutional Tribute to Global Governance: Overcoming the Chimera of the Developing-Developed Country Dichotomy," EUI Working Paper 2010/20, 2010, p. 2.

[4] Rosenau, J. N., "Governance in the 21st Century," *Global Governance*, Vol. 1, 1995, p. 13.

[5] Timmermans, Ch., "The EU and Public International Law," *European Foreign Affairs Review*, Vol. 4, 1999, p. 181.

[6] See, for example, Azoulai, L., "The *Acquis* of the European Union and International Organisations," *European Law Journal*, Vol. 11, 2005, p. 196.

[7] See, for example, Kronenberger, V. (ed.), *The European Union and the International Legal Order: Discord or Harmony?*, The Hague, T.M.C. Asser Press, 2001.

[8] See, for example, Wouters, J., Nollkaemper, A., and de Wet, E. (eds.), *The Europeanisation of International Law: The Status of International Law in the EU and its Member States*, The Hague, T.C.M. Asser Press, 2008; and Schuetze, R., "On 'Middle Ground'. The European Community and Public International Law," EUI Working Papers 2007/13, 2007.

personality of the EU,[9] the scope of its competences and capacities as an international actor,[10] the hierarchical status of international law in the EU legal order,[11] and the status of United Nations (UN) Security Council Resolutions in the European Communities' legal order.[12]

Inspired by this debate, this chapter seeks to turn the initial question around. In an attempt to contribute to the debate on improving the existing system of governance of global affairs, this chapter focuses on the question of why international law from the time of the establishment of the United Nations Organization has not developed the same dynamism as European Union law. The latter has progressed from the establishment of the European Coal and Steel Community (ECSC) and the European Economic Community (EEC), via the creation of the European Union to the entry into force of the Lisbon Treaty (LT). Based on the identification of common problems and following the method of parallel description, I will finally propose some areas for mutual learning between the European and the global frameworks of governance.

Greater Coherence and Unity: Towards a New Global Legal Order?

The Reform of the United Nations System in the International Context

Based almost exclusively on the relations between sovereign territorial nation states, the concept of international law and its consequent institutional design is no longer, and perhaps never has been, really capable of efficiently confronting the most important challenges that this world faces. There are many examples of the numerous ills resulting from the current "state" of global affairs, all of which require immediate and concerted action by the global community as a whole. Growing threats of a global dimension primarily concern the maintenance of peace and security,

9 See, for example, Wessels, R., "The International Legal Status of the EU," *European Foreign Affairs Review*, Vol. 2, 1997, p. 109.

10 See, for example, Cremona, M., "External Relations of the EU and the Member States: Competence, Mixed Agreements, International Responsibility, and Effects of International Law," EUI Working Papers 2006/22, 2006; Senti, R., "The Role of the EU as an Economic Actor in the WTO," *European Foreign Affairs Review*, Vol. 7, No. 1, 2002, p. 111.

11 See *supra* note 8.

12 See, for example, Tomuschat, Ch., "Case T 306/01, *Ahmed Ali Yusuf and Al Barakaat International Foundation v. Council and Commission*, judgment of the Court of First Instance of 21 September 2005; Case T-315/01, Yassin Abdullah Kadi vs. Council and Commission, judgment of the Court of First Instance of 21 September 2005," *Common Market Law Review*, Vol. 43, 2006, p. 537.

the increasing spread of poverty, the preservation of human health, and environmental degradation, which includes the topics of climate change and sustainable development.[13] The complexity of their causes and symptoms is unprecedented and, as an additional feature, each single problem appears to be inextricably linked to the sum of all the other problems. This explains the necessity for global and concerted action, in particular in view of the recent global financial crisis which, once more, has called to mind the increasing interdependence and the collective vulnerability of the inhabitants of this planet. Thus far, however, there are but few proposals that address these challenges through the reform of the major international organisations constituting the current international legal order. They include the UN,[14] the World Trade Organization (WTO)[15] and the G-20 in relation to international financial institutions in the context of the global financial crisis.[16] However, no consistent joint initiative for a reform of the entire architecture of the international legal order exists at this point in time. Moreover, the existing reform efforts themselves are highly fragmented because they fail to duly acknowledge the existence of other relevant international organisations where their respective policy fields intersect and relate to one another.

For instance, the "Delivering as One" Report by the UN High Level Panel on System-Wide Coherence never mentions the WTO in the context of institutional reform. The only reference made to the WTO is in the context of "coherence" at the national level.[17] This is regrettable given that the report seems to ignore the historical plans for the design of the UN system. In this respect, the preceding report by the Secretary General of the UN displays greater historical awareness when it states, as follows:

> In 1945, the framers of the Charter did not give the Economic and Social Council enforcement powers. Having agreed at Bretton Woods in the previous year to create powerful international financial institutions and *expecting that*

[13] For a very brief and incomplete account of the state of the planet, see the UN Millennium Goals Declaration, http://www.un.org/millennium/declaration/ares552e.pdf.

[14] See, for example, United Nations High Level Panel on Coherence, *Delivering as One: Report of the High-level Panel on United Nations System-wide Coherence in the Areas of Development, Humanitarian Assistance and the Environment*, UN GA A/61/583, 20 November 2006, http://daccess-ods.un.org/TMP/960320.8.html.

[15] See Sutherland P. *et al.* (eds.), *The Future of the WTO: Addressing Institutional Challenges in the New Millennium*, Geneva, WTO, 2004.

[16] G-20, *Declaration on Delivering Resources through the International Financial Institutions*, London, 2 April 2009, https://www.g20.org/Documents/Fin_Deps_IFI_Annex_Draft_02_04_09_-__1615_Clean.pdf.

[17] See United Nations High Level Panel on Coherence, *Delivering as One: Report of the High-level Panel on United Nations System-wide Coherence in the Areas of Development, Humanitarian Assistance and the Environment*, *op. cit.*, p. 47.

these would be complemented by a world trade organization in addition to the various specialized agencies, they clearly intended that international economic decision-making would be decentralized.[18]

Notwithstanding historical awareness of the intended but failed role of the Economic and Social Council, the predecessor of the WTO, the UN Secretary General's report is content with a simple call for the conclusion of the Doha Round negotiations.[19] Even internally, the UN system, pledging to be the global institution for the 21st century, is itself highly fragmented. In the report "Delivering as One" it is stated that "the United Nations needs to overcome its fragmentation and deliver as one through a stronger commitment to working together on the implementation of one strategy, in the pursuit of one set of goals".[20]

At the WTO level, the respective reform efforts appear slightly more productive in terms of "inter-institutional" awareness. The 2004 Report on the Future of the WTO dedicates six full pages to the issue of "coherence coordination with intergovernmental organizations" and shows much more sensitivity to the "horizontal coordination" between the WTO and competences of various UN specialised agencies.[21] Despite such political statements of good will, the improvement of the current system by establishing, for instance, a "hard" legal global institutional framework is not even considered. Instead, it merely limits itself to the granting of observer status to various related international organisations. Finally, the debate about reforming or strengthening the present international institutional financial framework in the wake of the global financial crisis is also more than disappointing. In the various documents made public by the G-20 meetings, there is generally no serious proposal for a radical reform of the global institutional architecture as a whole. Most initiatives focus on the financial sector and the financial institutions and their enduring effect is questionable.[22] Despite calls to reform the Bretton Woods Institutions and oblivious to the historical

---

18 See Report of the Secretary-General, *In Larger Freedom: Towards Development, Security and Human Rights for All*, UN GA Doc. A/59/2005, 21 March 2005, p. 44 [Italics added].

19 *Ibid.*, pp. 18 and 56.

20 See United Nations High Level Panel on Coherence, *Delivering as One: Report of the High-level Panel on United Nations System-wide Coherence in the Areas of Development, Humanitarian Assistance and the Environment, op. cit.*, pp. 9-10.

21 See Sutherland P. *et al.* (eds.), *The Future of the WTO: Addressing Institutional Challenges in the New Millennium, op. cit.*, pp. 35-40.

22 Cf. G20, *Communiqués*, http://www.g20.org/pub_index.aspx.

plan for an International Trade Organization (ITO)[23] and subsequent acts,[24] the role of the WTO is limited to calling for a completion of the Doha Round or the avoidance of WTO-inconsistent measures.[25] In turn, two recent studies of the International Monetary Fund (IMF) about lessons to be learned from the global financial crisis make no specific mention of the WTO.[26] Equally, the role of the Bank of the International Settlement of Disputes (BIS), as another organisation deemed relevant in this area, has also not found its way into the Declarations. This is regrettable because most global problems are precisely characterised by a strong degree of interdependence, the solution of which requires a coherent institutional and consistent governance framework for successful law and policy making.

In other words, like the international legal system, the current debate about reform of the central international institutions itself remains highly fragmented. The international organizations hardly take notice of each other in formulating reform proposals. Hence the current improvement efforts also lack ambition in terms of both scope and depth. In terms of content, the debate suffers from institutional and theoretical fragmentation and must therefore be considered insufficient for the task of meeting the needs of the global reality. As an exception, an encouraging

---

23 For an overview of the evolution of the GATT/WTO system from the ITO until the WTO and the implications for coherence, see, for example, Neuwirth, R. J., *The Cultural Industries in International Trade Law: Insights from the NAFTA, the WTO, and the EU*, Hamburg, Dr Kovač, 2006, pp. 79-102.

24 See, for example, the *Declaration on the Relationship of the World Trade Organization with the International Monetary Fund*, 15 April 1994, http://www.wto.org/english/docs_e/legal_e/34-dimf.pdf; *Declaration on the Contribution of the World Trade Organization to Achieving Greater Coherence in Global Economic Policymaking*, 15 April 1994, http://www.wto.org/english/docs_e/legal_e/32-dcohr.pdf; and the *Agreement between the WTO and the IMF and the World Bank*, Decision adopted by the General Council at its meeting on 7, 8 and 13 November 1996, WTO Doc. WT/L/194 and its Addendum, WT/L/194/Add.1, 18 November 1996, http://www.wto.org/english/thewto_e/coher_e/wtl194_e.doc.

25 See G20, *Seoul Summit Declaration*, 11-12 November 2010, http://www.g20.org/Documents2010/11/seoulsummit_declaration.pdf; G20, *Toronto Summit Declaration*, 26-27 June 2010, http://www.g20.org/Documents/g20_declaration_en.pdf; G20, *Leaders Statement*, The Pittsburgh Summit, 24-25 September 2009, http://www.g20.org/Documents/pittsburgh_summit_leaders_statement_250909.pdf; and G20, *Declaration Summit on Financial Markets and the World Economy*, 15 November 2008, pp. 4-5, http://www.g20.org/Documents/g20_summit_declaration.pdf.

26 See IMF Strategy, Policy, and Review Department, *Initial Lessons of the Crisis for the Global Architecture and the IMF*, 18 February 2009, http://www.imf.org/external/np/pp/eng/2009/021809.pdf; and IMF Monetary and Capital Markets Department, *Lessons of the Financial Crisis for Future Regulation of Financial Institutions and Markets and for Liquidity Management*, 4 February 2009, http://www.imf.org/external/np/pp/eng/2009/020409.pdf.

example of inter-organizational comity is provided by the *Report on G20 Trade and Investment Measures* which was prepared jointly by the UN Conference on Trade and Development, the WTO and the Organization for Economic Co-operation and Development (OECD).[27] This is clearly a positive practice which needs to be followed up in the future but also expanded in scope. In summary, the current reform efforts must certainly be characterised as inapt for meeting the challenges of the governance of global affairs in the 21st century, as long as the projected international legal system remains highly fragmented.[28] To further substantiate this argument, some of the major ills of the present international legal framework shall be briefly outlined.

The Fragmentation of the International Legal Order and the "Trade Linkage Debate"

Following the brief outline of the reform efforts of international organisations, it is also interesting to have a look at some related aspects of the academic debate in this matter. There exists a limited range of literature which addresses the deficiencies of the architecture underlying the international legal order. This literature can be described as dealing with the so-called "trade linkage debate", which addresses several pairs of "trade and [...]" problems.[29] The debate appears to stem from the dualistic mode of thinking which finds its expression in the old legal

27 UNCTAD, OECD, WTO, *Report on G20 Trade and Investment Measures*, 14 September 2009, http://www.unctad.org/en/docs/wto_oecd_unctad2009_en.pdf.

28 See, for example, International Law Commission (ILC), *Conclusions of the Work of the Study Group on the Fragmentation of International Law: Difficulties Arising from the Diversification and Expansion of International Law*, adopted by the International Law Commission at its Fifty-eighth session, in 2006, and submitted to the General Assembly as a part of the Commission's report covering the work of that session (A/61/10, para. 251) and International Law Commission (ILC), *Chapter IX: Fragmentation of International Law: Difficulties Arising from the Diversification and Expansion of International Law in United Nations*, Report of the International Law Commission, General Assembly, 54th session (29 April-7 June and 22 July-16 August 2002), UN Doc. A/57/10, pp. 237-242.

29 For only a few selected titles, see, for example, Polanyi, K., *The Great Transformation: The Political and Economic Origins of Our Time*, Boston, Beacon Press, 2001; Trachtman, J. P., "Institutional Linkage: Transcending 'Trade and ...'," *American Journal of International Law*, Vol. 96, No. 1, 2002, p. 77; Marceau, G., "Conflicts of Norms and Conflicts of Jurisdictions: The Relationship between the WTO Agreement and MEAs and other Treaties," *Journal of World Trade*, Vol. 35, No. 6, 2001, p. 1081; Mortensen, J. L., "The Institutional Requirements of the WTO in an Era of Globalisation: Imperfections in the Global Economic Polity," *European Law Journal*, Vol. 6, 2000, p. 176.

adage *expressio unius est exclusio alterius* (the choice of one part of an alternative excludes the other).[30]

The line of thinking just mentioned left a strong imprint on the international legal order in the form of an institutional rift between the UN system and the systems established under the General Agreement on Tariffs and Trade (GATT) and the WTO respectively. This rift was first created due to the tendency of the world's political organisations to lag behind the economic organisations,[31] and second, due to the failure of the establishment of an International Trade Organization (ITO) as proposed by the Havana Charter of 1947/48. The consequences of this failure persist today and manifest themselves in a lack of coherence between the UN specialised agencies on the one hand and the WTO on the other. As a consequence, the lack of coherence caused by the institutional rift is also responsible for varying degrees of inconsistency between different substantive provisions. This is, for instance, the case with the general exception clause of Article XX GATT, which exempts certain so-called "non-trade values", such as health, the environment, security concerns, human rights, and cultural products, from the scope of trade liberalisation undertaken under the WTO framework. This kind of regulatory method, however, appears to reflect an obsolete way of thinking and to be based on the wrong premises. It seems more appropriate to reason that there are no "non-trade values" since all the values mentioned under such categories are in fact, as reality shows, closely related to the area of trade. This is exemplified in the relation between culture and trade by virtue of cultural products, which are both "cultural and commercial in nature". The same holds for the link between trade and security in the case of "dual-use goods", which denominate goods that are normally used for civilian purposes but may also have military applications. In addition, most new technologies are dual in nature and combine goods and service characteristics. They even bear relevance to intellectual property rights. In this respect even the current multilateral trading system is already ill-equipped. The regulatory scopes of the GATT, the General Agreement on Trade in Services (GATS) and the Agreement on Trade-Related Aspects of Intellectual Property Rights (TRIPS) are too fragmented to tackle the problems related to most of these new technologies and realities. Last but not least, it is also exemplified in the link between trade and human rights, which must not be perceived as a separate body of laws but instead needs to be integrated into every aspect of law in accordance with the nature of human life that forms an integrated whole.

30 See also Neuwirth, R. J., "'United in Divergency': A Commentary on the UNESCO Convention on the Protection and Promotion of the Diversity of Cultural Expressions," *Heidelberg Journal of International Law*, Vol. 66, 2006, p. 829.

31 See Young, A. A., "Economics and War: A Presidential Address," *American Economic Review*, Vol. 16, No. 1, 1926, p. 7.

With regard to these observations, the present international legal order must be deemed inadequate, particularly as the unnecessary duplication of efforts and conflicts between international organisations thrive due to their proliferation.[32] In the absence of a coherent and consistent global legal framework, the trade linkage tries to put together what is, but should not be, separated. To allow the continuous separation of all these issues means to contribute further to the disintegration of the essential aspects in the life of a human being. Most of all, it neglects the status of the human being as the centre of all laws and in the service of whom laws ought to stand.

Unfortunately, even the academic debate is relatively modest in its proposals and still lacks creativity and fresh ideas that are capable of addressing these problems. For instance, it suffices to mention the separation in curricula of public from private international law, or the split of "international trade law" into distinct disciplines of the law of the WTO and the law of international commercial transactions. In view of the theoretical fragmentation, it is therefore hardly surprising to find fragmentation persisting at every level in practice. This shortcoming of the present international legal order is aggravated by the general exclusion of private actors from public international law. Their broad exclusion is being remedied too slowly in most areas. This can be illustrated by the slow development of human rights law at the international level.[33]

In view of these common problems, as a first step, it is necessary to restructure the entire institutional architecture of the UN system. In particular, it requires the establishment of a new institutional balance between its principal organs in order to better adapt them to the new realities. Only such a move will allow the formation of a truly global legal order. In concrete terms, it entails a merger of the WTO with the UN system but not before, and in parallel with, a major reform of the UN system itself. Additionally, it must also envisage the creation of a consistent global judicial framework possibly with some specialised tribunals, such as the International Criminal Court (ICC), the WTO's Dispute Settlement Body

---

32 See, for example, Romano, C. P. R., "The Proliferation of International Judicial Bodies: The Pieces of the Puzzle," *N.Y.U. Journal of International Law & Politics*, Vol. 31, 1999, p. 751; see also Dupuy, P.-M., "The Danger of Fragmentation or Unification of the International Legal System and the International Court of Justice," *N.Y.U. Journal of International Law & Politics*, Vol. 31, 1999; and Dupuy, P.-M., *L'unité de l'ordre juridique international, Cours général de droit international public (2000)*, Académie de Droit International de La Haye, *Recueil des cours de l'Académie de Droit International de La Haye*, Vol. 297, 2004.

33 See also Cancado Trindade, A. A., "The Consolidation of the Procedural Capacity of Individuals in the Evolution of the International Protection of Human Rights: Present State and Perspectives at the Turn of the Century," *Columbia University Human Rights Law Review*, Vol. 30, 1998, p. 1.

(DSB), the Human Rights Council and the International Tribunal for the Law of the Sea (ITLOS). The procedures before those specialised tribunals could be unified in the establishment of a two-tier appeal procedure to a truly global "world court".[34] Such plans must also duly consider a possible inclusion of the awards rendered by transnational arbitral courts.

A consistent global legal framework must equally give individuals, both legal and natural persons, a *locus standi*, i.e. the right to address a court in a matter that concerns them.[35] This proposal, as radical as it may seem, is not even new. The extension of the jurisdiction of the International Court of Justice (ICJ) to private individuals was already discussed in 1920 in the context of the creation of its predecessor, the Permanent Court of International Justice, albeit without success.[36] Today, such a right should be granted directly. The increasing number of international legal texts has direct ramifications or involves direct obligations for individuals, though without granting them the corresponding rights and appropriate legal remedies. In some cases this can also be granted indirectly: for instance, through the possibility of national courts to ask for a preliminary ruling from the world court. Such moves, however, are indispensable for reform of the present international legal framework with the aim of creating a new global legal order. This new legal order should be based on a structure of "global intelligence" which consists of a tight network of transnational relations between both private persons and various public entities recognising them as equal subjects of global law. Hence, it is a network similar to the structure of the brain, where the synapses are the junctions that are indispensable in the transmission and flow of information from one neuron to another. The equal recognition of private persons under a global law appears indispensable, in particular, because all legally relevant actions ultimately derive from them.[37] In analogy to the brain, access to global courts for private individuals not only allows the individual to defend her or his rights, but also provides useful information about the functioning of the system as a whole, and hence makes it possible for the judiciary, executive and legislature to fulfil their role better in adapting the laws to the society's present needs.

---

34 See also Nowak, M., "The Need for a World Court of Human Rights," *Human Rights Law Review*, Vol. 7, No. 1, 2007, p. 251.

35 See Art. 34 (1) of the Statute of the International Court of Justice, which reads: "Only states may be parties in cases before the Court".

36 Permanent Court of International Justice: Advisory Committee of Jurists, *Procès-verbaux of the Proceedings of the Committee*, 16 June-24 July 1920, The Hague, Van Langenhuysen Brothers, 1920, pp. 3, 6 and 7.

37 See the adage "[…] *et in omnes se effuderit gentes humanas*" formulated by Gentilis and cited in Lauterpacht, H., *Private Law Sources and Analogies of International Law*, London, Longmans, Green & Co, 1927, p. 11.

Last but not least, it can be argued that by finally linking the spheres of politics and economics in institutional terms, judgments by the World Court could also be enforced more efficiently by intertwining them with the benefits granted under the WTO regime. This would create a peaceful but at the same time efficient incentive to comply with the judgments issued by the World Court and thus breathe fresh air into a hitherto dusty institution. It must be noted, however, that each single change to the current system can only fully make sense when it is considered in the context of other changes. This is difficult to achieve but is the only way to deal with the present degree of complexity and inconsistency.

The Global Legal Order and Its Financial Aspects

The establishment of a global legal order meeting challenges of a global nature, as outlined above, requires change in practically all areas. One more area for action, which – in light of the current global financial crisis – bears great relevance, is the question of how the major organisations making up the global institutional framework will be financed. This question is intrinsically linked to the issue of how the emerging global financial and monetary system will be organised and, in turn, how it will be monitored by these institutions. A possible answer to both questions depends on a paradigm shift in the ways global society perceives the role and function of the globalising economy. The need for this shift is currently expressed most prominently in the concept of sustainable development. Ultimately, the sustainability of development can only come as a result of a more holistic approach to the governance of life and world affairs. In this context, there is an old idea that deserves serious discussion, which is the idea of a single world currency as proposed by John Stuart Mill:

> So much of barbarism, however, still remains in the transactions of the most civilized nations, that almost all independent countries choose to assert their nationality by having, to their own inconvenience and that of their neighbours, a peculiar currency of their own.[38]

In fact, a single world currency is not just an old idea but was already a reality for extended periods of human history. There were the examples of the Roman gold coinage aureus, followed by the later bezant, the British pound sterling or the Bretton Woods US dollar until 1971.[39] In fact, the idea was only recently picked up again by the Chinese government and

---

[38] Mill, J. S., *The Principles of Political Economy*, Kitchener, Ontario, Batoche Books, 2001, p. 718.

[39] See Mundell, R., "The case for a world currency," *Journal of Policy Modeling*, Vol. 27, 2005, p. 465.

backed by others.[40] In view of the increasing number of financial transactions carried out without printed money but via electronic transactions, even a credit card company has endorsed the idea of a "world currency" for its advertising campaign.[41] Certainly the idea of a global currency is still beyond the imagination of many and in particular those who think that ideas, money, and even newspapers stop at the border.[42] Such protagonists are still captured by the myth of the territorial nation state. They fail to accept that a world currency is in many ways already a reality. Similarly, for those who cannot separate themselves from "their" currency as a national symbol, a global monetary union of the major currencies (e.g. US dollar, euro, yen, RMB) could be envisaged. Equally, the example of the euro could be followed, with its coins displaying one side which is identical and the other side representing the national symbols or persons which usually adorn coins and banknotes.

These and related questions about the organisation of the financial and monetary global architecture must be considered together with the financing of the principal institutions involved in the governance and regulation of global affairs. In this context, an idea formulated by James Tobin in 1972 finally deserves anew our serious thought and immediate action. His idea consists of a call for "an internationally uniform tax on all spot conversions of one currency into another, proportional to the size of the transaction", otherwise known as the "Tobin Tax".[43] In 1996, the former Secretary General of the UN, Boutros Boutros-Ghali, endorsed the idea and proposed a Tobin Tax to finance the UN.[44] Such ideas and discussions appear more urgent than ever. The reasons for his assessment have only gained in significance since the time when Tobin wrote: "At present the world enjoys many benefits of the increased worldwide economic integration of the last thirty years. But the integration is partial and unbalanced; in particular private financial markets have become

---

40 See, for example, Bardeesy, K., "Calls grow to supplant dollar as global currency; France joins China, India and Russia in calling for a new reserve standard on the eve of the G8 summit," *The Globe and Mail* (Canada), 6 July 2009, p. B1.

41 See Visa World Currency Commercials, http://www.youtube.com/watch?v=MAI_mtNc-24.

42 See *Canada – Certain Measures Concerning Periodicals* (Complaint by the United States), WTO Doc. WT/DS31/R (Panel Report), 14 March 1997, para. 3.24, where it reads as follows: "Within a matter of a few decades, however, technological advances made it practical for foreign-based publishers to transmit editorial material electronically across the border into Canada and to publish split-run editions in Canada, thus avoiding the application of Tariff Code 9958".

43 Tobin, J., "A Proposal for International Monetary Reform," *Eastern Economic Journal*, Vol. 4, 1978, p. 155.

44 Brow, G. G. B., "The Tobin Tax: Turning Swords into Plowshares?," *Transnational Law and Contemporary Problems*, Vol. 9, 1999, p. 378.

internationalized much more rapidly and completely than other economic and political institutions".[45]

Most of all, the taboo of "supranational" taxes levied beyond the borders of the territorial nation state needs to be broken. Too many threats, dangers and nuisances cross borders freely. American and other nationals know too well that residing outside their country does not spare them the duty of declaring their income in their country of origin. Considering the need for greater independence, enhanced accountability and transparency of global institutions, a more sustainable source of funding is needed. In this respect, the UN Report "Delivering as One" restates the current situation as follows:

> Inefficient and ineffective governance and unpredictable funding have contributed to policy incoherence, duplication and operational ineffectiveness across the system. Cooperation between organizations has been hindered by competition for funding, mission creep and outdated business practices.[46]

Besides contributing to the efficiency, sustainability and coherence of global governance, a further benefit of such a tax would be to minimise the dangers inherent in risky financial speculations. Usually, taxation also has a social and behaviour-modifying function, putting limits on dangerous activities or activities potentially endangering others. Such activities include, for instance, driving a motorised vehicle, gambling, adventure sports, smoking and drinking. But what about speculating with the money of others and by doing so, threatening their housing, clothing or nutritional security? In other words, putting the very basis of their existence at stake.[47] Do such activities not call for a fiscal response? The answer appears to be in the affirmative, given that most financial transactions appear to be conducted for the sole sake of speculation instead of the raising of money for international trade and investment.[48] The BIS reported that the average daily global turnover in traditional foreign exchange markets had grown by an unprecedented 69% since April 2004, reaching US$3.2 trillion in 2007.[49] For 2007, this amounted to an annual total turnover of US$1168 trillion whereas the available numbers for the sum

45 Tobin, J., "A Proposal for International Monetary Reform," *op. cit.*, p. 155.

46 *Delivering as One: Report of the High-level Panel on United Nations System-wide Coherence in the Areas of Development, Humanitarian Assistance and the Environment*, *op. cit.*, p. 10.

47 See, for example, BBC News, "'Dire shortage' at UN food agency," 31 July 2009, http://news.bbc.co.uk/2/hi/in_depth/8179250.stm.

48 Brow, G. G. B., "The Tobin Tax: Turning Swords into Plowshares?," *op. cit.*, p. 361.

49 See Bank for International Settlements, *Triennial Central Bank Survey December 2007: Foreign Exchange and Derivatives Market Activity in 2007*, Basle, Bank for International Settlements, 2007, p. 1, http://www.bis.org/publ/rpfxf07t.pdf.

of world exports of merchandise and commercial as well as global foreign direct investment during the same time period only reached US$18.33 trillion.[50] These data clearly show that the sum total of foreign exchange transactions by far exceeds the sum total of transactions needed for international trade and investment.

Against this background such a global tax (or else "global insurance scheme" as it could be called), if only applied in the range of 0.1-1.0%, would not only generate considerable revenues but also help to mitigate the instability of financial markets.[51] Furthermore, if used appropriately, it could provide a sustainable source of funding for the principal activities of the organizations entrusted with the governance of global affairs. From this perspective, a global tax, whether on financial transactions, arms sales,[52] or other "(potentially) dangerous activities", would help to create positive synergies in the governance of global affairs. The precondition is that it is flanked by a coherent set of related measures and supported by a radical reform of the global institutional framework. Only then may it be possible to realise the objectives of a more peaceful, just and sustainable development on this planet. To this end, it is useful to turn to the experiment of the European Union and its experiences for some interesting insights.

The Legal Order of the European Union: A Continuous Striving for Unity and Coherence

The Single Institutional Framework

Similar to the international organisations set up under the aegis of the United Nations Charter, the predecessors of the European Union were

[50] World exports of merchandise and commercial services amount to US$ 13.57 trillion and US$ 3.26 trillion respectively; see WTO, *World Trade Report 2008: Trade in a Globalizing World*, Geneva, WTO, 2008, p. 7; and the amount of global foreign direct investment was estimated in 2007 to reach US$ 1.5 trillion; see UNCTAD, *Foreign Direct Investment Reached New Record in 2007*, UNCTAD/PRESS/PR/2008/001, 8 January 2008, http://www.unctad.org/Templates/webflyer.asp?docid=9439&intItem ID=1528&lang=1.

[51] See Schulmeister St., Schratzenstaller, M. and Picek, O., *A General Financial Transaction Tax: Motives, Revenues, Feasibility and Effects*, Research Study by the Austrian Institute of Economic Research (WIFO), March 2008, pp. 2-3, http://www.wifo.ac.at/wwa/servlet/wwa.upload.DownloadServlet/bdoc/S_2008_FINANCIAL_TRANSACTION_TAX_31819$.PDF.

[52] A tax on arms sales was for instance suggested by former French President Jacques Chirac; see Carter, R., "Chirac in call for global tax," *The EU Observer*, 21 September 2004.

established on the basis of classical international law.[53] This process of European integration, since its inception more than half a century ago, has been marked by a difficult journey towards greater unity and coherence leading to what we can term today the "European Union's legal order".[54] This is because during the early days of European integration the institutional setting for Europe's integration was highly fragmented. Two different methods of integration, a federalist-constitutional versus a functional one, or in other words a predominantly intergovernmental versus a predominantly supranational one, were pursued in two different institutional settings almost contemporaneously.[55] First the Council of Europe was established in 1949. The European Coal and Steel Community (ESCS) was established in 1952, followed in 1958 by the European Economic Community (EEC), as well as the European Atomic Energy Community (EURATOM). It was only in 1965, however, that the three so-called "European Communities", hitherto acting independently, received a common institutional framework by virtue of the 1965 Merger Treaty.[56] In subsequent years, the parallel processes of positive and negative integration, as well as widening and deepening undertaken in the framework of the three Communities, continued. These processes yielded a strengthening of the EU's institutional framework and contributed to greater coherence in law- and policy-making.[57] The institutional ties were complemented by a growing scope of competences. In addition, inter-institutional agreements concluded between the various EU organs further strengthened the institutional balance and helped to improve policy coordination.[58] This development culminated in the Maastricht Treaty (the Treaty on

---

53 This is, for instance, reflected in the publication of their founding treaties in the United Nations Treaty Series; Treaty Establishing the European Coal and Steel Community, signed at Paris, on April 18, 1951, 261 U.N.T.S. 142; Treaty Establishing the European Atomic Energy Community, signed in Rome on March 25, 1957, 294 U.N.T.S. 5 (entry into force: 1 January 1958); and Treaty Establishing the European Economic Community, signed in Rome on March 25, 1957, 294 U.N.T.S. 5 (entry into force: 1 January 1958).

54 See especially von Bogdandy, A., "The Legal Case for Unity: The European Union as a Single Organization with a Single Legal System," *Common Market Law Review*, Vol. 37, 1999, p. 887.

55 See Constantinesco, L.-J., *Das Recht der Europäischen Gemeinschaften: Das institutionelle Recht*, Baden-Baden, Nomos, 1977, pp. 115-122.

56 Treaty Establishing a Single Council and a Single Commission of the European Communities, 8 April 1965, *Treaty Series*, Vol. 15, No. 1, 1979 (Merger Treaty).

57 See also the discussion in Cremona, M., "Coherence through Law: What Difference Will the Treaty of Lisbon Make?," *Hamburg Review of Social Sciences*, Vol. 3, No. 1, 2008, p. 11.

58 See Hummer, W., "Interinstitutionelle Vereinbarungen und institutionelles Gleichgewicht," in W. Hummer (ed.), *Paradigmenwechsel im Europarecht zur Jahrtausendwende. Ansichten österreichischer Integrationsexperten zu aktuellen*

European Union (TEU)) which finally established the European Union's so-called "temple or pillar structure".[59] The Maastricht Treaty reinforced the aspiration for greater unity by virtue of Article 3, which stipulated: "The Union shall be served by a single institutional framework which shall ensure the consistency and the continuity of the activities carried out in order to attain its objectives while respecting and building upon the *acquis communautaire*".[60]

With the entry into force of the Lisbon Treaty on 1 December 2009 this aspiration for greater unity was further enhanced.[61] The amendments introduced by the Lisbon Treaty have, for instance, not only altered former Article 3 TEU but also explicitly granted the EU international legal personality and also ended the three-pillar structure together with other significant changes.[62] These changes, however, cannot disguise further problematic areas where arbitrariness and inconsistency reign.

In contrast to the situation at the international level, the EU's framework has made more progress in overcoming the "original sin" of a conceptual separation of politics from economics or what is falsely termed "trade" from "non-trade" matters. Additionally, the EU has also managed to integrate various cross-cutting areas better, such as those of a Common Foreign and Security Policy (CFSP) and of Justice and Home Affairs (JHA). The Lisbon Treaty also reduced the uncertainty surrounding the status of fundamental rights in the EU. Originally, the EU's predecessors were literally born as a *terrain vierge* with respect to fundamental rights provisions. Fundamental rights were indirectly taken into account by virtue of the case law of the European Court of Justice, reference to the European Convention for the Protection of Human Rights and Fundamental Freedoms (ECHR) and the case law of the (Strasbourg)

Problemlagen. Forschung und Lehre im Europarecht in Österreich, Wien, Springer Verlag, 2004, p. 116.

59 See also de Witte, B., "The Pillar Structure and the Nature of the European Union: Greek Temple or French Gothic Cathedral?," in T. Heukels, N. Blokker, and M. Brus (eds.), *The European Union after Amsterdam – A Legal Analysis*, The Hague, Kluwer Law International, 1998, pp. 51-68.

60 Note that to the difference of the English treaty version, which mentions "consistency," the French treaty version speaks of "*cohérence*," the German of "*Kohärenz*," the Italian of "*coerenza*," and the Spanish of "*coherencia*".

61 Treaty on European Union (TEU) and The Treaty on the Functioning of the European Union (TFEU), 9 May 2008, O.J. C 115/01, 2008 (consolidated version) [Lisbon Treaty (LT)].

62 See Art. 13 and Art. 47 Lisbon Treaty (LT); see also the Declaration concerning the legal personality of the European Union annexed to the LT; for brief overview over the differences between the Constitutional Treaty and the LT, see, for example, de Búrca, G., "The EU on the Road from the Constitutional Treaty to the Lisbon Treaty," Jean Monnet Working Paper 03/08, 2008, pp. 13-15.

Court of Human Rights, as well as resulting "from the constitutional traditions common to the Member States".[63] In December 2000, the Charter of Fundamental Rights of the European Union was solemnly promulgated, but, like the Universal Declaration on Human Rights of 1948, it lacked legally binding character. Hence, it was only on 1 December 2009 that the EU Charter finally assumed the same legal value as the Treaties and the EU was legally empowered to accede to the European Convention for the Protection of Human Rights and Fundamental Freedoms.[64]

In other areas and in regulatory terms, greater coherence is reflected also in the gradual shift from the use of "legal exceptions" to so-called "integration clauses" for the mitigation of conflicts between areas which were traditionally perceived as separate. This modification is well illustrated in the regulation of the areas of the environment, employment, culture, public health, consumer protection, and economic and social cohesion by integration clauses. These can be opposed to some exceptions to the prohibition of quantitative restrictions, such as those based on public morality, public policy or public security; the protection of health and life of humans, animals or plants; the protection of national treasures possessing artistic, historic or archaeological value; or the protection of industrial and commercial property.[65] The regulation of these grounds by virtue of an exception was evidently inspired by Article XX GATT 47 and reflects the traditional public international law approach. As another example of the striving for greater unity, the various integration clauses provide a regulatory tool that is capable of securing greater policy coherence.

In general, the progress in better coordinating the competences and strengthening the unity of the institutional framework of the EU has been substantial. Nonetheless, there are still several outstanding issues that need to be improved. For instance, there is no direct institutional link between the Council of Europe and the European Union, despite a vast overlap not only in the field of human rights, but also other areas, such as the regulation of audiovisual services.[66] This rift between the two

---

63 See Art. 6 Treaty on European Union (TEU), 29 December 2006, *Official Journal of the European Union*, OJ C 321 E/1, 2006 (consolidated version); see also Kunoy, B. and Dawes, A., "Plate Tectonics in Luxembourg: The *Ménage à trois* between EC Law, International Law and the European Convention on Human Rights Following the UN Sanctions Cases," *Common Market Law Review*, Vol. 46, 2009, pp. 73 *et seq*.

64 See Art. 6 LT; but see also the Protocol (No. 30) on the Application of the Charter of Fundamental Rights of the European Union to Poland and to the United Kingdom as well the various related Declarations.

65 See Art. 36 TFEU with Art. 11, 191, 147, 167 (4), 168 (1), 169 (2), and 175 TFEU.

66 See Quinn, G., "The European Union and the Council of Europe on the Issue of Human Rights: Twins Separated at Birth?," *McGill Law Journal*, Vol. 46, 2001, p. 849; for the work of the COE and the EU in the area of audiovisual services, see Azoulai, L.,

institutions may yet cause friction and conflicts in the future, and reflects the original differences in the method of integration in addition to the eternal tendency of separating politics from economics.[67] There is still room for further improvement in a great number of areas, as will be outlined below. So far, the EU legal order has been able to show that unity, in the sense of efficiency, legitimacy and coherence, does not have the same meaning as uniformity and centralisation of the governing structures. In terms of institutional unity and for a better balance of all stakeholders' interests it may be argued that it will require a path-breaking reform of the structure of the EU as it was envisaged by the failed project for the creation of a Constitution for Europe.

The Subsidiarity Principle and the Role of Private Individuals

In the context of the discussion on the unity of the European Union's institutional framework, it is important to mention the principle of subsidiarity. Enshrined in Article 5 of the Treaty on the Functioning of the European Union (TFEU), it stipulates as follows:

> In areas which do not fall within its exclusive competence, the Community shall take action, in accordance with the principle of subsidiarity, only if and in so far as the objectives of the proposed action cannot be sufficiently achieved by the Member States and can therefore, by reason of the scale or effects of the proposed action, be better achieved by the Community.[68]

Hence the subsidiarity principle, together with the principle of conferred powers and the principle of proportionality, is meant to ensure an efficient decision-making process by the mandate to address problems at the level where they arise and where they can best be dealt with. In this respect, it is regrettable that the subsidiarity principle is usually understood as a one-way conferral of powers in favour of the member states. Instead, I would argue for a more dynamic interpretation taking account of the possible changes in the regulatory environment. Such an interpretation implies the establishment of a standard process in a multilevel governance system, by which the best level of action is determined in a cooperative spirit and with due respect for the principle of complementarity aiming at the maximisation of synergies between different policy areas. This is clearly reflected first in the social doctrine of the Catholic Church, from where it originated. Together with the principles of the dignity of the human person, the common good, and solidarity, the principle

---

"The Acquis of the European Union and International Organisations," *European Law Journal*, Vol. 11, 2005, pp. 200-201.

67 See Young, A. A., "Economics and War: A Presidential Address," *op. cit.*

68 Ex Art. 5 Treaty Establishing the European Community (TEC) (consolidated version), 24 December 2002, OJ C 325/33, 2002.

of subsidiarity is part of a process of "progressively explaining them [the principles] in the attempt to respond coherently to the demands of the times and to the continuous developments of social life".[69] The broader implications of a more dynamic understanding of subsidiarity can be deduced from the following statement: "The principle of subsidiarity must not be seen just as a matrix for greater participation in decision-making, but also as an instrument in the reconstruction of solidarity and of the social fabric, to bring together the people who make up a given community".[70]

Support for a broader and more dynamic reading in the spirit of complementarity is also provided in the Preamble of the Lisbon Treaty: "Resolved to continue the process of creating an ever closer union among the peoples of Europe, in which decisions are taken as closely as possible to the citizen in accordance with the principle of subsidiarity".[71]

This paragraph reflects the great importance of the role of citizens (and private individuals). Their importance derives from their status as direct subjects of EU law.[72] This status is directly granted by what the European Court of Justice (ECJ) called the "European Constitutional Charter", which marks one important element distinguishing the European legal order from the present international legal order.[73] Subsidiarity, in its widest sense, therefore denotes the complementary relationship between the single European citizen (or private individual as both a natural and legal person) and the community of Europeans as a collective. This is also reflected in a statement by one of the founding fathers of the EU, Jean Monnet, who remarked that "*nous ne coalisons pas des États, nous unissons des hommes*".[74] The EU's underlying idea hence advocates a balance of power between the individual and greater polities, such as provinces, states or regional (as well as international) organisations. From such a dynamic and complementary understanding of subsidiarity also derives a different understanding of the principle of conferred powers. Instead of being seen as a static limitation on the powers of the Community, it

---

69 See Pontifical Council for Justice and Peace, *Compendium of the Social Doctrine of the Church*, Washington, USCCB, 2005, p. 77.

70 See the Intervention by the Holy See at the 13th Session of the UN Commission on Sustainable Development, Statement by H.E. Mons. Celestino Migliore, 20 April 2005, http://www.vatican.va/roman_curia/secretariat_state/2005/documents/rc_seg-st_20050420_xiii-comm-un_en.html, accessed 4 June 2013.

71 See Recital 13 Preamble of the LT, *supra* note 61.

72 See especially Art. 263 LT (ex Art. 230 TEC) and the judgment of the ECJ in ECJ (European Court of Justice) Case 6/64, *Costa v E.N.E.L.*, E.C.R. 585, 1964.

73 See ECJ Case 6/64, *Costa v E.N.E.L.*, E.C.R. 585, 1964, *op. cit.*, para. 3.

74 See Monnet, J., *Mémoires*, Paris, Fayard, 1976, p. 9. Translation: "We are not bringing states together, we are uniting people".

should be seen as an expression of the principle of legality, interpreted within a "particular conception of democratic legal culture, the culture of justification, in which decision-makers are obliged to justify their decisions".[75] Such an understanding would also support the expansive interpretation of community powers by the ECJ as well as mitigate the controversy around the residual powers clause enshrined in Article 352 TFEU (ex Art. 308 TEC). In sum, it would contribute to a better and more dynamic balance between the different actors making up the complex EU legal system, while at the same time limiting the creeping expansion of EU powers and serving the goals of simplification and consolidation of EU law.[76]

The spirit of complementarity is what can be found in the various instruments and principles establishing the unity of the EU legal order. The many positive steps in the direction of a true spirit of cooperation and solidarity notwithstanding, there is still ample room for improvement in terms of coherence. In the present context, coherence is understood as the balancing process in a search of complementarity between apparently divergent interests. Coherence may take the form of the compatibility of matters along a vertical or a horizontal line. Ultimately, complementarity between divergent interests is relevant to many types of relations, such as the relation between EU member states, between EU member states and their citizens, between the various EU organs themselves, or between the various policy areas within the former three Community pillars, to mention but a few.

The Finances of the European Union

Finally, one of the fundamental differences between the EU and international organisations is the way the European Union is financed. In accordance with classical international law, the European Economic Community was to be financed originally by financial contributions of the member states according to a system of fixed shares.[77] This was, however, considered to be a transitory situation since Article 201 of the Rome Treaty mentioned the possibility of replacing the member states' financial contributions by the Community's own resources. This provision came into effect following the institutional merger in 1965, when

[75] See Dyzenhaus, D., Hunt, M. and Taggart, M., "The Principle of Legality in Administrative Law: Internationalisation as Constitutionalisation," *Oxford University Commonwealth Law Journal*, Vol. 1, No. 1, 2001, p. 6.

[76] See Communication from the Commission to the Council and the European Parliament, *Simpler Legislation for the Internal Market (SLIM): A Pilot Project*, COM(96) 204 final, 8 May 1996.

[77] Art. 100 Treaty Establishing the European Economic Community, *supra* note 53.

the Council decided in 1970 to allocate financial resources of its own to the Communities.[78] The decision introduced agricultural duties and customs duties to serve as the Communities' own financial resources. In the following years, a complex system of the EC's own financial resources developed. Today, the budget of the EU is mainly financed by four autonomous sources, including agricultural duties, customs duties, a uniform rate valid for all member states on the value-added tax (VAT), and a levy on the member states' gross national income (GNI).[79] However, several special clauses apply to particular member states, which, together with the levy on the VAT and on the GNI, continue to cause strong controversy among member states. This was most recently the case during the negotiation of the financial perspective for the years 2007-13.[80]

Hence, it can be said that the financial autonomy of the EEC and subsequently the EU has set both organisations further apart from the practice of traditional international organisations, the latter usually being entirely financed by members' financial contributions. However, the financial autonomy of the EU is not yet complete in the sense that it is entirely free from member states' direct influence. This means that eventually, new resources have to be found which take the budget further out of the hands of member states' national interests. In this regard several ideas have been circulated which include taxes on civil aviation, CO_2 emissions, an excise duty on motor fuel for road transport or on alcohol and tobacco, and a corporate profit tax.[81] Equally, alternative sources could be pondered, like taxes on arms sales,[82] communications services (e.g. an SMS levy) or some other creative solution that has yet to be invented. An additional proposal concerned the introduction of a general financial transaction tax (similar to the original proposal by

78 70/243/CECA, CEE, Euratom: Décision, du 21 avril 1970, relative au remplacement des contributions financières des États membres par des ressources propres aux Communautés, OJ L 94/19, 1970, 28 April 1970.

79 See Art. 2 of the Council Decision of 7 June 2007 on the system of the European Communities' own resources (2007/436/EC, Euratom), OJ L163/17, 2007, 23 June 2007.

80 See, for example, Sciolino, E., "Shame and anger as EU budget talks collapse," *New York Times*, 20 June 2005, p. 1.

81 See also *Future Own Resources: External Study on the Composition of Future Own Resources for the European Parliament*, Directorate General Internal Policies, External Study on the Composition of Future Own Resources for the European Parliament, Directorate General Internal Policies, 28 June 2007, http://www.europarl.europa.eu/meetdocs/2004_2009/documents/dv/200/200706/20070628_own_resource_summary_en.pdf.

82 Carter, R., "Chirac in call for global tax," *The EU Observer*, 21 September 2004.

James Tobin).[83] In view of the recent troubles with the sovereign debt crisis in Europe and elsewhere, the support for such a tax is on the rise. In a 2010 communication, the Commission has put the focus of attention on the issue of a global financial transaction tax in order to secure that "the financial sector contribute[s] in a fair and substantial way to public budgets".[84] Backed by relevant European Parliament resolutions, this communication was followed by a proposal for a common system of a financial transactions tax to be implemented within the EU also, with a view to "creating a new revenue stream with the objective to gradually displace national contributions to the EU budget, leaving a lesser burden on national treasuries".[85]

Put briefly, the time has come for member states and European citizens to take notice of the "European reality" created by the establishment of a European Union currency, the euro, and to accept the introduction of an EU-wide tax. This could help not only to increase the efficiency but also the accountability of the EU. Furthermore, the tax could exercise a stabilising effect on the euro, as is currently needed in the context of the so-called "Greek debt crisis".[86] It is, however, imperative to note that such a move towards an EU-wide tax must be inextricably linked to a code of strict fiscal and budgetary discipline (like in the context of the Maastricht criteria for the European Monetary Policy), a reform of the European bureaucracy and the end of mismanagement and lack of transparency.[87] The objective of budgetary and fiscal discipline is crucial because of existing levels of excessive taxation prevalent in Europe. This is also expressed in the fact that some European political leaders, ignoring fiscal discipline altogether, appear to confuse "low-tax countries" with so-called "tax-havens"; the former levying lower taxes while the latter

---

83 European Parliament, *Motion for a Resolution on the 2 April 2009 G20 Summit in London*, B6-0186/2009, 16 April 2009, which urged the Commission "to submit proposals for the introduction of an EU-wide financial transaction tax, which could help finance investment in developing countries in order to help them overcome the worst consequences of the crisis and keep on track towards the achievement of the Millennium Development Goals".

84 Communication from the Commission to the European Parliament, the Council, the European Economic and Social Committee and the Committee of the Regions, *Taxation of the Financial Sector*, COM(2010) 549 final, 7 October 2010, p. 3.

85 Communication, Proposal for a Council Directive on a common system of financial transaction tax and amending Directive 2008/7/EC, COM(2011) 594 final, 28 September 2011, p. 3.

86 See, for example, Shellock, D., "Escalation of Greek debt crisis sparks volatility," *Financial Times* (London), 1 May 2010, p. 14.

87 For a report about the apparent practices of the European bureaucracy and realistic proposals for reducing costs and ending a lack of transparency, see Martin, H.-P., *Die Europafalle: Das Ende von Wohlstand und Demokratie*, München, Piper, 2009.

lack financial transparency and obstruct international cooperation in the field of taxes and finances.[88] As another important concern, the use of the revenues should primarily focus on the internal funding of the EU instead of the use of such funds for external development cooperation (as was also mentioned).[89] A first reason is that the concept of development cooperation is widely based on a flawed conception of so-called "developing-developed country dichotomy", which proves to be detrimental to the overall goals of global sustainable development.[90] Furthermore, the autonomy of the EU's budget should be secured internally before different EU external policies can be adopted and financed. In analogy to similar challenges at the global level and as a possibility for a mutual approach between the EU and the international legal order, European Council President Herman Van Rompuy and EU Commission President José Manuel Barroso have also expressed their opinions about a global transaction tax to the G-20 partners.[91] Even though the chances for the acceptance of the idea of a global financial transaction tax by the G-20 or all the UN members may appear dim at the moment, it may provide a first opportunity to contribute not only to a greater consistency and efficiency of each of the two orders but also to an even greater convergence between them in the future.

Conclusion

The analysis of some major deficiencies inherent in the international legal order is widely reflected in the challenges faced by the EU legal order. They differ only in terms of their scope and degree of integration. Essentially, they share a striving for greater consistency and coherence in view of the fragmentation of their policy and law-making procedures, which is widely manifest not only in their institutional design but also in the subsequent adoption of a great variety of regulatory tools and their normative content. The same is noticeable in the rift between institutions of a political nature and their economic counterparts. At the international level, this rift is exemplified in the missing institutional ties between the UN specialised agencies and the WTO. In Europe, a similar situation

88 See, for example, Watt, N. *et al.*, "G20: The deal: Tax havens: Renegade countries face naming, shaming and possible sanctions," *The Guardian* (London), 3 April 2009, p. 4.

89 Communication from the Commission to the European Parliament, the Council, the European Economic and Social Committee and the Committee of the Regions, *Taxation of the Financial Sector Taxation of the Financial Sector*, *op. cit.*, p. 2.

90 See Neuwirth, R. J., "A Constitutional Tribute to Global Governance: Overcoming the Chimera of the Developing-Developed Country Dichotomy," EUI Working Paper LAW 2010/20, 2010.

91 *Joint letter of President Van Rompuy and President Barroso on the G20 Summit in Cannes*, EUCO 93/11, Brussels, 7 October 2011.

is found externally with regard to the relation between the Council of Europe and the European Union, and, internally, between the various institutions and policy areas of the EU. The institutional fragmentation is matched by a series of substantive norms and legal instruments which may at times overlap, conflict or contradict each other to the detriment of greater coherence in law and policy making. The same problem is also noticeable in the respective difficulties in finding legal and legislative procedures that are able to successfully balance the interests between the individual and society as a whole. In this respect, at least, the individual is vested with a more prominent role in the legal order of the EU. Due to its greater institutional unity, which was reinforced by the entry into force of the Lisbon Treaty, both the horizontal balance of interests and the vertical delegation of powers is expected to function better. Similarly, the EU has achieved a slightly stronger degree of financial autonomy *vis-à-vis* its member states since, in addition to financial contributions from the member states, it was also vested with some financial resources of its own. The absence of the same degree of institutional unity and financial autonomy at the international level helps explain why the several reform initiatives undertaken by various international organizations lack coherence, consistency and ambition. This is why the different proposals of reform undertaken by various international organizations in isolation must be streamlined and coupled with a combined effort to reform the architecture of the international legal order as a whole. The realization of this goal, however, firstly presupposes a sincere global debate and secondly the adoption of a common language paving the way for the creation of a joint global platform, i.e. an institutional arrangement where various efforts can be grouped, the better to contribute to the enhancement of the governance of global and local affairs.

The European Union, Multilateral Taxation and the Inevitability of Contest and Tension[1]

Dr George GILLIGAN

University of New South Wales and University of Melbourne

Introduction

Taxation revenue is not only the lifeblood of governmental, and subsequently, numerous other organisational structures. Taxation infrastructure is additionally a key determinant of both micro- and macro-economic policy, and of the organization of commerce itself, within both the public and private sectors, and also between them. As such, taxation policy, practice and taxation-oriented business decision-making are often core elements of the tensions and conflicts that are perennial features of many trading contexts. However, increasingly the cumulative effects of developments in information technology, regulatory initiatives such as the liberalisation of capital markets and the broader influences of globalisation,[2] have produced more complex trading scenarios and thus the potential for more complex trading disputes and conflicts. As economic and political ties between many jurisdictions are deepening, nation states increasingly are playing a

1 This chapter builds on the paper "A Pretty Taxing Sort of Issue – The European Union as a Proactive Actor in Multi-Lateral Taxation Contests" presented at The Monash European and EU Centre Conference: "The External Relations of the European Union: Historical and Contemporary Perspectives," Melbourne, 24-25 September 2009.

2 Globalisation can be a contested concept and this chapter will not discuss the utility of various definitions of globalisation or how best to evaluate its impacts. There are many texts that analyse globalisation including: Bordo, M., Taylor, A. M. and Williamson, J. G., *Globalization in Historical Perspective*, Chicago, University of Chicago Press, 2003; Frieden, J. A., *Global Capitalism: Its Fall and Rise in the Twentieth Century*, New York, W.W. Norton and Company, 2006; Gray, J., *False Dawn: The Delusion of Global Capitalism*, London, Granta Books, 1998; Hirst, P. and Thompson, G., *Globalization in Question: The International Economy and the Possibilities of Governance*, Cambridge, Polity Press, 1998; Ohme, K., *The End of the Nation State*, New York, Free Press, 1995 and Scholte, J. A., *Globalization: A Critical Introduction*, Basingstoke, Palgrave Macmillan, 2005; Stiglitz, J., *Globalization and its Discontents*, New York, W.W. Norton and Company, 2003.

mediating role regarding the interests of much business that may be conducted within their spheres of influence. These developments are affecting contemporary understandings of sovereignty, as national political priorities become more intertwined with international politics and the requirements of international business.[3] A major consequence of these developments is that many regulatory structures and processes have become more internationalised and a variety of modes of governance are emerging that have a capacity for impacts of broad international scope. These shifts in regulatory power can be manifested in a global sense through bodies such as: the Basle Committee on Banking Supervision (BCBS); the International Association of Insurance Supervisors (IAIS); the International Organisation of Securities Commissions (IOSCO); and the World Trade Organisation (WTO). There are obviously more regional manifestations of regulatory praxis such as the activities of the Association of South East Asian Nations (ASEAN) and the European Union (EU). At its core, the absolute *raison d'être* of the EU is to reduce conflict, most especially armed conflict between European states. However, much of the activity of the EU, particularly through the European Commission (EC) and its ongoing efforts towards harmonisation, is not only to ameliorate tensions between member states where their interests may clash, but also to promote the interests of European member states collectively within international contexts. These dilemmas of balancing competing interests are illustrated sharply in the arena of taxation. Philippe Cattoir, someone who as administrator at the European Commission Directorate-General for Budget has a coalface experience of these tensions, expresses them in these terms: "Decision-taking in the taxation area at EU level is notoriously difficult. Taxation is at the heart of national sovereignty and one of the most protected 'chasses gardées' of the EU member states. Unanimous decisions on tax matters between the latter are therefore generally only obtained after long and difficult negotiations".[4]

In Europe, as elsewhere in the world, there are conflicting views on the relative legitimacy of many contemporary multilateral regulatory initiatives, some of which are taxation-driven. For example, the belief that some of its citizens (both natural and legal) have been avoiding their taxation obligations has prompted the EU to become more proactive in recent times in creating regulatory initiatives that aim to restrict the capability of its citizens to avoid these taxation obligations. The European

[3] These developments are growing in impact and some commentators such as Chayes and Chayes see sovereignty as a form of status with multiple elements. See Chayes, A., and Chayes, A. H., *The New Sovereignty: Compliance with International Agreements*, Cambridge, MA, Harvard University Press, 1995.

[4] Cattoir, P., *Taxation Papers – A History of the "Tax Package"*. The principles and issues underlying the Community approach, Luxembourg, Office for the Official Publications of the European Communities, 2007, p. 1.

Union Savings Tax Directive (EUSTD), discussed in more detail below, is an example of these anti-tax avoidance efforts. To an extent, the anti-tax avoidance activities of the EU, most especially through the EUSTD, have complemented the anti-tax avoidance efforts of other international organisations, in particular the Organisation for Economic Cooperation and Development (OECD). For the purposes of this chapter, what is of particular interest are the activities in recent years of the OECD with regards to what it terms *harmful tax practices* and the ramifications of its initiatives in this area (hereafter referred to as the OECDHTPI).[5] The OECD's work in this area has been carried largely through its Harmful Tax Practices grouping which is a subsidiary body of the OECD's Committee on Fiscal Affairs.[6]

The EU's strategy regarding the EUSTD has synergies with the OECDHTPI, and taken together, they are perhaps the most significant anti-tax avoidance multilateral regulatory initiatives of recent years. The ramifications of the ongoing Global Financial Crisis (GFC) have added further urgency to the objectives of these two separate initiatives. An analysis of how the EUSTD and the OECDHTPI have developed provide insights into not only how the changing pragmatic realities of political economy can influence how successful a multilateral regulatory initiative may be, but also how those same political economy realities illustrate rational-choice analysis at work as self-interest groupings position themselves in the rough and tumble of regulatory praxis. These self-interest groupings can be national-, regional- or sectoral-based, or an amalgam of all the above. The EUSTD and OECDHTPI can be utilised as a window to look at multilateral regulatory discourse in relation to financial services and taxation, in which an emerging issue seems to be whether erosion of sovereignty is becoming a price to be paid by at least some of those jurisdictions that want to participate in the global market for financial services. If this is indeed the case, then it raises interesting issues of legitimacy and how prevailing sets of power relations will manifest themselves within both national and international regulatory infrastructures of financial services. How the EU conducts itself within such a context can be informative about how it might be expected to act in other scenarios which have a global context, such as climate change.

---

5 The OECD has launched a number of initiatives which are discussed in more detail below and hereafter in this chapter the collated effects of the OECD initiatives on harmful tax practices will be referred to as the OECDHTPI.

6 For general background information regarding the structure of the OECD's efforts against Harmful Tax Practices, see http://www.oecd.org/tax/harmful/, accessed 25 July 2013.

Notions of legitimacy form the key theoretical construct for this chapter. It is essential not to assume legitimacy as a given, and instead recognise that legitimacy itself can be a complex and elastic concept. Legitimacy affects the character of power relations and can help explain systems of power. Not only how power works as an ongoing process, but also how it originates.[7] There are two types of "story" of legitimacy: one is a story of developmental stages; and the other is how self-confirming processes are at work within any settled power relations to reproduce and consolidate their legitimacy.[8] This cycle is never perfect or complete, and is open to contextual influences, whether those influences reside in arenas as diverse as the domestic political sphere or the international regulatory context.[9] Legitimacy is integral to any system of regulation or body of knowledge, and it can reside in positions of authority or in institutions.[10] However, it is a complex concept involving not only beliefs, but also: legality; judicial determination; and consent, both active and passive; and of course, perhaps most crucially with regard to the subject matter of this chapter, the potential for differential interpretation. This chapter considers legitimacy regarding the EUSTD and the OECDHTPI and their regulatory contexts from a range of perspectives, because legitimacy and consent can be culturally specific matters, and therefore subject to various and sometimes competing interpretations.[11]

Precisely because perceptions of legitimacy can be fluid in certain contexts and on certain issues, it is helpful to think of it as a continuum of belief and evaluation. Suchman offers three models of organizational legitimacy: (i) Pragmatic legitimacy – rooted in self-interested calculation, with an emphasis on notions of exchange and value; (ii) Moral legitimacy – normative evaluations are crucial, with an emphasis on notions of consequence, procedure, structure and personality; and (iii) Cognitive legitimacy – comprehensibility is crucial, with an emphasis on notions of predictability and plausibility. Although moving

7 For a critical discussion on legitimacy, see Beetham, D., *The Legitimation of Power*, London, Macmillan, 1991, pp. 38, 100-101.

8 *Ibid.*, pp. 98-99.

9 For analysis of how constructs of legitimacy can impact in international arenas, see Franck, T. M., "Legitimacy in the International System," *American Journal of International Law*, Vol. 82, No. 4, 1988, pp. 705-759; and Franck, T. M., *The Power of Legitimacy among Nations*, New York, Oxford University Press, 1990.

10 Tyler, T. R., *Why People Obey the Law*, New Haven, Yale University Press, 1990, p. 29.

11 For a critical analysis of how legitimacy issues can impact upon the regulatory structures and processes of financial services regulation, especially regarding the UK, see Gilligan, G. P., *Regulating the Financial Services Sector*, London, Kluwer Law International, 1999.

up the legitimacy scale from pragmatic to moral to cognitive is difficult, it can achieve more profound and self-sustaining levels of legitimacy.[12] Consequently, an analysis grounded in legitimation can be helpful when examining developments in regulation, because regulatory norms and standards can be local, national or international phenomena. As regulatory space and discourse becomes both more congested, and more contested, increasing importance is accorded to those actors perceived as possessing specialist knowledge and/or professional legitimacy. This professional knowledge often may be employed strategically in regulatory disputes. This tendency can be noted with regard to taxation, which as the case studies of the EUSTD and the OECDHTPI below indicate, increasingly is becoming a site of dispute between jurisdictions, international organisations and regional groupings.

The EUSTD – A Tale of Decreasing Tension in EU Tax Competition Policy?

The EUSTD is not the first multilateral taxation initiative by the EU. Indeed the issue of global taxation within the EU first was crystallised in a specific form by the EC in 1996.[13] At the informal Ecofin[14] meeting at Verona, Italy in April 1996: "[…] the Commission proposed a new and comprehensive 'global' view of direct taxation policy. […] Finance ministers welcomed the Commission paper 'Taxation in the European Union' and agreed on the need to consider these issues in a high-level discussion group".[15]

The core aims of the Ecofin taxation package were: stabilisation of member states' tax revenues; smooth functioning of the Single Market; and promoting employment.[16] The underlying philosophy of the 1996 document which has fed through to the EUSTD is that: "[…] repeated failure to achieve progress in tax co-ordination […] has gradually brought

12 Suchman, M. C., "Managing Legitimacy: Strategic and Institutional Approaches," *Academy of Management Review*, Vol. 20, No. 3, 1995, pp. 571-610.

13 Commission of the European Communities, *Taxation in the European Union*, SEC (96) 487 final, Brussels, 20 March 1996, http://ec.europa.eu/taxation_customs/resources/documents/taxation_sec(1996)487_en.pdf

14 Ecofin is the European Union's Council of Economic and Financial Affairs, whose membership comprises of Finance Ministers of the member states of the EU and representatives of the European Commission.

15 The European Commission, *Taxation and Customs Union. The Taxation Package*, Brussels, 1998, p. 1, http://europa.eu.int/comm/taxation_customs/taxation/information_notes/taxation_package/taxpack.htm.

16 Commission of the European Communities, *Taxation in the European Union*, Brussels, SEC (96) 487 final, *op. cit.*, p. 2.

a real loss of fiscal sovereignty by each member state in favour of the markets, through tax erosion".[17]

This clash between national fiscal sovereignty and market power is the core issue of political economy regarding EU-wide taxation policy initiatives. Following the meeting in Verona, a High Level Group, to be known as the Taxation Policy Group (TPG) was formed, chaired by the EC and comprising representatives of EU member states' Finance Ministers. However, the TPG experienced difficulty regarding the coordination of taxation policy in general and notions of harmful tax competition in particular: "Some Member States have made it clear that they looked for a more ambitious package, but extensive debate within the Council and the TPG has shown that, at present, this is not attainable given the initial reluctance of others to consider any move towards tax co-ordination".[18]

That some member states (almost definitely Austria and Luxembourg, and perhaps others) were reluctant initially to consider any move towards tax coordination is a clear indication of how difficult a task faced the EC and prime movers such as France in pushing for tax coordination reform. That there should be disagreement about these issues is unsurprising because the proposals had implications for the financial services sectors of EU member states. Also, regulatory innovation within the EU cannot blind itself to the pragmatic realities of a highly competitive global financial sector, in which jurisdictions, financial institutions and finance centres continually strive to maintain or increase their market share. Tax regimes and other systems of regulation are elements of the competition between different jurisdictions to attract capital. This economic, and simultaneously, political, imperative, is a major driver in the construction of systems of regulation that are sensitive to the requirements of investment capital. As such, it is a major justification for promoting regulatory reform, and indeed as we shall see below for various EU member states, for resisting regulatory reform. This social utility of regulation, or indeed of non-regulation, is acknowledged in the literature on social capital. Social capital can be interpreted as the norms, networks and typologies of trust that societies share in order to achieve shared objectives.[19] Social capital has been viewed as the resource of shared values that a society

17 *Ibid.*, p. 10.

18 Commission of the European Communities, *A package to tackle harmful tax competition in the European Union*, Brussels, COM(97) 564 final, 5 November 1997, p. 3, http://europa.eu.int/comm/taxation_customs/publications/official_doc/com/taxation/com_nov1997/en.pdf.

19 Putnam, R., "The Strange Disappearance of Civic America," *Policy* (Autumn), Vol. 12, No. 1, 1996, pp. 3-15.

has.[20] Taxation regimes are merely one or more cogs in the engines that jurisdictions build to generate social capital. Taxation regimes are especially important cogs though, not only for the generation of revenue, but also for their strategic capability to facilitate inward capital investment and other forms of entrepreneurial activity for the benefit of affected individuals, entities and society in general. Different jurisdictions (whether they are EU member states or not) will seek to produce social capital for themselves in different ways, and are more than likely to have different views on the types of taxation regimes they want to adopt in order to achieve these objectives. This is the core, and sometimes harsh, political and economic reality in which an agency such as the EC must function.

Nevertheless, the EC proposed that it should: "prepare a draft proposal for a Directive by April 1998".[21] The European Commission did, in fact, produce a proposal for a Directive in June 1998.[22] The central feature of the proposal was that:

> A dual approach was suggested; Member States in which the income was earned would have the choice between either: providing information to the other Member States about the investment income of their resident individuals, or applying a "withholding tax" at a minimum rate of 20% to such income arising to individuals resident in other Member States. The information and withholding tax were to be collected by the agent in the country paying the interest.[23]

A significant motivation for this dual model, often referred to as the co-existence model, was the resistance (on grounds of national interest) of both those member states with banking secrecy laws such as Austria and Luxembourg to adopting a EU-wide disclosure of information system and also the strong opposition of other jurisdictions, most notably the UK, to a compulsory withholding tax. During 1998 and 1999, there was continuing opposition (again motivated, unsurprisingly, by national self-interest), from various member states to certain proposals made by the EC. For example, in early 1999 the UK sought changes to the EU proposals in order to prevent a mandatory withholding tax and protect

---

20 Fukuyama, F., "The Great Disruption," *The Atlantic Monthly*, Vol. 283, No. 5, 1999, pp. 55-80.

21 Commission of the European Communities, *A package to tackle harmful tax competition in the European Union*, Brussels, *op. cit.*, p. 5.

22 Commission of the European Communities, *Proposal for a Council Directive to Ensure a Minimum of Effective Taxation of Savings Income in the Form of Interest Payments within the Community*, COM(1998) 295 final, 4 June 1998, http://europa.eu.int/comm/taxation_customs/proposals/taxation/proposal_savings/ojc-en.pdf.

23 The European Commission, *Taxation and Customs Union. The Taxation Package*, Brussels, 1998, *op. cit.*, p. 3.

London's Eurobond market.[24] The UK argued strongly for its position regarding the Draft Directive on Savings at the Lisbon European Council in March 2000, where EU member states agreed on a timeframe to secure political agreement by June 2000 and adoption of the Directive before 31 December 2000.[25] The discussion of this chapter is testimony to the fact that the latter objective was not achieved. Nevertheless, there was some progress in 2000, as seen by the agreement reached by Heads of State and Government at the Santa Maria de Feira European Council in June 2000 that endorsed: "[…] a step-by-step development towards realisation of the exchange of information as the basis for the taxation of savings income of non-residents […] so as to achieve full agreement on the adoption of the Directives and the implementation of the tax package as a whole as soon as possible and no later than by the end of 2002".[26]

It is significant that the European Council pushed out its deadline for adoption of the Directive by a further two years, from its position of only three months earlier in Lisbon. In doing so, they were acknowledging the difficulties of not only securing a common position amongst EU member states, but also recognising the complexities associated with competing regulatory regimes (most notably Switzerland and the US), outside the EU.[27] Also, it is significant that the Council should express such a strong preference for an approach based on exchange of information. This position was reported widely in the world media as a victory for the UK in the combative environment that often is intra-EU politics.[28] Indeed, in the UK House of Commons in the best traditions of enlightened self-interest and the sustaining of subsidiarity within the maelstrom of EU political push and shove, Prime Minister Tony Blair trumpeted this aspect of the Feira agreement as "a personal triumph for the Chancellor. This is a comprehensive agreement which fully protects the competitiveness of the City".[29]

However, on the very same day that Prime Minister Tony Blair was glowing in the aftermath of his self-proclaimed UK triumph, Austrian

---

24 There was widespread media coverage of this issue. For example: "In Bondage," *The Economist*, 17 April 2001, p. 87; and Jamieson, B., "Withhold and Wither," *The Weekly Telegraph*, 14-20 April 1999, p. 43.

25 Commission of the European Communities, *Report from the Commission, Progress on Financial Services, Second Report*, COM(2000) 336 final, 30 May 2000, p. 22, http://europa.eu.int/comm/internal_market/en/finances/actionplan/progress2en.pdf.

26 *Santa Maria de Feira European Council, Presidency Conclusions*, 19 and 20 June 2000, p. 7, http://ue.eu.int/Newsroom/LoadDoc.asp?BID=76&DID=62050&from=&LANG=1.

27 The effects of these international pressures are discussed in more detail below.

28 For example, see Bagwell, S., "UK Claims Victory on Measures to Counter Tax Evasion," *The Australian Financial Review*, 19 June 2000, p. 10.

29 *Hansard*, HC, PM, *Statement to the House*, Column 339, 21 June 2000.

Finance Minister Karl-Heinz Grasser, in an interview with the news agency Reuters, was declaring the agreement as a triumph for Austria, because the EU formally had moved away from its intention to abolish bank secrecy throughout the EU. Minister Grasser also expressed doubt as to whether the agreement could work in practice because he felt that Switzerland and other low-tax countries would not relax sufficiently their bank secrecy laws to permit equivalent exchange of information with EU authorities.[30] The Ecofin meeting in Brussels in November 2000 was a critical circuit breaker in the evolution of the EUSTD and was recognised as such in the media.[31] Luxembourg capitulated regarding seeking exemption for its money market funds but had a "victory" in that those countries applying the withholding tax option in the transitional period would retain 25% of the revenues and not 10%, as under earlier proposals.[32] However, there were provisos surrounding the overall agreement. Austria and Luxembourg's support was dependent upon "a binding decision on the roll-back of the sixty-six measures within the framework of the Code of Conduct".[33] Also, there was the very significant issue that the overall agreement was built on the understanding that the EU could persuade the US, Switzerland and other jurisdictions to adopt similar measures.

Nevertheless, in July 2001, the Commission withdrew its 1998 proposal for a Savings Directive,[34] and issued a new proposed Directive,[35] based on the Ecofin agreement, hammered out in Brussels in November 2000.[36] The EC sought to strengthen their push for the proposed Directive by issuing supporting publications.[37] The EC argued strongly that: it was

---

30 http://www.reuters.com/, 21 June 2000.

31 *2312 Council – Ecofin*, Brussels, 26 November 2000, Press: 453 Nr: 13861/00, http://ue.eu.int/Newsroom/LoadDoc.asp?MAX=21&BID=93&DID=64233&LANG=1.

32 *The Australian*, "EU tax hopes up as 'mouse' demurs," 26 November 2000, p. 26.

33 *2312 Council – Ecofin*, Brussels, 26 November 2000, *op. cit.*, p. 5.

34 Commission of the European Communities, *Proposal for a Council Directive to ensure a minimum of effective taxation of savings income in the form of interest payments within the Community*, COM(1998) 295 final, *op. cit.*

35 Commission of the European Communities, *Proposal for a Council Directive to ensure effective taxation of savings income in the form of interest payments within the Community*, COM(2001) 400 final, 18 July 2001, http://europa.eu.int/comm/taxation_customs/proposals/taxation/com2001400/com2001400_en.pdf.

36 *2312 Council – Ecofin*, Brussels, 26 November 2000, *op. cit.*, p. 5.

37 Commission of the European Communities, *Commission adopts new proposal on taxation of cross-border savings income*, Brussels, 18 July 2001, IP/01/1026, http://europa.eu.int/comm/taxation_customs/publications/official_doc/IP/ip011026/ip011026_en.pdf; and Commission of the European Communities, *Savings tax proposal: frequently asked questions*, Brussels 18 July 2001, MEMO/01/266, http://europa.eu.int/comm/taxation_customs/publications/official_doc/IP/ip011026/memo01266_en.pdf.

not seeking tax harmonisation;[38] that the proposal would not cause a shift of business out of the EU;[39] and that member states did not cooperate sufficiently well in exchanging information on cross-border interest on savings.[40] Member states reached political agreement at the Ecofin meeting of 21 January 2003 and it was adopted formally on 3 June 2003.[41] The EUSTD's application was dependent on equivalent measures being adopted in six non-member countries: Andorra, Liechtenstein, Monaco, San Marino, Switzerland and the United States. Similarly, equivalent measures were required in ten associated or dependent territories of the UK and the Netherlands: Anguilla, Aruba, British Virgin Islands, Cayman Islands, Guernsey, Isle of Man, Jersey, Montserrat, Netherlands Antilles, and the Turks and Caicos Islands. Gradually between 2003 and 2005 agreements were reached with these jurisdictions and the EUSTD became active from 1 July 2005.

So the EUSTD had finally arrived, with the political in-fighting of the 2003-2005 period being much less fierce than during the previous three years. However, it is still not applied uniformly to all jurisdictions and its success to date may be symbolic more than pragmatic. Transitional arrangements still exist for Austria, Belgium and Luxembourg (who were all strident critics of the EUSTD when it was first mooted), and the transitional arrangement will not end until Andorra, Liechtenstein, Monaco, San Marino and Switzerland can guarantee comprehensive exchange of information. The EUSTD has been relatively easy to circumvent for the more sophisticated market operators using vehicles such as trusts and foundations. Klautke and Weichenreider found that there were enough loopholes (exempt bonds included) for tax evaders to avoid EUSTD obligations at no extra cost to their activities.[42] One should not be too surprised by this given not only the ambitious nature of the EUSTD, but also the problematic contexts of EU Directives themselves in that there is always going to be some interpretative leeway for member states in how they choose to enact Directives into national law systems. The latter process is almost always affected by notions of self-interest and the implications of subsidiarity.

---

38 Commission of the European Communities, *Savings tax proposal: frequently asked questions*, Brussels 18 July 2001, *op. cit.*, p. 1.

39 *Ibid.*, p. 2.

40 *Ibid.*, p. 3.

41 Commission of the European Communities, *Council Directive on taxation of savings income in the form of interest payments*, COM(2003), 3 June 2003, p. 48.

42 Klautke, T. and Weichenreider, A. J., "Interest Income, Tax Evasion, the EU Savings Directive, and Capital Market Effects," *CESifo Working Paper Series*, No. 2300, 1 May 2008, http://papers.ssrn.com/sol3/papers.cfm?abstract_id=1135532.

The EC itself has struggled to gauge the effectiveness of the EUSTD and establish data benchmarking.[43] The measurement difficulties faced by the EC are summed up by Zipfel in these terms:

> Many Member States do not, for example provide any information on the amount of the taxpayers' foreign and domestic interest income (which [the tax-payers] state in their returns), the number that provide information or those that opt for withholding tax. Moreover, they typically specify only the total amount of withholding tax and the total number of reports issued since 2005. What is more, longer time series are available only for items that cover a scope larger than that of the Directive. As a result there is no ideal benchmark available.[44]

So, in essence, the EUSTD should be viewed as just one element in the ongoing struggle by nation states and international organizations such as the EU to secure the stability of taxation revenues and increase levels of transparency and accountability in the financial affairs of their citizens, both legal and natural persons. Of crucial importance with regard to the EUSTD in general, and the pace and shape of its statutory evolution in particular, has been the changing international environment relating to tax competition between jurisdictions and prevailing expectations of transparency and exchange of information between countries. The ongoing global financial crisis and the election of President Barack Obama to replace President George W. Bush in the White House have been substantial catalysts for change. These effects are discussed in more detail in the conclusion to this chapter. First, it is interesting to examine the impact of another significant international actor in international tax matters, the OECD, because in recent years its activities in relation to harmful tax practices have been influential in how the EU has been able to promote and establish the EUSTD.

The EUSTD in the International Taxation Policy Context

During the same period that the EC has been trying to promote support for the EUSTD and its predecessor, there have been increasing efforts by a number of international organizations such as the OECD, the Financial Action Task Force (FATF), the Financial Stability Forum (FSF), and also

---

43 See European Commission, *Commission Staff Working Document. Refining the present coverage of Council Directive 2003/48/EC on taxation of income from savings*, [SEC(2008)559]; and European Commission, *Report from the Commission to the Council, in accordance with Article 18 of Council Directive 2003/48/EC on taxation of savings income in the form of interest payments*, [COM(2008)552].

44 Zipfel, F., *EU Savings Taxation Directive, One piece in the puzzle of cross-border tax policy*, Deutsche Bank Research, 2009, p. 6, http://www.dbresearch.com/PROD/DBR_INTERNET_EN-PROD/PROD0000000000243300.pdf;jsessionid=6B2EF7F30A50BD66479DC541E40C7AC7.srv12-dbr-com.

by a large number of nation states to counter money laundering, tax evasion and the financing of terrorism. These efforts were given greater urgency in the aftermath of the terrorist attacks on New York and Washington, DC on 11 September 2001. During 2000, 2001 and 2002, the OECD, FATF and FSF separately engaged in specific listing initiatives that have become widely referred to as blacklists.[45] This is because, in the main, they have highlighted what the FATF, FSF or OECD have seen as problematic, or non-cooperative, jurisdictions that currently are operating in global financial markets. Of particular relevance for the EUSTD has been the OECD's Project on Harmful Tax Practices (OECDPHTPI). In May 2000, the OECD declared that the following thirty-four jurisdictions met the OECD's technical criteria as tax havens: Andorra, Anguilla, Antigua and Barbuda, Aruba, Bahamas, Bahrain, Barbados, Belize, British Virgin Islands, Cook Islands, Dominica, Gibraltar, Grenada, Guernsey/Sark/Alderney, Isle of Man, Jersey, Liechtenstein, Liberia, Maldives, Marshall Islands, Monaco, Montserrat, Nauru, Netherlands Antilles, Niue, Panama, Samoa, Seychelles, St Lucia, St Christopher & Nevis, St Vincent and the Grenadines, Tonga, Turks & Caicos, US Virgin Islands and Vanuatu.[46] In April 2002, the OECDPHTPI published its second blacklist and classified as "unco-operative tax havens": Andorra; Liberia; Liechtenstein; Marshall Islands; Monaco; Nauru; and Vanuatu.[47]

Due to word-length constraints this chapter is unable to chart all the twists and turns of the OECDHTPI.[48] However, there were a number of key issues that not only symbolized the struggle between the OECD and its alleged tax havens and other offshore finance centres (OFCs), but also have implications for the EUSTD and how the EU functions in multilateral tax contexts. First, the lack of support for the listing processes by many of those listed was not surprising and typifies what some legitimacy

45 For a critical analysis of the listing initiatives, especially as they apply to offshore finance centres, see Gilligan, G. P., "Overview:" Markets, Offshore Sovereignty and Onshore Legitimacy," Chapter 1, in D. Masciandaro (ed.), *Global Financial Crime, Terrorism, Money Laundering and Offshore Centres*, Aldershot (UK) and Burlington (US), Ashgate Publishing, 2004, pp. 7-60.

46 Organisation for Economic Co-operation and Development, *Towards Global Tax Co-operation, Report to the 2000 Ministerial Council Meeting and Recommendations by the Committee on Fiscal Affairs, Progress in Identifying and Eliminating Harmful Tax Practices*, Paris, 2000.

47 Organisation for Economic Co-operation and Development, *The OECD Issues: The List of Unco-operative Tax Havens*, Paris, 18 April 2002, http://www.oecd.org/EN/document/0, EN-document-103-nodirectorate-no-12-28534–22,00.html.

48 For a more detailed discussion of the OECDHTPI, see Gilligan, G., "The Regulatory Dance in Tax Competition – A Case Study in Multi-Lateral Governance," *Monash University Department of Business Law & Taxation Research Paper*, No. 11, 2008, http://ssrn.com/abstract=1090118.

theorists might refer to as "a lack of compliance pull". Under this construct of compliance pull, the more legitimate a rule, initiative or regulatory framework is perceived to be by those who are subject to its effects, the greater the level of compliance they will be accorded. Similarly, the lower the levels of legitimacy accorded to specific rules, the lower will be the levels of compliance accorded. Interestingly, the compliance-pull-and-legitimacy relationship is an interactive one, so that increasing levels of compliance pull will strengthen the legitimacy and compliance levels achieved by rules/initiatives, and decreasing levels of compliance pull will have the opposite effect.[49] The interactive compliance pull-and-legitimacy relationship has been important with respect to the OECDHTPI and eventually decided their relative ultimate success.

A key factor in that process was the manner in which small offshore finance centres gathered together and utilized the concept of legitimacy to shape the discourse of their relationship with the OECD and which led to the establishment of the Global Forum on Taxation. The Global Forum sought to bring together in more cohesive ways how the OECD, certain OECD members and many of those jurisdictions likely to be affected by the OECDHTPI interact on tax competition issues.[50] The Global Forum has met on numerous occasions, including Berlin in June 2004, where it produced a policy document to progress efforts towards achieving a level playing field.[51] The Berlin meeting stated that the term

> "high standards" refers to the principles of transparency and effective exchange of information accepted by the Participating Partners, which principles are reflected in the 2002 Model Agreement on Information Exchange on Tax Matters. [...] Central to the concept of a global level playing field is that it is fundamentally about fairness. A convergence of existing practices of information exchange to meet high standards would achieve a global level playing field.[52]

Interestingly, the Berlin Global Forum also acknowledged that in the taxation area: "competition be on the basis of legitimate commercial considerations",[53] which might be interpreted as something of a victory for some of the blacklisted jurisdictions and their supporters.

---

49 For a discussion of the compliance-pull-legitimacy interaction, see Raustalia, K. and Slaughter, A. M., "International Law. International Relations and Compliance," in W. Carlsnaes, T. Risse *et al.* (eds.), *Handbook of International Relations*, London, Sage Publications, 2002, p. 541.

50 http://www.oecd.org/EN/document/0,,EN-document-103-nodirectorate-no-12–36128-22,00.html.

51 OECD Global Forum on Taxation, Berlin 3-4 June 2004, *A Process for Achieving a Global Level Playing Field*, 4 June 2004, Final, http://www.oecd.org/ctp/harmful/31967501.pdf, accessed 25 July 2014.

52 *Ibid.*, p. 3.

53 *Ibid.*

Nevertheless, the OECD also can claim some success, because as noted by OECD Secretary-General Angel Gurria in June 2009, all 84 countries surveyed by the Global Forum had endorsed the OECD Standards of Transparency and Exchange of Information and agreed to implement them.[54]

Also, it is perhaps of note regarding the progress of the EUSTD that the OECD should have considered Liechtenstein and Monaco so unfavourably. Traditionally France has exerted strong influence over Monaco, especially in the area of Monaco's external affairs. Similarly, traditionally Liechtenstein has had very close relations with Switzerland; both favour banking regimes that offer secrecy and that is significant in the context of the EUSTD. What is undeniable regarding the progress of the EUSTD is that factors external to the EU have been crucial, most especially efforts by the EC to persuade the US and Switzerland to adopt similar positions on exchange of information issues. In October 2001 Ecofin authorised the EC to negotiate with the US, Switzerland, Liechtenstein, Monaco, Andorra and San Marino to secure agreement that these jurisdictions would adopt equivalent measures to the EUSTD.[55] Despite the efforts of the EC, there was much uncertainty surrounding the position of the US on the EUSTD during the Bush administration, as interest groups sought to influence the administration's tax policy. A number of lobby groups such as the National Taxpayers Union (NTU),[56] and the Centre for Freedom and Prosperity (CFP),[57] have contributed to debates on tax competition. The NTU helped to organise international coalitions to oppose the efforts of the EU and OECD on harmful tax competition, including *The Saint Louis Declaration*, which denounces the efforts of the EU and OECD in this area as oppressive.[58] Like the NTU, the CFP is based in Washington, DC, and it has argued fiercely against the OECDPHTPI and the EUSTD. Similar to the NTU, the CFP has portrayed both the EUSTD and the OECDPHTPI as inimical to notions of individual freedom, harmful to

54 OECD, *Moving forward on the global transparency and tax information exchange agenda*, Berlin, 23 June 2009, http://www.oecd.org/newsroom/movingforwardontheglobaltransparencyandtaxinformationexchangeagenda.htm.

55 *2376 Council – Ecofin*, 16 October 2001, Luxembourg, Press: 364 Nr: 12831/01, http://ue.eu.int/Newsroom/LoadDoc.asp?MAX=21&BID=93&DID=68158&LANG=1.

56 The National Taxpayers Union was founded in the US in 1969 and has 335,000 members. It is an influential lobby group in the US and is a founding member of the World Taxpayers Association. The NTU produces regular newsletters and other information on taxation matters. See http://www.ntu.org.

57 The CFP produces regular newsletters and articles on these issues. See http://www.freedomandprosperity.org.

58 National Taxpayers Union, *Taxpayers of the World Unite: 33 Groups across the Globe Denounce EU/OECD Tax Cartel Scheme*, http://www.ntu.org/01conf/PO10615StLouisDec.html.

concepts of free trade, damaging to growth and therefore against the national interest of the US.[59]

The CFP has had considerable levels of support within the US Congress, some of whom were implacable in their opposition to the EUSTD throughout 2002. For example, House Government Reform Committee Chairman Dan Burton in a letter to then US Treasury Secretary Paul O'Neill urged vigorous opposition to Information Exchange Schemes.[60] Media reports quoted Congressman Jim DeMint of South Carolina in a letter to Secretary O'Neill when he described the EU's agenda on information exchange as "[…] bad tax policy and bad economic policy […]" and "a threat to America's competitive position in the world economy".[61] Similarly, Pennsylvania Senator Rick Santorum, who also served as Chairman of the Republican Conference, asked Secretary O'Neill to be: "[…] sceptical toward the European Union's proposed Savings Tax Directive […] As a low-tax country by industrial world standards, the United States has little if anything to gain by participating in a tax cartel designed to help high-tax nations […]. Governments, like private businesses, should be subjected to the discipline of market competition".[62]

However, there have been conflicting interpretations offered about how the Bush administration viewed the EUSTD. For example, media reports in June 2002 stated that the EU had claimed in a communiqué that: "Contacts at political and technical level have been held with the United States, Monaco, Andorra, San Marino and Liechtenstein. These states have expressed their willingness to cooperate with the European Union."[63] However, the CFP offered a very different interpretation:

59 The CFP regularly publishes on these issues. For example: *CFP Weekly Update*, May 23 2001 Edition, http://www.freedomandprosperity.org/update/u05-23–01/u05-23–01.shtml; and Mitchell, D. J., *CFP Strategic Memo, To: Leaders of Low-Tax Jurisdictions and Supporters of Tax Competition, Financial Privacy, and Fiscal Sovereignty*, 16 June 2001, http://www.freedomandprosperity.org/Papers/m06-16–01/m06-16–01.shtml.

60 *Center for Freedom and Prosperity Weekly Update*, "House Government Reform Committee Chairman Dan Burton Urges Vigorous Opposition to Information Exchange Schemes," 22 February 2002, http://www.freedomandprosperity.org/ltr/burton/burton.shtml.

61 Godfrey, M., "The US Starts to Recognize EU 'Information Exchange' Problem," 20 June 2002, *tax-news.com*.

62 *Center for Freedom and Prosperity Weekly Update*, "Third Ranking Republican in U.S. Senate Denounces the EU's Savings Tax Directive," 12 February 2002, http://archive.freedomandprosperity.org/update/u02-12–02/u02-12–02.shtml#2, accessed 4 June 2012.

63 Godfrey, M., "EU claims that US supports Savings Tax Directive," *Tax-news.com*, 27 June 2002.

> The Center for Freedom and Prosperity was told Tuesday by several senior Bush Administration sources that the United States has rejected any participation in the European Union (EU) savings tax directive. According to one highly placed White House official, "We are not signing the European Union's 'savings tax directive.' There is ZERO support in the Administration for signing".[64]

What we see here is similar to the situation described earlier of the agreement reached on the Draft Directive at the Santa Maria de Feira Council in June 2000, when UK Prime Minister Tony Blair and Austrian Finance Minister Karl-Heinz Grasser offered alternative social constructions of the same sets of political and economic realities, in order to legitimate their actions to their separate constituencies. The EU and CFP are engaging in competing social constructions of the same issue. The CFP offers an explanation of why their interpretation of the same events should contrast so sharply with that of the EU in these somewhat pejorative terms:

> In all likelihood, this confusion may be the result of struggles inside the Administration. The career bureaucrats at Treasury and the IRS are ideological zealots and they fully support the EU Savings Tax Directive. […] Similarly, it is not surprising that the President's political appointees and economic advisers vehemently deny that the U.S. is supporting the EU's proposed cartel. These men and women generally support competitive markets […].[65]

The CFP analysis may have been prescient if media reports in September 2002 and a CFP press release of October 2002 were to be believed. One senior White House official speaking on condition that he was not identified told a meeting of conservative political groups that "[…] the administration would not support the European Union's information-sharing directive: [The Commission] want to get us to sign on in order to badger the Swiss into signing, and get the Swiss to sign on to badger us"[66] And:

> Moving to erase any ambiguity, the Bush Administration reiterated its opposition to a European Union proposal that would require nations to collect and share private financial information on non-resident investors. Larry

---

[64] *CFP Press Release*, "CFP Hails Death of EU Savings Tax Directive, Bush Administration Rejects Tax Cartel," July 24 2002, http://www.freedomandprosperity.org/press/p07-24–02/p07-24–02.shtml.

[65] Mitchell, D., *CFP Strategic Memo, To: Supporters of tax competition, financial privacy, and fiscal sovereignty, Re: Who is in Charge: President Bush or IRS Bureaucrats?*, 26 June 2002, http://www.freedomandprosperity.org/memos/m06-26–02/m06-26–02.shtml.

[66] Alden, E., Guerrera F. and Shlaes, A., "US opposes sharing information on Savings Taxation: White House Advisers come out against European request for data on foreign-held accounts," *Financial Times*, 26 September 2002.

Lindsey, the President's senior economic advisor and Director of the National Economic Council, firmly stated that "the Administration does not support the EU Savings Directive – there is zero interest in it".[67]

Both these statements are significant and illustrate the gaming that goes on in the political economy of taxation, but for the purposes of this analysis it is especially important to note the Switzerland/US/EC interaction. The Bush administration was essentially hostile towards the EUSTD but did not trumpet this position in the media, whereas the US Department of the Treasury and the Internal Revenue Service were much more supportive. As discussed earlier, whether the EUSTD became a reality was contingent on how these regulatory tensions played out in terms of relative support, or at least lack of obstruction from various quarters, including Switzerland, the US, Luxembourg and a number of dependent territories such Jersey, Guernsey and the Cayman Islands. In the end, as was discussed earlier, sufficient international support was forthcoming and the EUSTD has been in active service for more than three years now, albeit as noted above with question marks over its relative efficacy.

Conclusion

What conclusions might one draw from this discussion? First, the EUSTD, the OECDHTPI and the support and the opposition that they both have attracted from various parties over the years show the forces of globalisation and increasing interdependence between nation states at work.

Second, it is important to remember that different jurisdictions have different perceptions about what are their respective legitimate positions on increased transparency in taxation and other financial contexts.

Third, normative issues are crucial when seeking to understand issues of compliance, whether at the local, national or international level. The pivotal importance of reflexive legitimacy should be at the forefront of EU strategies as it seeks to build on the EUSTD and pursues further regulatory innovation in the fields of taxation administration[68] and mutual assistance in the recovery of taxes.[69]

---

67 *CFP Press Release*, "White House Reiterates Opposition to EU Savings Tax Cartel: Free-Market Leaders Hail Administration Stance," 29 October 2002, http://www.freedomandprosperity.org/press/p10-29–02/p10-29–02.shtml.

68 European Commission, *Proposal for a Council Directive on administrative cooperation in the field of taxation*, COM(2009)29, 2009.

69 European Commission, *Proposal for a Council Directive concerning mutual assistance for the recovery of claims relating to taxes, duties and other measures*, COM(2009)28, 2009.

Fourth, the powerful influence of Adam Smith's *Invisible Hand* is omnipresent.[70] That is to say, market forces themselves, and in particular, the decisions and choices of the consumers of financial services. Under this paradigm of regulatory arbitrage, exchanges and finance centres understandably exploit what they perceive as their cost or other structural advantages, such as a particular jurisdiction's system of company law, or levels of transparency, in order to gain competitive advantage.

Fifth, there is an urgent and growing need for more and continuing empirically informed research on the efficacy of international regulatory initiatives such as the EUSTD and OECDHTPI, and there have been some econometric studies in the area of tax competition. For example, Janeba and Schjelderup found that increasing tax competition is likely to bring overall positive effects to the welfare of communities, because although the supply of public goods would decrease, so too would rents to politicians.[71] Sorensen investigated the difficulties associated with international tax coordination and found that approaches need to be global rather than regional to achieve any significant positive effect.[72] Brauner also stresses the benefits of a global approach and in a conclusion that favours current OECD initiatives, advocates the benefits of a single set of international tax rules via gradual rule-harmonization effects, led preferably by the OECD.[73]

Sixth, it is the various political economy contexts which are most influential, such as the ongoing global financial crisis. The G20 meeting in London in April 2009 pledged to take action against non-cooperative jurisdictions including tax havens and to protect national taxation revenues.[74] These new realities were re-affirmed by the G8 meeting in the Italian city of L'Aquila, in July 2009, where the major nations committed to further efforts in international tax and prudential cooperation and

70 Smith, A., *The Wealth of Nations*, London, T. Nelson and Sons, 1884.

71 Janeba, E. and Schjelderup, G., "Why Europe Should Love Tax Competition – and the U.S. Even More So," *NBER Working Paper*, No. 9334, Cambridge, MA, 2002, http://www.nber.org/papers/w9334.pdf.

72 Sorensen, P. B., *International Tax Coordination: Regionalism Versus Globalism*, *CESifo Working Paper*, No. 483, Munich, 2001, http://papers.ssrn.com/sol3/papers.cfm?abstract_id=273359.

73 Brauner, Y., *An International Tax Regime in Crystallization – Realities, Experiences and Opportunities*, New York, NYU Law School, *Public Law Research Paper*, No. 43, 2002.

74 Group of 20, *The Global Plan for Recovery and Reform*, London, 2 April 2009, http://www.g20.org/Documents/final-communique.pdf.

in combating illicit financing.[75] President Obama has a legislative history of activism against bank secrecy and tax avoidance. For example, in February 2007 he was one of the co-sponsors of the *Stop Tax Haven Abuse Act 2007*.[76] So, the current US administration is much more likely to support the proactive anti-avoidance efforts of the EU in multilateral taxation contexts than the previous Bush administration. The impacts of these political and economic pressures are stimulating increasing levels of international tax cooperation. For example, there are literally hundreds of Tax Information Exchange Agreements (TIEAs) being concluded worldwide between a host of jurisdictions, some including previously more reluctant jurisdictions such as Liechtenstein, Monaco and Switzerland.[77] Also, there is continuing global activity by international organizations to increase mutual assistance in the taxation arena. One example is the announcement by the OECD and the Council of Europe that they are amending the Convention on Mutual Administrative Assistance in Tax Matters.[78]

It is highly likely that these trends will continue and that the EU will be an increasingly significant actor in multilateral taxation contexts. National tax authorities globally – not just in Europe – are owed significant amounts that are being filtered through international financial markets. Reconciling the competing claims of nation states for tax revenues, finance centres for market access and financial institutions for freedom to operate is a substantial challenge. Consequently issues of national sovereignty need to be factored heavily into the development of international initiatives, and the input of affected jurisdictions sought in an inclusive manner so as to generate appropriate checks and balances into international taxation regulatory infrastructures and praxis. Such a legitimacy emphasis will be integral for multilateral taxation regulatory efforts such as the EUSTD and the OECDHTPI to have realistic hopes of mitigating tension, reducing contestation and achieving continuing success.

---

75 Group of Eight, *Responsible Leadership for a Sustainable Future*, 8 July 2009, http://www.g8italia2009.it/static/G8_Allegato/G8_Declaration_08_07_09_final,0.pdf.

76 U.S. Congress – *S.681 Stop Tax Haven Abuse Act, a bill to restrict the use of offshore tax havens and abusive tax shelters to inappropriately avoid Federal taxation*, 17 February 2007, http://www.opencongress.org/bill/110-s681/show.

77 For example, Australia's recent TIEA with Monaco is its twenty-third; Commonwealth of Australia, *Australia signs Tax Information Agreement with Monaco*, 7 April 2010, http://ministers.treasury.gov.au/DisplayDocs.aspx?doc=pressreleases/2010/059.htm&pageID=003&min=njsa&Year=&DocType=.

78 Organisation for Economic Co-operation and Development, *Tax: Revised OECD, Council of Europe treaty will boost multilateral cooperation*, 6 April 2010, http://www.oecd.org/document/33/0,3343,en_2649_37427_44892193_1_1_1_1,00.html.

Part VI

Conclusions

The European Rescue of the Empire or the EU as Ferment of Change in International Relations?

Pascaline WINAND

Monash University and Université libre de Bruxelles

The EU as Ferment of Change in the World?

On July 1st 2013, Croatia joined the European Union. In Australia, EU Ambassador David Daly hailed its entry into this "democratic peace and reconciliation club" as a "great day for Europe and for the world". The EU was well deserving of its Nobel Peace Prize, he insisted. Born as "a political project for peace and reconciliation after the Second World War", it had succeeded in reinforcing democratic values in Europe.[1] The previous year, the EU Ambassador to India had written an article in *The Times of India* entitled "Nobel Years of Peace in Europe" in which he explained the EU approach to promoting reconciliation and democratic values in a continent which had been frequently ravaged by war.[2] Both speeches were very much in tune with the Norwegian Nobel Committee's praise of the EU for its contribution "to the advancement of peace and reconciliation, democracy and human rights in Europe". The Committee commended the EU and its forerunners for bringing about reconciliation between former enemies, introducing democracy in Greece, Portugal and Spain, strengthening democracy in central and eastern Europe and fostering reconciliation in the Balkans. Today, Croatia is a member of the EU and accession talks have been opened with Serbia. It does seem, then, that the EU, in the words of the Nobel Committee, is playing a role in helping "transform most of Europe from a continent of war to a continent of peace".[3] The Committee

1 Daly, D., "Speech given by H.E. David Daly, Ambassador and Head of Delegation of the European Union to Australia on the occasion of the Accession of Croatia to the European Union," 1 July 2013.

2 Cravinho, J., "Nobel Years of Peace in Europe," *The Times of India*, 11 December 2012, p. 20.

3 The Norwegian Nobel Committee, Oslo, 12 October 2012, http://www.nobelprize.org/nobel_prizes/peace/laureates/2012/press.html.

stopped short, however, of describing the EU as a factor of peace in the world beyond Europe.

In his contribution to this book, Ambassador Daly emphasizes that candidate countries to EU membership had consistently seen their GDP increase as they joined the EU, while foreign direct investment and trade rose as they progressively adopted the EU *acquis communautaire*. But is there more to EU enlargement than promoting prosperity and stability in an expanding club of European nations? For former European Commissioner Chris Patten, EU enlargement has been "the most successful foreign policy pursued by Europe". It not only played a key role in fostering open markets in central and eastern Europe, but also in reinforcing democracy.[4] This begs the question, however, of whether the EU also has had a role in promoting peace, reconciliation and security beyond Europe. Europe has been the breeding ground for two world wars. We could argue that by the very fact of playing a stabilizing economic and political role in the region, European integration is contributing to peace in the world at large. It does so by enlarging to include new members but also by striving, with varying degrees of success, to stabilize its neighbourhood towards the East and South through multilateral networks of political and economic cooperation. But some EU policy-makers and policy entrepreneurs such as Jean Monnet have long considered the positive influence of the EU as extending beyond the beneficial effects of the stabilization of its own region.

In 1963, Jean Monnet, one of the masterminds behind the creation of the first European Community, the European Coal and Steel Community (ECSC), described the European unification process as a "ferment of change" in international relations. Its revolutionary but peaceful action was not to be confined to Europe. For him and his collaborators in the Action Committee for the United States of Europe,[5] European integration was not about fostering the emergence of a European nationalism, or the creation of a new great power, but rather about promoting "a method to introduce change in Europe and consequently in the world". "European unity", wrote Monnet, "is not a plan; it is not a theory; it is a process that has already started and which aims to bring people and nations together so they can jointly adapt to circumstances in constant evolution".[6] Monnet's method was to foster peaceful change in Europe and in the

4 Patten, C., *Not Quite the Diplomat: Home Truths about World Affairs*, London, Allen Lane, 2005, p. 152.

5 Winand, P., "Le Comité d'Action pour les États-Unis d'Europe de Jean Monnet," in *Vingt ans d'action du Comité Jean Monnet 1955-1975, Notre Europe, Problématique européenne*, No. 8, May 2001.

6 Monnet, J., "A Ferment of Change," *Journal of Common Market Studies*, Vol. 1, No. 3., March 1963.

world through pragmatic, step-by-step action. It involved the creation of common institutions, common policies in Europe and beyond, which would then bring about a sense of common responsibilities and objectives. Recent pronouncements by EU officials would seem to have taken a leaf from Monnet's book, in expounding the philosophy of incremental change in international relations, as well as from academic literature – particularly neo-functionalism – analysing the evolution and nature of the EU. This is perhaps not surprising as some EU officials themselves are well versed in such literature, having studied with some of its proponents and authors.[7]

The "First Non-imperialist Empire in History" and a World of Partnerships and Regions

In 2003, forty years after Monnet wrote his article in the *Journal of Common Market Studies*, in the wake of the Iraq war which had triggered conflicting responses on the part of EU member states, the European Council adopted a European Security Strategy (ESS), "A Secure Europe in a Better World". Drafted by High Representative for Common Foreign and Security Policy Javier Solana, the document depicted the EU as inherently peaceful, prosperous, stable, based on the rule of law and democracy. The EU was portrayed as a global player by the sheer size of its economic power and the forces it deployed "in places as distant as Afghanistan, East Timor and the DRC" [Democratic Republic of Congo]. The ESS also saw the EU becoming a "more credible and effective actor" as European interests increasingly converged and EU mutual solidarity strengthened. The EU would make its mark on the international stage by confronting global threats through a mixture of non-military and military instruments and strategies. Among these were the promotion of trade and development, support offered for effective multilateralism and democracy, and strategic partnerships with key actors such as Japan, China, Canada and India. The EU was to contribute to strengthen global governance not only by backing the United Nations, the World Trade Organization (WTO) and international financial institutions but also regional organizations such as the Organization for Security and Cooperation in Europe (OSCE), the Council of Europe, NATO, the Association of Southeast Asian Nations

---

7 White, J. P. J., "Theory Guiding Practice. The Neofunctionalists and the Hallstein EEC Commission, *Journal of European Integration History*, Vol. 9, No. 1, 2003, pp. 111-131; Warzoulet, L., "Relancer la CEE avant la chaise vide. Néofonctionnalistes vs. fédéralistes au sein de la Commission européenne (1964-1965)," *Journal of European Integration History*, Vol. 14, No. 1, 2008, pp. 69-86; Bajon, P., "The European Commissioners and the Empty Chair Crisis of 1965-66," *Journal of European Integration History*, Vol. 15, No. 2, 2009, pp. 105-124; Peterson, J., "José Manuel Barroso. Political Scientist and ECPR Member," *European Political Science*, Vol. 7, No. 1, 2008, pp. 64-75.

(ASEAN), the Common Market of the South (MERCOSUR) and the African Union. But for it to have more of an impact in the world and more political weight, the ESS recommended developing more active EU policies in crisis management and conflict prevention, increasing its military efficiency and diplomatic capability and bringing more coherence to its foreign, security and defence policies. In the end, only an "active and capable European Union would make an impact on a global scale" and "in doing so, [...] contribute to an effective multilateral system leading to a fairer, safer and more united world". All in all, the ESS contributed to the impression that the EU was already a global player, but needed to become more coherent, more capable and more active in the world to increase its influence further beyond the economic realm. To become more of what Monnet would have called a "ferment of change" in international relations by helping to build a more peaceful "international order based on effective multilateralism", the EU must first gain in efficiency and strength.[8]

In 2006, European Commission President José Manuel Barroso went one step further. He described the EU as "the first non-imperialist empire in history". He saw it as different from other empires, however. Although it had the dimension of empire, it had not been made by force, by the diktat of a centre, but "through the free agreement of all the participants". It was "reconciliation through peace, democracy and freedom", an "empire of freedom and peace". Raised eyebrows at the mention of "empire" by a national from a former colonial power notwithstanding, the more interesting point is that Barroso felt that the reunification of Europe in peace and prosperity via enlargement had implications well beyond Europe. It gave the EU "the legitimacy to make its mark on the new forms of governance taking shape in the international community", to "promote its universal values" and to "bring [its] true weight to bear on world affairs". According to the Commission President, the EU had the mission to "build a world of partnerships" as it had "by definition [...] a multilateral culture, a culture of constructive compromise in both its international affairs and its external relations with its major partners".[9] For Barroso, through a kind of rebirth via European reconciliation and reunification, the EU would soon

8 "A Secure Europe in a Better World, European Security Strategy," Brussels, 12 December 2003.

9 Barroso, J. M., speech at the opening session of the ECSA-World Conference "Europe's challenges in a globalized world," Global Jean Monnet Conference, Brussels, 23 and 24 November 2006, European Commission, Luxembourg, Office for Official Publications of the European Communities, 2007. For a later speech, see also Barroso, J. M., "European Union is 'non imperial empire'" (long version), 10 July 2007, https://www.youtube.com/watch?v=-I8M1T-GgRU, and Charter, D., "Call for Vote on Europe Empire," *The Times*, 11 July 2007.

find itself in a position to regain a leading position and promote its own model in the world.

Likewise, the European Commission has shown its support for a world of regions, patterned in part on its own blueprint for integration. For example, the Commission has stated that the EU backed ASEAN efforts "to build a closer relationship among its member countries" as "European history bears testimony to the fact that greater integration is the best guarantee of stability and prosperity, and South-East Asia can find inspiration in this".[10] Group-to-group cooperation with organizations such as ASEAN or MERCOSUR, as well as support for interregional or transregional fora such as the Asia-Europe Meeting (ASEM), have been seen as ways of enhancing global prosperity and stability by preventing conflicts. This in turn would benefit EU security and prosperity, and enhance its recognition on the international stage, as more regions seek to emulate the EU model.[11] According to this vision, the wider adoption of the EU recipe for peaceful change seems to know no bounds. Integration, by a kind of "contagion effect", spreads the EU partnership of regions throughout the world in a step-by-step process, reminiscent of Monnet's "ferment of change" method and neo-functionalist analyses, writ large. The impression is that the EU is intent on using its recipe for peace in Europe on a wider scale and spreading the rule of law and democracy in the world by using methods similar to those it has used to achieve peace and stability within its own borders.

Today, EU officials insist that the expansion of the Union equals the expansion of its political influence and that this, in turn, can only be good for the world as it leads to the expansion of peace and security worldwide. In the words of Ambassador Daly, with Croatian accession, the "world's largest Single Market and trader" became even bigger, but with it also came an expansion of the "area of peace and security of the EU" in the world as the EU saw its political clout further increase. EU officials also frequently point, as does Ambassador Daly, to the benefits of the EU to the world in helping foster more environmentally responsible policies and contributing to "political, security, humanitarian and development aid". We are reminded that "the EU and its Member States give over 55% of all development aid worldwide".[12]

10 European Commission, Directorate General External Relations, "EU/ASEAN 2007: Celebrating 30 Years of Relations. Impressive achievements – even more potential," Brussels, Publications Office, 2007.

11 Winand, P., "The EU, ASEAN and the Challenges of the 21st Century: Conclusions and Recommendations," in D. Novotný and C. Portela (eds.), *EU-ASEAN Relations in the 21st Century*, Basingstoke, Palgrave Macmillan, 2012.

12 Daly, D., "Speech given by H.E. David Daly," *op. cit.*

Notwithstanding such up-beat pronouncements by EU officials about the role of the EU in the world, we must dig deeper and ask if external actors see the EU as a significant contributor to security, and more particularly, human security. Is it perceived as having contributed to spreading – in the words of the Nobel Committee – "peace and reconciliation, democracy and human rights", not just in Europe, but also beyond this region? Do external actors view the EU as a model to be emulated? Has the EU proved adept in adapting to "circumstances in constant evolution" as Monnet had it? Is it seen as a "ferment of change" and a positive factor for change in international relations?

Combining Historical and Contemporary Perspectives

When we embarked on this project, we set out to research the external relations of the EU in historical and contemporary perspectives. We asked how the EU and its predecessors had been seen by non-EU actors since their creation in the 1950s and how the attitudes of actors external to the EU had evolved over time. We also asked to what extent the EU's view of itself – or at least the image EU policy-makers project towards the outside world of the EU as a growing economic, political and strategic player on the world scene – had been shared by actors external to the EU. Confronting the EU conception of its own role with the perceptions of external actors, would, we hoped, help to sketch the contours of the evolution of its presence on the international scene and of its nature as a polity. This, in turn, might lead to policy recommendations and policy changes as EU policy-makers see themselves also via the mirror image that is reflected back at them by external actors.

Although there has been interest in recent years in studying how the EU interacts with external actors and is perceived by them,[13] there still

[13] Lucarelli, S., "The European Union in the Eyes of Others: Towards Filling a Gap in the Literature," *European Foreign Affairs Review*, Vol. 12, No. 3, 2007, pp. 249-270; Lucarelli, S. and Fioramonti, L. (eds.), "The External Image of the European Union," GARNET Working Paper Series 62, http://www.gartnet-eu.org/index.php?id=27, accessed 1 December 2010; Elgström, O., "Leader of Foot-Dragger? Perceptions of the European Union in Multilateral International Negotiations," Swedish Institute for European Policy Studies Report 1, www.sieps.se/publ/rapporter/bilagor/20061.pdf; Chaban, N., Elgström, O., and Holland, M., "The European Union as Others See it," *European Foreign Affairs Review*, Vol. 11. No. 2, 2006, pp. 245-262; Holland, M., Ryan, P., Nowak, A., and Chaban, N. (eds.), *The EU through the Eyes of Asia: Media, Public and Elite Perceptions in China, Japan, Korea, Singapore and Thailand*, Warsaw, University of Warsaw, 2007; Chaban, N., and Holland, M. (eds.), *The European Union and the Asia-Pacific: Media, Public and Elite Perceptions of the EU*, London/New York, Routledge, 2008; Chaban, N., Holland, M., and Ryan, P. (eds.), *The EU through the Eyes of Asia: New Cases, New Findings*, Singapore/London, World Scientific, 2009.

is a dearth of analysis on how the attitudes of external actors towards European integration and cooperation have evolved over time. Historians have researched the American role in European integration and the evolution of American attitudes towards it since the Second World War.[14] They have also researched the enlargement negotiations of the European Communities, European projects and policies towards Africa, including the concept of *Eurafrique*, as well as the Yaoundé and Lomé Conventions and their links with the evolution of EEC development policy.[15] Yet not many studies focus on how the creation of the European Communities and their policies have been perceived by external actors, and certain periods have been under-researched. Few studies combine in-depth historical and contemporary perspectives in analysing the attitudes of external actors to the EU and its predecessors. As a result, relatively little is known about how the international community has viewed and been impacted by the creation and evolution of the European Communities and their successive avatars. And yet this knowledge is crucial to gain a better understanding of the evolution of the presence[16] of the EU on the international stage and the impact of some of its policies in bilateral relations with third countries and international frameworks. Knowing the image and impact of the EU abroad is essential to understanding what it is, and how it has evolved, not just from the point of view of its policy-makers, but from that of the international community.

As Wolfram Kaiser has argued, collaboration between contemporary historians and political scientists in European Studies has been impeded by a number of factors. Historians have tended to be wary of theoretical political science approaches, while some political scientists, particularly of the rational choice tradition, have mostly overlooked the detailed empirical studies of European integration historians. The availability of archives has also played a role, with political science analysis of contemporary European developments forging ahead while diplomatic

---

14 For an overview of contributions of specialists on the role and attitudes of the US towards European integration, see Gilbert, M., "Partners and Rivals: Assessing the American Role," in W. Kaiser and A. Varsori (eds.), *European Union History. Themes and Debates*, Basingstoke, Palgrave Macmillan, 2010, pp. 169-189.

15 Bitsch, M.-T. and Bossuat, G. (eds.), *L'Europe unie et l'Afrique. De l'idée d'Eurafrique à la Convention de Lomé I*, Brussels, Bruylant, 2005; See Garavani, G., "Foreign Policy beyond the Nation-State: Conceptualizing the External Dimension," in W. Kaiser and A. Varsori (eds.), *European Union History*, *op. cit.*, pp. 193, 196.

16 Presence is defined as follows: "Presence conceptualizes the ability of the EU, by virtue of its existence, to exert influence beyond its borders. An indication of the EU's structural power, presence combines understandings about the fundamental nature, or identity of the EU and the (often unintended) consequences of the Union's internal priorities and policies," Bretherton, Ch. and Vogler, J., *The European Union as a Global Actor*, London/New York, Routledge, 2006, p. 24.

historians waited for archival material to become accessible under the 30-year rule. As a result, there has been little cross-fertilization between the contemporary historians of European integration and political scientists, and the two groups have mostly ignored one another. This is to be deplored, as political scientists can learn much from historical research to understand how European integration has changed over time and to explain what the EU is today, also from the point of view of external actors. Likewise, historians can benefit from cross-disciplinary collaboration to produce less descriptive, "more analytically sophisticated historical narratives of European integration" which draw on social sciences concepts and theories. Particularly promising for collaboration are approaches such as historical institutionalism or policy-network analysis. Historical institutionalism emphasizes the role of original policy and constitutional decisions in leading to long-term path-dependencies, which limit policy-making choices. As such, it shows the importance of "history as an independent variable for explaining present-day EU politics". Working together, historians and political scientists have also used policy-network analysis to reconstruct EU policy-making over time.[17] Both types of analysis can be used equally to study the evolution of the role of the EU on the international scene, how it has been perceived or influenced by external actors and how external actors have been influenced by EU actors.

Thus Flora Anderson's chapter analyses the influence of a network of American social scientists with close ties to American policy-makers on American policy towards European unity. Following in the footsteps of scholars who have studied the influence of neo-functionalist authors on policy-makers, she argues that these social scientists not only contributed to shaping American policy towards Europe but also to the official discourse of EU officials on the origins of the EU. American social scientists were part of a much broader transatlantic network, however. As Pascaline Winand has shown, the network included policy entrepreneurs such as Jean Monnet who had close ties with both American and European policy-makers and was particularly influential in the US during the 1950s and early 1960s. In a cross-fertilization process, influence went both ways as American and European policy-makers, lawyers, businesspeople, economists, members of think tanks, journalists and academics shared views on what constituted an acceptable peace settlement and what role a united Europe should play in maintaining peace and security in Europe.[18]

[17] Seidel, K., "From Pioneer Work to Refinement: Publication Trends," and W. Kaiser, "From Isolation to Centrality: Contemporary History Meets European Studies," in W. Kaiser and A. Varsori (eds.), *European Union History*, *op. cit.*, pp. 41, 54, 56 and 63.

[18] Winand, P., *Eisenhower, Kennedy and the United States of Europe*, New York, St. Martin's Press, 1993; Winand, P., "'American 'Europeanists', Monnet's Action

But we must go further than collaboration between political scientists and historians and extend collaboration to other disciplines. For example, this book includes contributions from legal and business scholars such as Rostam Neuwirth and George Gilligan, both writing with a keen eye to the importance of historical development. There is indeed much potential for collaboration between historians and scholars from other disciplines in unveiling the complicated evolution of international institutions so as to better understand, as historian Wilfried Loth put it, "the present [...] in the light of the past"[19] and make practical proposals for the reform of the international legal order rooted in a sophisticated analysis of the current situation.

Multiarchival, Multilevel, Multilayered, Multicountry, Comparative and Discursive Approaches

The book also follows some of the latest trends in current historical and contemporary research on the EU by using multiarchival, multilevel, multilayered, multicountry, comparative and discursive approaches. Rather than focusing exclusively on the national archives of a single EU country, several studies in this book utilize both national archives – or other archives available at the national level – from several EU member states and archives from EU institutions, while also, when accessible, using the archives of non-EU countries. Thus Marie Julie Chenard, in her study of the European Community's policy towards China in the early 1970s, uses archives from the Churchill Archives Centre in Cambridge, the British National Archives, the French *Archives Nationales Contemporaines* and the *Politisches Archiv des Auswärtigen Amts*. In his chapter on Japan and the EEC in the 1970s, Hitoshi Suzuki draws on material from the German Federal Archives, the archives of the Ministry of Foreign Affairs of Japan, secondary sources from the Ministry of International Trade and Industry (MITI) and *Keidanren*, as well as from the Historical Archives of the EU. Laura Kottos' comparative study of the attitudes of three imperial powers – France, Belgium and the UK – draws on sources documenting the attitudes of national and European pressure groups towards European overseas territories in the lead up to the creation of the EEC. Ferdinand Leikam's analysis of Commonwealth Africa, Britain and the EEC Association system uses material from the British National Archives, the Historical Archives of the European Commission, African newspapers and secondary sources. British National Archives and the National

Committee and British Membership," in G. Wilkes (ed.), *Britain's Failure to Enter the European Community 1961-1963*, London, Frank Cass, 1997, pp. 164-190.

19 Loth, W. (ed.), *Experiencing Europe. 50 Years of European Construction 1957-2007*, Baden-Baden, Nomos, 2009, p. 14.

Archives of Australia are Andrea Benvenuti's preferred sources in analysing the attitudes of Australia towards the establishment of the EEC. In his study of American perceptions of EC enlargement during the 1960s and early 1970s, Max Guderzo draws on a variety of material including from the Lyndon B. Johnson Library, the American National Archives in Maryland, the *Foreign Relations of the United States* documents and the Historical Archives of the European Union. Flora Anderson uses the Harvard University Archives to examine the contribution of two prominent American social scientists to the American vision of Europe in the 1940s and 1950s. Natalia Chaban and Sarah Christie, on the other hand, have chosen to adopt a multilayered perspectives approach. Drawing on the official correspondence in the New Zealand National Archives and print media, they focus on images and perceptions of the EU in the 1950s through the prism of New Zealand elites and newsmakers.

From a more contemporary perspective, Serena Kelly draws on interviews with political, business, media and civil society elites as well as public opinion surveys to understand how the EU is perceived in New Zealand. As for Gudrun Wacker, Daniel Novotný, Emilian Kavalski, Rémy Davison, Rostam Neuwirth and George Gilligan, they all ground their analysis of the current period in its historical context. Drawing on secondary literature and documents from the European Commission, the Council of the European Union, the European Council on Foreign Relations as well as public opinion polls and surveys, Gudrun Wacker shows how the relationship between the EU and the Asia-Pacific region has changed from the 1970s to the 21st century. From a relationship focused on economics, trade and development aid, she explains how EU-Asian relations progressively matured into a more political relationship based on the increased economic clout of Japan, the four "tiger states" and China. Her analysis offers a cogent account of the evolution of EU policy towards Asia and, in particular, the current overemphasis of the EU on its strategic partnership with China and the comparative lack of attention it devotes to other partners such as ASEAN and India. Likewise, Daniel Novotný roots his analysis of Indian perspectives on the EU in an analysis of a succession of "strategic triangles" promoted by dominant powers in the region to keep a system of "manageable instability". He shows how British colonial rule over India cultivated intolerance between the Hindu and Muslim communities, while, during the Cold War, the policies of the Soviet Union, China and the United States led to instability between India and Pakistan. He explains how the current "strategic triangle", with China partnering with Pakistan and the United States developing its partnership with India, leaves the EU out of the "'triangular' and 'multi-cornered' relations in South Asia." Adopting a discursive approach, Emilian Kavalski uncovers the historical genealogy of EU-India relations through an analysis of official EU documents as well as Indian governmental, press media, academic and other sources. This allows him, for example, to identify some quirks in EU-India relations, such as a tendency on the part of the EU to see India "through the prism of British imperial lens"[20] and its failure to understand India's current interests in a more pragmatic fashion. Going back to the 1990s and the early years of the 21st century and using NATO, US, and European publications, Rémy Davison explains the co-evolution of NATO and the EU in a post-Cold War, post-September 11, 2001 context. He highlights the origins of points of policy convergence and divergence among transatlantic allies on the role of NATO, including in countering terrorism. Last but not least, from a lawyer's perspective, Rostam Neuwirth draws on a variety of sources from the EU, the United Nations, the Group of 20, the Organisation for Economic Co-operation and Development (OECD), the United Nations Conference on Trade and Development (UNCTAD), the WTO and the International Monetary Fund (IMF). He shows how the current fragmentation of the international legal order has its origin in the conditions of its creation after the Second World War and the subsequent evolution of international institutions. By comparison, he explains how the EU has evolved a more integrated institutional framework and legal order which does not separate trade and non-trade matters, is more financially autonomous than other international organizations and vests the individual citizen with a more prominent role. In his detailed discussion of multilateral regulatory initiatives in anti-tax avoidance in the EU and the OECD, George Gilligan uses a similarly wide array of sources from the EU, the US, the OECD, the G20, and the Deutsche Bank.

Broadening the Range of Actors and Time Periods

What these studies reveal is the importance of studying a range of actors, both within and beyond the EU in order to gain a better understanding of its role on the international scene. They also show the need to study time periods which have not so far been the focus of much historical investigation but which offer interesting observations on the evolution of attitudes of EEC countries towards the external world. Thus, Laura Kottos' insightful examination of the period leading to the creation of the EEC suggests that France, Belgium and the United Kingdom all sought to continue their empires by transforming them, be it via an association system of overseas territories with the EEC or, for the UK, by relying on the Commonwealth framework. Thus, France sought to salvage its empire by incorporating it into Europe. In a way, it could be argued that the EEC

[20] Dixit, J. N., "Cooperation with Europe," *Indian Express*, 10 July 2000.

association system, to paraphrase Alan Milward, was perhaps a European Rescue of the Empire, at least to some EEC member states.

The analyses of Davison, Neuwirth and Gilligan show the interest of studying the EU by placing it within its historical context and situating its evolution in parallel with that of international and regional institutions and fora for international cooperation such as the UN, the OECD, NATO, UNCTAD, the WTO, the IMF, the G20 and the Council of Europe. Such studies can reveal different approaches and lack of coordination between regional and international institutions and fora on issues crucial to human security. They can further suggest how solutions to international problems might best be found either at the global or at the regional level, or a combination of both, while highlighting the role of the EU in comparison with, and in relation to, a range of international organizations.

Analysing the attitudes towards the EU of non-EU countries with or without a colonial past is equally important to understand the role of the EU in the world and the impact of the creation of the European Communities on the evolution of the international system. Several scholars have analysed American attitudes towards European integration,[21] but much less is known about the impact of the European Communities on developing countries. In this book, Ferdinand Leikam argues that in Africa, the EEC Association System affected Commonwealth African countries both before and after the UK joined the EEC, and "served as a framework for the relations between Europe and Africa until 1975 and beyond".[22] In line with Leikam, several authors in this book emphasize the importance of studying the attitudes of countries towards the EEC that were not part of its association system rather than focusing, as have a number of historical studies, on relations of the EEC with the (former) African colonies of its original six member states, particularly France. This means not only broadening the scope of investigation beyond the EEC and the countries associated with it under the Treaty of Rome, the Yaoundé Conventions, the Lomé Conventions and, more recently, the Cotonou Partnership Agreement, but also examining periods leading up to the EEC Treaty or pre-dating UK accession to the European Communities. Thus, Leikam focuses on the 1957-1975 period and shows how the creation of the EEC and its association system triggered fears of trade discrimination in British colonies and Commonwealth countries in Africa. They feared not just the prospects of higher EEC tariffs against

21 See, for example, Winand, P., *Eisenhower, Kennedy and the United States of Europe*, *op. cit.*; Lundestad, G., *"Empire" by Integration. The United States and European Integration 1945-1997*, Oxford, OUP, 1998; Guderzo, M., *Interesse nazionale e responsabilità globale. Gli Stati Uniti, l'Alleanza atlantica e l'integrazione europea negli anni di Johnson 1963-1969*, Florence, Aida, 2000.

22 See Leikam, F. in this volume.

the outside world but also to be placed at a competitive disadvantage *vis-à-vis* colonies included in the EEC association system. Leikam also demonstrates the importance of going beyond a study of the relations of the EEC with specific African countries and investigating their interplay within the broader context of international frameworks such as UNCTAD and the Organization of African Unity (OAU). Thus, discussions on the deeply unpopular reverse preferences in the markets of associated countries, which the EEC required in exchange for preferential access to its market, were held in UNCTAD in the 1960s. Subsequently, in the early 1970s, in the context of the successful re-application of the UK to join the EEC, the OAU effectively managed to establish a common position of both African francophone associates and anglophone "associables". Together with the European Commission's signal of its lack of enthusiasm for reverse preferences, the mediating role of the OAU in helping African countries to find a common position towards the EEC succeeded in swaying EEC member states, and particularly France, away from reverse preferences.

The Importance of Institutions

In the manner of Leikam, Marie Julie Chenard and Hitoshi Suzuki show the importance of the institutional interplay within the EU, and between EU institutions and external actors, to explain policy outcomes. Marie Julie Chenard demonstrates how the European Parliament and the European Commission made good use of the EC evolving China policy to increase their importance in the EC decision-making process. Thus the European Parliament – in spite of it being perceived in the 1970s as a "talking shop" – succeeded in keeping diplomatic relations with China on the agenda of both the Council of Ministers and the European Commission. In turn, the European Commission gave a high priority to relations with China with an eye to the British referendum on membership in the EC, and, especially, the need to assert its political role *vis-à-vis* the recently established European Council. Hitoshi Suzuki shows how the European Commission, faced with an influx of Japanese goods and diverging reactions among EC member states largely seeking to restrict Japanese exports to the EC, sought instead to expand EC exports into Japan by persuading Japan to open its markets. Although it met with less success with the Ministry of International Trade and Industry (MITI) and *Keidanren*, the Commission, benefiting from the support of the Danish Chairman of the EC Council of Foreign Ministers, managed to bring on board the Japanese Ministry of Foreign Affairs (MOFA) and to sign a joint communiqué with Japan, which specified guidelines for resolving the trade balance. Suzuki thus shows the importance of inter-institutional dynamics on both the EC and the Japanese side, and, in particular, the unifying role of the Commission in seeking agreement within the EC, and, to a lesser extent, in facilitating agreement on the Japanese side.

In a similar vein, Andrea Benvenuti makes clear how the ambivalent attitude of the Australian government to the EC in the lead-up to the creation of the EEC can largely be explained through internal dynamics and bureaucratic politics within the Australian government. The dominant role of the Department of Trade (DT) *vis-à-vis* other departments in Australian policy towards Western Europe, he argues, effectively ensured that economic, rather than political considerations would prevail in policy towards the creation of the EEC. Taking the EU and MERCOSUR as examples, Edward Moxon-Brown focuses on inter-regional institutional borrowing and its effect on policy. He shows how institutional templates borrowed by one region produce different outcomes than in the original regional setting. Thus, recipes that work in one context may not be appropriate to another. Finally, Rostam Neuwirth shows the importance of analysing regional institutions in conjunction with the co-existing international institutions. Diagnosing an institutional fragmentation between the UN and the GATT/WTO systems, at both the theoretical and practical level, most clearly exemplified by missing institutional links between the two systems, he finds similar problems between the EU and the Council of Europe.

Combining historical and contemporary approaches can thus yield interesting observations on the role of the EU and its predecessors on the international scene. It can also reveal what studying the EU can teach us about the functioning of regional and international institutions, their role, their evolution and their potential reform. In light of our findings so far we now turn to the examination of the role and perceptions of the EU in the 21st century.

The EU in the 21st Century

In review, do external actors see the EU as a significant contributor to peace, security and reconciliation in the world? Do they view the EU as a model and if so, in which fields? Is the EU seen as a positive "ferment of change" in international relations with a capacity for constantly adapting to new circumstances? These are questions that we were prompted to ask at the beginning of this chapter.

In the academic community, both in Europe and abroad, academics have underlined the role of the EU in promoting peace and security in the world by providing access to the EU market, by promoting regional integration and through actions which reinforce human security. In 2003, American political scientist Andrew Moravcsik argued that the "single most powerful instrument for promoting peace and security in the world today, is the ultimate market access: admission or association with the EU trading bloc".[23] For other authors, the EU is contributing to peace and security in the world by its actions or even its very presence, with some regional organizations beyond Europe following its example.[24] Gudrun Wacker shows that the EU has contributed to peace and stability in East Asia by providing assistance and funding to support "post-conflict reconstruction, nation-building, institution-building, security sector reform, and police training".[25] The EU is also portrayed as exerting a powerful influence on the reform of international institutions. Nicoletta Pirozzi has shown how, in the wake of the Lisbon Treaty, the EU succeeded in obtaining reinforced observer status in the UN General Assembly (GA). The resolution allowing for this status includes a provision that considers granting similar rights to other regional organizations that have observer status in the GA, based on prior agreement between the member states of such organizations.[26] In a similar vein, for Rostam Neuwirth, the growing coherence and unity of the EU legal order and, particularly its success in overcoming the artificial separation between so-called "trade-" and "non-trade" matters which plagues the international legal order, could provide inspiration for a badly needed reform of international institutions.

The EU as a Model and a Significant Global Actor?

Does this mean that the EU is seen as a model to be emulated by external actors? Our research indicates that the EU is perceived by some of India's highest-placed government officials as a successful experiment in the reconciliation on a continental scale of peoples and states with a violent past. From a Southern Asian perspective, regional economic integration and institutional arrangements based on a consensual decision-making mode, together with the respect of national identities, are all commendable features of the EU experiment in multilateral cooperation. As such, the EU is regarded by some officials as an example to be emulated in South Asia, perhaps pointing the way to a South Asian Union that would go beyond the South Asian Association for Regional Cooperation

[23] Moravcsik, A., "Striking a New Transatlantic Bargain," *Foreign Affairs*, No. 28, Vol. 4, 2003, p. 85.

[24] Bretherton, Ch. and Vogler, J., *The European Union as a Global Actor*, *op. cit.*

[25] See Wacker, G. in this volume.

[26] Pirozzi, N., "The EU's Contribution to the Effectiveness of the UN Security Council between Presence and Impact," in J. Krause and N. Ronzitti (eds.), *The EU, the UN and Collective Security. Making Multilateralism Effective*, London, Routledge, 2012, pp. 94-95.

(SAARC) and bring stability to the region.[27] In Latin America, Edward Moxon-Browne shows that, although the EU has a less distinctive profile than the US, and knowledge and perceptions of the EU vary considerably between sub-regions in Latin America, the EU has indeed provided a model for regional integration in some sub-regional organizations. This has been relatively more the case in countries of the Southern Cone than in Central America. Thus, certain features of the EU, such as passport-free travel, the Structural and Cohesion Funds, consultative councils allowing for more civil society participation in political processes, or even institutions, have been emulated by regional organizations in the Southern Cone. In addition, while the United States is seen as making a greater contribution than the EU as a global actor in democracy, free trade, peace and development cooperation, Brazilians tend to consider the EU as the major contributor to world peace, in contrast to the US. Brazilians also see the EU as "a force upholding multilateralism" and as a "guarantor of a more multipolar international system". Interestingly, opinion poll data in Latin America shows that "the more favourable the opinions are of the EU, the more robust the support for regional integration in Latin America".[28]

But there are limits to external actors' perceptions of the EU as a model to be emulated. A recent book on EU-ASEAN relations has shown that even though ASEAN sees the EU as an important trading and investment partner and a way of helping balance powerful neighbours such as China and the USA in the region, the EU is not seen as a model to be emulated. The EU is to be tapped for good ideas, for example, on economic integration and environmental change, but is seen as too different from ASEAN to be a model for integration. Its preference for a highly institutionalized, legalistic approach to integration and the relatively similar economic development of its member states is contrasted with ASEAN's preference for a more informal grouping and its huge disparities in economic development. ASEAN has accordingly tried to develop its own model. As for the EU's image as an example of reconciliation, although ASEAN elites do see the EU as a successful experiment in the peaceful resolution of disputes, they see ASEAN itself as having achieved reconciliation in its own right, owing little to the EU model.[29]

The picture of the EU on the international scene is not all rosy. Rémy Davison explains the roots of disagreements between the US and the EU

[27] See Novotný, D., Kavalaski, E., Jain, R. in this volume and Winand, P., Vicziany, M. and Datar, P., *The European Union and India: Rhetoric or Meaningful Partnership?*, Cheltenham, Edward Elgar, 2014.

[28] See Moxon-Browne, E. in this volume.

[29] Winand, P., "The EU, ASEAN and the Challenges of the 21st Century: Conclusions and Recommendations," *op. cit.*

on how to fight terrorism in NATO and beyond and shows that there were doubts on the part of the US about the capacity or the willingness of the EU to confront international crises, whether that be independently or together with other actors. In the Asia-Pacific, Serena Kelly shows how New Zealand and Singapore mostly view the EU as an important economic power and less as a normative actor able to export its values beyond the economic realm. The emphasis of the EU on peace, stability, democracy, human rights, development policies and the environment is not always met with the reception expected by EU leaders. In particular, Kelly explains that while the EU does appear as a peaceful entity in Singapore and relatively more as an environmental actor and a democratic entity in New Zealand, the EU has experienced difficulties in branding itself as a defender of human rights in these two countries. Although this may be due in part to the tendency for ASEAN countries to view the EU promotion of human rights in the region as "a form of neo-colonialism", there is a clear need for improved communication of the EU on its role as a normative actor. Her findings match those of Natalia Chaban, Martin Holland and Lai Suet-yi who, in a recent study, found that in China, India, Singapore, Thailand, Malaysia and the Philippines the EU is perceived mostly as an economic global power, and relatively less so as a diplomatic, normative, military or development actor. Although the EU sees itself as "the world's leading development player", the elites of China and Malaysia see things differently, even though these countries benefit substantially from EU development aid.[30]

The EU's lack of coherence further contributes to undermine the perception of its role as a significant global actor. Following the passage of the Lisbon Treaty the EU now possesses legal personality and a newly created European External Action Service. Both of these developments would be expected to enhance its coherence in the area of external relations. At the same time, however, the EU has embarked on an ambitious enlargement which has had the effect of bringing in its train more diversity and less coherence. Thus, Karolina Pietras shows how EU enlargement has also meant less EU cohesion as Europeans from East and West have struggled to find a common identity. In turn, Wacker, Novotný, Jain and Kavalski all portray the EU as lacking political coherence, when seen from an Asian perspective. Gudrun Wacker shows how difficult it is to have a unified EU policy towards China, as EU member states pursue diverging approaches and compete with one another in their efforts to woo the Asian giant. In the eyes of Indian elites, the EU is mostly perceived as

[30] Chaban, N., Holland, M. and Suet-yi, L., "Asian Views of the EU. Dysfunctional Relations?," in N. Witzleb, A. Martínez Arranz, and P. Winand (eds.), *European Union and Global Engagement: Institutions, Policies and Global Engagement*, Cheltenham, Edward Elgar, forthcoming in 2015.

a coherent economic actor but also as an incoherent political and security one. The EU indeed appears plagued by internal political strife and its claims to be a model of integration for the external world dissolve in its own difficulties to exert itself as a unified actor. The Indian chapters also highlight frustrations in dealing with the complex bureaucratic structure and procedures of the EU.

Lack of coherence and institutional complexity within the EU further combine with external factors in making it difficult for the EU to project a credible and effective image on the world stage. How the EU is perceived in comparison with other key actors in a region can indeed teach us much about its global role. So, too, can the importance the EU accords to certain countries, as compared to others. Thus, in Latin America, the EU competes for attention in public opinion with the United Nations, the North American Free Trade Agreement (NAFTA), MERCOSUR, other Latin American countries, Japan, and especially, the United States.[31] In Asia, the perception of the importance of the EU pales in comparison with that of a powerful actor such as the United States with a more unified stance in international affairs and more direct geopolitical interests in the region. In India, the EU is seen as having little to offer in terms of military security and as lacking a strategic vision of India-EU relations. By contrast, the US is India's main security partner, having "clearly chosen India to be the balancer of Asia"[32] and adopted a much more decisive approach in supporting Indian security interests and aspirations to become a great power. Further complicating EU efforts to achieve a common stance towards Asia are different viewpoints in EU member states on the extent to which the EU should coordinate policies with the US, together with a tendency to mostly follow its lead in the Asian region. Yet, as long as the EU merely appears to follow the US lead in Asia, its relevance to Asia (and the US) will appear as insignificant, even though many Asian countries would welcome its increased role as a counterweight to the US in the region.[33] In addition, the EU focus on China relative to India, primarily motivated by economic and trade considerations, is perceived negatively in India. Delhi points to India's democratic credentials, which China lacks, and its fast-growing economy.

The difficulty for the EU in asserting itself as a credible actor on the world stage, particularly in "hard" security issues, is compounded by significant disagreements between the EU and external actors on substance. In Asia, Indian elites are bemused by the EU focus on soft power

---

31 See Moxon-Brown, E. in this volume.

32 Kaur, K. and Mann, B. S., *South Asia: Dynamics of Politics, Economy and Security*, New Delhi, Knowledge World, 2006, p. 173.

33 See Wacker, G. in this volume.

instruments to achieve security, a position which is largely incompatible with their own focus on *Realpolitik* considerations in a highly unstable region. They find potential for further economic collaboration between the EU and India, and little convergence in terms of common strategic interests. Added to this are diverging conceptions of multilateralism and differences of opinion on how to cope with global challenges to human security such as climate change. In this light, it is no wonder that the EU-India strategic partnership, initiated by the European Commission, has mostly been branded in India as "empty rhetoric rather than a content-driven strategy".[34] Nor is it surprising if recent EU-India summits and meetings have yielded only meagre results. The complexity of the EU decision-making process, compounded by India's no-less-complex administrative architecture, together with a lack of agreement between India and the EU on substance, have effectively stymied the prospects of what could be a much more mutually rewarding relationship.

Shadow of the Past, Internal and External Factors

This would seem to point to the need for the EU to focus more on substance and less on process and declaratory posturing with its partners, including in the Asia-Pacific. To do so, the EU needs to reflect on how it is perceived by external actors and why it is that they see it as they do. In no small part, their perceptions may be influenced by the shadow of the past. This includes lingering memories of European colonialism, of the effect of the European Communities association system, of successive EC/EU enlargements and of the creation of the Common Agricultural Policy on outsiders. More positively, the perceptions of external actors may also tally with the hopes the creation of the European Communities has raised for reconciliation on a war-ravaged continent in which two world wars originated, and for similar reconciliation processes in the wider international community.

The perceptions of the international community *vis-à-vis* the EU are also influenced by factors internal to the EU. The complexity of EU decision-making, the difficulty in reconciling the views of EU member states on key external relations issues and the effects of the European financial and debt crisis, which have been felt well beyond the EU, all contribute to the image of the European Union. For example, a research project[35]

34 Duran, D. C., "The EU-India Strategic Partnership. What's New?," *IPCS Article 2222*, 27 February 2007, http://www.ipcs.org/article/india-the-world/the-eu-india-strategic-partnership-whats-new-2222.html, accessed 27 September 2014.

35 See the PowerPoint presentation "New Zealand vs. Australia: Views on Europe in Crisis from Down Under" by Dr Serena Kelly (National Centre for Research on Europe, University of Canterbury), Dr Eva Polonska and Dr Patrick Kimunguyi (Monash European and EU Centre, Monash University) at the Jean Monnet Chair

on the EU in the eyes of Australasia has shown how EU internal divisions work against its image as a great power or a leader in international politics, with large EU member states appearing as the voices of the EU. The EU financial and debt troubles have also prompted Australian elite commentators to encourage Europeans to look to Australia for lessons on how to run their banking system.

The perceptions of external actors are equally influenced by factors external to the EU and the regional dynamics and interests at play in specific regions.[36] To become a more credible actor on the world stage, the EU needs to gain a better understanding of endogenous dynamics, interests and perceptions particular to certain countries and regions. This is important to engage more deeply and significantly on substance with its external partners, who may hold different views on democratization, human rights, supranationalism and multilateralism, for example. At the same time, the EU, having only awakened relatively late to the growing economic, political and strategic importance of Asia, needs better to recognize the significant power shift towards Asia and further increase its visibility and engagement in the region.[37] The recently created European External Action Service has kept the focus on Japan, China and India as the EU's three strategic partners in Asia and the EU has continued to develop relations with regional or transregional frameworks such as ASEAN and ASEM. Yet, there is a need for a strategic vision for the whole of Asia with less emphasis on countless meetings and more focus

Annual Seminar *Communicating Europe in Times of Crises*, 13 April 2012, University of Canterbury, which showcased the findings of the transnational research project "The EU in the Eyes of Asia-Pacific: Post-Lisbon Reflections (2011-12)" from ten countries in the region supported by a Jean Monnet Lifelong Learning initiative of the European Commission Directorate-General of Education and Culture, and the Asia-Europe Foundation (ASEF). See also the PowerPoint presentation "Communicating the European Union to Australia: The EU Communication Strategy and its Reception Down Under" by Dr Eva Polonska (Monash European and EU Centre) at the *Jean Monnet National Symposium on Australia-EU Relations – Time for a Reappraisal?*, co-hosted by the Monash European and EU Centre and the School of Social and Political Sciences of the University of Melbourne, Monash University, 26 April 2013. See also Polonska-Kimunguyi, E., and Kimunguyi, P., "Communicating the European Union to Australia: The EU Information Strategy and its Reception Down Under," *Baltic Journal of European Studies*, Vol. 3., No. 3, 2013, pp. 127-152.

36 For example, a 2012 Australian Government document evidenced a tendency for Australia, given its location in the Asia-Pacific, to over-focus on Asia, thereby understating the importance of its trade, investment, political and security relations with the EU and transregional fora such as ASEM, see Australian Government, *Australia in the Asian Century*, White Paper, Canberra, Commonwealth of Australia, October 2012.

37 See Wacker, G. in this volume. See also *Australia in the Asian Century*, *op. cit.*, and Geeraerts, G., "EU-China Relations" and Kubo, H., "EU-Asia Trade Relations," in T. Christiansen, E. Kircher and P. Murray (eds.), *The Palgrave Handbook of EU-Asia Relations*, Basingstoke, Palgrave Macmillan, 2013, pp. 492-505, pp. 247-261.

on efficiency, coherence, adequate resources and knowledge of the particular circumstances of EU partners in specific regions.[38]

"Benign imperialism" or "Eurocentric cultural imperialism"[39] towards formerly colonized areas of the world will not do. A better understanding of the image of the EU rooted in in-depth research of the evolution of the perceptions and impact of the EU in the international community could go a long way in informing EU external policies. To paraphrase Jean Monnet, the EU needs to show itself capable of adapting to new circumstances in constant evolution. To do this, the EU needs to look squarely at its image in the world at the national, regional and international levels and to focus its interactions with external actors less on procedure and more on substance.

---

38 Cameron, F., "The Evolution of EU-Asia Relations: 2001-2011," in T. Christiansen, E. Kircher and P. Murray (eds.), *The Palgrave Handbook of EU-Asia Relations*, *op. cit.*, pp. 30-43.

39 Moxon-Brown, E., in this volume; Sjursen, H., "The EU as 'Normative' Power: How Can This Be?," *Journal of European Public Policy*, Vol. 13, No. 2, March 2006, p. 248.

Index

"European Policy"

"European Policy" is an interdisciplinary series devoted to the study of European integration in a broad sense. Although mostly focusing on the European Union, it also encourages the publication of books addressing the wider, pan-European context, as well as comparative work, including other forms of regional integration on the world scene. The core disciplines are politics, economics, law, and history. While being committed to high academic standards, "European Policy" seeks to be accessible to a wide readership, including policymakers and practitioners, and to stimulate a debate on European issues. Submissions will normally undergo a thorough peer-review process. The series publishes both in English and in French.

Series Editor: **Pascaline WINAND,**
Professor and Jean Monnet Chair in European Integration and International Relations (Monash University, Australia)

Recent Titles

No.51: *The EU and the Political Economy of Transatlantic Relations,* Finn LAURSEN (ed.), 2012, 321 p., ISBN 978-90-5201-900-0

No.50: *Obama, US Politics, and Transatlantic Relations. Change or Continuity?,* Giles SCOTT-SMITH (ed.), 2012, 332 p., ISBN 978-90-5201-876-8

No.49: *The Making of the EU's Lisbon Treaty. The Role of Member states,* Finn LAURSEN (ed.), 2012, 324 p., ISBN 978-90-5201-812-6

No.48: *Energy and the Environmental Challenge. Lessons from the European Union and Australia,* Lillian WYLIE and Pascaline WINAND (eds.), 2011, 415 p., ISBN 978-90-5201-765-5

No.47: *New Europe, New World? The European Union, Europe and the Challenges of the 21st Century,* Alfonso MARTÍNEZ ARRANZ, Natalie J. DOYLE & Pascaline WINAND (eds.), 2010, 283 p., ISBN 978-90-5201-604-7

No.46: *Switzerland – European Union. An Impossible Membership?,* René SCHWOK, 2009, 155 p., ISBN 978-90-5201-576-7

No.45: *The EU in the Global Political Economy,* Finn LAURSEN, 2009, 352 p., ISBN 978-90-5201-554-5

No.44: *America, Europe, Africa / L'Amérique, l'Europe, l'Afrique. 1945-1973,* Éric REMACLE & Pascaline WINAND (eds./dir.), 2009, 329 p., ISBN 978-90-5201-529-3

N° 43: *Le paysage européen de la sécurité intérieure,* Pierre BERTHELET, 2009, 573 p., ISBN 978-90-5201-473-9

No.42: *In Pursuit of Influence. The Netherlands' European Policy during the Formative Years of the European Union, 1952-1973,* Anjo G. HARRYVAN, 2009, 284 p., ISBN 978-90-5201-497-5

N° 41: *Les États-Unis et l'unification monétaire de l'Europe*, Dimitri GRYGOWSKI, 2009, 472 p., ISBN 978-90-5201- 489-0

N° 40: *Le Traité de Rome histoires pluridisciplinaires. L'apport du Traité de Rome instituant la Communauté économique européenne,* Sandrine DEVAUX, René LEBOUTTE & Philippe POIRIER (dir.), 2009, 210 p., ISBN 978-90-5201-500-2

No.39: *European Integration from Rome to Berlin 1957-2007. History, Law and Politics,* Julio BAQUERO CRUZ & Carlos CLOSA MONTERO (eds.), 2009, 286 p., ISBN 978-90-5201-464-7

No.38: *European and Turkish Voices in Favour and Against Turkish Accession to the European Union,* Christiane TIMMERMAN, Dirk ROCHTUS & Sara MELS (eds.), 2008, 149 p., ISBN 978-90-5201-428-9

N° 37: *Centre et centrisme en Europe aux XIXe et XXe siècles. Regards croisés,* Sylvie GUILLAUME et Jean GARRIGUES (dir.), 2006, 288 p., ISBN 978-90-5201-317-6

N° 36: *Vers une Europe fédérale ? Les espoirs et les actions fédéralistes au sortir de la Seconde Guerre mondiale,* Bertrand VAYSSIÈRE, 2006 (2nd printing 2007), 416 p., ISBN 978-90-5201-353-4

N° 35: *Institutionnaliser l'évaluation des politiques publiques. Étude comparée des dispositifs en Belgique, en France, en Suisse et aux Pays-Bas,* Steve JACOB, 2005, 271 p., ISBN 978-90-5201-078-6

No.34: *Visions, Votes and Vetoes. The Empty Chair Crisis and the Luxembourg Compromise Forty Years On,* Jean-Marie PALAYRET, Helen WALLACE & Pascaline WINAND (eds.), 2006, 344 p., ISBN 978-90-5201-031-1

No.33: *Networks of Empire. The US State Department's Foreign Leader Program in the Netherlands, France, and Britain 1950-70,* Giles SCOTT-SMITH, 2008, 516 p., ISBN 978-90-5201-256-3

N° 32: *Le droit institutionnel de la sécurité intérieure européenne,* Pierre BERTHELET, 2003, 324 p., ISBN 978-90-5201-193-6

www.peterlang.com

For the avoidance of doubt, input of the whole or any part of this publication into any generative artificial intelligence model, chatbot, program, software or technology is expressly prohibited without the prior written consent of the publisher.